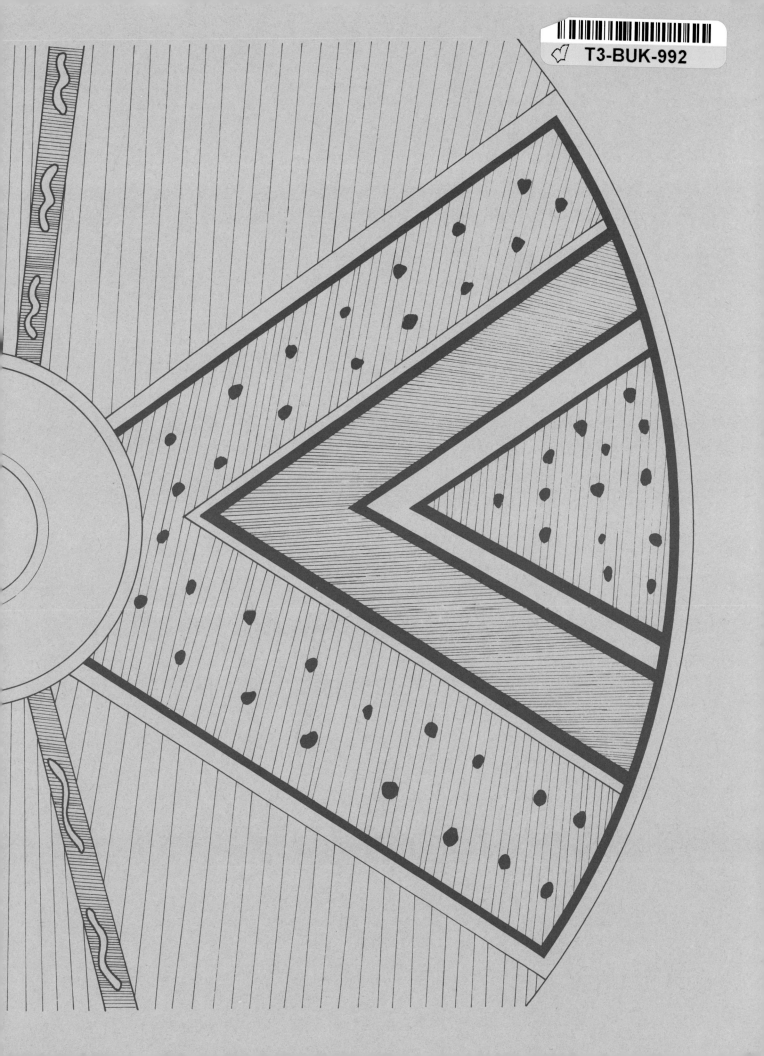

PACHACAMAC

Max Uhle, circa 1900 (The University Museum Photo Archives neg. no. 137258)

University Museum Monograph 62

PACHACAMAC

A reprint of the 1903 edition by Max Uhle

and

PACHACAMAC ARCHAEOLOGY: RETROSPECT AND PROSPECT

an Introduction by

Izumi Shimada

Published by

THE UNIVERSITY MUSEUM
of Archaeology and Anthropology
University of Pennsylvania
Philadelphia
1991

Design, editing, production
Publications Department
The University Museum

Printing
Science Press
Ephrata, Pennsylvania

Colophon and endpapers
Georgianna Grentzenberg

Library of Congress Cataloging-in-Publication Data

Uhle, Max, 1856-1944.
   Pachacamac : a reprint of the 1903 edition / by Max Uhle. And,
Pachacamac archaeology : an introduction / by Izumi Shimada.
         p.   cm. -- (University museum monograph ; 62)
   Originally published (1st work): Philadelphia : Dept. of
Archaeology, University of Pennsylvania, 1903.
   Includes bibliographical references.
   ISBN 0-924171-09-X
   1. Pachacamac Site (Peru)   2. Excavations (Archaeology)--Peru-
-Lurín River Valley.   I. Shimada, Izumi.   Pachacamac archaeology.
1991.   II. Title.   III. Title: Pachacamac archaeology.   IV. Series.
985'.25--dc20   91-25823
                                                                                   CIP

Table of Contents

Part I

A New Introduction to Max Uhle's *Pachacamac*

Part II

Reprint of Max Uhle's *Pachacamac*

Illustrations

Figures

Plates

Tables

Acknowledgments

The successful republication of this volume owes much to the concern and efforts of many people. I thank Clark Erickson and Karen Vellucci for their continuing support. For their helpful comments on this essay, I am grateful to my colleagues Patricia Lyon and John H. Rowe. Patricia Knobloch generously offered insights from her ongoing analysis of the Pachacamac-style ceramics. María Rostworowski clarified various ethnohistorical matters. Ponciano Paredes, resident archaeologist at the Pachacamac National Archaeological Monument and his collaborator, Régulo Franco, kindly provided the isometric projection drawing of Pyramid with Ramp 2. James M. Vreeland shared information regarding burials excavated by Julio C. Tello and his colleagues. Paul Jaeckel assisted with the compilation of the bibliography. As usual, Melody Shimada gave up her time to go over my manuscript. The American Museum of Natural History allowed me to reproduce Bandelier's map of Pachacamac (Pl. 1). Plates 2, 3, 5, and 6 were provided by the Servicio Nacional Aerofotográfico del Perú.

Izumi Shimada

Foreword

I have a sense of identification with, or some kind of an attachment to, the site of Pachacamac. It was the first place I ever excavated in Peru. This was back in 1941, when I had gone there as an assistant to William Duncan Strong, who was in charge of one of the archaeological projects being carried out by the Institute of Andean Research in Latin America in 1941-1942. Strong had been invited to dig at Pachacamac by Julio C. Tello, then Peru's leading archaeologist, who was himself carrying out excavations and restorations at the site. In preliminary discussions with Tello, we had indicated that we would like to do some stratigraphic digging in deep refuse to see if we could verify and refine the chronology that Max Uhle had established for Pachacamac back at the turn of the century. Tello told us that he knew "just the place." The place turned out to be a huge refuse heap, which, in its semidecayed condition, resembled a great black, dusty-looking haystack. It was situated just below the Inca Temple of the Sun and almost certainly, at least in its upper levels, would start us at the terminal end of whatever stratigraphic story we might come up with. We moved a lot of dirt and potsherds in this dig through the "haystack," which did, indeed, prove to be an Inca Period deposit, and we went on down below this into an earlier occupation that we were to identify as pertaining to the "interlocking style," or the Early Lima culture (see Strong and Corbett 1943). This Early Lima culture, as I came to find out, was the one that Uhle had identified as his Early, or pre-Tiahuanaco, Period at Pachacamac.

We—Strong, John Corbett, and I—were digging at Pachacamac during the chill and foggy winter months of July until October of 1941. I can recall now, sitting up on the Sun Temple hill near our dig during the lunchtime break and looking out over the vast, dun-colored ruins of Pachacamac, marveling at the energy and drive that had fired Max Uhle to do all that he had done at that site back in 1896-1897. It so happened that just before we started work at Pachacamac I had had the pleasure of meeting Uhle. I should explain that, in 1939, Uhle had come to Peru to attend the XXVII International Congress of Americanists. While he was there, Germany invaded Poland, ushering in World War II, and Uhle was marooned in Peru. He was still there in 1941, and Strong and I encountered him one day on the steps of the National Museum for Archaeology when that institution was located on the Avenida Alfonso Ugarte in Lima. Uhle, then in his eighties, was carrying a copy of a huge book, which turned out to be his own *Pachacamac* monograph. He had been permitted to borrow it from the museum library and was taking it home to his quarters in Bellavista. I remember wondering at the time just what research he was pursuing—or was he, perhaps, just taking a "sentimental journey" into the past? I had not seen a copy of *Pachacamac* before, and as we were to start our own digging at the site in a few days, it seemed advisable to me to have a look at what the master had done. Fortunately, Uhle didn't keep the copy—quite possibly the only one in all Peru at that time—out of the library, and when he returned it, I was allowed to borrow it and to enlighten myself about the site and the man.

The 1903 text of Max Uhle's *Pachacamac* was the finest single-site archaeological report in Americanist studies of its time. In it Uhle combined architectural and grave stratigraphy with ceramic grave-lot seriational analyses to establish a firm archaeological sequence. He then went beyond this to integrate his Pachacamac sequence into a wider chronological frame of reference for Peruvian-Bolivian archaeology. They weren't thinking in terms of archaeological culture area or co-tradition in Peru in those days, but what Uhle was beginning to construct was the chronology chart for such an area. It should be pointed out that this was the first such cultural-chronological scheme for a major New World area. In 1903 Mesoamerica, or the Southeastern United States, by contrast, was not to have such working frames of chronological reference for another twenty to thirty years. John H. Rowe (1954), in the subtitle of his biographical memoir of Uhle, refers to him as "The Father of Peruvian Archaeology." No one can quarrel with this designation; I would want only to go further and add that Uhle was a key figure in the development of archaeology for all the Americas.

It should be noted that by the time Uhle wrote *Pachacamac* he was an experienced archaeologist and very much a professional. For a thorough biographical background of Uhle one should turn to the Rowe memoir cited above. Here, briefly, we can note that Uhle was a product of the high tradition of late-nineteenth-century German scholarship. Born of upper-middle-class parents in Dresden in 1856, he took a doctorate in linguistics at the University of Leipzig in 1880. While employed at the Dresden Museum, from 1880 until 1888, he continued his linguistic researches and also examined, analyzed, and wrote about the museum's rich ethnographic collections. In 1888, he received an appointment at the Königliches Museum für Völkerkunde in Berlin, where he became increasingly interested in South America. He collaborated with Alphons Stübel—a man who had spent many years studying and photographing the ruins of Tiahuanaco in Bolivia—in writing and publishing a monograph on that site, *Die Ruinenstätte von Tiahuanaco* (Stübel and Uhle 1892). From this, Uhle gained an intimate knowledge of the art style of Tiahuanaco as well as of the styles of the later Inca civilization.

In 1892, he went to South America for the first time and saw, among other things, the ruins of Tiahuanaco. In those early years, 1892-1896, he traveled extensively in Bolivia, Argentina, and Peru, and made observations in linguistics, ethnography, and archaeology. In 1896-1897, he was given the opportunity to spend a full year exploring and digging at Pachacamac. Thus, at age forty, well trained and well traveled in the subject and areas of his interests, and with ideas about Peruvian archaeology already formed and forming in his mind as the result of his Tiahuanaco studies, Uhle was prepared to excavate in one of the largest and most complex archaeological sites in the area. As his report, *Pachacamac*, shows, he made the most of his opportunity.

Uhle continued archaeological fieldwork in Peru after the Pachacamac excavations, surveying and excavating in both coast and highlands, north and south. These studies, especially his grave excavations in the Moche Valley on the North Coast (Uhle 1913), further

solidified his Peruvian chronology, a chronology that has been added to and refined but that, in its major outlines, still stands some eighty years after Uhle outlined it at Pachacamac.

While in no way detracting from Uhle's accomplishments, it should be noted that his fourfold chronology of (1) the Early Period, (2) the Tiahuanaco Period, (3) the Late Period, and (4) the Inca Period also owes much to A. L. Kroeber (1925a, 1925b; Strong 1925; Gayton and Kroeber 1927; Gayton 1927), who, working with Uhle's field notes and collections, brought order to much of the data that Uhle himself had never published. Finally, the major modifications of this chronological structure since Uhle's time have been, so to speak, at the "bottom" of the chart, the additions being an Early, or Chavín, Horizon, preceding the Early Period cultures; an Initial Ceramic Period, preceding this Early Horizon; and a long preceramic era before the Initial Ceramic Period.

Uhle finished his work in Peru in 1911, after which he accepted a position in Chile to carry out archaeological work in that country. He did this until 1919, then went to Ecuador in a similar capacity and stayed there until 1933, when he returned to Germany. He did important work in both of these countries, providing in each a good foundation for systematic archaeological research. In neither, however, was he able to repeat his Peruvian success in establishing a lasting chronological framework. The reason for this lack of success in Chile and Ecuador was that he had only the top "horizon" for his chronologies, that of the Inca Period; in neither country was there a satisfactory Tiahuanaco horizon, or any other earlier horizon, and this limited his ability for broad chronological generalization. In effect, he found himself outside the "Peruvian co-traditional" sphere, as this was to be defined a good many years later (Bennett 1948).

I had the pleasure of seeing Uhle once again, after that brief encounter on the steps of the National Museum. This was in early 1942, when I invited him to visit us during our excavations at Ancón, a site, or an archaeological zone, where he had worked extensively more than thirty years before (see Rowe 1954:18-19). Shortly thereafter, he was able to return to his homeland, and he died in Germany in 1944.

Gordon R. Willey
Harvard University
March 1990

Pachacamac Archaeology: Retrospect and Prospect

by

Izumi Shimada

Background

The Pachacamac volume by Max Uhle is undoubtedly the best-known and single most-important publication by this German scholar, who is generally regarded as the father of scientific archaeology in the Andes (Rowe 1954). The volume as originally published in 1903 is impressive not only on its scholastic merits (see Foreword) but also in its physical size, measuring 51 x 38 x 2.8 cm and 5. 79 kg (12.75 lbs) in weight. With its early publication date and relatively small print run, the volume has become quite rare even among large university libraries and is most often kept in noncirculating rare-book collections. One wonders how many students of Andean archaeology in recent decades have had an opportunity not just to handle this volume but to scrutinize its contents carefully. Even a quick glance at his accurate 1:2000 scale site map is quite informative and eye-opening when compared with the map that Adolph Bandelier had made just four years earlier (Pl. 1) and with a modern aerial photograph (Pl. 2). Although much deference is paid to this volume and its author in modern literature, I have the impression that this owes more to the assumption of their proven importance in the history of New World archaeology than to firsthand familiarity with its contents and significance.

Efforts to have this classic work republished by The University Museum of the University of Pennsylvania stem from my long-standing interest in Andean ceremonial and urban centers and my belief that the significance of the site and associated cultures of Pachacamac have not been properly appreciated. It has become clear to me that better understanding of Pachacamac is crucial to my own field research in Batán Grande on the North Coast of Peru, the inferred capital of the Vatican-like Middle Sicán religious polity. In fact, much the same can be said about various studies undertaken within the past decade or so at other major contemporaneous ceremonial centers on the coast (e.g., Cahuachi [South Coast], Maranga [Central Coast], Moche and Pacatnamú [North Coast]; Fig. 1), and about the problematics of the Middle Horizon (Table 1; A.D. 550-900, divided into 4 Epochs) in general.

Given these considerations, it seemed well worthwhile to pursue republication of the volume. Discussions toward this end began in 1984 with Robert Dyson, Director of The University Museum at the University of Pennsylvania, and Barbara Murray, then Director of Publications at the Museum. The effort came to fruition some six years later with Karen Vellucci, the current Director of Publications.

This volume faithfully reproduces original texts and photos. The notable reduction in overall size of the new volume (about one-third of the original) results primarily from a diminution of the wide margins around the texts in the original. The crucial site map is reproduced in its original size.

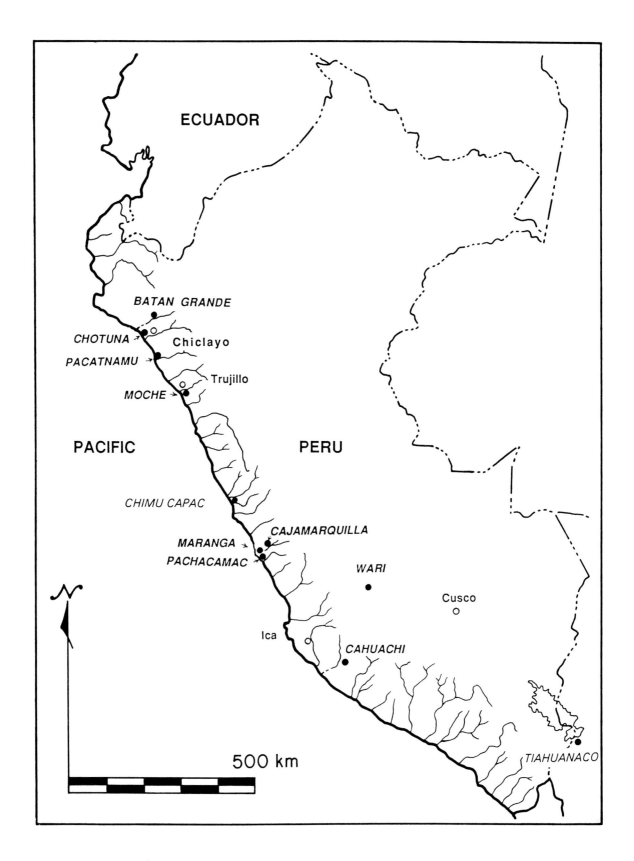

ECUADOR

BATAN GRANDE

CHOTUNA

Chiclayo

PACATNAMU

Trujillo

MOCHE

PACIFIC

PERU

CHIMU CAPAC

CAJAMARQUILLA

MARANGA

PACHACAMAC

WARI

Cusco

Ica

CAHUACHI

500 km

TIAHUANACO

Figure 1. Map showing the location of Pachacamac and its contemporaneous ceremonial centers in the Central Andes. Drawing by Izumi Shimada.

CHRONOLOGICAL TABLE FOR SELECTED ARCHAEOLOGICAL REGIONS OF THE CENTRAL ANDES

YEARS	PERUVIAN REFERANT CHRONOLOGY	UPPER PIURA VALLEY	LAMBAYEQUE	CAJAMARCA BASIN	MOCHE VALLEY	SANTA VALLEY	CALLEJÓN DE HUAYLAS	CENTRAL COAST	ICA VALLEY	AYACUCHO
1500	LATE HORIZON	CHIMU INCA	SICAN INCA		CHIMU INCA	LATE TAMBO REAL	INCA INFLUENCE	INCA INFLUENCE PACHACAMAC IV	INCA INFLUENCE ICA	INCA INFLUENCE
	LATE INTERMEDIATE PERIOD AD 900 - 1476	CHIMU / (LATE SICAN) / (MIDDLE SICAN) / PIURA	SICAN CHIMU / LATE SICAN / MIDDLE SICAN / EARLY SICAN	FINAL CAJAMARCA / LATE CAJAMARCA	CHIMU / EARLY CHIMU	EARLY TAMBO REAL / LATE TANGUCHE (SICAN INFLUENCE)	LOCAL STYLES	CHANCAY / PACHACAMAC III	ICA	TANTA 'URCO / ARQALLA
1000										
	MIDDLE HORIZON AD 550 - 900	VICUS/MOCHICA (MOCHICA I-V)	MOCHE V / MOCHE IV	MIDDLE CAJAMARCA	EARLY CHIMU / MOCHE V / MOCHE IV	EARLY TANGUCHE (WARI INFLUENCE) / GUADALUPITO (MOCHE III-IV)	HONCO / WARI INFLUENCE	WARI DERIVED PACHACAMAC II / PACHACAMAC II A–B / NIEVERIA	DERIVED WARI-PACHACAMAC / WARI-INFLUENCED / NASCA 8 / NASCA 7	VINAQUE / CHAKIPAMPA A, B / WARI / HUARPA
500										
AD / BC 0	EARLY INTERMEDIATE PERIOD 400 BC - AD 550	VICUS / ENCANTADA	MOCHE III / MOCHE I, II? / GALLINAZO	EARLY CAJAMARCA / INITIAL CAJAMARCA / LAYZON / EARLY LAYZON	MOCHE III / MOCHE II / GALLINAZO / SALINAR	LATE SUCHIMANCILLO (LATE GALLINAZO) / EARLY SUCHIMANCILLO (EARLY GALLINAZO) / VINZOS / RECUAY	RECUAY / WHITE-ON-RED / HUARAS	LIMA (MARANGA-INTERLOCKING) PACHACAMAC I / BAÑOS DE BOZA (WHITE-ON-RED)	NASCA / OCUCAJE/PARACAS	HUARPA / RANCHA
500	EARLY HORIZON 1400 - 400 BC		CHAVIN INFLUENCE (JANABARRIU) / CUPISNIQUE	LATE HUACALOMA	CUPISNIQUE	CAYHUAMARCA	JANABARRIU / CHAKINANI / URABARRIU / CHAVIN	ANCON (CHAVIN)	DISCO VERDE	CHUPAS / KICHKAPATA / WICHQANA
1000										
1500	INITIAL PERIOD - 1400 BC			EARLY HUACALOMA				HALDAS	ERIZO	ANDAMARCA

This edition begins with a Foreword by Gordon R. Willey, Bowditch Professor (Emeritus) of Mexican and Central American Archaeology and Ethnology, Harvard University. Based on his personal acquaintance with Max Uhle and fieldwork at Pachacamac in 1941, he offers a succinct characterization of the historical significance of Uhle and the Pachacamac volume to the growth of New World archaeology.

My essay traces the roughly ninety years of scientific archaeology at Pachacamac and, to a lesser degree, in its vicinity on the Central Coast (defined here as comprised of Ancón and the three contiguous valleys of Chillón, Rimac, and Lurín) since Uhle's original fieldwork to define changing research personnel, issues, methodologies, and attendant perceptions and understanding of the site and the associated cultures. It is a selective rather than exhaustive review, focusing on four research areas where notable advances have been made:

1. Refinement of Uhle's basic Peruvian area-wide chronological outline through a series of stratigraphic excavations and detailed stylistic analyses of ceramics, including grave lots Uhle excavated.

2. Definition of the form, organization, function, and chronology of major architecture within the Pachacamac National Archaeological Monument through clearing and excavations by Peruvian national institutions and investigators.

3. Elucidation of the ideological and sociopolitical bases for the local, regional, and pan-Andean importance of Pachacamac for Incaic and pre-Incaic eras extending back into the Middle Horizon through detailed ethnohistorical research.

4. Comparative studies at contemporaneous "ceremonial centers" on the coast for better understanding of their interrelationships with Pachacamac, and the pan-Andean processes that may have been responsible for the ebb and flow of Pachacamac.

Finally, from the vantage of this long-term perspective, future research tasks and directions are charted. The accompanying bibliography is not intended to be exhaustive, but includes the most significant archaeological and complementary ethnohistorical studies on the site and related cultures subsequent to publication of the original volume. Aerial and ground-level photos, as well as drawings of the structures excavated and/or reconstructed since Uhle's excavation, document the changing appearance of the site. Tables 1-4 summarize and correlate various competing chronologies for the site and associated cultures.

Ceramic Analyses and Chronology Building

Efforts continue to refine the basic pan-Peruvian cultural chronology that Uhle established on the basis of his excavations at Pachacamac. Discussion here focuses on efforts to better define his "early regional" and "Tiahuanaco-influenced" styles and their broader cultural significance.

EARLY REGIONAL STYLES

(EARLY INTERMEDIATE PERIOD; PACHACAMAC I)

In his discussion of excavations carried out at archaeological sites around the modern city of Lima, Uhle (1910) defined a distinct "early regional" ceramic style called Proto-Lima. "Proto-" denoted "pre-Tiahuanaco influence," and "Lima" reflected his impression that the style was autochthonous and had enjoyed considerable popularity and prestige around the Lima region. Though Uhle (see pp. 28-29) encountered a handful of Proto-Lima sherds among the Tiahuanaco and Epigonal graves and between the adobes in the Pachacamac (Pachakamaj) Temple back

in 1896, he had not recognized their significance; initially, he was inclined to think of them as post-Tiahuanaco in date (Kroeber 1926:296).

Through his 1904 excavation at the site of Cerro de Trinidad in the lower Chancay Valley some 55 km northeast of the city of Lima, Uhle (1910) recognized the Proto-Lima as a distinct early regional style preceding Tiahuanaco influence.

In analyzing Uhle's collections from these two sites, Alfred L. Kroeber (1926) applied the term "Interlocking" to materials from Cerro de Trinidad, as these motifs were popular there on ceramics and murals, reserving Proto-Lima for related but somewhat later materials from the Nievería cemetery near the neck of the Rimac Valley. Uhle (1926:296) earlier had subsumed materials from both sites within his Proto-Lima. In her analysis of ceramics from Nievería, Anna Gayton (1927) followed Kroeber in calling them Proto-Lima in style. Kroeber (1954) continued his distinction between Interlocking and Proto-Lima in his report on the materials from Huaca Juliana (also called Pucllana) and Maranga (situated within modern metropolitan Lima).

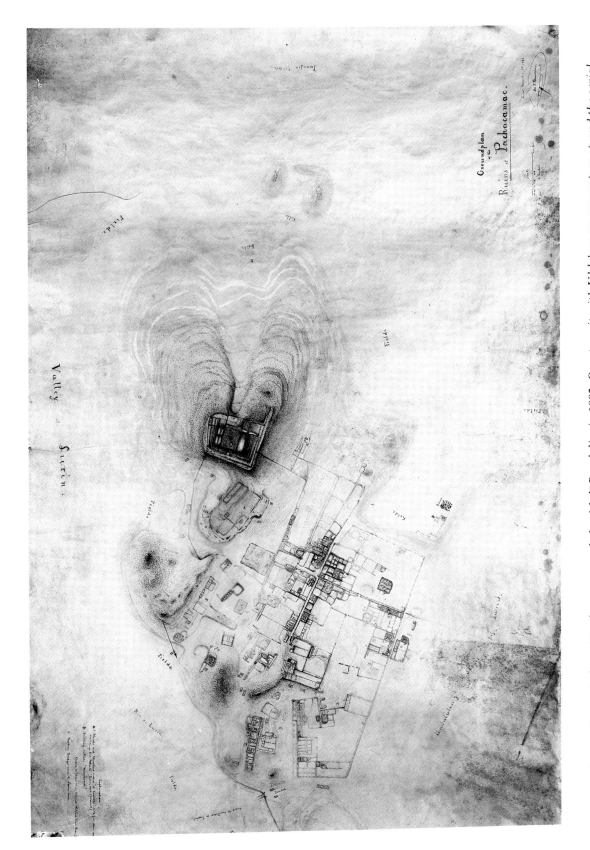

Plate 1. Ground plan of Pachacamac made by Adolf Bandelier in 1892. Compare it with Uhle's more accurate map and the aerial photographic mosaic (Pl. 2). (Courtesy of the Department of Library Services, American Museum of Natural History. Neg. no. 312536)

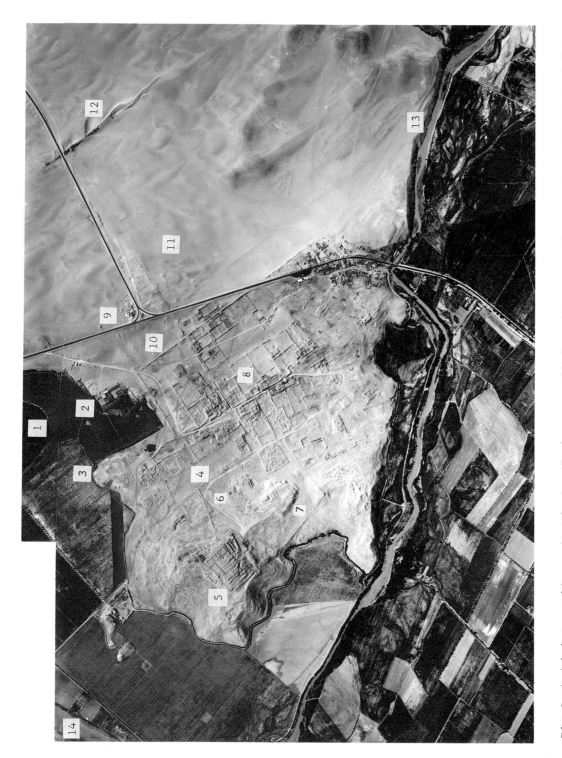

Plate 2. Aerial photographic mosaic of the site of Pachacamac and its immediate surroundings near the mouth of the Lurín River. (1) the Laguna de Urpi Wachak (The Ducks' Lagoon); (2) what Uhle called the Mamacona Convent and Tello called the Temple of the Moon; (3) identified by Tello as the Temple of Urpi Wachak; (4) the "Pilgrims' Plaza"; (5) the Temple of the Sun; (6) the Pachacamac Temple; (7) the "Old Temple of Pachacamac"; (8) the general area where the "Pyramids with Ramp" are found; (9) a modern highway; (10) what Uhle referred to as the Old City Wall; (11) the barrio, an extensive sand-covered area believed to have been the principal residential sector of the site; (12) the "great perimeter wall" of the site; (13) the Lurín River; and, (14) the Pacific Ocean. (Courtesy of the Servicio Aerofotográfico Nacional del Perú. Proyecto 6512-57 and 5-649; taken in 1958)

The distinction reflects Kroeber's general recognition of a significant stylistic change that occurred at the end of the long-lived regional style of the Early Intermediate Period (subdivided into eight Epochs; see Table 1) on the Central Coast. This early regional style is today commonly known as Lima and spans much of the Early Intermediate Period within the referent Peruvian chronology. It is characterized by predominantly geometric, highly abstracted designs painted in white and outlined in black against plain red-slipped background (e.g., intersecting straight lines, stylized figures with triangular or forked heads and serrated bodies). Though relatively rare, highly stylized fish or marine animals were also painted. The style forms a notable contrast to the predominance of representational (pictorial) and curvilinear decorations of the famous contemporaneous Mochica and Nasca styles that flourished on the North and South Coasts of Peru, respectively.

Concurrent with the above analyses of Uhle collections, efforts continued in the field to verify and refine the Uhle chronological scheme through excavations. As part of a long-term program of scientific and cultural cooperation between American republics, the Institute of Andean Research, working under the auspices of the Office of the Coordinator of Inter-American Affairs, sponsored fieldwork at Pachacamac and Cerro de Trinidad in 1941 (see Foreword; Strong and Corbett 1943). Both involved "intensive stratigraphic excavations in rubbish heaps with the primary purpose of defining ceramic types and sequences" (Strong 1942:182; Strong and Corbett 1943:31). Working alongside the Anthropological Museum team under the direction of Julio C. Tello, William D. Strong and John Corbett (1943:62-78; at times aided by Gordon R. Willey) excavated two deep cuts into a large refuse heap below and south of the west (main) entrance to the Temple of the Sun at Pachacamac. They found two major occupations: (1) the top 2 m of deposits containing abundant Inca and Late Intermediate Period ceramics and (2) some 8 m of deposits containing essentially Early Intermediate Period ceramics ("Pachacamac Interlocking" and related "types," including some "White-on-Red" and "Negative" painted ceramics). Associated with the latter was an adobe-and-stone structure and a number of nearby tombs. One tomb was remarkable in that some 100 skeletons were crowded within, together with several large jars and decorated cooking pots (Strong and Corbett 1943:41; Newman 1947). The structure was later abandoned and buried with debris that contained primarily Early Intermediate Period ceramics.

Curiously, Strong and Corbett used arbitrary, horizontal levels in excavating sloping deposits, thereby obscuring or disrupting critical associational data (Patterson 1974:66-67). In analyzing the materials from

the bottom 8 m, they did not recognize many stylistic differences and applied the type-variety technique rather than the approach advocated by Uhle, Kroeber, and more recently by Rowe (1959, 1961, 1962) that emphasizes association and units of contemporaneity.

In spite of their disregard of archaeological association, Strong and Corbett were able to define the ceramic sequence quite well, largely because of the distinctive character of the styles represented therein and findings made at other sites, notably by Uhle (1910; Kroeber 1926) and Willey (1943) at Cerro de Trinidad in the Chancay Valley. Willey's excavation in a thick, consolidated refuse heap yielded complementary results, with abundant Interlocking style ceramics underlaid by related Chancay White-on-Red pottery and a tomb. Thus, the Pachacamac sequence was extended backward in time by the addition of the White-on-Red style, and the relative order of Interlocking and White-on-Red styles was clearly defined. Thus, Strong and Corbett were able to show the pre-Tiahuanaco date of Pachacamac Interlocking and the probable presence of occupations by local populations during the Early Intermediate Period.

Overall, combined with data generated by Uhle and Willey, they established a regional chronology considerably more refined than that of Uhle: (from the most recent) (1) Inca Polychrome/Inca Associated styles, (2) Black and White on Red (Uhle's Late Coastal style), (3) Black-White-Red Geometric (Uhle's Late Pre-Inca style), (4) Epigonal, (5) Coastal Tiahuanaco, (6) Early Lima, (7) Pachacamac Interlocking, (8) Pachacamac Negative, (9) Pachacamac White-on-Red, and (10) Pachacamac Punctate and Incised. Though they were uncertain as to the chronological positions of the last three types, they had a general (and largely accurate) intuition that they pre-dated Pachacamac Interlocking. The punctate and incised ceramics may well date back to the final portions of the Early Horizon (see Table 1; Strong and Corbett 1943:77, Fig. 19; Stothert 1980:286). At the same time, their usage of the term "Early Lima" is quite inclusive and corresponds to what Kroeber and Gayton called "Proto-Lima" (see Table 2). Strong and Corbett (1943:87) assumed "general contemporaneity" of the "eclectic" and "variable" Early Lima style or stylistic complex. Precise chronological and stylistic differentiation within the complex came much later (see below).

Concurrent fieldwork in contemporaneous inland sites began to clarify the substantive aspects of the Lima culture but at the same time added to the existing terminological confusion. In 1925, Jijón y Caamaño (1949) carried out the first extensive archaeological excavations at the impressive site of Maranga in the lower Rimac Valley. It became apparent that most of the constructions at this site dated to the Early Intermediate Period. In describing Proto-Lima ceramics (à la Uhle)

TABLE 2
**Lima-Style
Terminological Correlation**

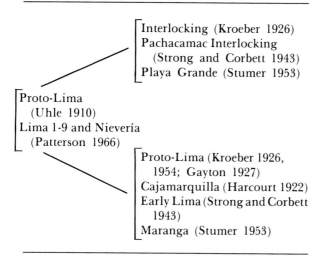

Interlocking (Kroeber 1926)
Pachacamac Interlocking
    (Strong and Corbett 1943)
Playa Grande (Stumer 1953)

Proto-Lima
    (Uhle 1910)
Lima 1-9 and Nievería
    (Patterson 1966)

Proto-Lima (Kroeber 1926,
    1954; Gayton 1927)
Cajamarquilla (Harcourt 1922)
Early Lima (Strong and Corbett
    1943)
Maranga (Stumer 1953)

associated with construction phases defined in one of the major mounds, Jijón y Caamaño (1949; see Patterson 1966:35) established a series of typological units designated "Maranga," "Interlocking," and "Cajamarquilla" in their presumed chronological order, with the last being latest and corresponding to the materials recovered from Nievería (see Table 2). The name "Cajamarquilla" was applied by Raoul d'Harcourt (1922; Table 2) in his description of ceramics from the vicinity of Cajamarquilla and Nievería. Both sites are located near the neck of the Rimac Valley. The former site was a major "urban" settlement with numerous contiguous rectangular rooms of *tapia* (or *adobón*, rammed earthen blocks) walls along narrow streets. Predominantly, these ceramics manifest strong Wari influence dating to the initial portion of the Middle Horizon (see Table 1). Thus, in contrast to the efforts of Kroeber and others, Jijón y Caamaño's inclusive usage of the term "Proto-Lima" (much like Uhle's usage) failed to properly recognize significant transformations of the "early regional style."

Input from foreign archaeologists to Peruvian archaeology dwindled during the interim period between the completion of the Institute of Andean Research field projects and the initiation of the Fulbright exchange program that brought a new generation of American scholars to Peruvian archaeology (Schaedel and Shimada 1982:361). One exception is Louis M. Stumer, who resided in Lima and had the independent means to pursue archaeology. Data from his extensive surveys and excavations of sites in the contiguous Rimac and Chillón Valleys (1954a, b), as well as excavations at the major Early Intermediate Period

habitation site of Playa Grande in Ancón (ca. 30 km north of Lima; 1953), formed the basis of his settlement pattern reconstruction (1954c) and stylistic and chronological analyses of the regional Early Intermediate Period cultures and their transformations during the early Middle Horizon (1953, 1954c, 1956).

In regard to the chronological issues at hand, along with Ernesto E. Tabío (1957, 1965), who also excavated Playa Grande, Stumer (1953, 1954c) began using the term "Playa Grande" to describe the Early Intermediate Period ceramics of the Central Coast, in the same way that the existing terms "Interlocking" and "Pachacamac Interlocking" were used (Table 2). In his excavation at Vista Algre (near the neck of the Rimac Valley), Stumer (1958) documented superposition of the Nievería style ceramics above those of the "Playa Grande" style but chose to call the former "Classic Maranga" (Fernández 1960). Stumer's "Maranga," then, is roughly the equivalent of "the Proto-Lima of Kroeber and Gayton and the Cajamarquilla styles of d'Harcourt and Jijón y Caamaño...." (Table 2; Patterson 1966:35).

As Patterson (1966:35) laments:

> The distinction between the Playa Grande and Maranga styles is not altogether clear. In any event, [Lima] pottery style has far too many names, and many of the names refer to typological rather than chronological distinctions that exist within the style. At present, there are problems involved in using all the names.

Thomas Patterson's dissertation work (1966), based on survey and test excavation of archaeological sites (1962-1963) between Pachacamac in the south and Lomas Lachay (Chancay Valley) in the north (with emphasis in the lower Chillón Valley and in the vicinity of Ancón just to the north), resulted in a significant refinement and terminological systematization of the regional Early Intermediate Period styles. In establishing his seriation, Patterson analyzed ceramics for synchronic patterns or interrelationships among vessel shape, decoration, and manufacturing technique by emphasizing association in contemporaneous contexts. Ceramics were also examined for diachronic processes of persistence and change, or how one phase evolved into the next by emphasizing similarities and stratigraphic positions (Patterson 1966:1-2; Rowe 1961).

Patterson (1966:36) revived the term "Lima" to describe this style as it "has priority in the archaeological literature... and approximately describes the area of known geographical distribution of the style." In his chronological scheme, Lima style is subdivided into nine phases, starting with Lima 1 in Early Intermediate Period 5 and ending with Lima 9 in Middle Horizon 1A (a span of ca. A.D. 250-600). The last three phases are the most problematical, as each is identified on the basis of a relatively small number (ca. 90) of sherds surface-collected at one site. These Lima phases follow four phases of Miramar style in the Ancón region and lower Chillón Valley (ca. 50 B.C. to A.D. 250; MacNeish et al. 1975:48) and are followed by the Nievería style of Middle Horizon 1B. The Miramar style is closely related to what Willey (1943) identified as Chancay White-on-Red (also known as the Baños de Boza style; Table 1), found in the Chancay Valley just north of Ancón. Overall, Patterson's detailed stylistic study clearly demonstrated the largely autochthonous and continuous nature of Miramar and Lima styles that had been long suspected by earlier investigators. Absolute dates for both Miramar and Lima styles are based on only a handful of radiocarbon dates and cross-dating with the better-dated South Coast referent chronology (Table 1), and thus should be regarded as tentative. However, it is unlikely that Lima style extended up to A.D. 800 (see Bueno 1982:26; Lumbreras 1974:119; see Table 3).

Patterson (1966:130-132, 1974) reanalyzed the materials recovered by Strong and Corbett (1943) in their excavations at the Temple of the Sun using his seriation and properly defining association. Thus, instead of the two major occupations identified by Strong and Corbett, Patterson was able to present a much more detailed occupational history for the area around the Temple of the Sun at Pachacamac:

> The presence of sherds belonging to the third and fourth phases of the Lima style at the bottom of the debris underlying the structure [immediately overlying the sterile zone] suggests that there may have been a small habitation site in the area at the time.... [I]t is clear that there was a major occupation that began at the time when Lima 7 pottery was being made. At the time of the Lima 8 or 9 style, a structure with adobe-brick and stone walls was built.... The structure was covered with a fill containing Lima 9 pottery at some later time.
>
> (Patterson 1966:114, 1974:67-68)

It appears, then, that the Temple of the Sun was built at least in part over an existing late Lima construction. Patterson (1966:115, 1974:69-70) suggests that, during Lima 8 and 9 (terminal Early Intermediate Period, ca. A.D. 500-550?), there was another major mound some 250 m east of the one found by Strong and Corbett beneath the Temple of the Sun. He notes its similarities in primary construction material (hand-shaped small rectangular adobe bricks, or adobitos) and overall configuration with those of major structures associated with Lima-style pottery at the sites of Copacabana, La Uva, Maranga, and the Huaca Juliana in the nearby Chillón and Rimac Valleys to the north.

Though attribution of the east mound to the Lima culture seems to be widely accepted (e.g, Bueno 1974/1975, 1982; Paredes 1987/1988), as we shall see later, there is confusion as to whether it corresponds to what historical documents call the Pachacamac Temple. The designation "Pachacamac" is a Quechua term imposed by the Incas for the chief pre-Incaic local deity called "Ichimay" or "Ichma" (inter alia; transcribed by Spaniards as Irma). The physical location of the Pachacamac Temple where this pre-Incaic cult was focused is now thought to have shifted over time.

With excavations carried out in the 1960s and 1970s by Arturo Jiménez Borja and Alberto Bueno (see below), the sample of Lima-style pottery at Pachacamac expanded considerably, but without significant refinement in its stylistic chronology (e.g., Lavallée 1966). In fact, Patterson's seriation is employed only sporadically, and the earlier, simpler Playa Grande-Maranga distinction continues to be widely employed in archaeological literature (e.g., Bueno 1974/75, 1982; Lavallée 1966; Lumbreras 1974). This preference also reflects the emphasis given to the site of Maranga in the Lima culture (see below).

TIAHUANACO-INFLUENCED STYLES

(MIDDLE HORIZON EPOCHS 1 AND 2; EARLY PACHACAMAC II)

Major advances also have been made in clarification of Uhle's "Tiahuanaco-influenced" styles and cultures at Pachacamac. It is apparent from the above comments on ceramics from Cajamarquilla and Nievería that, since the time of Uhle, it was widely recognized that the Central Coast experienced a major cultural transformation at the onset of the Middle Horizon that saw the arrival of "Tiahuanaco influence." However, clarification of the exact timing, source, and nature of this "influence" came much later.

In this regard, the most important contribution has been made by Dorothy Menzel (1958, 1964, 1968, 1969, 1977), who, by means of detailed stylistic analysis of ceramics, defined the problematical highland influence as having been the Wari (Huari) culture disseminating out of its capital at the urban site of Wari in the Ayacucho Basin (Fig. 1) through two waves (Middle Horizon Epochs 1B and 2A) of military conquest for religious proselytizing. Earlier identification of the source as "Tiahuanaco" (the main site of Tiahuanaco, or Tiwanaku, is situated on the south shore of Lake Titicaca on the Bolivian altiplano; see Fig. 1) is understandable given certain stylistic and iconographic similarities with Wari art. Menzel (1964:60, 67) suggests that the mythical themes that came to characterize Wari ceremonial ceramics were introduced into

TABLE 3
Evolución Social en el Valle de Lurín

PERIODOS NACIONALES	FORMACIONES SOCIALES	PATRONES DE ASENTAMIENTO	ZONAS ARQUEOLOGICAS
Imperio (1440-1533 d.n.e.)	**Lurín VII** Tawantinsuyo	**Pachacamac IV** Arquitectura Casas de Palacios Enclave Templos	Nieve-Nieve-Avillay-Huaycán II Mamacuna Pachacamac‹ Taurichumbi Templo del Sol
Formaciones Señoriales (1200-1470 d.n.e.)	**Lurín VI** Ichimay	**Pachacamac III** Pueblos Rurales en el Valle Pirámides con Rampa Frontal Ciudad Cultista Regional	Huaycán I-Chontay en Cieneguilla Pachacamac‹ Cuadrángulos/Depósitos Pirámides con rampa
Formaciones Urbanas (800-1200 d.n.e.)	**Lurín V** Wari/Complejo Lurín	**Pachacamac II** Arquitectura en Adobón Cuadrángulos Suroeste Entierros/Cerámica Wari	Construcciones adyacen- Pachacamac‹ tes al Montículo Suroeste Basurales Sur Cementerio I
Formaciones Regionales (100-800 d.n.e.)	**Lurín IV** Maranga	**Pachacamac I** Aldeas Locales Centros Cultistas Locales	Quebrada Grande en Cieneguilla
Formaciones Agroalfareras Epoca Desarrollada (1200-100 a.n.e.)	Complejo Tablada V **Lurín III** Complejo Tablada IV Chavín	Reciclajes Externos 2 Reciclajes Externos 1 Enclaves Cultistas	Pachacamac—Adobitos Urpiwachak Pachacamac—Montículo Suroeste Panel-Villa El Salvador-Tablada Tablada-Villa El Salvador-Panel Malache Cardal III Curayacu
Epoca Inicial Locales (2000-1200 a.n.e.)	Complejo Curayacu Complejo Manchay Bajo	Aldeas Sedentarias Centros Ceremoniales	⌈Manchay Bajo II ⌊Mina Perdida II Cardal II
Formativo (4000-2000 a.n.e.)	**Lurín II** Tablada de Lurín III	Conjuntos Ceremoniales "U" Aldeas Configurativas en Lomas Villas Incipientes en Lomas	⌈Manchay Bajo I ⌊Mina Perdida I Cardal I Tablada de Lurín Norte Piedra Liza Mal Paso Tablada de Lurín
Epoca Reciente (7000-4000 a.n.e.)	**Lurín I** Tablada de Lurín II Tablada de Lurín I	Campamentos/Refugios Campamentos en Lomas	Conchales distribuidos en toda la Tablada de Lurín Tablada de Lurín Norte

(Taken from A. Bueno M. 1982, Table 1)

the Ayacucho region by local men who learned the new religion, perhaps at Tiahuanaco, and brought it back, and that direct exchange between these two religious art styles may have taken place as late as Epoch 2A (see Cook 1983; Isbell 1983; Isbell and Cook 1987).

Working from the vantage of her familiarity with Wari style ceramics together with Stumer's (1958) finds at Vista Alegre, Menzel (1964:31-32) formally defined the Nievería style as the innovative result of fusion of Lima and intrusive highland styles during Middle Horizon Epoch 1B.

Of particular importance to our study is Menzel's definition of Pachacamac style based mainly on ceramic specimens from Pachacamac published by Uhle (1903, reprinted in this volume), Baessler (1902-1903) and Schmidt (1929), supplemented with examples from Ancón (Strong 1925) and Nievería cemeteries (Gayton 1927). The inferred emergence of this style in Epoch 2A is said to reflect the rise of the site of Pachacamac (with its physical focus presumably at what Uhle called Pachacamac Temple) as the most prestigious and influential religious center of the Peruvian coast (Menzel 1964:70). Two phases, Pachacamac A and B, are recognized, with the more conservative A corresponding to Middle Horizon Epoch 2A and the more stylistically variable and advanced B assigned to Epoch 2B (Menzel 1964:70; see Table 1). In the terminology of Peruvian colleagues (Paredes 1985), Menzel's Pachacamac A and B are subsumed within Pachacamac II (Tables 2, 3).

The style is composed of features selected from the local antecedent Nievería style, Epoch 2 "Atarco" (a South Coast stylistic variant), and the Viñaque and Derived Conchopata and Robles Moqo styles of highland Wari origin (Menzel 1964:36-38, 53-55). Lumbreras (1974:157) sees "strong influences from the earlier Lima style" in respect to extensive modeling and vessel form, in particular, in the "globular bottle with a long conical spout joined to the body by a handle."

One of the main icons of the Pachacamac style is the "Front-faced Deity." Called the "Male Deity" by Menzel (1964:19, 1977:33, 55; see Uhle's Fig. 16, p. 26), this is an elaborate, full-bodied, front-face anthropomorphic figure with supernatural attributes, holding staffs in his hands, and may represent the sun (and/or perhaps thunder). It is often accompanied by auxiliary figures shown in profile called "attendants" or "angels" (Menzel 1964:20). This deity occupied the dominant position in the Wari and Tiahuanaco iconographies and is thought to have been the visual symbol of their sovereignty (Cook 1985, 1987).

The most distinctive feature of the Pachacamac style is the mythical figure that Menzel (1964:59-60, 1977:31) calls "Pachacamac Griffin" (Fig. 2; see Uhle's Figs. 17b, 19, and Pl. 4.4), a supernatural being with an eagle head and winged feline body, who was apparently an attendant to the Front-faced Deity (Knobloch n.d.). Lumbreras (1974:157) considers the bird to be a falcon. The Griffin is essentially a local synthesis of earlier highland Wari mythical themes. The Pachacamac B griffin differs from that of Phase A, for example, in missing the belt on the hip and bars or lines in the center of the limbs (representing bones?; Knobloch n.d.). Limbs are often shown with simple paw lines, rather than human hands and feet, and the headdress is omitted or considerably simplified. The bodiless mythical eagle head is also said to be "exceedingly common in Phase B and is confined to the Pachacamac style" (Menzel 1964:61). In Epoch 2B, the Pachacamac Griffin was not "represented in religious art centered in other parts of the [Wari] Empire" (Menzel 1977:31). The feline-headed being was apparently eliminated in the Pachacamac B style.

Knobloch (n.d.) suggests that various supernatural creatures including the Pachacamac Griffin and the Front-faced Deity icons "formed a complete mythological explanation for the sun and stars in which supernatural creatures could run across the earth, fly into the night sky and return to earth, thereby accompanying and attending to the sun deity."

With her rather limited data base of published and unpublished Middle Horizon Pachacamac ceramics (both with and without gravelot association), Menzel (1964:61) saw room for further refinement in analysis of the Pachacamac style with a larger sample. Her Epoch 2A sample, including 3 gravelot associations, contained 6 sherds and 16 vessels, whereas the Epoch 2B sample included 10 gravelot associations.

Some important results are emerging from ongoing analysis of the Pachacamac style by Patricia Knobloch, who has enlarged the data base by inclusion of excavated, unpublished vessels. Knobloch (1987, personal communication) points out that the W. Gretzer and A. Baessler collections of Pachacamac pottery at the Museum für Völkerkunde in Berlin are far larger than the ninety-one vessels suggested in the Baessler (1902/1903) and Schmidt (1929) publications. In fact, the inclusion of all relevant vessels from these collections, according to Knobloch (1987, personal communication), would more than double the data base used by Menzel, who only studied published photographs. It should be noted, however, that there is a distinct possibility that a certain portion of these early collections, though perhaps attributed to the site of Pachacamac because of its fame, was not derived from there.

Knobloch (1987, personal communication) found that the Pachacamac style was not restricted to Middle Horizon Epoch 2 as Menzel thought and defined an early version, designated Pachacamac I, for Epoch 1B. This style is characterized by the Pachacamac Griffin,

PACHACAMAC GRIFFIN (MIDDLE HORIZON 2A)

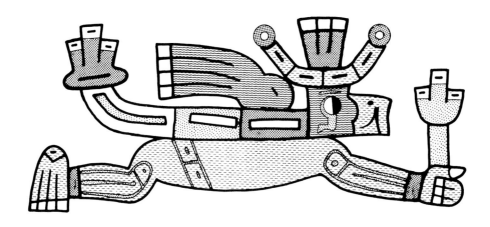

PACHACAMAC GRIFFIN (MIDDLE HORIZON 2B)

WHITE   GREY   BLACK   CREAM   BROWN   DARK
                                                  BROWN

Figure 2. (A) Roll-out drawing of a rather complete version of the Pachacamac Griffin, taken from a Pachacamac A style vessel at the Museum für Völkerkunde, Berlin (VA 19059); (B) roll-out drawing of the Pachacamac Griffin, taken from a Pachacamac B style vessel at the Museum für Völkerkunde, Berlin (VA 19175). Note the simplification from the preceding. It is no longer shown with the staff or "bonelike" details on the limbs. Drawing by the author.

human figures, and the Front-faced Deity. On this basis, she (1987, personal communication) suggests that Pachacamac "earned the reputation of a pilgrimage site during Middle Horizon 1 with priestly individuals who proselytized the new mythology."

EPIGONAL STYLES

(MIDDLE HORIZON EPOCHS 3 AND 4; LATE PACHACAMAC II)

Chronological anchoring and explicit stylistic definitions of the widely distributed and influential Wari and Wari-related styles have allowed cross-dating of various regional styles, for example, the Teatino style of the Ancón and Chancay (Bonavia 1962; Menzel 1977: 45, 47; also see Kaulicke 1983). In addition, they have brought better understanding of what Uhle (p. 21) called "Epigone" styles, which imply "less distinguished successors of an illustrious generation" (Oxford English Dictionary 1971). The Epigonal styles that essentially belong to Middle Horizon Epochs 3 and 4 were commonly inferior in craftsmanship to those of the preceding era and typically simplified, localized, less formal versions of the Wari and Pachacamac or their related styles in Epoch 2. For example, Lyon (1966:41) summarized the general trend in the regional ceramics of Ica on the South Coast between Epochs 2 and 4 as "simplification." The above general characterization also applies to Central Coast epigonal styles known by names such as Teatino, Pachacamac II-D, Middle Ancón II (see Tables 1, 3, 4; see also Kaulicke 1983:7; Kroeber 1926, 1944; Strong 1925; Willey 1943). They seem stylistically quite similar having simple, nonrepresentational line patterns in two or three colors (red, white, black) and Patterson (MacNeish et al. 1975: 62) proposes subsuming them under the rubric of Chillón style. Menzel (1977: 47) sees these styles to "have been partly inspired by stylistic innovations of the coast to the north."

LATE COASTAL STYLES

(LATE INTERMEDIATE PERIOD; PACHACAMAC III)

Chronological and stylistic differentiation for the succeeding Late Intermediate Period is still imprecise. In addition, there is a strong tendency to base archaeological interpretation on ethnohistorical data (see below). The veracity of the latter is implicitly assumed rather than independently tested by the former.

Though various styles are identified within the Pachacamac III period in Table 2, their chronological and stylistic definitions have not been adequately presented. Such definitions are essential in support of inferences on the ethnic and geographical identities of regional polities and religions said to have been represented at the site of Pachacamac during this time period. The Geometric Tricolor style in Table 2 corresponds to the Three-color Geometric or Black-White-Red Geometric of the early Late Intermediate Period defined by Kroeber (1926) at Chancay, Strong (1925; his Late Ancón I) at Ancón, and Strong, Willey and Corbett (1943) at Pachacamac. It is described by Patterson and Lanning (1964:116) as highly characteristic of the Chancay Valley and less common farther south. As defined by these investigators, it combines earlier Epigonal elements with innovative use of white background paint and geometric red and black designs (Strong and Corbett 1943:89).

In the Lurín Valley, the Three-color Geometric evolves into the White-on-Red Ichimay (also called Huancho; see, e.g., Iriarte 1960) style believed to date to the time the *Señorío* (ethnic polity) of Ichimay dominated the valley, including the site of Pachacamac (ca. thirteenth to fifteenth centuries; Bueno 1982:41; Feltham 1983, 1984). The Ichimay style resembles the contemporaneous Black-on-White Late Chancay style (Horkheimer 1963) in its use of bichrome and modeling to represent a range of animal and human forms (Bueno 1982:41-42). At the same time, it differs in having a reddish coarse paste as opposed to off-white paste of the latter that was very well fired. These two styles have clearly distinct distributions; the former is found as far south as Mala, Cañete, and Chincha on the South-Central Coast (Bueno 1982:41-42), whereas the latter is found primarily along the coast from Huacho, Chancay, Ancón, and the northern bank of the Chillón Valley. Patterson and Lanning (1964:116; MacNeish et al. 1975:62) note that the southern Chillón shared its pottery style with the Rimac Valley just to the south. They (1964) note that this bipartite ceramic distribution matches ethnohistorical descriptions (particularly those of Father Bernabé Cobo) of the linguistic and sociopolitical separation of the Central Coast into two groups. Pachacamac clearly belonged to the southern group; Late Chancay pottery has not yet been found at Pachacamac (Bueno 1982:42). Thus, Patterson (MacNeish et al. 1975: 62) infers that after A.D. 1050 "the influence of the Pachacamac oracle became more localized" on the southern Central Coast.

ABSOLUTE CHRONOLOGY

In contrast to the refinements achieved in stylistic dating, absolute dating of eight constituent epochs of the Early Intermediate Period and the four epochs (1-4) and their subdivisions (A and B) of the Middle Horizon is still tenuous at best. There are only a handful of pub-

TABLE 4
Chronological Correlation for Pachacamac

DATE	CULTURE	PHASE	CERAMIC STYLE	MAJOR TEMPLES	ICONOGRAPHY OF PACHACAMAC
1500	Inca	B	Provincial Inca		
	Pachacamac IV	A	Imperial Inca	Temple of the Sun	
1400					
		III	Ichma/Yauyos	Pyramids	
1300			Chancay N/B		
	Ichimay	II	Ichma Bichrome	with	Replica Wooden
1200	**Pachacamac III**		Geometric Tricolor		Icons
			Ichma Plain	Ramps	
1100		I	Epigonal Tricolor		
1000				P T	
		D	Epigonal Styles	A E	
900				I M	
	Huari	C	"Local" Huari	N P	Double-faced
800	**Pachacamac II**			T L	
		A-B	"Classic" Huari	E E	Wooden Icon
700				D	
		V	Nievería		
600				O T	
		IV	Maranga	L E	
500				D M	
				P	
400				L	
	Lima	III	Playa Grande	E	
300	**Pachacamac I**			OF	Stone Icon?
200				P	
				A	
100				C	
A.D.		II	Tablada de Lurín	H	
				A	
B.C.				C	
100				A	
				M	
200				A	
		I	Baños de Boza	C	
300			(B/R)		
400					

(Based on P. Paredes B. and R. Franco J. 1987)

lished dates for the entire span of Early Intermediate Period on the Central Coast. Specific dates presented earlier for Miramar and Lima styles should be taken as tentative dates.

Epoch 1A (Lima 9) has no radiocarbon dates and presumably spans ca. A.D. 550-600. Middle Horizon 1B Nievería appears to span ca. A.D. 600 to 700 or as late as 750 on the basis of cross-dating with the securely radiocarbon-dated terminal phase of the Mochica culture (Moche V) on the north coast (see Shimada 1990). Nievería ceramics were recovered by the Italian Mission led by Claudio Sestieri (1964, 1971) in the "Grupo Tello" portion of the site of Cajamarquilla close to the Nievería cemetery. However, detailed associational data are not described for the two published dates (R-302, 1160 ± 50 [790 ± 50 a.d.], Trench 1, Huaca A, associated with black pottery, terminal Lima?; R-301, 1100 ± 100 [850 ± 100], charcoal found with Nievería and late Lima ceramics; Alessio et al. 1967:363) and thus they cannot be reliably assigned to the Middle Horizon 1B. The most problematical are Middle Horizon Epoch 2A (emergence of Pachacamac A; see Anders 1990:35-37 for discussion of possible contemporaneity of Epochs 1B and 2A ceramics) and 2B (the second wave of Wari expansion and their subsequent decline at the end of the epoch), and the Wari occupation at the site of Wari itself (see Isbell 1988), as there are only a few reliable radiocarbon dates.

The Middle Sicán blackware bottles that Uhle excavated in front of the Pachacamac Temple are Middle Horizon Epoch 3 in style dating to ca. A.D. 1000. In fact, Middle Sicán style on the northern North Coast can be securely dated to ca. A.D. 900-1100 on a basis of internally consistent set of some two dozen radiocarbon dates (Shimada 1990). This would mean that Middle Horizon Epoch 2 is up to 200 years long and two subdivisions for the Epoch seem inadequate. At the same time, one needs to be aware of the potentially serious problem of equating time and style; stylistically contemporaneous ceramics of geographically distinct regions (e.g., Ayacucho and North Coast) may diverge considerably in absolute date possibly due to conservatism or time lag in spread of the style.

Absolute dating of the Late Intermediate Period is not much better than for the preceding periods. Ichimay (Huancho) style has a couple of dates: Tx-2370, 780 ± 60 BP [1170 ± 60 a.d.] for charcoal from a tomb within a residential sector of the Monterrico Grande Oeste 1 site some 8 km east of Lima, and Tx-2449, 700 ± 50 BP [1250 ± 50 a.d.] for cotton cloth fragments and organic remains from Mummy Bundle No. 60 derived from Rinconada Alta, La Molina 5 km east of Lima (Valastro et al. 1978:270-271). They compare reasonably well with historically derived dates of the thirteenth to the fifteenth century (Bueno 1982:41).

Table 5 compiles published radiocarbon dates for the site of Pachacamac. The first three young dates for the Pyramid with Ramp No. 2 presumably reflect reoccupation during the historical era, whereas the remaining three assays point to the Late Intermediate Period. Because the associated ceramics have not been described, these three dates cannot be compared with the two other Late Intermediate dates above. Further, these dates for Pyramid with Ramp 2 were obtained at the radiocarbon laboratory of the Catholic University in Lima, which in the past has produced some problematical dates. These dates should be considered tentative until confirmed by independent dating by another laboratory. The three dates for the Temple of the Sun are quite variable and were derived nearly forty years ago shortly after the introduction of the radiocarbon-dating technique using samples collected from secondary refuse contexts. The remaining dates may be somewhat more reliable. In general, the available radiocarbon dates do not help us refine the stylistic seriation.

Defining Architectural Organization, Function, and Chronology at Pachacamac

The site of Pachacamac has long attracted tourists and scholars alike from all over the world for a variety of reasons. Daggett (1988:13-14) explains that "though the size and complexity of the site, as well as its proximity to Lima, are obvious lures to potential investigators, the true significance of Pachacamac lies in the length and nature of its occupation. From its founding around the first century A.D. to its occupation by the Spanish in the sixteenth century, this site played an important role in first local, then regional, then pan-regional ceremonial activities." In addition, the site boasts good preservation of archaeological remains, impressive architecture set against the contrasting sceneries of the arid coastal plateau, the Lurín River, and the Pacific, and a distinctive and widespread art style of its own. The site was in many ways a highly appropriate setting for Uhle's pioneering fieldwork that helped establish the basic pan-Peruvian chronological framework.

Understandably, Pachacamac has been one of Peru's most cherished and well-known national monuments. Yet following Uhle's pioneering excavation, there was

TABLE 5
Radiocarbon Dates for Pachacamac

Pachacamac Temple (Painted Temple)[1]:

LAB NO.	PROVENANCE	DATES	COMMENTS
PUCP-83	Floor, Grid B, Central Atrium	1180 ± 70 BP (770 ± 70 a.d.)	remains of *lúcuma* wood pole inside the circular pedestal base

Pyramid with Ramp, No. 2[2]:

SAMPLE	PROVENANCE	DATES	COMMENTS
I-B-11	principal entry, Grid B-11	140 ± 80 BP (1810 ± 80 a.d.)	wood, possible door lintel
II-J-2	Forecourt, Grid J-2	A. 110 ± 40 BP (1840 ± 40 a.d.) B. 230 ± 80 BP (1720 ± 80 a.d.)	small wooden window bars
II-E-5	Forecourt, Grid E-5	250 ± 80 BP (1700 ± 80 a.d.)	wooden post in refuse pile
III-C-4	"Pyramid," Grid C-4	600 ± 70 BP (1350 ± 70 a.d.)	wooden lintel of vaulted niche
VI-D-4	Smaller pyramidal structure, Grid D-4	654 ± 80 BP (1396 ± 80 a.d.)	wooden post remains on floor
IX-E-6	Auxiliary buildings, Grid E-6	660 ± 160 BP (1290 ± 160 a.d.)	burnt, worked wood found on terrace

Temple of the Sun (all dated at the Lamont Laboratory)[3]:

LAB NO.	PROVENANCE	DATES	COMMENTS
L-123a		3800 ± 200 BP (1849 ± 200 a.d.)	marine shell (mostly *Concholepas* and *Mytilus*) associated with Inca and Provincial Inca ceramics; collected by D. Strong in 1941
L-123b		900 ± 150 BP (1051 ± 150 a.d.)	organic materials consisting of cords, mats, reed and *junco* grass; associated with Inca ceramics (?)
L-123c		500 ± 120 BP (1451 ± 120 a.d.)	remains of llama and other animals' skin; associated with Inca ceramics

Other Contexts[4]:

IVIC-182B		1280 ± 85 BP (670 ± 85 a.d.)	woven net; Middle Horizon?
Hv-351		990 ± 40 BP (960 ± 40 a.d.)	charcoal
U-156		640 ± 180 BP (1310 ± 180 a.d.)	cloth from a looted burial
IVIC-182A		modern	wood

[1]Paredes and Franco 1985:80.
[2]Paredes and Franco 1987:7.
[3]Ravines and Alvarez 1967:21.
[4]Ravines 1982:164-165.

a long hiatus in on-site fieldwork until 1938. Descriptions of the site of Pachacamac that appeared during this period (e.g., Urteaga 1914; Villar Cordova 1935) offered some architectural details not found in Uhle's publication, but in general no significant new insights. Monsignor Pedro E. Villar Cordova's (1935:207-221) synthesis of Central Coast archaeology, for example, while recording some new details of the Temple of Sun's construction and painting, presents only an impressionistic description of the site and cultural reconstructions based on sixteenth- and seventeenth-century documents and Uhle's prior findings. In fact, during these years much of the archaeological attention on the Central Coast (Uhle's included) was directed to major sites in adjacent areas to the north (e.g., Maranga, Cajamarquilla, and Cerro de Trinidad).

THE NATIONAL MUSEUM ACTIVITIES AND DISCOVERIES AT THE PACHACAMAC TEMPLE

In 1938, the National Museum (with field direction by Albert Giesecke, an American economist with no training in archaeology) initiated the first cleaning and reconstruction project of the monumental structures at Pachacamac (Antúnez de Mayolo 1938; Casa Vilca 1939; Muelle and Wells 1939:265). The project seems to have been modeled after the reconstruction projects being carried out at major Mexican sites and was intended to preserve the site, particularly from the wanton destruction of *huaqueros* (grave looters) and allow public visitation (Anon. 1938). It was also motivated by government interest in creating a special attraction for those attending the VIIIth Pan American Congress (1938) and the 27th International Congress of Americanists (1939) in nearby Lima (Anon. 1938; Muelle and Wells 1939:265). The project soon came under fire by Julio C. Tello, perhaps the best-known and highly influential Peruvian archaeologist, who saw it as quite destructive and wanting in technical direction and control (Anon. 1938). The subsequent debate as to the merits of the project is summarized by Daggett (1988:14-15).

The National Museum project, nonetheless, did yield some important discoveries. Cleaning of the northeast side of the Temple of the Sun (a trapezoidal five-tiered platform mound constructed by the Incas atop the highest portion of the site; Pl. 3) revealed an elevated portico and the associated vestibule, as well as two stone staircases that guided traffic toward the summit from the base of the mound. In addition, Giesecke found storerooms atop the summit with many well-preserved original contents, including Inca cloth, maize, hot peppers, and peanuts (Casa Vilca 1939). The thrust of the work at the summit, however, was

clearing and reconstruction of the inferred "Temple of the Sun Sanctuary" with central, trapezoidal windows, as well as symmetrically opposed altars and wall niches. The sanctuary is believed to have been the setting for worshiping the sun (Casa Vilca 1939).

Perhaps the best-known discoveries of the National Museum team are those made at what Uhle called the Pachacamac Temple (9 levels of terraces; ca. 115 x 55 m x 9 m high; Fig. 3; Pl. 4). Since the time of Uhle's (pp. 11, 13, 20-21) fieldwork, this large terraced mound (ca. 100 m long x 40 m wide at the top) situated just to the north of the Temple of the Sun had been known for its polychrome murals of birds and other creatures decorating the terrace faces. As this was the only ornately painted structure he found at the site, Uhle regarded this as the finely painted house where the *Conquistadores* led by Hernando Pizarro found the venerated idol in 1533. Thus, Uhle named it the Pachacamac Temple (today called Painted or Polychrome Temple; see below).

On the northwest side of the Pachacamac Temple, the National Museum team exposed new frescoes that were recorded and analyzed by Jorge Muelle (Muelle and Wells 1939), who had studied art before turning to archaeology. Muelle found that different portions of the temple preserved painting of different styles and times. Small Altar D in the entry to the Hall of the Columns at the temple, for example, had sixteen superimposed layers of painting (Muelle and Wells 1939:277-278). Plate 4 shows the terraces on the northwest side where portions of schematic representations of fish and plants (maize?) painted in either pink or yellow (the other color used as the background; both ochre) are still recognizable. The walls and four columns in the Hall of Columns, however, were painted light blue, the only location where this color is known to occur at the site (Muelle and Wells 1939:266). Without some conservation measures, however, these exposed paintings are destined to disappear.

The fortunate recovery of painting brushes and bags containing pigments has allowed a detailed reconstruction of painting techniques and pigments (Muelle and Wells 1939; Bonavia 1974, 1985). Paints were applied by means of large balls of cotton on plastered adobes or rocks; motifs were applied by brushes (human hair) and later outlined with black lines to make the figures stand out more (Muelle and Wells 1939:274, 277).

Paintings are difficult to date, in part due to their fragmentary and superposed nature. Bonavia (1985:146-147) dates the exposed paintings to the Late Intermediate Period and Late Horizon. Given the range of burials Uhle found in front of this temple, it is likely that this temple dates back to sometime in the Middle Horizon.

Perhaps the most unexpected find was that of a "wooden idol" among the rubble in front of the

Plate 3. Oblique angle aerial view of the Temple of the Sun, looking west toward the Pacific. (Courtesy of the Servicio Aerofotográfico Nacional del Perú. Photo no. 0-1621; taken in 1943)

Plate 4. Remains of polychrome frescoes on the north terraces of the Pachacamac (Courtesy of the author. Taken in June 1989)

PLAN OF THE "PAINTED PYRAMID,"
PACHACAMAC

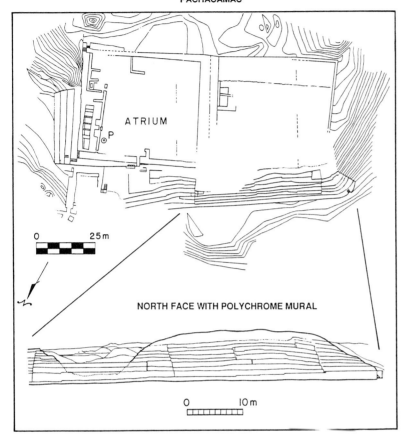

Figure 3 (left). Plan of the Pachacamac Temple ("Painted Pyramid") showing constructions atop the platform and the location of the best-preserved polychrome mural. "P" represents the circular pedestal for a wooden column. Composite drawing made by the author from topographic map by Carlos Farfán (Paredes 1985:79) and Figure 5 in Muelle and Wells (1939: 273). Compare it with Uhle's plan (what he called Pachacamac Temple).

Figure 4. Middle Horizon 2B(?) style carving on the wooden idol found at the base of the Pachacamac Temple. Redrawn by the author from the original in Jiménez Borja (1985:47, Photo 4).

temple. The idol, measuring 234 cm long and 27 cm in diameter (see various views shown in Antúnez de Mayolo 1938; Bueno 1982:39; Kosok 1965:39, Fig. 2; 45, Fig. 11; Jiménez Borja 1985:47, his Photos 3 and 4; Paredes 1985:79), consists of three parts: (a) the uppermost section (58 cm high and 15 cm wide) with a standing figure, (b) mid-section with elaborate carving measuring 122 cm high, and (c) the bottom portion without any ornamentation (54 cm high). The figure atop the pole is in reality a composite of what Antúnez de Mayolo (1938) identifies as a pair of "male" and "female" figures back-to-back. Jiménez Borja (1985:46) considers it to be two males. Bueno (1974/1975:189) regards it as a pair of male-female Siamese twins. Each is shown with its own face and pair of legs, but the torso and arms are shared. The "male" wears a dress decorated with a maize motif, and the "female" is adorned with what Antúnez de Mayolo (1938) believes to be a yucca motif. Below the figure, the mid-section of the pole has intricate carving in the round (Fig. 4) that shows, among others, a pair of seated animals facing each other, a simplified Pachacamac-style griffin(?), a smaller version of the same "male" figure described above, and double-headed serrated arcs.

Bueno (1974/1975:189; 1982:38-39) considers the idol to be an "epigonal" reinterpretation (more naturalistic and terrestrial in character) of earlier Wari motifs and assigns it to Pachacamac III (eleventh to twelfth century A.D.). However, strong influence of an earlier North Coast religious tradition can be seen, and stylistically the idol can be dated earlier to Middle Horizon Epoch 2B (ca. A.D. 800-900?). The pairs of seated animals with spotted body markings is quite reminiscent of what Menzel (1977:63; also Fig. 8 in Shimada 1990:315) calls the "Moon Animals" of the North Coast tradition. These are mythical creatures with attributes of various animals such as foxes and felines. Menzel (1977:62) notes that the Moon Animal "came to be treated interchangeably with the Feline Star Animal" of Wari religion as they are both sky spirits in animal form. The double-headed serrated arcs, on the other hand, are Middle Horizon Epoch 2 versions of the North Coast Sky Serpent, which ends in Wari style mythical appendage heads. In a typical Middle Horizon North Coast sky scene, the Sky Serpent arches over a feline spirit animal. Overall, the carving appears to have strong linkage to celestial creatures and forces that affected terrestrial life. Jiménez Borja (1985:42) regards the idol as the *axis mundi* and symbolic of the "tree of life."

Given that the temple was in use in 1533, the wooden idol was apparently either handed down from generation to generation since its carving sometime late in the Middle Horizon or represents a more recent copy of the original. Bueno (1982:38), like many scholars before

him, considers the idol found by Giesecke to be the same one encountered by the Spaniards in 1533 atop the Pachacamac Temple. Importantly, the idol was found in rubble by Giesecke together with a door built of wooden sticks (both exhibited at the Pachacamac Site Museum). The door was covered on both sides with cotton cloths. One shows a complex scene depicting *Strombus* (trumpet shell) surrounded by marine creatures, birds and plants, and the other is plain, adorned with *Spondylus* (thorny oyster) shell, just as the eyewitness, Miguel Estete, described (Bueno 1974/1975:175, 1982:36-37). Accordingly, the idol is identified as the icon of the local, pre-Inca deity Rma or Ichimay.

Antúnez de Mayolo (1938) interprets the idol iconography on the basis of a historic legend about the mother and the son created by Pachacamac (a creator god in Quechua) and the death of the son who is subsequently regenerated (see Rostworowski 1981:44-45 for details); that is to say, the idol symbolizes Pachacamac the deity and his power over the life forces.

Bueno (1974/75:189, 1982:37-41) offers another, more elaborate interpretation. He sees the carving as combining human, animal, plant, and celestial components in an allegoric representation of mythical and natural cosmogonies. The Siamese twins symbolize unification of female and male sexes that results in procreation and fertility, and thus the creator and protector deities of the coastal inhabitants, Ichimay (renamed Pachacamac by the Incas) and his wife, Urpi Wachak, the nucleus of the cult centered at Pachacamac. He believes the heavy "agrarian" connotation of the idol was matched by the marine life depicted on the associated wooden door. Bueno (1982: 40) stylistically dates the wooden door to the fourteenth to fifteenth century, preceding Inca arrival.

Overall, many of the discrepancies found among competing interpretations of the idol iconography stem from divergent usages of historically recorded myths and folklore, and they effectively illustrate the difficulty in deciphering the deep cultural meanings of any Prehispanic art.

The program of clearing, mapping, and excavation at the Pachacamac Temple that began in 1983 under the direction of Ponciano Paredes found a fragment of *lúcumo* (*Lucuma obovata*) wood at the center of the remains of a circular clay pedestal (with greenish blue paint 20 cm high and 27 cm diam) in the central atrium (Paredes and Franco 1985:80). The pedestal is surrounded by a stone circle 30 cm high and 67 cm in diameter. Paredes and Franco hypothesize that the wood is a fragment of an icon representing one of the ethnic groups inscribed to the cult of Pachacamac. The wooden remains yielded a C-14 date of 1180 ± 70 BP (770+70 a.d.; PUCP-83).

ANTHROPOLOGICAL MUSEUM ACTIVITIES UNDER JULIO C. TELLO

Julio C. Tello, as the director of the Anthropological Museum in Magdalena, Lima (which he founded in 1938), began his fieldwork at Pachacamac in May 1940 with the help of his colleagues and students (Rebeca Carrión Cachot, Toribio Mejía Xesspe, Julio Espejo Nuñez, Luís Ccosi Salas and Cirilio Huapaya; Anon. 1940a, b; Tello 1940a, b, 1943; 1960:30). His excavation and reconstruction projects continued intermittently until his death in 1947. In undertaking this project, Tello seems to have been intrigued by the possibility that recently uncovered cut masonry at Pachacamac might have been of Chavín origin. This stems from his overriding interest in the Chavín culture, "la cultura matriz de la civilización andina" in his estimation.

Unfortunately, he wrote no technical report with details of the work he directed at Pachacamac. The following brief description is based on information extracted piecemeal from brief notices he and others wrote in periodicals and newspapers, and from sections in his general cultural syntheses of the Andean civilization (Anon. 1940a, b; Tello 1940a, b, 1942, 1943, 1960).

In general, the Anthropological Museum project under his direction was more structured than the earlier National Museum work and started with survey, mapping, and test pits of various sectors of the site to document known structures and discover new materials and architecture. It is apparent that Tello, like Uhle before him, was well aware that the site of Pachacamac was two to three times greater in extent than suggested by visible structures. Tello knew that during dry spells structures would emerge in the low-lying area west of the "ceremonial sector" (see below) toward the Pacific shore. His survey extended as far north as the major adobe "Outer Wall" of the site that runs perfectly parallel to what Uhle called the "Old City Wall" some 900 m to the south. Tello saw this perimeter wall as a ceremonial road used by priests and worshipers to walk between various religious structures and ceremonial precincts of the site. He considered the many lengthy walls found on the slopes of Andean foothills, including the famous "Santa Wall" in the Santa Valley on the North Coast, to have served a similar function of linking religious centers of the coast and highlands and rejected the argument that their function was defensive. At Pachacamac, there are walls 3-5 m wide and Uhle (pp. 57-59) himself speaks of "roadways over the walls." However, Uhle's comment pertains to the "Pyramids with Ramps" and associated walled enclosures (see below). Tello's view of the perimeter wall is questionable; there are a number of ground-level, walled streets that linked major sectors of the site, and it is not clear which religious structures

and ceremonial precincts would have been served by his ceremonial road.

Tello's fieldwork was largely focused on clarification of architectural organization, function, and chronology of major constructions found in one of the four major sectors Uhle recognized at the site (see Pl. 2); the western "ceremonial" sector with its series of "pyramids" (strictly speaking, "pyramids" at Pachacamac are multilevel or terraced platform mounds) or "temples" and associated plazas. This sector is also known as the "Max Uhle" Group. Three other sectors in Tello's terminology are (1) the central zone containing "great mansions" or "walled palaces," (2) the eastern "urban" sector with relatively well-built, "minor mansions" with clearly defined doorways and patios but without enclosing walls, and (3) the least explored and understood northern sector of extensive *barrio*, or "suburbs."

Tello considered "walled palaces" to be communal residences of elite social groups similar to those found at Chan Chan, the capital of the Chimú Kingdom on the North Coast. In regard to the structures in the eastern urban sector, both Uhle and Tello seem to be uncertain about their true significance and function. On the other hand, they both agree that the *barrio* located in the largely sand-covered area north of what Uhle called the Old City Wall (see his base map) was where the residences and cemeteries of the masses were. Even Uhle's (p. 62) casual surface survey through the *barrio* revealed abundant ceramic fragments and other refuse in peripheral portions of the site. Yet, the *barrio* does not appear in Uhle's base map of the site.

In his clearing and excavation on the northwestern base of the Temple of the Sun, Tello unearthed stone-lined terraces and staircases under thick Incaic refuse layers. Farther below (east of the Pachacamac Temple), Tello exposed an extensive rectangular plaza (ca. 200 x 50 m) with fine fitted masonry borders and a stone-lined pit identified as an *ushnu* (for ritual offerings), and a set of two parallel rows of bases of columns that probably supported roofs. Surrounding the plaza were remains of numerous, small, superimposed structures with layers of sand and refuse separating successive periods of occupation. They are believed to represent a series of temporary occupations by pilgrims. The plaza is accordingly known as the Plaza of the Pilgrims.

Probably Tello's best-known work at Pachacamac is the excavation and extensive reconstruction in and around the convent of Mamacona ("Chosen Women" of the Inca Empire who served the state church; Pl. 5). This structure is also described as the Temple of the Moon. In the low-lying area (much like sunken gardens or *mahamaes*) just south and west of the convent Tello found a network of cisterns and aqueducts built of square hewn stones to take advantage of seeping

Plate 5. Oblique angle aerial view of the reconstructed Convent of Mamacona, looking north. (Courtesy of the Servicio Aerofotográfico Nacional del Perú. Photo no. 0-1623; taken in 1943)

water. Water was carried by aqueducts to the Urpi Wachak, or Ducks' Lagoon. Tello felt that in this manner water was collected for the population of the site, gardens, and animals. Though Tello felt that his newly discovered stone constructions dated back some 2,000 years, they are Incaic in origin. His assumption that fine masonry was "archaic" misled him. In his brief descriptions, stratigraphic information is incomplete or ignored (Fung 1963). Thus, it is difficult to ascertain the significance of his intriguing observations, for example, that slightly modified stone constructions antedate those of small hand-shaped adobe bricks (*adobitos*, presumably Early Intermediate Period in date). His claim that "worked stone constructions" at the lowest stratigraphic positions were associated with

"Chavín" like incised ceramics also remains to be properly documented.

The best-known legacy of Tello's work is the fully reconstructed Convent, what Rowe (1947:434) describes as "one of the most striking Inca remains on the coast." This was one of the first large-scale architectural reconstructions undertaken in Peru, and Tello has been criticized for his "imaginative" reconstruction (Bueno 1974/1975:175-176; compare the condition of the convent as Uhle saw it [Uhle's Pls. 2, 21] with Pl. 5 in this essay).

Tello was quite intuitive and decisive in functional identification of major structures at Pachacamac. Relying heavily on legends and a sketch map of the site of Pachacamac made in 1793 by Josef Juan (see Kosok

1965:40, his Fig. 3; also Jiménez Borja 1985:54, his Photo 7), Tello (1960:29-30) claimed that what Uhle identified as the Pachacamac Temple was actually the Painted Temple. Tello felt that what today is known as the Lima Temple (a poorly preserved mound built of small hand-shaped adobes some 250 m east of the Temple of the Sun; see below) was the actual Pachacamac Temple. The Painted Temple is identified on Tello's site map (1960) as the Temple of Urpi Wachak, dedicated to the cult of Urpi Wachak, wife of Pachacamac.

IDENTIFYING THE PACHACAMAC TEMPLE AND DELINEATING EARLY INTERMEDIATE PERIOD (PACHACAMAC I) AND MIDDLE HORIZON OCCUPATIONS (PACHACAMAC II)

Tello's identification of the Pachacamac Temple seems paradoxical given the murals, wooden idols, and other discoveries made at Uhle's Pachacamac Temple prior to the onset of Tello's work at Pachacamac and their match with eyewitness accounts. In addition, Josef Juan's rough sketch shows only one mound (there were actually two) north of the Temple of the Sun.

To properly assess Tello's intuition, we must review the available data on pre-Middle Horizon occupation at Pachacamac. On the basis of his seriation of Lima-style ceramics recovered by Strong and Corbett at the bottom of the refuse heap stratigraphy, Patterson (1966:114, 130-132) suggests that initial occupation around the Temple of the Sun may have begun around Lima Phases 3 and 4 (mid-Early Intermediate Period). Further, Patterson (1966:132) observes that there may have been a major occupation beginning around Lima 7 (latter portions of the Early Intermediate Period). During Lima 8 or 9, the terminal portions of the Early Intermediate Period, a structure with adobe-brick and stone retaining walls was built, which was, in turn, buried probably when the Incas constructed the Temple of the Sun (east side below the 4th and 5th terraces; Patterson 1966:114).

In terms of scale of construction, the most impressive Early Intermediate Period structure seems to be what Tello identified as the Pachacamac Temple. It is sometimes called the Lima Temple to emphasize its date of construction, inferred from associated ceramics, construction form, technique, and materials (e.g., yellow plaster and small, hand-shaped, rectangular adobes).

Data that lend considerable support to Tello's intuition come from a program of clearing and excavation at the Lima Temple that began in November 1986 under the direction of Paredes and Franco (1987/1988) with a grant from the Augusto N. Wiese Foundation.

The Lima Temple is a large, irregularly shaped mound covering about 16,500 m^2 in area and standing some 25 m high. Its peculiar shape is believed to have been modeled after small offshore islands that held funerary and ritual importance for the coastal dwellers (Paredes and Franco 1987/1988:26). The temple mound, in reality, consists of two major superimposed structures: a terraced stone-clay mortar mound built on a natural sand-and-rock hill overlain by another mound built of adobitos. The later construction has been designated as "Old Pachacamac Temple." Although much of the exterior has been eroded or damaged by earlier looting, the Temple top consists of access and entry, a patio with benches, "sacred chamber," "offering platform," "Platform of the Gallinazos [a type of vulture]," and "Recinto de la Conopas." Conopas refer to small stone or metal objects embodying the guarding spirits of humans, animals or plants that they represent. Paredes and Franco (1987/1988:26) differentiated three phases of occupation atop the temple, each characterized by a different color floor and/or wall finishes: yellow, white, and polychrome (red-black-yellow-white) for the Early (ca. A.D. 100-400?), Middle (ca. A.D. 400-600?), and Late (ca. A.D. 600-700) phases, respectively. Through these three phases of renovations the sacred chamber remained in the same location in the central depression atop the temple, suggesting strong ideological and ritual continuities throughout the Early Intermediate Period. The basis for the preceding dating, however, is not clear, as associated artifacts have not yet been described.

Altogether, it appears that the Lima Temple, the structure beneath the Temple of the Sun, and the associated quadrangular walled enclosure (ca. 470 x 400 m) formed the ceremonial nucleus of the Lima occupation at Pachacamac. It seems quite certain that the religious and ceremonial importance of Pachacamac dates back to the Early Intermediate Period, perhaps to the very beginning of its occupation.

Apparently, at the beginning of the Middle Horizon (not clear whether Epoch 1A [Lima 9] or 1B [Nievería]; Paredes and Franco 1987/1988: 27), access passages and much of the construction atop the temple were buried. With the introduction of the Wari religion, the ceremonial focus of Pachacamac apparently shifted to a new temple (see below). Yet, the presence of offerings of stone conopas of maize ears in association with Epigonal and later ceramics in the Recinto de los Conopas suggests that the Old Pachacamac Temple may have regained some of its original importance with the loss of prestige of Wari religion sometime at the end of Middle Horizon Epoch 2B.

During the Middle Horizon, the ceremonial focus at Pachacamac apparently shifted to Uhle's Pachacamac

Temple. Through his own excavation and clearing, Paredes (1985) defined at least two major phases in the long history of Pachacamac Temple. He (1985:73-74) found that the temple had an old foundation with offering terraces on the east and north sides, and a large closed atrium at the top with central doors facing the north wall that was painted red. Paredes calls this red-painted construction the "Ichimay Temple," or "Red Temple." Though technical details of the excavation have not yet been published, it appears that Paredes's Red Temple corresponds to the buried "Old Temple" that Uhle (pp. 19-20; see his Figs. 3.5, 4, 5) found in 1896 beneath the Pachacamac Temple. The Red Temple was apparently built with rock quarried from an on-site sedimentary rock outcrop, supplemented by *adobitos* razed from the Old Pachacamac Temple just to the east. Yet, as Jiménez Borja and Bueno (1970:14) point out, the presence of Lima burials in front of the Pachacamac Temple raises a distinct possibility that there is yet another buried Lima temple.

A later expansion of the offering terraces to the northwest correlates with initiation of the tradition of polychrome frescos at the Pachacamac Temple. This "Polychrome Temple" (Paredes 1985:74) phase spans numerous superimposed frescos on constructions built largely with adobes believed to have been made in the swampy littoral area and Urpi Wachak Lagoon.

As enumerated earlier, various lines of evidence suggest that the Polychrome Temple became the Pachacamac Temple, the religious focus of the site of Pachacamac, sometime during the Middle Horizon, at least as early as Epoch 2 (on the basis of the stylistic date of the wooden idol and burials Uhle excavated in front of the Temple). That this temple was in use at the time of the Spanish arrival is supported by both eyewitness accounts and Paredes's (1985:78-79) recovery of Inca and Hispanic (colonial or later) materials in the central atrium atop the temple. On the basis of Menzel's study (1964) and with analogy to the known dissemination centers of Wari religion that were located in areas of great local and regional prestige (e.g., Pacheco, Conchopata, and Moche), Patterson (1966:115) hypothesizes that the Pachacamac Temple was built during Middle Horizon Epoch 1B between the two temples that had already established their prestige in the preceding Early Intermediate Period, the Old Pachacamac Temple and the one beneath the Temple of the Sun.

To minimize the terminological confusion, the following shorthand summary of the above discussion is offered:

Early Intermediate Period: Tello's Pachacamac Temple = Lima Temple = Paredes's Old Pachacamac Temple (with the Adobitos Temple overlying the Stone Temple)

Middle Horizon (Epoch 1B or 2A) to Late Horizon: Uhle's Pachacamac Temple = Paredes's Painted Temple, which subsumes the earlier Ichimay, or Red, Temple and the later Polychrome Temple

Data that have accumulated since Uhle's fieldwork now allow us roughly to delineate the extent and nature of occupation at Pachacamac spanning the Early Intermediate Period and Middle Horizon.

The date and nature of the earliest occupation at the site is still vague. Jiménez Borja (1985:41) refers to a "Chavín" occupation in the nearby modern village of Lurín. Initial occupation of this ceremonial sector may be pushed back into the Early Horizon or even to the Initial Period, depending on the dating of the Stone Temple beneath the Old Pachacamac Temple. Jiménez Borja (1985:41) argues that there is a hiatus between the "Chavín" and Lima occupations. On the other hand, Bueno (1982:23) considers that those who utilized Pachacamac Negative and White-on-Red ceramics first occupied the area around the Temple of the Sun, preceding the Lima occupation. Given the small quantities and secondary contexts from which these ceramic fragments were derived, the preceding inference should be regarded as quite tentative.

Lima occupation appears to have covered the southwestern portion of the site from the Old Pachacamac Temple to the Pachacamac Site Museum cutting through the southern corner of Tello's "walled palace" sector (ca. 1 km east-west and 0.6 km north-south). The inferred temple beneath the Temple of Sun was built using small, hand-shaped, cubic adobe bricks. Bueno (1974/1975:181-182; 1982:23-24) believes that the Lima Temple was built somewhat later using slightly differently shaped, small bricks. Additional Lima constructions are the "Adobitos" Group structures in front of the Pachacamac Site Museum excavated in 1964-1965 by Arturo Jiménez Borja and Alberto Bueno (Jiménez Borja and Bueno 1970:13; Bueno 1974/1975:176; 1982:24; Lavallée 1966). The excavation revealed a "small temple" built with materials and techniques characteristic of Lima structures (e.g., *adobitos*, parallel rows of wooden pillars for roof support; Vásquez 1984). In addition, it featured a centrally situated, rectangular, stepped courtyard. Six successive occupation floors, each associated with distinct Lima-phase ceramics (from Lima 4 to 9), were defined.

Bueno (1982:24; Jiménez Borja 1970:14) also notes that the circular, buried mound called the Urpi Wachak Temple (ca. 500 m northwest of the Temple of the Sun; Pl. 2), as well as a small building on the north side and below the Incaic Mamacona Convent were built with *adobitos*. Lima-style pottery has also been recovered from the low-lying area around the Urpi Wachak Lagoon and over 3 m below surface in a pit excavated next to the Pyramid with Ramp 1 in the central "walled palace" sector (Bueno 1982:24). Patterson

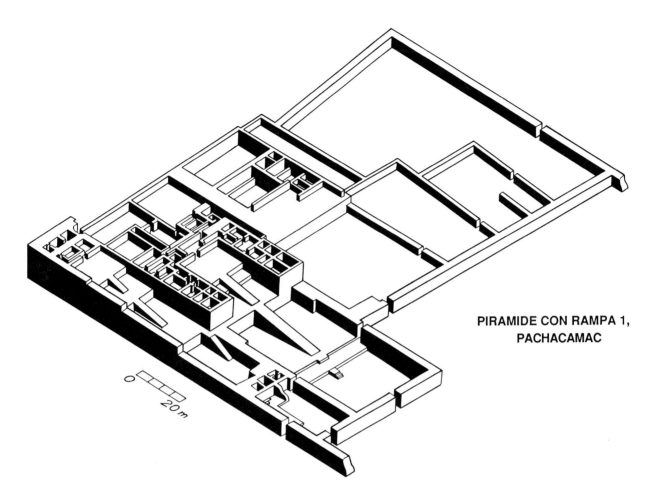

**PIRAMIDE CON RAMPA 1,
PACHACAMAC**

0

20 m

Figure 5. Isometric projection drawing of the "Pyramid with Ramp" No. 1. Redrawn by the author from Figure 3, Paredes and Franco (1987:6).

(1966:115) suggests the major north-south street at Pachacamac, which is nearly aligned with the center of the Lima Temple, may also have been established at the same time as the temple.

Delimitation of the area occupied during the Middle Horizon at Pachacamac (e.g., see the map on Bueno 1982:28) is largely a matter of speculation based on some local ceramics attributed in time to the Middle Horizon. We do not know whether Pachacamac A and B style ceramics, the symbol of Pachacamac's prestige during Middle Horizon Epoch 2, were manufactured at the site or elsewhere. As evident from this review, other than the handful of burials Uhle excavated in front of the Pachacamac Temple, relevant physical evidence is indeed scarce. In fact, perhaps with the exception of the Pachacamac Temple, not a single structure can be conclusively shown to be Middle Horizon in its date of construction.

PYRAMIDS WITH RAMP AND LATE INTERMEDIATE PERIOD

(PACHACAMAC III)

With the collapse of the Wari empire and abandonment of Cajamarquilla, the Late Intermediate Period is seen as a time of Pachacamac resurgence accompanied by unprecedented intense construction activity (perhaps begun as early as Middle Horizon Epoch 3; Jiménez and Bueno 1970:15-16). According to Uhle (p. 57; see his Pls. 9.2 and 10.3), "Among the foremost in number and prominence" at Pachacamac are what he called "terraced" or "castle houses" built during this period. These are situated along the two major intersecting streets (north-south and east-west). Based on the complex internal divisions within large enclosing walls with limited access, Uhle (pp. 57-59) regarded them as chiefs' palaces, and discounted the significance

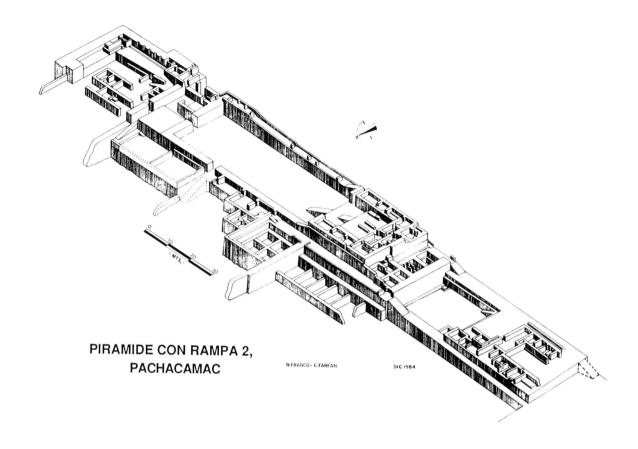

PIRAMIDE CON RAMPA 2,
PACHACAMAC   R.FRANCO - C.FARFAN.   DIC. 1984

Figure 6. Isometric projection drawing of the "Pyramid with Ramp" No. 2. Courtesy of Ponciano Paredes.

of massive mounds with central ramps. Today, how-ever, they are known as the Pyramids with Ramps.

Other than some limited excavations, Tello left them for future research. Indeed, beginning in 1958, the Pyramid with Ramp 1 (Fig. 5) and surrounding con-structions (now known as the Jiménez Borja area), in-cluding the major north-south street, became the focus of the fieldwork by Arturo Jiménez Borja, a Peruvian architect with a longstanding interest in archaeology but no formal training in it (Jiménez Borja 1985; Jiménez Borja and Bueno 1970; Bueno 1974/1975:176).

The "Pyramid," in reality, is a large, multilevel, ter-raced mound with centrally placed short, direct ramps linking one level to the next (Figs. 5, 6; Pls. 5, 6) built at the far end of a rectangular walled enclosure with limited, indirect access. This basic configuration and placement (but with varied orientation) is repeated with different scale in the 15 "pyramids with ramp" identified thus far in the central portion of the site

(Paredes 1988:42; see Bueno 1982:33; Jiménez Borja 1985).

On the basis of the two excavated Pyramids with Ramp (No. 1 or "JB" in 1958-1960 and No. 2 in 1981-1983 both under the direction of Jiménez Borja [Paredes 1988:42]; both are partially restored), a tenta-tive characterization of their internal organization, oc-cupational history and nature, as well as construction techniques and features may be presented. Paredes and Franco (1987:5-7; see also Jiménez Borja 1985:41-42; Paredes 1988:44) list the diagnostic architectural fea-tures of the "Pyramids with Ramp" as follows: (1) tor-tuous principal entry off a street, (2) forecourt within principal walled enclosure, (3) centrally placed, U-shaped principal monumental platform mound ("pyramid" or "Gran Audiencia") that may reach a height of some 15 m above the associated courts as in the case of Pyramid with Ramp 2), with (4) relatively short, straight, central ramps surrounded by (5) rectan-gular or square rooms that may have served diverse

Plate 6. Frontal view of the "Pyramid with Ramp," No. 1. (Courtesy of the Servicio Aerofotográfico Nacional del Perú. Photo no. Rn-9908; taken in 1960)

functions such as storerooms for ritual goods and costumes, funerary chambers, and reception/waiting rooms, and (6) other contiguous, auxiliary structures, including (7) walled enclosures with hindcourts. Lastly, wide and narrow streets along or atop the major walls were used for communication within (including different levels of the enclosure) and without. For example, a 6-m wide wall-top street on the north side of the forecourt connected the fore- and hind-courts of Pyramid with Ramp 2 (Paredes 1988:47). On the other hand, the south side of the forecourt had a narrower parapeted wall-top street with various cross walls that prevented easy movement (Paredes 1988:47). In other words, the centrally situated Pyramid was accessible directly through the central ramps, or indirectly via the two wall-top streets.

The foundations of these pyramids and associated structures were built of two types of materials; sandstone quarried at outcrops at the site was used to level the uneven surface and formed the foundation upon which adobe bricks and *tapias* were placed. Paredes (1988:47, 53-54) suggests that Inca-period use of *tapias* was an expedient solution to a labor shortage resulting from Inca-imposed demographic and administrative reorganization of the Lurín Valley. As a group, these "pyramids" are relatively well preserved, though adobes made with the local marshy soil of the Urpi Wachak Lake do not weather well. Clearing of rubble along the walls defining the principal entry of Pyramid with Ramp 2 (see Uhle's Pl. 10.2) revealed entries with lintels and corner posts of *caña de guayaquil* (*Bambusa* sp.), *lúcumo* (*Lucuma obovata*), *molle*

(*Schinus molle*), and *algarrobo* (*Prosopis juliflora*; Paredes 1988:45). Small rectangular niches on the side walls of the principal entry were also found (Paredes 1988:45). Clearing of the nicely plastered Pyramid-top room complex showed niches and doorways with wooden lintels. The patio surrounded by the room complex was roofed with *totora* reed (*Typha domingensis*) underlain by cane bound with cord.

These walled compounds had long, complex constructional histories, with the Pyramids with Ramp serving as the stable nuclei of growth and modifications for much of their histories. The form and orientation of associated streets were attendant to their changing configurations as courts, storage buildings, and auxiliary structures were added to the pyramidal core over time. For example, the sunken hindcourt west of Pyramid with Ramp 2 has superimposed floors, remains of impermanent structures, and a water deposit, which may have been used over a long span of time by temple servants who, apart and largely hidden from more solemn, ceremonial areas to the east, engaged in domestic activities (Paredes 1988:53). Also, many of the wide wall-top streets projecting outward from the Pyramid with Ramp enclosures seem unfinished, suggesting that the growth of the central sector of Pachacamac may have been abruptly arrested by the arrival of the Incas or Spaniards.

It was pointed out earlier that some Lima-style pottery was found over 3 m below the surface in the Pyramid with Ramp 1 area. However, to date there has been no definite indication that the construction of the Pyramids originated in the Early Intermediate Period. Paredes (1985:74; 1988:51) sees the numerous renovations documented at the Painted Temple (e.g., expansion from the Red Temple to Polychrome Temple, and up to sixteen layers of frescos) correlating with twelve successive layers of plaster discerned atop the Pyramid with Ramp 2. In addition, Paredes (1985:74) notes similarity between the red paint found on one of the earliest plaster layers of the Pyramid with Ramp 2 and that of the Red Temple. Much of the former, however, were not painted or at least show no paint today. In essence, Paredes (1988:51) sees the original constructions of the Pyramids with Ramp as contemporaneous with the Painted Temple (late Middle Horizon). In Pyramid with Ramp 2, the original configuration is believed to be best preserved in the posterior or western half of the enclosure (Paredes 1983:52). Later additions, raising, and/or enlarging wall-top streets and rooms using stones and *tapias* are attributed to the Late Intermediate Period Ichimay and Late Horizon Inca occupations.

In the forecourt of Pyramid with Ramp 2, in addition to evidence of its use in the last century for animal corrals, Ichimay and Inca ceramics were found among the accumulated refuse (Paredes 1988:46; Paredes and Franco 1987:5). Further, fragments of imported Cusco Inca ceramics were found scattered on the floors of the small rooms atop Pyramid with Ramp 2 (Paredes 1988:48). Paredes (1988:51) regards Inca-period occupants responsible for graffiti on plastered wall faces and the use of some areas (e.g., parapeted wall-top street) for trash.

Overall, in spite of the tendency to emphasize these walled enclosures with the pyramidal core as Late Intermediate Period (Pachacamac III) local developments (Bueno 1974/1975:186-187, 1982:32-35; Jiménez Borja 1985), the above lines of evidence suggest that these structures and the central sector of the site were occupied perhaps continuously since the Middle Horizon (if not late Early Intermediate Period) to the Spanish Conquest. On the northern North Coast, similar T-shaped, monumental, multilevel platforms are widely found and are attributable to the Middle Sicán culture ca. A.D. 900-1100 (Table 1; see, e.g., Huacas Miguelito and Teodora in the Zaña Valley [see Figs. 4-7 in Kosok 1965:141-142], Huaca Chornancap and Taco or Eten in the lower Lambayeque Valley [see Figs. 3 and 4 in Donnan 1990:251-252; Pl. XIX, Fig. 1 and Pl. XXX, Fig. 2 in Kroeber 1930], and Huacas El Corte, Rodillona, and El Moscón in Batán Grande [Figs. 16-17 in Shimada 1985a:102-103]). Though freestanding without accompanying walled enclosures, these platforms were, at the same time, built by means of superimposed lattices of filled and sealed adobe chambers much as Pachacamac's Pyramids with Ramp (Cavallaro and Shimada 1988:76-81; Paredes 1988:50, 52; Shimada and Cavallaro 1986:55-63). Given various lines of evidence indicating that beginning in Middle Horizon Epoch 3 Pachacamac came under strong Middle Sicán influence (discussed later), the Pyramids with Ramp within walled enclosures may be seen as a late Middle Horizon synthesis of North and Central Coast architectural traditions. Paredes (1988:49) sees the prototype of the wall-top circulation and walled enclosures as present at Cajamarquilla.

Views regarding the overall significance of these Pyramids with Ramps have been heavily influenced by historical data (see below) that speak of a relatively peaceful time before the arrival of the Incas on the Central Coast and control of the site of Pachacamac by the local *Señorío* of Ichimay. It appears that Pachacamac was the most influential ceremonial center on the Central Coast and received labor services and tribute of a wide range of material goods from agricultural communities and polities on the Central Coast, adjacent highlands, and beyond.

With the above background information, Jiménez Borja (1985:41-42; Jiménez Borja and Bueno 1970:16), and Bueno (1974/1975:186-187, 1982:32-35) argue that the Pyramids with Ramp were *edificios provinciales y familiares*, the ceremonial-civic structures of the provincial ethnic polities and lords that worshiped the cult of Pachacamac or had some binding obligations to serve it with labor and material goods. Their placement below the Pachacamac Temple is believed to be symbolic of the deference accorded to the temple. Overall architectural layout of the *edificios provinciales* permitted control of physical movement and heightened the sense of importance of making the long ascent to the top of the "pyramid." Jiménez Borja (1985:42) views this "ascent" as symbolic of the transition from terrestrial, mortal life to a celestial, mythical realm. Large open forecourts and substantial enclosure walls accentuated the dramatic visual effect of these T-shaped terraced mounds. Varied orientations of the pyramids and their ramps are inferred to indicate the homelands of these provincial polities (e.g., Rimac, Chillón, and Chancay valleys, Cieneguilla and Huarochrí in the middle and headwaters of the Lurín Valley, respectively). In this regard, the presence of textiles and ceramics of various Late Intermediate styles on the Central Coast is briefly mentioned, but it is not clear whether a specific style is confined to a specific enclosure or whether these styles are contemporaneous.

The unity seen among the fifteen Pyramids with Ramp implies the Ichimay *Señorío* and the cult of Pachacamac had considerable political and/or ideological power. Thus, smaller versions of these walled-in compounds found at various sites on the Central Coast are interpreted as their local outposts. Similarly, these polities are seen together to have formed a confederacy and sociopolitical hierarchy to maintain the cult and the ceremonial center of Pachacamac. The social and economic networks thus formed are, in turn, thought to have promoted interethnic trade with the site of Pachacamac serving as a "port-of-trade." Prestige, as well as social and economic foundations of the cult of Pachacamac, would thus be strengthened.

In general, archaeological findings point to the Pyramids' ritual functions. Excavation of the forecourt in Pyramid with Ramp 2 (Pl. 6) yielded a dense accumulation of refuse, leading Paredes and Franco (1987:5; cf. Jiménez Borja 1985:47) to suggest that the space was used for public celebration and exchange. Apparently Tello found *Spondylus* shells and wrapped guinea pigs in his excavation of the back patios of various Pyramids with Ramp presumably left by pilgrims (Paredes 1985:74). Numerous guinea pigs wrapped in maize and *achira* (*Canna edulis*) were also found by Giesecke in his clearing of the Pachacamac Temple summit, suggesting that such offerings may have been widespread during the late Prehispanic era. Many of the small structures in grid layouts flanking and/or behind the Pyramids with Ramp are thought to have stored tributary goods. Preserved *ají* peppers (*Capsicum anuum*) and maize were found in a

storeroom complex on the west side of the Pyramid with Ramp 2 (Paredes 1988:52). Jiménez Borja (1985:42) suggests that the stored goods were used by the residents of these enclosures to underwrite costly, periodic architectural repairs and renovations, and rituals and celebrations related to both the cult of Pachacamac and their own provincial religions. He envisions laborers engaged in repairs and renovations as provisioned using stored goods.

Bueno (1974/1975:187) argues that the walled-in parcels of land bordering the *edificios provinciales* were reserved for polities that might later join this confederacy built around worship of the Pachacamac cult. Jiménez Borja (1985:42) rejects this notion in favor of the view that these spacious enclosures were used to process cotton and dry maize, *ají* peppers and other agricultural produce brought to the site to be stored. In fact, shelled maize kernels and seeded *ají* were found scattered over the superimposed clay floors (Jiménez Borja 1985:42). Drying on or storing in saline sand would have spoiled them (Jiménez Borja 1985:54). *Ají* peppers and maize in Pyramid with Ramp 2 storerooms were found mixed in clean alluvial sand presumably brought from a nearby river (Paredes 1988:52). Test excavations in some of these peripheral walled-in areas have shown firepits and associated ash lenses, postholes, and Ichimay ceramic fragments, suggesting that the laborers engaged in temple maintenance and processing of agricultural produce may have resided there (Paredes 1988:55).

There are indications that some of the smaller rooms adjacent to the above enclosed spaces were used for craft production, including pottery making (Jiménez Borja 1985:42). Jiménez Borja even suggests that a smaller version of the Pachacamac Temple wooden idol found in one of the adjacent streets may reflect "commerce" dealing with mementos of the pilgrimage to Pachacamac.

There are other tantalizing bits of evidence that may shed additional light on the nature of occupation and functions of the Pyramids with Ramps and associated enclosures. For example, Jiménez Borja (1985:50) speaks of the 1958 discovery of a wooden die in the form of a truncated pyramid during the clearing of Pyramid with Ramp 1. Each of the four angled faces bears one to four incised lines (Jiménez Borja 1985:50). In the same year, two stone tablets with small holes on one side were found near the side entrance to the enclosure of the Pyramid, and an additional stone and three clay tablets with parallel rows of holes were later found at another Pyramid with Ramp. On the basis of explanations found in colonial documents, Jiménez Borja (1985:50-51) suggests that the recovered tablets were used in determining the duration and order of funerary rituals so as to facilitate the transition of the deceased from the living to the mythical realms.

Unfortunately, potentially significant bits of information such as the above are presented without contextual and chronological data, making it difficult to assess these inferences. Archaeological findings seem to be secondary to historical data in the interpretations discussed above.

LATE HORIZON OCCUPATIONS
(PACHACAMAC IV)

As seen already, fieldwork by Giesecke and Tello at Pachacamac helped to define the nature and extent of Inca occupation. Jiménez Borja and Bueno also made significant contributions. In 1962 Jiménez Borja was named director of the Pachacamac Site Museum and was given broad authorization to conduct clearing, excavation, and reconstruction at any part of the site. In 1963, he exposed the zigzagging principal stairway to the Temple of the Sun situated in the center of its east side (Bueno 1974/1975:176). During 1965-1967, Jiménez Borja and Bueno (who joined in 1964) directed the clearing and consolidation of the north corner, west face, and Terraces III and IV of the Temple of the Sun (Bueno 1974/1975:177; Jiménez Borja and Bueno 1970:17). In 1967 and 1968, they excavated the inferred "Palace of the *Curaca Tauri Chumpi*, [the Inca governor of Pachacamac at the time of Spanish Conquest]," and surrounding Late Horizon residential structures situated near the bridge over the Lurín River (Jiménez Borja and Bueno 1970:17; Bueno 1982:48-50).

The Tauri Chumpi Palace is a large architectural complex consisting of two large courtyards surrounded by rooms, platforms, storage cells, and other structures linked by corridors and ramps (Bueno 1982:48). The complex also features two tall towers that may have functioned as watchtowers (Bueno 1982:48).

Combined with historical data, the Inca occupation at the site is relatively well known. Its occupation covers much of the site south of Uhle's Old City Wall, with the heaviest density of refuse and structural build-up evident in the area between the Temple of the Sun and the Tauri Chumpi Palace (Bueno 1982:46-48). Major Inca constructions include the Temple of the Sun, the Convent of Mamacona, the Pilgrims' Plaza, and the Tauri Chumpi Palace. In addition, we have seen that there was extensive Inca refuse and architectural modification of Pyramid with Ramp enclosures in the central sector of the site. The area around the Pachacamac Site Museum also has remains of Inca occupation (Lavallée 1966:227-231). Referring to the excavation of Pyramid with Ramp 1 by Jiménez Borja, Rowe (1963:17) emphasizes the presence of "over a meter of very dirty Inca refuse," some of which had entered even into a gap in the damaged portion of the south wall of the forecourt. He (1963:17) concludes: "There is no question that this building was in a ruinous condition when the Incas began to use it as a dump." Miguel Estete, one of the first Spanish visitors to Pachacamac (in 1533), also noted that much of the site was in ruins in his time (Rowe 1963:17). In this respect, the presence of imported Cusco Inca sherds at Pyramid with Ramp 2 calls for our attention; does it indicate the physical presence of Inca elite or simply a gift given to local ethnic elite still occupying the Pyramid? Could it be that Late Horizon occupation of the central sector was limited to transient and occasional pilgrims and that most of the temple servants who maintained the *edificos provinciales* no longer resided at the site? The nature and composition of Inca occupation in the central sector remain to be elucidated.

Ethnohistorical Approach to Late Prehispanic Pachacamac

It is evident from this review, that both the sixteenth- and seventeenth-century colonial writings and their modern analyses have had a major impact on what we know about and how we perceive the site and associated cultures of Pachacamac. The number of relevant publications is rapidly increasing. In this section comments are restricted to a few notable studies and general trends among recent ethnohistorical studies.

Even before Uhle's fieldwork, nineteenth-century visitors to Pachacamac (e.g., Markham 1956; Middendorf 1894; Rivero and von Tschudi 1855; Squier 1877; Wiener 1880) compared their observations to those of sixteenth- and seventeenth-century writers (e.g., Cieza de León, Bernabé Cobo, Miguel de Estete, Hernando de Santillan; see the list on pp. ix-x; see more recent compilations in Bueno 1974/1975, 1982; Espejo 1941; Jiménez Borja 1985; Jiménez Borja and Bueno 1970). In fact, confirmation of historical observations (e.g., identification of the Pachacamac Temple) is a task that on-site fieldwork has addressed for many years. In this regard, historical data has tended to confine archaeological fieldwork to defining notable features of a few monumental structures.

In general, the heavy reliance on historical data established early in the history of Pachacamac archaeology has been continued, if not accentuated, to this day. In some cases, such data have guided not only the selection of excavation loci but also the analysis and interpretation of recovered materials and data (e.g., consider those related to the Tauri Chumpi Palace and the Pyramids with Ramp). The veracity of historical data is implicitly assumed and proper assessment of other plausible views minimized, thereby placing archaeological inquiries subordinate to historical data. Uhle (p. 85) himself provided a good illustration of this problem when, mustering archaeological and forensic evidence, he convincingly argued that women interred in the Cemetery of the First Southeast Terrace of the Sun Temple at Pachacamac were of high status and "did not die a natural death"; that they were ceremonially sacrificed by strangulation in honor of the Sun. The discovery not only provided the first good empirical evidence for human sacrifice in Peru but served as a caution against uncritical acceptance of claims made in chronicles (J. H. Rowe, personal communication 1990; see also Means 1931:432-434).

Reliance on historical documents also has had subtle but important impact in archaeological time perception. Historical documents that relate to pre-Inca domination of the Central Coast (prior to A.D. 1460-1470; Rowe 1945, 1948) often do not specify the relevant time frame. María Rostworowski (e.g., 1972, 1974, 1975, 1977, 1981) has ventured forth to push the origins of late Prehispanic institutions and patterns on the Central Coast back in time to the Early Intermediate Period and Middle Horizon with the hope that archaeologists will confirm her inferences.

Her inferences reflect her conviction that Prehispanic Peruvian coastal societies possessed sociopolitical and economic organizations quite distinct from those of the adjacent highlands in having a more marked division of labor. In general, she sees the Early and Late Intermediate Periods without domination of highland-based polities to be a time when a fundamentally coastal pattern prevailed on the coast. Her leads have stimulated a number of collaborative archaeological field projects, including those pertaining to Inca and pre-Inca management of the valuable coca-growing *yunga* zone in the upper Chillón Valley (Dillehay 1977, 1979; Feltham 1984; Marcus and Silva 1988; MacNeish et al. 1975:62-65; Rostworowski 1988). At the same time, it is not an easy task to field-test these inferences as it requires identification of the relevant institutions (and even ethnic groups) and demonstration of their continuity over time. There is the definite danger of regarding these ethnohistorically derived chronological inferences as factual or reliable without adequate independent testing. As noted earlier, we need much better archaeological dating of the later portions of the Middle Horizon and the entire span of the Late Intermediate Period.

On a more positive side, recent ethnohistorical studies focusing on local folklore and administrative, litigation, and ecclesiastical records have shed much light on intangible aspects of late Prehispanic Pachacamac and the Central Coast. For example, texts collected by Francisco de Avila during his involvement in the eradication of idolatry have been extensively analyzed for, among others, reconstruction of interethnic relationships (e.g., Millones 1982; Rostworowski 1977, 1981, 1983, see below; Spalding 1984; see also Duviols 1983; Villar Cordova 1933). Such studies are based on the premise that struggles between regional deities are sanctified histories of actual human struggles over the control of various resources. However, the question of how one determines the applicability of such a premise is not clear.

Rostworowski has been the single most important force in the advancement of coastal ethnohistory in recent decades. She (e.g., 1972, 1973, 1975, 1977, 1978, 1980, 1981, 1983, 1988) has been responsible for much of what we know about the *Señorío* of Ichimay; the evolution and nature of Ichimay and Pachacamac; the deities, social, and economic networks underlying the cult of Ichimay; and ethnic relationships on the Central and South-Central coasts during the Late Intermediate Period (and perhaps into the Middle Horizon). For example, in her study of late Prehispanic *Señoríos* of the Central Coast and its highland hinterlands, some of the above points are summarized:

> En la Costa Central, el núcleo religioso de Pachacamac aglutinaba a varios pequeños cacicazgos de los valles de Lima y Lurín, bajo el nombre del Señorío Ychma. El Santuario ejercía una profunda influencia religiosa no solo en los valles centrales y sur centrales, sino en varias regiones serranas; sin embargo cabe hacer hincapié que este predominio era más devocional que político.
>
> El Señorío de Ychma comprendía a varios curacazgos menores asentados en el mismo valle, entre ellos se contaba a los Manchay y Guaycán, mientras el cacicazgo de Sisicaya a pesar de componerse de gente yunga estaba dominado por los Yauyos y en tiempos toledanos formaba parte de las Guarangas de Huarochirí. Cerca de Pachacamac se situaba el pueblo de pescadores de Quilcay y más al sur (en las lomas) se hallaban los Caringas.

She has stimulated complementary archaeological research and generated topics for many more such investigations. For example, Rostworoski (1972) hypothesizes that the Pachacamac priests carried out religious proselytizing in distant lands to expand the cult of Pachacamac and to extract tribute in goods and services. Documentary evidence suggests that the primary method employed for these ends was not conquest but rather the threat of Pachacamac, the deity who among his various attributes controlled damaging earthquakes with a movement of his head (Rostworowski 1975, 1981). Thus, Pachacamac priests were able to extract considerable quantities of goods that were presumably deposited in storage rooms in and around the Pyramids with Ramp. Although Jiménez Borja and Bueno (Jiménez Borja 1985; Jiménez Borja and Bueno 1970) have given the latter part of this reconstruction some empirical support, documentation and further clarification of the inferred processes of proselytizing by threat pose a serious methodological challenge to archaeology. In addition, historical statements pertaining to the sociopolitical and territorial organization within the *Señorío* of Ichimay are essentially static descriptions that do not offer a clear picture as to whether the given configuration remained stable and for how long. Once again, to answer these questions archaeologically is no simple task (see Feltham 1984).

Another worthwhile archaeological research issue is based on Rostworowski's (1977:44) assertion that an Ichima group from the Central Coast were in a settlement named Ayarucho or Cullum Ychima in Preincaic Cusco. The existence of this ethnic name in Cusco, together with findings from the historical linguistic studies of Gary Parker (1972) and Alfredo Torero (1970), form the basis for her suggestion. Parker and Torero argue that the Inca tongue of Quechua originated on the Central Coast and later spread into the highlands and to Chincha (Puerto Viejo) on the South Coast. Rostworowski (1977:46), in fact, sees these Quechua speakers in Chincha to be "merchants" sponsored by the Pachacamac priests participating in coastal maritime trade. These traders are believed to have obtained the *Spondylus* shell used in rituals at Pachacamac. Though tantalizing, archaeological verification of this historical linguistic reconstruction poses serious methodological problems.

Some of the issues raised by the preceding reconstruction are discussed in Patterson's (1985) study of how the caretakers of the principal shrine at Pachacamac expanded their power base through establishment of branches outside the "home base" territory of Ichma (Lurín Valley) during Inca domination of the Andes. In the process, he shows, much as Rostworowski (1977) had done earlier, the effectiveness of a fine-grained analysis of ethnohistorical materials (particularly the Quechua text *Dioses y Hombres de Huarochirí* and its analysis by Spalding 1984), including field inspection of relevant locations.

Patterson (1985:170) asserts that "the power of Pachacamac was based on its alliances with the Inca royalty,... and on its control of ideology which was the cement that held Andean societies together." The symbiotic and mutually reinforcing relationship between Pachacamac and the Incas is apparent. Alliance between these two entities meant an impressive blend of long-established and widely known religious reputation and prestige, on the one hand, and the recent but rapidly expanding and proven political-military might and territorial ambition, on the other. Each could count on the strength of the other in furthering its cause. The Inca state sponsored establishment of Pachacamac branches beyond the imperial frontier as such expansion served both; Pachacamac gained in prestige and religious tribute, while helping to lay the groundwork for rapid and efficient incorporation of areas by the Incas. Netherly (1977:302) relates an example of the Pachacamac oracle's requesting the Inca king to establish a branch oracle in the "Chimor" (Moche) Valley on the North Coast. The site of the new oracle, described as "*la huaca* [sacred place] *grande del río*," is perhaps the Huaca del Sol (so-called Pyramid of the Sun) at the site of Moche. This *huaca* retained religious prestige long after the demise of the Mochica, and it is where Wari ritual offerings were made (Menzel 1977:37-41).

Changes in the functioning of the Pachacamac shrine resulting from its interaction with the Incas show how ideological terms were used by the priests for legitimizing the establishment of branches and attendant exploitation of local peasant populations (tribute payment and labor service). In other words, control of ideology is seen as the power base of the Pachacamac priests. Interaction between the Wari state and Pachacamac during Middle Horizon Epoch 2 may have taken a similar form.

Comparative Perspectives

Much of the above discussion focuses on the site of Pachacamac. This section addresses primarily the regional and pan-Andean significance of Pachacamac from the late Early Intermediate to the end of the Middle Horizon (ca. A.D. 450-1000). The preceding section has already covered the Late Intermediate Period and Late Horizon.

PACHACAMAC IN THE EARLY INTERMEDIATE PERIOD CENTRAL COAST

Though a number of settlement pattern studies have been carried out on the Central Coast, it is still difficult to define the nature of articulation between Pachacamac and surrounding areas in the PreIncaic era. Through plotting of the distribution of ceramics manufactured at different locations, Patterson, McCarthy, and Dunn (1982) presented a model of the interaction and resource base of Early Intermediate Period sociopolitical groups in the Lurín Valley. Pachacamac does not receive particular attention. Earle's (1972) follow-up survey resulted in a model of Early Intermediate Period sociopolitical developments in the mid-Lurín valley. Site distribution and estimated population size were defined using a six-phase chronological scheme. Earle (1972:476) concluded that Phase 6 saw "a sudden and drastic population relocation and cultural (political) orientation toward the Lima state developing at that time to its fullest in the Rimac." However, attributing the observed change to "Lima state" expansion was premature as the critical Phase 6 (equivalent of Lima 7-9 in Patterson's seriation) may span a couple of centuries. As seen above and below, during this span, there was a series of other major changes affecting the Central Coast. Further, the "Lima state" was never explicitly or substantively defined.

Stumer (1954c:143-145) found the settlement typology and developmental sequence that Schaedel (1951) developed for the North Coast quite applicable to the Rimac Valley. Unfortunately, his single-valley perspective did not allow testing of Schaedel's observations on relationships between contiguous valleys. Schaedel (1951) argued that when small and large valleys form contiguous pairs (e.g., La Leche and Lambayeque, Moche and Chicama), the larger valley becomes the breadbasket for the pair, and the smaller valley becomes the setting for urban development and major ceremonial centers. Smaller valleys with greater hydraulic and political unity are seen to dominate their more fragmented, larger neighbors (Schaedel 1951; Moseley 1982). However, this observation does not apply to the Rimac-Chillón or the Rimac-Lurín pairs; it is the large Rimac Valley that boasts major ceremonial and urban centers such as Maranga and Cajamarquilla.

Conklin and Moseley (1988:154) suggested that Cajamarquilla and Pachacamac were urban and ceremonial centers, respectively, of the Lima culture. However, Early Intermediate Period habitation at Cajamarquilla, though considerable, appears to be largely confined to the terminal Epoch 8 (mostly Lima 8 and 9; Patterson 1966:112; Bueno 1974/1975; Sestieri

1964, 1971). It is doubtful whether there was any significant earlier occupation (e.g., Lanning 1967:118; Stumer 1954c:144). For earlier Epochs, the site of Maranga is a much stronger candidate to have been the major ceremonial *and* population center of the Lima culture (e.g., Agurto 1984; Canziani 1987). Covering about 150 hectares and having a planned layout, the site boasts some dozen monumental platform mounds, including Huaca San Marcos with basal dimensions of 300 x 120 m and 30 m height, surrounded by rows of small rooms and walled enclosures. The scale of Lima "ceremonial" structures and the extent of associated habitation at Pachacamac seem pale in comparison. It is likely that the time-honored oracle in the Rimac Valley that still held much sway at the time of the Inca empire dated back to the Early Intermediate Period. At the same time, we should keep in mind that these mounds are not necessarily precisely or reliably dated to have formed a synchronic, integrated whole.

It is important to note that Lima 8 and 9 (essentially Early Intermediate Period Epoch 8 and Middle Horizon Epoch 1A) was a time of significant cultural transformation on the Central Coast. It seems that Maranga was largely abandoned at this time and became a burial ground, while Cajamarquilla saw a major surge in construction activity and perhaps population size lasting up to Middle Horizon Epoch 2A (MacNeish et al. 1975: 52-54; Patterson 1966:112). At Pachacamac, the two known major Lima constructions, the Old Pachacamac Temple and the structure beneath the Temple of the Sun with its associated, peculiar mass grave, date to the same time.

Based on pollen and soil records from the Central Highland basin of Ayacucho, MacNeish, Patterson, and Browman (1975:53-54; see also Paulsen 1976 for a similar but more generalized view) suggested that the observed population shift within the Rimac Valley was a response to a series of major fluctuations in the precipitation pattern between about A.D. 450 and 550. It is believed (MacNeish et al. 1975:53-54) that during the early part of this time span (prior to A.D. 500) Central Coast population reached its maximum, largely owing to a sustained period of increased availability of irrigation water resulting from above-average precipitation levels in the adjacent highlands. However, precipitation returned to normal or subnormal levels starting about A.D. 500 with a consequential decline in water availability on the coast and abandonment of marginal and lower valley lands and settlements.

Recently, annual precipitation records (spanning the past 1,500 years), based on ice cores drilled at the Quelccaya Glacier south of Cusco, were analyzed in an effort to clarify the nature of environmental conditions and forces underlying the major transformation of the Mochica (Moche) culture that occurred during its Phase

IV-V transition (corresponding to the Lima 8 and 9 transition; Schaaf 1988; Shimada et al. 1991). Among notable changes observed at this time on the North Coast was the unprecedented population nucleation at valley necks that would have allowed ready control of water for the entire valley. The Quelccaya precipitation records in general lend strong independent support to the above reconstruction by MacNeish, Patterson, and Browman (1975:52-54). The Quelccaya data indicate that much of the sixth century A.D. for the Peruvian Andes (which is under the same general climatic regime) was a period of prolonged climatic anomalies, including a couple of El Niño events and droughts spanning A.D. 524-540 and 562-594 (Shimada et al. 1991). The latter drought was remarkable for its severity, duration, and abrupt onset, and must have significantly reduced the water available on much of the Peruvian coast. It is argued that the observed settlement shifts were responses to the significant and prolonged shortage of water (Shimada et al. 1991). These responses, however, were not necessarily abrupt or synchronic; some communities may have relocated in response to the first drought, and others may have remained only to succumb to the second, longer drought.

Earle's observation of settlement shift in his Phase 6 also should be reexamined in light of the data presented above. More precise dating of relevant sites and examination of their relationship to water sources are needed. Similarly, the construction of a Lima temple beneath the Temple of the Sun at Pachacamac may also have related to this "Time of Trouble." If so, the Cajamarquilla population, in spite of the distance that separated them, would have been spiritually dependent on Pachacamac.

THE WARI-PACHACAMAC INTERACTION DURING MIDDLE HORIZON EPOCH 1B AND 2A

The arrival of Wari religious ideas at Pachacamac, inferred to have occurred sometime in Middle Horizon Epoch 1B, capitalized on the prestige and organizational setup of Pachacamac for further dissemination. It was a widespread Wari (in fact, a common Andean) practice to reoccupy and convert established prestigious religious sites (e.g., La Mayanga [Batán Grande], Moche, Pañamarca, Pachacamac, Pacheco) as secondary dissemination points of its religion (e.g., Menzel 1964, 1977; Patterson 1966:115; Schaedel 1972:24). The strategy served to symbolize the dominance of the new over the old and establish its legitimacy among local populations. By capitalizing on extant institutions for proselytizing and/or extraction of tribute and labor services, Wari attempted to ex-

ploit and integrate diverse economic, social, and ethnic groups. The last is critical to any religion that aspires to a pan-Andean coverage.

There has been longstanding debate on the means employed for dissemination of Wari objects and ideas (see Isbell 1988 and Schreiber 1987 for reviews). An alternative to Menzel's vision of religiously motivated conquests is that of commercial expansion. On the basis of his observation that Lima pottery manifests evidence of pre-Middle Horizon contact with the Central Highlands, Bueno (1974/1975:180; Jiménez Borja and Bueno 1970:14) argues that Wari influence was first channeled through a local Lima group and that later, with Wari expansion (presumably Middle Horizon Epoch 1B), Cajamarquilla became a Wari colony and concurrently gained importance as the regional commercial center. Bueno (1974/1975:184; Jiménez Borja and Bueno 1970:15; see Shady and Ruíz 1979) sees Cajamarquilla under Wari administration as a ceremonial center that regularly served as a "great interregional market" with perhaps as many as 20,000 people at times. Although Cajamarquilla saw intense construction activity under the Wari, Pachacamac is seen as a local Wari burial ground. In this scenario, it was Wari traders from Cajamarquilla that incorporated the Lurín Valley into the expanding Wari commercial empire.

It is not clear when "pre-Middle Horizon" contact with the Central Highlands occurred or what lines of evidence support his "commercial" hypothesis and vision of Cajamarquilla as the regional market. We await publication of results from ongoing fieldwork at Cajamarquilla under the direction of Jiménez Borja and future study at the Middle Horizon (primarily Epoch 2) Wari site of Socos situated in the *chaupiyunga* (zone of year-round sun and warmth that allows cultivation of a wide range of crops, including coca) in Chillón Valley (Isla and Guerrero 1987). Considering the widespread Wari practice of taking over preexisting, prestigious religious centers, it is likely that the Middle Horizon Epoch 1B Wari outpost within the Rimac Valley was the site of Maranga and not Cajamarquilla (Menzel 1977:46).

Menzel (1964:70; 1977:46) argues that Pachacamac attained great religious prestige with its physical focus presumably at the Pachacamac Temple sometime early in Epoch 2A as a consequence of the reorganization of the Wari empire. Though Pachacamac supplanted Maranga as the "principal religious center" of the Central Coast, the presence of "pottery in the tradition of the Nievería style" at the former "suggests that the Rimac and Lurín Valleys may have been under a single administration at that time" (Menzel 1977:46). At this point, we know little of what happened to Maranga and who might have administered these valleys. Menzel sees a certain degree of Pachacamac autonomy from

Wari dominance during Epoch 2A in distinct treatment of mythical themes in Pachacamac style. In addition, the presence of a bowl with a Pachacamac A griffin within the ceramic offering cache found in Sausal (Donnan 1968) "shows that as early as Epoch 2A the Pachacamac griffin was a rival figure in the religious world of [Wari] and that its influence had made itself felt as far north as the Chicama Valley" (Menzel 1968: 88) on the North Coast.

It is quite likely that Epoch 2A religious dissemination to the North Coast was preconditioned by as yet unclear contact between the North and Central coasts during Epoch 1B (perhaps as early as 1A). During this time, Moche V textiles and ceramics (polychrome Mochica motifs on double-spout bottles) are found on the Central Coast (e.g., Conklin 1979; Stumer 1958), the Central Coast technique of filled adobe chambers for monumental construction appears in the Lambayeque Valley (Shimada and Cavallaro 1986), and finely made, thin-walled blackware vessels become popular in both areas (Shimada n.d.b; Stumer 1957).

PACHACAMAC AUTONOMY AND EXPANSION DURING THE MIDDLE HORIZON EPOCH 2B

Pachacamac appears to have increased its autonomy from Wari dominance considerably during Epoch 2B:

The distribution and influence of pottery in the Pachacamac B style indicates that Pachacamac established a great sphere of influence of its own in Epoch 2B, one which extended north to Chicama, south to Nasca, and inland to Huancayo in [central highlands]. It is possible that Pachacamac was the capital of an independent state, governing part of this area in full sovereignty, but much more likely that it remained subject to [Wari] and exercised its influence through an oracle, as it did under Inca rule, when its sphere of influence was at least equally large.

(Menzel 1964:71)

During Epoch 2B, in Menzel's opinion, Pachacamac was the most prestigious and influential religious center on the Peruvian coast but had minimal impact in the highlands, where Wari Viñaque was widely distributed.

Recently, Menzel's vision of the religious schism and political autonomy of Pachacamac has been questioned because of the discovery at the Moraduchayuq compound within the site of Wari of "representations of the 'Pachacamac Griffin' as well as other icons and ceramic decorations best known at Pachacamac" (Isbell 1988:188). However, their broader context, or how

common these "representations" are within and outside this compound at Wari, is still not clear, making it difficult to assess the significance of the discovery. It would not be surprising to find at Wari enclaves of representatives (including possible traders) from contemporaneous cultures such as Cajamarca, Tiahuanaco, and Pachacamac using their own ceramics. In fact, imported kaolin Middle Cajamarca ceramics have been found at Wari and nearby Wari state settlements (e.g., Bennett 1953; Isbell 1972, 1977; Ravines 1969).

In a later publication, Menzel again emphasized Pachacamac autonomy in Epoch 2B. South of Pachacamac, the strength of its religious art is most evident in the Ica Valley in the form of a local variant known as Ica-Pachacamac that replaced the earlier syncretic Nasca-Wari religion; in fact, the regional dominance of the Ica-Pachacamac style is believed to reflect the presence of a Pachacamac branch oracle in Ica (Menzel 1977:53).

In understanding the nature and means of Epoch 2B Pachacamac expansion to the north, Uhle's excavated funerary ceramics from Chimú Capac (now largely destroyed through looting) in the Supe Valley on the North-Central Coast are critical. These ceramics included provincial variants of highland Wari forms that were largely restricted to the capital region of Ayacucho (Menzel 1977:31). In addition, Pachacamac B-style vessels were scarce at Chimú Capac in notable contrast to the coastal region farther south. Thus, Menzel concluded that

Chimu Capac probably functioned as a strategic outpost of the [Wari] government, designed to curb the growing power of two serious coastal rivals to [Wari] power, Pachacamac and an important center of religion and worldly power on the north coast. The danger from these rivals may have been particularly acute in Middle Horizon Epoch 2B because they showed signs of merging into a cultural, and therefore potentially political, alliance.

(1977:31)

In spite of the presence of a Wari outpost at Chimú Capac, textiles and ceramics bearing Pachacamac religious icons are found much farther north at Pacatnamú, at the mouth of the Jequetepeque River (see below), and at sites in the Batán Grande region in the central La Leche Valley (see Fig. 1). These sites are ca. 650 and 740 km northwest of Pachacamac, but Chimú Capac is just 180 km distant.

At various sites in Batán Grande, Early Sicán (Middle Horizon Epoch 2; A.D. 700-850) blackware single-spout bottles with globular bodies (nearly identical to those of the Pachacamac style as described earlier by Lumbreras 1974:157) recovered from burials and fill are decorated with raptorial bird faces with prominent

L PACHACAMAC

Plate 7. Early Sicán blackware bottle with raptorial bird face decorating the base of its short spout. The face is associated with humanlike ears with holes presumably for ear spools. (Photograph courtesy of the author. Vessel no. 2320, Museo Brüning, Lambayeque)

beaks much like those of the Pachacamac Griffin (Pl. 7; also see Figs. 8-10 in Shimada 1990:315-316). Some are quite explicit in detail and generally well made; others are crude imitations.

At Pacatnamú, excavations of graves by Heinrich Ubbelohde-Doering (1967, 1983; also Keatinge 1978) yielded a number of decorated cotton textiles stylistically and iconographically very similar to those looted (part of the van den Zypen Collection at the Museum für Völkerkunde in Berlin and the Gaffron Collection at the Chicago Art Institute) and excavated (Uhle's Pl. 8, Figs. 17-19; see also Engelstad 1986) from graves at Pachacamac. Shared motifs include double-headed birds (Ubbelohde-Doering 1967:84). Though both Ubbelohde-Doering and Keatinge fail to date the

Pacatnamú textiles, by means of cross-dating with those excavated by Uhle, we suggest a Middle Horizon Epoch 2 date.

Pacatnamú may have had a special relationship with Pachacamac during Middle Horizon Epoch 2. It may well have been the source of North Coast influence that the Wari outpost at Chimú Capac was intended to block during this time. Pacatnamú presents striking similarity to Pachacamac in its location, architectural forms, composition, and layout as well as inferred function. It occupies a fan-shaped edge of an extensive desert plain that overlooks the Pacific to the west and the Jequetepeque River to the south and east (see Donnan and Cock 1986; Eling 1987; Hecker and Hecker 1977, 1985; Keatinge 1977, 1982; Keatinge et al. 1975; Ubbelohde-Doering 1967, 1983). In other words, Pachacamac and Pacatnamú both occupy dramatic spots where the ocean, land, and sky seem to come together, a sort of *axis mundi* (see Paredes 1988:42).

Pacatnamú is divided into four sectors defined by three concentric walls running roughly east-west. The two innermost sectors comprise the City of the Temples, with some 30 one- and two-level platform mounds with short central ramps interconnected by major north-south streets. The outer two walls define an extensive "suburb" with numerous inferred residential structures. Though it does not seem to have had any distinct religious art, it was prestigious enough to receive burials (both single and mass) and cache offerings of various cultures (Mochica, Pachacamac, Middle Sicán, Chimú, and Chimú-Inca spanning the Early to Late Intermediate Periods in the city and suburb (Donnan and Cock 1986; Eling 1987; Flores 1984; Keatinge 1978; Ubbelohde-Doering 1967, 1983). On the basis of similarities in their geographical positions, inferred ceremonial and funerary functions, architectural composition and layout, among others, Keatinge (1978:40; see also Ubbelohde-Doering 1967:84) suggests that "perhaps Pacatnamú and Pachacamac represent shrines of different deities who nevertheless were part of the same pantheon."

Attempts to establish branch oracles or shrines by taking over preexisting, prestigious religious centers may well explain the leapfrog-like distribution of the Pachacamac stylistic-iconographic cluster on the North Coast. In this regard, it may be significant that both Pacatnamú and Batán Grande were important regional Moche V religious centers (e.g., Shimada 1982, 1990, n.d.b; Ubbelohde-Doering 1967, 1983) that marked the northern and southern borders of the Moche V heartland, and thus would have been well suited to become Pachacamac branch shrines.

PACHACAMAC AND LONG-DISTANCE MARITIME TRADE

Another factor worth considering in regard to the leapfrog-like distribution of Pachacamac "influence" is the possibility that it sponsored long-distance maritime trade in sumptuary-ritual items with north coastal Peru and coastal Ecuador. Perhaps the most widely valued and traded ritual item in the Central Andes during the Middle Horizon was *Spondylus*, a brightly colored thorny oyster shell harvested primarily off coastal Ecuador. In contrast to prior, highly restricted usage, beginning with the Middle Horizon it came to be used in appreciable numbers in ritual contexts throughout much of the Central Andes (Shimada n.d.a, b; Shimada et al. n.d.). On the North Coast, for example, although during the Early Intermediate Period only the sumptuous Mochica burials included *Spondylus* shell offerings (e.g., those from Sipán; Alva 1988), during the Middle Horizon, a series of *Spondylus* workshops emerged (e.g., Moche V Pampa Grande [e.g., Shimada 1982], Huaca El Dragón [Schaedel 1966; Middle Horizon Epoch 2 or 3? See below], and perhaps atop Cerro Blanco overlooking the site of Moche [Menzel 1977:40-41]). This notable surge might have been occasioned by the adverse effects of the thirty-two-year-long drought (the most intense and longest drought recorded in the past 1,500 years) that suddenly beset the Central Andes starting A.D. 562 (Shimada et al. 1991, n.d.). The shell may have been widely used in rituals to appease deities for the return of water.

Pachacamac may have taken over the sponsorship role left vacant by the demise of the Mochica polity centered at Pampa Grande ca. A.D. 700-750 (the end of Middle Horizon Epoch 1B). In this case, Pacatnamú and Batán Grande would have served as secondary dissemination points for both *Spondylus* and the Pachacamac religion. The ability of these centers to provide the valued shell would have reinforced the prestige and power of the Pachacamac religion. To date, however, we identified no Middle Horizon Epoch 2 *Spondylus* caches or workshops at these centers.

MIDDLE HORIZON EPOCH 3 TRANSFORMATION

It has been argued that Wari political fortune began to wane at the end of Epoch 2B and the capital city of Wari was largely abandoned by early Epoch 3 (Menzel 1964:72). There are few radiocarbon dates to specify when Wari lost its political primacy or viability. Also, the responsible conditions and forces are not clear, just as it is difficult to specify whether the decline was rapid and/or uniform across the large Wari domain. In this regard, it is interesting that Patterson (1966:112) sees Cajamarquilla as abandoned before Epoch 2B Wari expansion (assuming that burials at the nearby Nievería cemetery reliably reflect the Cajamarquilla demography), while occupation continued at Pachacamac throughout Epoch 2 (Menzel 1964:72; Patterson 1966:112).

Whether or not Pachacamac had indeed established political autonomy from Wari, the former's religion began "as a direct new transplant of [Wari] religion to the coast" (Menzel 1977:53); thus the collapse of the Wari empire must have had a profound and prompt adverse effect on Pachacamac and its religion. Menzel (1964:73) notes that during Epoch 3 "the sphere of influence of Pachacamac was much reduced" to well within the Central Coast, and production of its once prestigious pottery considerably declined. Concurrently, Knobloch (n.d.) observed evidence of a "gradual abandonment of Wari [derived] mythology and assimilation of north coast Mochica culture at Pachacamac." One of the oldest Middle Horizon burials (Epoch 2B?) excavated by Uhle contained a damaged textile that showed the Front-faced Deity wearing a distinctly North Coastal T-shaped plume headdress and animal-headed rays (Knobloch n.d.). We already noted North Coast elements in the wooden idol excavated at the base of the Pachacamac Temple.

The nature and breadth of cultural changes that began in Epoch 3 (perhaps as early as late Epoch 2B) can be well appreciated in data collected by Uhle at the extensive settlement of Ancón (just to the north of Lima) established in Middle Horizon 1B perhaps to serve as a fishing center for Wari settlements farther inland (Menzel 1977:42-43). Though Ancón lacked the monumental architecture found at contemporaneous Cajamarquilla and Pachacamac, it was a major "necropolis" for much of the Central Coast from Middle Horizon 1B through the Late Horizon as evidenced by stratigraphic superposition of various styles related to those found in the Chancay and Rimac Valleys as well as at Pachacamac (Kaulicke 1983; Menzel 1977: 42). As such, numerous graves there have provided an excellent basis for the regional chronology and means to gauge the changing role and status of Pachacamac on the Central Coast.

Although during Middle Horizon Epoch 1B elite burials at Ancón show strong ties to society in the Rimac Valley, in subsequent Epoch 2A highly distinguished burials with new Pachacamac-Wari pottery appear, reflecting the emergence of Pachacamac as the principal religious center of the Central Coast (Menzel 1977:46). However,

> With the end of Epoch 2B, the influence of the Pachacamac and Rimac Valley virtually disappeared from the record of pottery styles of

Ancón.... The large-scale disappearance of the Pachacamac-[Wari] tradition reflects the collapse of power of Pachacamac with the end of the [Wari] Empire. Occasional derivatives of [Wari] forms occur at Ancón, but resemble some of the derivatives of [Wari]-style vessels from Chimu Capac, rather than those of the Pachacamac-[Wari] tradition.... It appears that as the power of Pachacamac vanished, the influence of a new order at Chimu Capac and north increased at Ancón.

(Menzel 1977:47)

In general, there was an appreciable qualitative and quantitative diminution in grave goods and constructions during Middle Horizon Epochs 3-4 and into the early Late Intermediate Period as compared with the first two Middle Horizon epochs. Gold and silver ornaments as well as stuffed cloth false-mummy bale heads all became rarer, and graves became shallower and/or simpler in structure (Menzel 1977:44-45). The burial rites of the preceding era "invested with pomp and ceremony" gradually came to an end (Menzel 1977:44). At the same time, Epoch 3 and 4 religious art on ceramics and painted cloth from Ancón show definite similarities to those from Chimú Capac and farther north (e.g., "Sky God" with an arching headdress).

These and other changes at Ancón are likely to be related to the changing balance of power along much of the coast following the Wari cultural decline and Pachacamac's loss of prestige. In Middle Horizon Epoch 3, the direction of "influence," which formerly radiated north out of Pachacamac along the coast, was clearly reversed; now the Central Coast came under strong stylistic and ideological influence from the North Coast. It is suggested here that Menzel's Middle Horizon Epoch 3 (perhaps as early as Epoch 2B) "North Coast center of influence" was the Sicán Precinct in the Batán Grande National Archaeological Monument in the central La Leche Valley (Fig. 7; Shimada 1985a:100, n.d.a). The Precinct is the inferred Vatican-like capital of the Middle Sicán state-level religious polity (Shimada 1985a:100, n.d.a), encompassing some dozen monumental mounds (including Huaca Rodillona measuring 100 x 100 m and 43 m high) within a T-shaped area of ca. 1,500 m east-west and 1,000 m north-south).

The demise of the Wari polity and consequent loss of prestige of Pachacamac coincides in time with the "cultural florescence" of Sicán culture (Middle Sicán; A.D. 900-1100) characterized by a distinct religious art that combined selected motifs and themes from earlier Mochica, Wari, and Pachacamac art into a new overall configuration. The central Sicán deity known as the Sicán Lord is typically represented by a masklike flat face with features adopted from Wari's Front-faced

Deity, but, at the same time, it is often accompanied by the North Coast mythical creatures (Shimada 1990:326, fn. 7, n.d.a).

Middle Sicán is also characterized by (a) the resurgence and importance of monumental platform mound temples, (b) large elite shaft tombs, (c) industrial scale, local smelting, and metalworking of copper alloys, and (d) maritime trade with coastal Ecuador (Shimada 1985a, b). The political and economic power wielded by the Middle Sicán elite is apparent in the size and number of temples constructed and an unprecedented accumulation of precious metals and other sumptuary goods (e.g., *Spondylus* shell, emerald, and pearls) found in some shaft tombs (Carcedo and Shimada 1985:62-65; Shimada 1990:321-346; Shimada and Cavallaro 1986:51).

The prestige of the Middle Sicán religion and polity can also be gauged by the presence of its distinct blackware bottles decorated with ideologically charged motifs at Pacatnamú, Ancón, and Pachacamac (Cleland and Shimada n.d.), and how they overshadowed local ceramics and were imitated in the upper Piura and lower Chicama valleys that bordered the Middle Sicán heartland (La Leche to Jequetepeque Valleys, inclusive). For example, in his excavation in front of the Pachacamac Temple, Uhle (Uhle's Pls. 8.7 and 8.10) recovered two Middle Sicán blackware bottles that appear to have been imported (Pl. 7). Other imported vessels and local derivatives are also found on much of the Peruvian coast between Chicama and Pachacamac (e.g., Larco 1948:43; Pl. IX, Vessel 4 in Kroeber 1926 [Chanchan]; Fig. 269 in Wilson 1988:511 [Santa Valley]). The southward spread of monochrome blackware covering the entire North and North-Central Coast sometime early in Middle Horizon Epoch 3 is also believed to be associated with the Middle Sicán expansion (Lyon n.d.). It essentially supplanted polychrome ceramics (tricolor ceramics persisted) of the preceding Epoch as the prestigious ceramics.

Another important Epoch 3 change concerns longdistance maritime trade along the Pacific coast. Though evidence for inferred trade linking Pachacamac, the North Coast, and Coastal Ecuador during Middle Horizon Epoch 2 is still tenuous, the case for Middle Sicán-coastal Ecuador maritime trade during Epochs 3-4 is much stronger and has been described in some detail elsewhere (e.g., Shimada 1985a:118-124, 1990:366-369, n.d.a). Frequent and explicit depictions of *Spondylus* shell and its harvest in Middle Sicán ceramics and metal objects and largescale ritual offerings of the shell in burials and architecture, together with the presence of Sicán ceramics at the major *Spondylus* harvest center of Isla de La Plata off the Ecuadorian coast, all point to the intimate involvement of the Middle Sicán polity and religion in

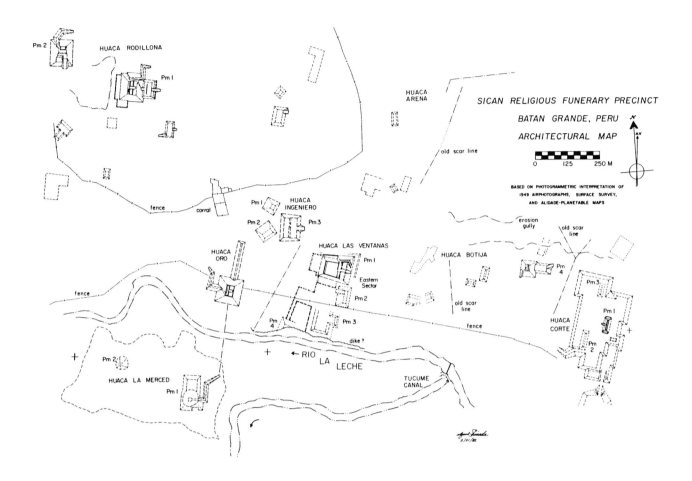

Figure 7. Architectural plan of the Sicán Precinct in the Batán Grande Archaeological Complex. Compare the T-shaped platform mounds of Pachacamac with those of Huaca Rodillona, Ingeniero (also called El Moscón), Las Ventanas, and El Corte. Drawing by the author.

procurement and distribution of the shell. It is suggested that, in exchange for the shell, copper and copper alloys produced in quantities in the Batán Grande region using local ore and fuel were offered to the metal-poor Ecuadorian coast. In addition, such sumptuary items as pearls and emeralds were obtained from the north.

The above Epoch 3 trade network probably involved other sponsors and benefactors elsewhere on the coast and highland hinterlands, for example, Huaca El Dragón with *Spondylus* workshops. Though some attribute these workshops to Middle Horizon Epoch 3 the basis of the associated frieze styles and iconographies, their dating is still tenuous (see Donnan 1990:283-295; Helsley 1985; Schaedel 1966:452-458) largely because of difficulties in cross-dating increasingly divergent North Coast art with the Ica Master Sequence (see Shimada 1990:313).

If the maritime trade linking Pachacamac, North Coast, and Coastal Ecuador in fact existed in Middle Horizon Epoch 2, it is likely that Pachacamac's would have declined at the end of Epoch 2 along with its religious prestige and political power. Just as Pachacamac may have taken over sponsorship of *Spondylus* trade at the end of Middle Horizon Epoch 1B, the Middle Sicán polity is thought to have assumed its administration in Middle Horizon Epoch 3 and to have dominated until its demise around A.D. 1050-1100.

The South Coast during Middle Horizon Epochs 3 and 4 had no religious-political power or center comparable to Pacatnamú and the Sicán Precinct. Overall, Menzel's (1977:51) characterization of Pachacamac's changing relationships with the surrounding areas seems to be still largely valid: "During the later culture history of the coast of ancient Peru the peoples of the Rimac and Lurín Valleys formed a cultural pivot, receiving influences from the coastal cultures to the north and south, as well as influencing these cultures at times."

Starting around the thirteenth century, the emergent Chimú state probably came to be the principal North Coast sponsor of maritime trade (Shimada n.d.a; Schaedel 1990), while the specialized Chincha traders described in a colonial document published by Rostworowski (1970; Murra 1975) managed the actual operation of the trade, including navigation. Rostworowski (1977:46, 1989:218) considers it possibility that the Chincha traders were subservient to the cult and oracle of Pachacamac before the Inca empire took control of the trade.

PACHACAMAC AND COASTAL RELIGIOUS CENTERS

Pachacamac, Pacatnamú, and the Sicán Precinct share a number of important common features, including a notable concentration of monumental constructions that have religious character. At the Sicán Precinct and Pachacamac, excavations atop mounds have revealed colonnades and associated enclosing walls with elaborate murals. In addition, these sites enjoyed longevity, boasting nearly continuous occupation from at least the Early Intermediate Period to the Late Horizon. That they enjoyed prestige well beyond the local or even regional scope over much of this long time span is suggested by the presence of various contemporaneous ceramic styles. M. Eliade (1974) and Victor Turner (1974), among others, have noted that widespread and durable religions are characterized by

ideologies emphasizing inclusiveness and acultural openness. Yet, the extent to which the importance of these sites depended on the acceptance of and devotion to associated ideologies (including the concept of *huaca*; see Jiménez Borja 1985), or threats (e.g., alluding to the "anger" or "retribution" of the patron deities, or even taking sacred icons of troublesome groups "hostage"), or some other factors (e.g., taking advantage of established prestige) is uncertain.

Though integral parts of a functioning settlement, "residential" and "ceremonial" sectors are segregated by distance and/or physical barriers. Pachacamac and Pacatnamú have major walls separating their inferred residential sectors. In the case of the Sicán Precinct, there are no walls separating Huaca Arena, the nearest associated habitational area. In terms of interaction and the residents' perception, the nearly 1 km distance that separated the Sicán Precinct and Huaca Arena may not have differed much from walls at Pachacamac and Pacatnamú. We are speaking here of a concentric or sectorial settlement system in which peripherally situated settlements were in constant communication and had a set of long-term social and ritual obligations to the religious center. In this view, the nucleus is a center not in terms of population density or size but rather in terms of interaction (see Wheatley 1972). Thus, it is critical that the size, composition, and permanence of the resident population be established for all three sites (see Silverman 1985, 1986).

The above list based on coastal data provides a starting point toward more complete characterization of Central Andean ceremonial centers or ceremonial cities.

Future Research Tasks and Directions

This review has elucidated a number of important future research tasks and directions for Pachacamac archaeology.

One pressing task is publication of technical details and results of fieldwork carried out thus far at Pachacamac and nearby sites. As noted by Willey in his Foreword, Uhle's original *Pachacamac* report was in many ways without peer for its time; yet, it was A. L. Kroeber (e.g., 1926) and his students at the University of California at Berkeley (Gayton 1927; Strong 1925) who clarified association, classified and described Uhle's materials, and generally made them accessible and meaningful. We await full publication of Uhle's remaining documents, including field maps showing the exact recovery location of artifacts (see Rowe 1954:23), as well as artifacts recovered or attributed to

Pachacamac within the Baessler and Gretzer collections now at the Museum für Völkerkunde in Berlin and elsewhere.

At the same time, our attention should not be confined to ceramics. Ina Van Stan's long-term study of Pachacamac textiles now housed at The University Museum of The University of Pennsylvania culminated with the publication of *Textiles from Beneath the Temple of Pachacamac, Peru* (1967; also see Van Stan 1957, 1961a, 1961b, 1963, 1965; Engelstad 1986). Her study as a whole provides a fine structural characterization of a portion of the Pachacamac textile collection at The University Museum. However, many textiles remain to be illustrated and analyzed, and together with advances made in ceramic analysis, they promise to be valuable for stylistic and iconographic studies of the Pachacamac style (Knobloch 1989, personal communication, n.d.). Engelstad's (1986) recent analysis of a group of grave tablets and shirt fragments from Pachacamac, in fact, effectively illustrates how weaving techniques and materials may shed new light on the changing relationship between Pachacamac, on the one hand, and the Wari empire and the North Coast, on the other.

Much the same can be said about the need to publish results of the work that J. C. Tello and A. Jiménez Borja directed at Pachacamac during 1940-1947 and 1958 up to the 1980s, respectively. In regard to Tello's work, the brief notices that appeared in newspapers and periodicals simply do not provide the necessary details of excavations and clearing or their results. It is hoped that relevant portions of the fieldnotes and other documentation that Tello willed to the San Marcos National University, Lima, will be published, following the example of *Páginas Escogidas* (Tello 1967). In regard to Jiménez Borja's clearing and excavations among Pyramids with Ramp, tantalizing bits of information appear in a few, scattered publications (see Lavallée 1966). Though Paredes's (1988) summary article is informative and useful, we eagerly await full publication of broader contextual and associational data.

Related to the above publication efforts, we need systematization of terminologies employed in describing architecture and ceramics. Each archaeologist that worked at the site seems to have imposed his own names for major sectors and structures, and an effort was made in this essay to minimize this terminological confusion.

Since the days of Uhle's original study, Pachacamac has been commonly described as a "sacred" or "religious" city. What do these designations mean in terms of constituent institutions, their residents, and their activities, functions, and physical locations? Uhle and Tello's divisions of the site seem to have been derived largely from an assumed relationship among the form, size, and function of the most visible structures. Yet the degree and nature of architectural variability within and between sectors still have not been established. What can we really say about the social and economic structure and organization of the resident population at any one point in time? What were the specific roles played by the residents of Tello's "palaces" or "citadels," "minor mansions," and *barrios*? How were they supported? Other than some tantalizing ethnohistorical leads for late Prehispanic eras, archaeology has not contributed many concrete answers.

Our knowledge of the *barrio*, or "suburb," an extensive sand-covered area north and northeast of the Old City Wall, remains the most limited and tenuous. Tello (1960) regarded this area as the "dwellings of the common people" because of the extensive distribution of refuse and minor structural remains. At least for the Pachacamac IV period, portions of this area were used as cemeteries (Bueno 1982:47). It is not clear whether or not the burials there were of the resident "common people." Given the long-standing religious importance of Pachacamac, it would not be surprising if bodies were brought there from some distance to be buried.

Surprisingly, there has not been any attempt to take advantage of the large number of human burials that have been excavated at Pachacamac and the "Necropolis" and other sites within the extensive desert plain known as Tablada de Lurín to elucidate regional population structure and dynamics. Over the last three decades or so, numerous human skulls have been collected at the Necropolis de la Tablada de Lurín by Josefina Ramos de Cox (e.g., 1960, 1964, 1972) and Mercedes Cardenas (1969, 1970). With more systematic collection and recording (including postcranial bones; see Paredes 1984), the Necropolis should yield valuable demographic data. Such a study may be compared to M. Newman's (1947) analysis of seventy-two skeletons from Pachacamac.

In any case, one major task is to gain a holistic understanding of this "ceremonial city" through a balanced sampling of different areas and adoption of a systemic perspective. To this end, it is essential to elucidate the physical extent and organization, functions, history, and nature of occupation in the "suburb." Only when armed with such knowledge can we fruitfully discuss the internal dynamics of Pachacamac as a ceremonial city. Bonavia (1985:137) laments that "it is a great pity that work has been concentrated in a single sector [ceremonial] of Pachacamac, while the rest remains covered by sand, partly destroyed forever, and now spoiled by poorly conceived reconstructions." It is hoped that a workable balance between academic and public/touristic interests can be achieved in selection of future clearing and excavation loci.

For a better understanding of the physical transformation of the site over time, we need better definition of the physical extent of the site, additional deep stratigraphic cuts, and continuing refinement of ceramic and architectural seriations. Tello was uncertain of the full extent of the site and as late as 1967-1968 efforts were still being made to define it (Bueno 1974/1975:177). Also, Bueno's (1982) broad-stroke characterization of site growth within the Old City Wall was done within a four-phase (Pachacamac I-IV) framework with single phases spanning anywhere from about 100 to 700 years, too imprecise to clarify the factors and mechanisms that brought about the transformation. Chronological control is quite problematical between the late Middle Horizon to early Late

Intermediate Period, a time span for which ethnohistorical data are of limited utility.

Ongoing analysis of the Pachacamac style by P. Knobloch should improve our chronological control of the Middle Horizon on the Central Coast. Her long-term aim is to integrate, to the extent possible, Uhle's original notes, catalogs, reports, and excavated ceramics housed in three museums (the Robert Lowie Museum, University of California at Berkeley; The University Museum of Archaeology and Anthropology, the University of Pennsylvania, Philadelphia; and the Museum für Völkerkunde, Berlin) in order to amplify the descriptive repertoire of the Pachacamac style and to refine Menzel's stylistic chronology. New insights, in conjunction with those gained from more recently discovered Wari artifacts (see, e.g., Anders 1990) will allow refinement of the Middle Horizon chronology and further exploration into the sociopolitical dimensions of the stylistic interaction among contemporaneous Pachacamac, Tiahuanaco, and Wari peoples.

Fuller publication of the numerous burials (many stratigraphically superimposed) excavated at Ancón over the past 100 years, since the time of Reiss and Stübel (1880-1887), would help various aspects of Pachacamac archaeology. For example, excavations of burials at Ancón in the 1940s by teams from the National Museum of Anthropology and Archaeology under the direction of J. C. Tello recovered some 2,500 burials (J. M. Vreeland, personal communication, 1980). Greatly amplified burial data could help further clarify not only coastal Middle Horizon chronology but also Pachacamac's changing relationship with the Wari empire and the sociopolitical hierarchy of regional ethnic groups. In addition, unpublished Ancón gravelots hold much promise in elucidating the formation and sociopolitical correlates of Epigonal styles that have not to date received much attention.

Efforts are also needed to develop independent dating of architecture that would allow effective cross-dating of physically detached monumental constructions that have been excavated to date. Seriation of adobe forms (e.g., *adobito* versus *adobón*, or *tapia*) or wall abutment and bonding analysis are often too imprecise and are subject to errors stemming from recycling, reconstructions, and/or conservatism. However, architectural features identified by Paredes and Franco (1987:5) as being diagnostic for the Pyramids with Ramps seem appropriate as the basis for their "similiary seriation" of specific architectural attributes. Raffael Cavallaro (1988:53-83) has demonstrated the effectiveness of this approach in his re-analysis of the *Ciudadelas* at the Chimú state capital of Chan Chan that share some important features with the Pyramids with Ramps (e.g., impressive perimeter walls, formal layout, presence of storage cells) in addition to being partially contemporaneous.

Whether the physical distance between the temple and given Pyramids with Ramps correlates with the order of their construction or position within the sociopolitical hierarchy at the site remains to be seen. Similarly, we may consider the possibility of dual organization of the Pyramids with Ramps (see Cavallaro 1988:84-97).

Deep stratigraphic cuts are needed to clarify the extent and nature of Lima and pre-Lima occupation at Pachacamac. Whether the initial occupation at Pachacamac dates back to the "Chavín" or "Archaic Horizon" (the first millennium B.C.) as Tello suspected remains to be documented. Also, clarification of chronological and functional relationships among documented and suspected Lima period mounds in the southern "ceremonial" sector would be essential in defining the establishment of the ceremonial center at Pachacamac. Were the severe climatic anomalies of the mid- to late sixth century A.D. responsible for the establishment or relocation of any Lima temple? How stratigraphic sequences at different parts of the site relate to one another has not been defined. To date, in spite of problems stemming from their disregard of the natural stratigraphy and archaeological association, those excavated by Strong and Corbett (1943) are the only properly described and published stratigraphic cuts at Pachacamac.

Pachacamac, being one of the best-known and important monuments of Peru, has sometimes led investigators to become overly focused on the site in and of itself. However, in reality, Pachacamac has held varying degrees of importance at local (Lurín Valley), regional (Central Coast and neighboring highlands), and even Andean levels for much of the last 1,500 years or so of its prehistory. Its prestige appears to have been significantly boosted when it was transformed to become the regional dissemination center of Wari religion. It may even have achieved ideological and political autonomy apart from the Wari. With the demise of the Wari empire and concurrent expansion of the Middle Sicán polity on the North Coast with its innovative Mochica-Wari "fusional" religion, Pachacamac's importance was reduced to the regional level. However, even during the subsequent dominance of the North Coast by the Chimú Kingdom, Pachacamac was able apparently to hold sway over much of the Central Coast and the adjacent highlands as the key regional religious center. The later formation of a symbiotic alliance between Pachacamac and the expanding Inca empire around A.D. 1476 (Menzel and Rowe 1966:68) provided the legitimacy and political power to reestablish its pan-Andean prestige and importance.

A better understanding of the conditions and forces underlying the ebb and flow of Pachacamac over time and space remains a major research task. In this regard, it is vital that we continue integrated archaeological-ethnohistorical research into the ideological, economic, and sociopolitical foundations of Pachacamac, for example, the inferred maritime trade in sumptuary goods that may have linked various major religious centers on Peruvian coast with coastal Ecuador. How did the trade change over time from the Middle to Late Horizon? Did Pachacamac serve as the hub of the trade at any point in time? Menzel (1977:46) suggests that the administrative unification of the Lurín and Rimac valleys in Middle Horizon 2A may relate to the formation of an intervalley irrigation system. If so, who administered it and what was the productivity of the associated field system? Also, we still do not have adequate knowledge of how the famed oracle in the Rimac Valley interacted with that of Pachacamac; were they rivals?

Clearly, no one research group can be expected to deal with the local, regional, and Andean dimensions of Pachacamac over time with the same thoroughness. We need a team approach (e.g., ethnohistorians and archaeologists jointly conducting field surveys) and bet-ter communication (e.g., occasional roundtables) between those working at Pachacamac and contemporaneous sites on the Central Coast and those working farther afield, particularly at other notable religious centers. There is no doubt that in recent decades detailed ethnohistorical studies have made significant contributions to understanding of the social and ideological aspects of late Prehispanic Pachacamac and the Central Coast in general. However, archaeological interpretations have been too often heavily dependent on historical data with their assumed veracity. Archaeologists and historians alike have extrapolated historical data as far back as the beginning of Middle Horizon with the hope that others would verify such inferences. It is hoped that both sides will develop a realistic view of one another's potentials and limitations.

The preceding comments are by no means an exhaustive list of future research tasks and directions. It shows, however, that even after a century of research there are still many basic issues to be resolved. It is also a reflection of the complexity and significance of the site and associated cultures of Pachacamac. It is hoped that the publication of this edition will serve to stimulate additional research surrounding Pachacamac.

Bibliography

Agurto, Santiago

1984   *Lima Prehispánica.* Municipalidad de Lima Metropolitana, Lima.

Alessio, M., F. Bella, F. Bachechi, and C. Cortesi

1967   University of Rome Carbon-14 Dates V. *Radiocarbon* 9:198-217.

Alva, Walter

1988   Discovering the New World's Richest Unlooted Tomb. *National Geographic* 174(4):510-549.

Anders, Martha B.

1990   Maymi: un Sitio del Horizonte Medio en el Valle de Pisco. *Gaceta Arqueológica Andina* 5(17):27-39.

Anon.

1938   Las Excavaciones en Pachacamac y la Arquitectura Religiosa de los Valles de Lima. *El Comercio* (September 21). Lima.

1940a   Valioso Descubrimiento Arqueológico en Pachacamac. *El Comercio* (July 16). Lima.

1940b   El Doctor Julio C. Tello nos Habla de los Descubrimientos Realizados en las Ruinas de Pachacamac. *El Comercio* (July 18). Lima.

Antúnez de Mayolo, Santiago E.

1938   Una Visita a las Ruinas de Pachacamac. *El Comercio* (November 13), afternoon ed. Lima.

Baessler, A.

1902/1903

        Ancient Peruvian Art; Contributions to the Archaeology of the Empire of the Incas. Translated by A. H. Keane, 4 parts. Berlin.

Bennett, Wendell C.

1948   The Peruvian Co-Tradition. In *A Reappraisal of Peruvian Archaeology*, ed. W. C. Bennett. Memoir 4, pp. 1-7. Society for American Archaeology.

1953   *Excavations at Wari, Ayacucho, Peru.* Yale University Publications in Anthropology 49. New Haven.

Bonavia, Duccio

1962   Sobre el Estilo Teatino. *Revista del Museo Nacional* 31:43-94.

1974   *Ricchata Quellcani: Pinturas Murales Prehispánicas.* Banco Industrial del Perú, Lima.

1985   *Mural Painting in Ancient Peru.* Translated by Patricia J. Lyon. Indiana University Press, Bloomington.

Bueno, Alberto

1974/1975

        Cajamarquilla y Pachacamac: Dos Ciudades de la Costa Central del Perú. *Boletín Bibliográfico de Antropología Americana* 36:171-201. Instituto Panamericano de Geografía e Historia, D. F. México.

1982   *El Antiguo Valle de Pachacamac: Espacio, Tiempo y Cultura.* Editorial Los Pinos, Lima.

Canziani, José

1987   Análisis del Complejo Urbano Maranga Chayavilca. *Gaceta Arqueológica Andina* 4(14):10-17.

Carcedo, Paloma, and Izumi Shimada

1985   Behind the Golden Mask: Sicán Gold Artifacts from Batán Grande, Peru. In *Art of Precolumbian Gold: Jan Mitchell Collection*, ed. Julie Jones, pp. 60-75. Weidenfeld and Nicolson, London.

Cardenas, Mercedes

1969   Necrópolis de Tablada de Lurín, Area 313: Cistas No. 1 y No. 2. *Arqueología PUC*, no. 3:75-86. Instituto Riva-Agüero, Pontificia Universidad Católica del Perú, Lima.

1970   Dos Ceramios Naturalistas en Tablada de Lurín: Informe de las Tumbas 1 y 3 del Area 22. *Arqueología PUC*, no. 6:1-11. Instituto Riva-Agüero, Pontificia Universidad Católica del Perú, Lima.

Casa Vilca, Alberto

1939   Las Ruinas de Pachacamac. *Boletín de la Sociedad Geográfica de Lima* 56(2):95-99.

Cavallaro, Raffael, and Izumi Shimada

1988   Some Thoughts on Sicán Marked Adobes and Labor Organization. *American Antiquity* 53:75-101.

Cleland, Kathryn M., and Izumi Shimada

n.d.   Sicán Bottles: Marking Time in the Peruvian Bronze Age. *Andean Past*. In press.

Conklin, William J.

1979   Moche Textile Structures. In *The Junius B. Bird Pre-Columbian Textile Conference, May 19th and 20th, 1973*, eds. A. P. Rowe, E. P. Benson, and A. Schaffer, pp. 165-184. The Textile Museum and Dumbarton Oaks, Washington, DC.

Conklin, William J., and Michael E. Moseley

1988   The Patterns of Art and Power in the Early Intermediate Period. In *Peruvian Prehistory*, ed. Richard Keatinge, pp. 145-163. Cambridge University Press, Cambridge.

Cook, Anita, G.

1983   Aspects of State Ideology in Huari and Tiahuanaco Iconography: The Central Deity and the Sacrificer. In *Papers from the 1st Annual Northeast Conference on Andean Archaeology and Ethnohistory*, ed. D. H. Sandweiss, pp. 161-185. Cornell University Latin American Studies Program, Ithaca, NY.

1985   *Art and Time in the Evolution of Andean State Expansion*. Ph.D. dissertation, Department of Anthropology, State University of New York, Binghamton.

1987   The Middle Horizon Ceramic Offerings from Conchopata. *Ñawpa Pacha* 22-23:49-90.

Daggett, Richard E.

1988   The Pachacamac Studies: 1938-1941. In *Multidisciplinary Studies in Andean Anthropology*, ed. Virginia J. Vitzthum, pp. 13-21. Michigan Discussions in Anthropology 8. University of Michigan, Ann Arbor.

Dillehay, Tom D.

1977   *Tawantinsuyu*, Integration of the Chillón Valley, Peru: A Case of Inca Geo-Political Mastery. *Journal of Field Archaeology* 4:397-405.

1979   Pre-Hispanic Resource Sharing in the Central Andes. *Science* 204:24-31.

Donnan, Christopher B.

1968   An Association of Middle Horizon Epoch 2A: Specimens from the Chicama Valley, Peru. *Ñawpa Pacha* 6:47-113.

1990   The Chotuna Friezes and the Chotuna-Dragon Connection. In *The Northern Dynasties: Kingship and Statecraft in Chimor*, eds. Michael E. Moseley and Alana Cordy-Collins, pp. 275-296. Dumbarton Oaks, Washington, DC.

Donnan, Christopher B., and Guillermo A. Cock (editors)

1986   *The Pacatnamú Papers*. Vol. 1. Museum of Cultural History, University of California, Los Angeles.

Duviols, Pierre

1983   El Contra Idolatría de Luís de Teruel y una Versión primeriza del Mito de Pachacamac-Vichama. *Revista Andina* 1:385-392.

Earle, Timothy

1972   Lurín Valley, Peru: Early Intermediate Period Settlement Development. *American Antiquity* 37:467-477

Eliade, Mircea

1974   *Patterns in Comparative Religion*. Translated by Rosemary Sheed. New American Library, New York.

Eling, Herbert

1987   *The Role of Irrigation Networks in Emerging Societal Complexity During Late Prehispanic Times, Jequetepeque Valley, North Coast, Peru*. Ph.D. dissertation, Department of Anthropology, University of Texas, Austin.

Engelstad, Helen

1986   A Group of Grave Tablets and Shirt Fragments from Pachacamac. *Ñawpa Pacha* 24:61-72.

Espejo, Julio

1941   Cuentos, Leyendas y Anécdotas Relacionadas con las Ruinas de Pachacamac. *Chaski* 1(3):67-71.

Feltham, Jane P.

1983   *The Lurín Valley, Peru, A.D. 1000-1532.* Ph.D. dissertation, Institute of Archaeology, University of London, London.

1984   The Lurín Valley Project—Some Results for the Late Intermediate and Late Horizon. In *Current Archaeological Projects in the Central Andes: Some Approaches and Results,* ed. A. Kendall, pp. 45-73. British Research Council International Series 210.

Flores, Isabel

1984   Telas Pintados de Pampa de Faclo, Pacatnamú. *Gaceta Arqueológica Andina* 3(12):6-7.

Fung, Rosa

1963   Las Ideas Evolucionistas en las Interpretaciones Arqueológicas. *Revista del Museo Nacional* 32:203-208.

Gayton, Anna H.

1927   *The Uhle Collections from Nievería.* University of California Publications in American Archaeology and Ethnology 21(8):305-329. Berkeley.

Gayton, Anna H., and Alfred L. Kroeber

1927   *The Uhle Pottery Collections from Nazca.* University of California Publications in American Archaeology and Ethnology 24(1). Berkeley.

Harcourt, Raoul d'

1922   La céramique de Cajamarquilla-Nievería. *Journal de la Société des Américanistes de Paris,* n.s., 14:107-118.

Hecker, Gisela, and Wolgang Hecker

1977   *Archäologische Untersuchungen in Pacatnamu, Nord-Peru.* Gebr. Mann Verlag, Berlin.

1985   *Pacatnamú y sus Construciones: Centro Religioso Prehispánico en la Costa Norte Peruana.* Verlag Klaus Dieter Vervuert, Frankfurt.

Helsley, Anne M.

1985   *The Friezes of Huaca El Dragón: An Interpretation.* Master's thesis, Department of Anthropology, University of Texas, Austin.

Horkheimer, Hans

1963   Chancay Prehispánico: Diversidad y Belleza. *Cultura Peruana* 23(175-178):62-69.

Iriarte, Francisco

1960   Algunas Apreciaciones sobre los Huanchos. In *Antiguo Peru: Espacio y Tiempo,* compiled by Ramiro Matos, pp. 259-263. Editorial Mejía Baca, Lima.

Isbell, William H.

1972   Huari y los Orígenes del Primer Imperio Andino. In *Pueblos y Culturas de la Sierra Central del Perú,* eds. D. Bonavia and R. Ravines, pp. 53-65. Cerro de Pasco Corporation, Lima.

1983   Shared Ideology and Parallel Political Development: Huari and Tiwanaku. In *Papers from the 1st Annual Northeast Conference on Andean Archaeology and Ethnohistory,* ed. Daniel Sandweiss, pp. 186-208. Cornell University Latin American Studies Program, Ithaca.

1988   City and State in Middle Horizon Huari. In *Peruvian Prehistory,* ed. Richard Keatinge, pp. 164-189. Cambridge University Press, Cambridge.

Isbell, William H., and Anita Cook

1987   Ideological Origins of an Andean Conquest State. *Archaeology* 40(4):26-33.

Isla, Elizabeth, and Daniel Guerrero

1987   Socos: Un Sitio Wari en el Valle de Chillón. *Gaceta Arqueológica Andina* 4(14):23-28.

Jijón y Caamaño, Jacinto

1949   *Maranga, Contribución al Conocimiento de los Aborígenes del Valle del Rimac, Perú.* La Prensa Católica, Quito.

Jiménez Borja, Arturo

1985   Pachacamac. *Boletín de Lima* 7(38):40-54.

Jiménez Borja, Arturo, and Alberto Bueno

1970   Breves Notas acerca de Pachacamac. *Arqueología y Sociedad,* No. 4, pp. 13-25. Universidad Nacional Mayor de San Marcos, Lima.

Kaulicke, Peter

1983   *Gräber von Ancón, Peru: Nach den Arbeiten von W. Reiss/A. Stübel, M. Uhle, R. Ravines, G. R. Willey und C. Huapaya.* Verlag C. H. Beck, München.

Keatinge, Richard W.

1977   Religious Forms and Secular Functions: The Expansion of State Bureaucracies as Reflected in Prehistoric Architecture on the Peruvian North Coast. *Annals of the New York Academy of Sciences 293:229-245.* New York.

1978   *The Pacatnamu Textiles. Archaeology* 31:30-41.

1982   The Chimu Empire in a Regional Perspective: Cultural Antecedents and Continuities. In *Chan Chan: Andean Desert City,* eds. M. E. Moseley and K. Day, pp. 197-224. School for American Research.

Keatinge, Richard W., D. Chodoff, D. P. Chodoff, M. Marvin, and H. Silverman

1975   From the Sacred to the Secular: First Report on a Prehistoric Architectural Transition on the North Coast of Peru. *Archaeology* 28:128-129.

Knobloch, Patricia J.

n.d.   Artisans of the Realm: Art of the Wari Empire and Its Contemporaries. In *Ancient Art of the Andean World,* eds. Shozo Masuda and Izumi Shimada. Iwanami, Tokyo. In press.

Kosok, Paul

1965   *Life, Land and Water in Ancient Peru.* Long Island University Press, New York.

Kroeber, Alfred L.

1925a   *The Uhle Pottery Collections from Moche.* University of California Publications in American Archaeology and Ethnology 21(5). Berkeley.

1925b   *The Uhle Pottery Collections from Supe.* University of California Publications in American Archaeology and Ethnology 21(6). Berkeley.

1926   *The Uhle Pottery Collections from Chancay.* University of California Publications in American Archaeology and Ethnology 21(7):265-304. Berkeley.

1930   *Archaeological Explorations in Peru, Part II: The Northern Coast.* Field Museum of Natural History, Anthropology Memoirs 2(2). Chicago.

1944   *Peruvian Archaeology in 1942.* Viking Fund Publications in Anthropology 4. Chicago.

1954   *Proto-Lima: Middle Period Culture of Peru.* Fieldiana, Anthropology 44. Chicago Natural History Museum, Chicago.

Lanning, Edward P.

1967   *Peru Before the Incas.* Prentice-Hall, Englewood Cliffs, NJ.

Larco Hoyle, Rafael

1948   *Cronología Arqueológica del Norte del Perú.* Sociedad Geográfica Americana, Buenos Aires.

Lavallée, Danièle

1966   Una collección de cerámica de Pachacamac. *Revista del Museo Nacional* 34:220-246.

Lumbreras, Luís G.

1974   *The Peoples and Cultures of Ancient Peru.* Translated by Betty J. Meggers. Smithsonian Institution Press, Washington, DC.

Lyon, Patricia

1966   Innovation Through Archaism: The Origins of the Ica Pottery Style. *Ñawpa Pacha* 4:31-61.

n.d.   Andean Art and Its Cultural Implications. In *Ancient Art of the Andean World,* eds. Shozo Masuda and Izumi Shimada. Iwanami, Tokyo. In press.

MacNeish, Richard S., Thomas C. Patterson, and David L. Browman

1975   *The Central Peruvian Prehistoric Interaction Sphere.* Papers of the Robert S. Peabody Foundation for Archaeology, No. 7. Phillips Academy, Andover, MA.

Marcus, Joyce, and Jorge E. Silva

1988   The Chillón Valley "Coca Lands": Archaeological Background and Ecological Context. In *Conflicts over Coca Fields in Sixteenth Century Peru* by María Rostworowski, pp. 1-52. Memoirs of the Museum of Anthropology, University of Michigan No. 21. Ann Arbor.

Markham, Clements R.

1856   *Cuzco: A Journey to the Ancient Capital of Peru, with an Account of the History, Language, Literature, and Antiquities of the Incas.* Chapman and Hall, London.

Means, Philip A.

1931   *Ancient Civilizations of the Andes.* Charles Scribner's Sons, New York.

Menzel, Dorothy

1958   Problemas en el Estudio del Horizonte Medio de la Arqueología Peruana. *Revista del Museo Regional de Ica* 9(10):24-57.

1964   Style and Time in the Middle Horizon. *Ñawpa Pacha* 2:1-105.

1968   La Cultura Wari. In *Las Grandes Civilizaciones del Antiguo Perú* 6:184-197. Companía de Seguros y Reaseguros Peruano-Suiza, Lima.

1969   New Data on the Huari Empire in Middle Horizon Epoch 2A. *Ñawpa Pacha* 6:47-114.

1977   *The Archaeology of Ancient Peru and the Work of Max Uhle.* Robert H. Lowie Museum of Anthropology, University of California, Berkeley.

Menzel, Dorothy, and John H. Rowe

1966   The Role of Chincha in Late Pre-Spanish Peru. *Ñawpa Pacha* 4:63-76.

Middendorf, Ernest W.

1894   *Peru II: Das Küstenland von Peru.* Robert Oppenheim, Berlin.

Millones, Luís

1982   Brujerías de la Costa/Brujerías de la Sierra: Estudio Comparativo de Dos Complejos Religioso en el Area Andina. In *El Hombre y su Ambiente en los Centrales*, eds. Luís Millones and Hiroyasu Tomoeda, pp. 229-274. Senri Ethnological Studies 10. National Museum of Ethnology, Senri.

Moseley, M. E.

1982   Introduction: Human Exploitation and Organization on the North Andean Coast. In *Chan Chan: Andean Desert City*, eds. M. E. Moseley and K. C. Day, pp. 1-24. University of New Mexico, Albuquerque.

Muelle, Jorge C., and Robert Wells

1939   Las Pinturas del Templo de Pachacamac. *Revista del Museo Nacional* 8:275-282.

Murra, John V.

1975   El Tráfico de *Mullu* en la Costa del Pacífico. In *Formaciones Económicas y Políticas del Mundo Andino*, pp. 255-267. Instituto de Estudios Peruanos, Lima.

Netherly, Patricia J.

1977   *Local Level Lords on the North Coast of Peru.* Ph.D. dissertation, Department of Anthropology, Cornell University. University Microfilms International, Ann Arbor.

Newman, Marshall T.

1947   *Indian Skeletal Material from the Central Coast of Peru.* Papers of the Peabody Museum of American Archaeology and Ethnology, Harvard University 27(4). Cambridge, MA.

Oxford English Dictionary

1971   *The Compact Edition of the Oxford English Dictionary*, Vol. 1: A-O, s.v. "Epigone."

Paredes B., Ponciano

1984   El Panel (Pachacamac): Nuevo Tipo de Enterramiento. *Gaceta Arqueológica Andina* 3(10):8-9, 15.

1985   La Huaca Pintada o El Templo de Pachacamac. *Boletín de Lima* 7(41):70-77.

1988   Pachacamac—Pirámide con Rampa No. 2. *Boletín de Lima* 10(55):41-58.

Paredes B., Ponciano, and Régulo Franco

1985   Excavaciones en La Huaca Pintada o El Templo de Pachacamac. *Boletín de Lima* 7(41):78-84.

1987   Pachacamac: Las Pirámides con Rampa, Cronología y Función. *Gaceta Arqueológica Andina* 4(13):5-7.

1987/88
        Excavaciones en El Templo Viejo de Pachacamac. *Willay*, nos. 27-28:25-27. Cambridge, MA.

Parker, Gary J.

1972   Falacias y Verdades acerca del Quechua. In *El Reto del Multilingüismo en el Perú*, pp. 111-121. Instituto de Estudios Peruanos, Lima.

Patterson, Thomas C.

1966   *Pattern and Process in the Early Intermediate Period Pottery of the Central Coast of Peru.* University of California Publications in Anthropology 3. Berkeley.

1974   Pachacamac Revisited: Some Comments on Methods of Interpreting Archaeological Evidence. In *Perspectives in Palaeoanthropology*, ed. Asok K. Ghosh, pp. 65-71. Firma K. L. Mukhopadhyay, Calcutta.

1985   Pachacamac: An Andean Oracle under Inca Rule. In *Recent Studies in Andean Prehistory and Protohistory*, eds. D. Peter Kvietok and Daniel H. Sandweiss, pp. 159-176. Cornell University Latin American Studies Program, Ithaca.

Patterson, Thomas C., and Edward P. Lanning

1964   Changing Settlement Patterns on the Central Peruvian Coast. *Ñawpa Pacha* 2:113-123. Berkeley.

Patterson, Thomas C., J. P. McCarthy, and R. A. Dunn

1982   Polities in the Lurín Valley, Peru, During the Early Intermediate Period. *Ñawpa Pacha* 20:61-82.

Paulsen, Allison

1976   Environment and Empire: Climatic Factors in Prehistoric Andean Culture Change. *World Archaeology* 8:121-132.

Ramos de Cox, Josefina

1960   Necropólis de la Tablada de Lurín. In *Antiguo Peru: Espacio y Tiempo*, compiled by Ramiro Matos, pp. 251-257. Editorial Juan Mejía Baca, Lima.

1964   *Nota sobre una Nueva Forma Cerámica y Material del Periodo Intermedio Temprano en la Costa Central del Perú.* Publicación del Instituto Riva Agüero, Pontificia Universidad Católica del Perú, Lima.

1972   Estratos Marcadores y Niveles de Ocupación en la Tablada de Lurín, Lima. *Arqueología PUC* 13:7-30. Instituto Riva-Agüero, Pontifica Universidad Católica del Perú. Lima.

Ravines, Rogger

1969   Un Depósito de Ofrendas del Horizonte Medio en la Sierra Central del Perú. *Ñawpa Pacha* 6:19-45.

1982   *Panorama de la Arqueología Andina.* Instituto de Estudios Peruanos, Lima.

Ravines, Rogger and Juan J. Alvarez

1967   Fechas Radiocarbónicas para el Perú. *Arqueológicas* 11. Museo Nacional de Antropología y Arqueología, Lima.

Reiss, W., and A. Stübel

1880-87
        Peruvian Antiquities: The Necropolis of Ancon in Peru; A Series of Illustrations of the Civilization and Industry of the Empire of the Incas. Translated by A. H. Keane. 8 parts. New York.

Rivero, Mariano Eduardo, and Johann J. von Tschudi

1855   *Peruvian Antiquities.* Translated by Francis L. Hawks. A. S. Barnes, New York.

Rostworowski, María

1970   Mercaderes del Valle de Chincha en la Epoca Prehispánica: Un Documento y Unos Comentarios. *Revista Española de Antropología Americana* 5:135-177.

1972   Breve Informe sobre el Señorio de Ychma o Ychima. *Arqueología PUC* 13:37-51. Instituto Riva-Agüero, Pontificia Universidad Católica del Perú, Lima.

1973   Urpay Huachac y el "Símbolo del Mar." *Arqueología PUC* 14:13-22. Instituto Riva-

        Agüero, Pontificia Universidad Católica del Perú, Lima.

1974   Plantaciones Prehispánicas de Coca en la Vertiente del Pacífico. *Revista del Museo Nacional* 39:193-224. Lima.

1975   Pescadores, Artesanos y Mercaderes Costeños en el Perú Prehispánico. *Revista del Museo Nacional* 41:311-349.

1977   *Etnía y Sociedad: Ensayos sobre la Costa Central Prehispánica.* Instituto de Estudios Peruanos, Lima.

1978   *Señorios Indígenas de Lima y Canta.* Instituto de Estudios Peruanos, Lima.

1980   *Guarco y Lunahuaná: Dos Señoríos Prehispánicos, Costa Sur-Central del Perú.* *Revista del Museo Nacional* 44:153-214.

1981   *Recursos Naturales Renovables y Pesca, Siglos XVI y XVII.* Instituto de Estudios Peruanos, Lima.

1983   *Estructuras Andinas del Poder: Ideología Religiosa y Política.* Instituto de Estudios Peruanos, Lima.

1988   *Conflicts Over Coca Fields in Sixteenth-Century Peru.* Memoirs of the Museum of Anthropology, University of Michigan No. 21. Ann Arbor.

1989   *Costa Peruana Prehispánica.* Instituto de Estudios Peruanos, Lima.

Rowe, John H.

1945   Absolute Chronology in the Andean Area. *American Antiquity* 10:265-284.

1947   Obituary: Julio C. Tello. *American Journal of Archaeology*, 2d series (51):433-434.

1948   The Kingdom of Chimor. *Acta Americana* 6:26-59.

1954   *Max Uhle, 1856-1944, a Memoir of the Father of Peruvian Archaeology.* University of California Publications in American Archaeology and Ethnology 46(1). Berkeley.

1959   Archaeological Dating and Cultural Process. *Southwestern Journal of Anthropology* 15:317-324.

1960   Cultural Unity and Diversification in Peruvian Archaeology. *Man and Culture: Selected Papers of the Fifth International Congress of Anthropological and Ethnological Sciences*, compiled by Anthony F. C. Wallace, pp. 627-631. Philadelphia.

1961   Stratigraphy and Seriation. *American Anti-quity* 2(3):324-330.

1962   Stages and Periods in Archaeological Inter-pretation. *Southwestern Journal of Anthropology* 18(1):40-54.

1963   Urban Settlements in Ancient Peru. *Ñawpa Pacha* 1:1-28.

Schaaf, Crystal Barker

1988   *Establishment and Demise of Moche V: Assessment of the Climatic Impact.* Master's thesis, Extension School, Harvard University, Cambridge.

Schaedel, Richard P.

1951   Major Ceremonial and Population Centers in Northern Peru. In *The Civilizations of Ancient America: Selected Papers of 29th International Congress of Americanists*, ed. Sol Tax, pp. 232-243. University of Chicago Press, Chicago.

1966   La Huaca El Dragón. *Journal de la Société des Américanistes* 42:383-496.

1972   The City and the Origin of the State in America. *Actas y Memorias del 39 Congreso Internacional de Americanistas* 2:15-33.

1990   El comercio en el antiguo Perú. In *Historia, Antropología y Política: Homenaje a Angel Palerm*, ed. Modesto Suarez, Tomo I, pp. 163-189. Alianza Editorial Mexicana, Universidad Iberoamericana, D.F. México.

Schaedel, Richard P., and Izumi Shimada

1982   Peruvian Archaeology, 1964-80: An Analytic Overview. *World Archaeology* 13:359-371.

Schmidt, M.

1929   *Kunst und Kultur von Peru.* Impropyläen-Verlag, Berlin.

Schreiber, Katharina J.

1987   From State to Empire: The Expansion of Wari Outside the Ayacucho Basin. In *The Origins and Development of the Andean State*, eds. J. Haas, S. Pozorski and T. Pozorski, pp. 91-96. Cambridge University Press, Cambridge.

Sestieri, Pellegrino Claudio

1964   Excavations at Cajamarquilla, Peru. *Archaeology* 17(1):12-17.

1971   Cajamarquilla, Peru: The Necropolis of the Huaca Tello. *Archaeology* 24(2):101-106.

Shady, Ruth, and Arturo Ruíz

1979   Evidence for Interregional Relationships During the Middle Horizon on the North-Central Coast of Peru. *American Antiquity* 44:676-684.

Shimada, Izumi

1981   Temple of Time: The Ancient Burial and Religious Center of Batán Grande, Peru. *Archaeology* 34(5):37-4.

1982   Horizontal Archipelago and Coast-Highland Interaction in North Peru. In *El Hombre y su Ambiente en los Andes Centrales*, eds. Luís Millones and Hiroyasu Tomoeda, pp. 137-210. Senri Ethnological Studies 10. National Museum of Ethnology, Senri, Japan.

1985a   La Cultura Sicán: Una Caracterización Arqueológica. In *Presencia Histórica de Lambayeque*, compiled by Eric Mendoza, pp. 76-133. Editorial y Imprenta DESA, S.A., Lima.

1985b   Perception, Procurement and Management of Resources: Archaeological Perspective. In *Andean Ecology and Civilization*, eds. Shozo Masuda, Izumi Shimada and Craig Morris, pp. 357-399. University of Tokyo Press, Tokyo.

1990   Cultural Continuities and Discontinuities on the Northern North Coast of Peru, Middle-Late Horizons. In *The Northern Dynasties:Kingship and Statecraft in Chimor*, eds. Michael E. Moseley and Alana Cordy-Collins, pp. 297-392. Dumbarton Oaks, Washington, DC.

n.d.a   The Regional States of the Coast During the Late Intermediate Period: Archaeological Evidence, Ethnohistorical Record and Art Outline. In *Pre-Inca States and Inca Kingdoms*, ed. Laura Laurencich Minelli. Editoriale Jaca Book, Milan. In press.

n.d.b   *Pampa Grande and the Mochica Culture.* Ms. under review.

Shimada, Izumi, and Raffael Cavallaro

1986   Monumental Adobe Architecture of the Late Pre-Hispanic Northern North Coast of Peru. *Journal de Société des Américanistes* 71:41-78.

Shimada, Izumi, C. B. Schaaf, Lonnie G. Thompson, and E. Mosley-Thompson

1991   Cultural Impacts of Severe Droughts in the Prehispanic Andes: Application of a 1,500-year Ice Core Precipitation Record. *World Archaeology* 22:247-270.

n.d.   Onset of the Middle Horizon and Severe Droughts in the Peruvian Andes: New Perspectives from Ice Core Data. *Boletín de Lima.* In press.

Silverman, Helaine

1985   Cahuachi: simplemente monumental. *Boletín de Lima* 7(41):85-95.

1986   *Cahuachi: An Andean Ceremonial Center.* Ph.D. dissertation, Department of Anthropology, University of Texas, Austin.

Spalding, Karen

1984   *Huarochirí: An Andean Society under Inca and Spanish Rule.* Stanford University Press, Stanford.

Squier, E. George

1877   *Peru, Incidents of Travel and Exploration in the Land of the Incas.* Harper and Brothers, New York.

Stothert, Karen

1980   The Villa Salvador Site and the Beginning of the Early Intermediate Period in the Lurín Valley, Peru. *Journal of Field Archaeology* 7:279-295.

Strong, William D.

1925   *The Uhle Pottery Collections from Ancon.* University of California Publications in American Archaeology and Ethnology 21(4). Berkeley.

1942   Recent Archaeological Research in Latin America. *Science* 95:179-183.

Strong, William D., and John M. Corbett

1943   A Ceramic Sequence at Pachacamac. In *Archaeological Studies in Peru, 1941-1942,* by William D. Strong, G. R. Willey, and J. M. Corbett, pp. 27-122. Columbia Studies in Archaeology and Ethnology 1(3). New York.

Strong, William D., Gordon R. Willey, and J. M. Corbett

1943   *Archaeological Studies in Peru, 1941-1942.* Columbia Studies in Archaeology and Ethnology 1(3). New York.

Stübel, Alphons, and Max Uhle

1892   *Die Ruinenstätte von Tiahuanaco im Hochlande des Alten Peru.* Karl W. Hiersemann, Leipzig.

Stumer, Luis M.

1953   Playa Grande: Primitive Elegance in Pre-Tiahuanaco Peru. *Archaeology* (1):42-48.

1954a   The Chillón Valley of Peru: Excavation and Reconnaissance, 1952-53, Part 1. *Archaeology* 7(3):171-178.

1954b   The Chillón Valley of Peru: Excavation and Reconnaissance, 1952-53, Part 2. *Archaeology* 7(4):220-228.

1954c   Population Centers of the Rimac Valley of Peru. *American Antiquity* 20:130-148.

1956   Development of Peruvian Coastal Tiahuanacoid Styles. *American Antiquity* 22:59-69.

1957   Céramica Negra del Estilo Maranga. *Revista del Museo Nacional* 26:272-289.

1958   Contactos Foráneos en la Arquitectura de la Costa Central del Perú. *Revista del Museo Nacional* 27:11-30.

Tabío, Ernesto E.

1957   Excavaciones en Playa Grande, Costa Central del Perú, 1955. *Arqueológicas* 1(1). Museo Nacional de Antropología y Arqueología, Lima.

1965   *Excavaciones en la Costa Central del Perú, 1955-1958.* Departamento de Antropología, Academia de Ciencias de la República de Cuba, La Havanna.

Tello, Julio C.

1940a   Pachacamac. *El Comercio* (August 4). Lima.

1940b   Pachacamac. *Chaski* 1(2).1-4.

1942   Origen y Desarrollo de las Civilizaciones Prehistóricas Andinas. *Actas del XXVII Congreso Internacional de Americanistas,* Tomo 1, pp. 589-714. Lima.

1943   Memoria Sucinta sobre los Trabajos Arqueológicos Realizados en las Ruinas de Pachacamac durante los Años 1940 y 1942. *Memoria de la Junta Departamental Pro-Desocupados de Lima (1939, 1940 y 1941).* Lima.

1960   *Guía de las Ruinas de Pachacamac.* Tipografía Peruana, Lima.

1967   *Páginas Escogidas.* Selection and Prologue by T. Mejía Xesspe. Universidad Nacional Mayor de San Marcos, Lima.

Torero, Alfredo

1970   Lingüística e Historia de la Sociedad Andina. In *Anales Científicos* 8(3-4):321-364. Universidad Nacional Agraria, La Molina, Lima.

Turner, Victor W.

1974   *Dramas, Fields, and Metaphors: Symbolic Action in Human Society.* Cornell University Press, Ithaca, NY.

Ubbelohde-Doering, Heinrich

1967   *On the Royal Highways of the Incas.* Thames and Hudson, London.

1983   *Vorspanische Gräber von Pacatnamú, Nordperu.* Materialien zur Allgemeinen und Vergleichenden Archäologie, Band 26. Deutsches Archäologisches Institut, Verlag C. H. Beck, München.

Uhle, Max

1910   Uber die Frühkulturen in der Umgebung von Lima. *Proceedings of the 16th International Congress of Americanists,* Zweite Häfte, pp. 347-370. A. Hartleben's Verlag, Wien and Leipzig.

1913   Die Ruinen von Moche. *Journal de la Société des Américanistes de Paris* 10:95-117.

1926   Report on Explorations at Chancay. In *The Uhle Pottery Collections from Chancay,* ed. A. L. Kroeber, pp. 292-303. University of California Publications in American Archaeology and Ethnology 21(7). Berkeley.

Urteaga, Horacio H.

1914   Pacha Camac en Ruinas. In *El Perú; Bocetos Históricos; Estudios Arqueológicos, Tradicionales é Histórico-Criticos,* pp. 7-17. Casa Editora E. Rosay, Lima.

Valastro, S., Jr., E. M. Davis, and A. J. Varela

1978   The University of Texas at Austin Radiocarbon Dates XII. *Radiocarbon* 20:245-273.

Van Stan, Ina

1957   A Peruvian Ikat from Pachacamac. *American Antiquity* 23:150-159.

1961a   Miniature Peruvian Shirts with Horizontal Neck Openings. *American Antiquity* 26:524-531.

1961b   Ancient Peruvian Textile Arts: Patchwork and Tie-Dye from Pachacamac. *Expedition* 3:34-37.

1963   A Problematic Example of Peruvian Resist-Dying. *American Antiquity* 29:166-173.

1965   A Triangular Scarf-like Cloth from Pachacamac, Peru. *American Antiquity* 30:428-433.

1967   *Textiles from Beneath the Temple of Pachacamac, Peru: A Part of the Uhle Collection of the University Museum, University of Pennsylvania.* Museum Monographs 7. The University of Pennsylvania, Philadelphia.

Vásquez, Segundo

1984   La Waka Pucllana. *Gaceta Arqueológica Andina* 3(9):8-9.

Villar Cordova, Pedro E.

1933   Folk-lore de la Provincia de Canta (en el Departamento de Lima): El Mito "Wa-kon y los Willka" referente al Culto Indigena de la Cordillera de "La Viuda." *Revista del Museo Nacional* 2(3):161-179.

1935   *Las Culturas Pre-Hispánicas del Departamento de Lima.* Edición auspiciada por la Municipalidad de Lima, Lima.

Wheatley, Paul

1972   The Concept of Urbanism. In *Man, Settlement and Urbanism,* eds. P. J. Ucko, R. Tringham, and G. W. Dimbleby, pp. 601-637. Duckworth, London.

Wiener, Charles

1880   *Pérou et Bolivie, Récit du Voyage.* Librairie Hachette, Paris.

Willey, Gordon R.

1943   Excavations in the Chancay Valley. In *Archaeological Studies in Peru, 1941-1942,* by William D. Strong, Gordon R. Willey and J. M. Corbett, pp. 123-195. Columbia Studies in Archaeology and Ethnology 1(3). New York.

Wilson, David J.

1988   *Prehispanic Settlement Patterns in the Lower Santa Valley, Peru.* Smithsonian Institution Press, Washington, DC.

Building a Scale Reconstruction Model of the Sun Temple at Pachacamac

In the spring of 1990 Dr. Ruben E. Reina asked me to make a reconstruction model of the Incan Sun Temple at Pachacamac as it might have appeared in AD 1500 before the conquest of Peru. This model serves as an element in the Pre-Columbian section of the exhibit "The Gift of Birds: Featherwork of Native South American Peoples" at The University Museum.

The Sun Temple is a massive skewed rectilinear structure which rises from a 12-acre base in 4 stepped layers of solid terraces constructed partly of stone and mainly of soft adobe brick, in the manner of a square wedding cake. Although the temple itself is only 25 meters high, it perches at the apex of a 75-meter-high acropolis-like hill on the southern edge of the ceremonial center of Pachacamac, the most dominant local feature. Many small buildings were constructed on the wide, generous terraces of the temple, presumably to house priests of Inti, pilgrims, and a support staff. A stairway snaked its way up the NE face from level to level, arriving ultimately at the top, or plateau level, where the two large sun shrines stood. These stairways were probably elaborately decorated with fish, bird, and human motifs in several colors. Casements at landings suggest the presence of doors to restrict access to upper levels. The vertical terrace walls were tinted with red paint to catch the rays of the rising and setting sun and also may have had figurative paintings on them which have long since washed away.

The SW face presents a complex of descending galleries and courts facing the Pacific Ocean, which breaks below in frothy wave bands only 600 meters from the base of the hill. Recent excavations beneath the courts have revealed ancient cubiform adobe brick structures, indicating earlier temples on the site. Down the hill to the north is a polychrome painted temple and nearby the unexcavated ruins of an ancient temple dedicated to the stern-faced local god, Pachacama. Incan and Pre-Incan mummies have been found buried in the dry gray earth on the flanks of the temples in wrappings of fine woven fabrics, accompanied with feather decorations and jewelry made of bone, shell, and gold. Some of these artifacts will be in the exhibit.

The Spanish Conquistadores came into the sacred district of Pachacamac soon after 1533. They demolished the Sun Temple looking for gold. Since then, 450 years of wind and water erosion and the feet of countless tourists have reduced the site to a dusty mound of rubble with only a few walls and terraces intact to indicate its former glory.

The task of restoring the temple has proven challenging. A slumped mound of eroded earth with a few walls here and there is not what one would call precise architectural information. Luckily, Max Uhle made a careful survey, plans, and elevations of the site for The University Museum in 1896. This plan has provided me with the basis upon which to extrapolate a reconstruction model. In addition, the observations of early Spanish chroniclers have been helpful in imagining the original structure. I also confered with Dr. John Hyslop, an expert on coastal Incan architecture at the American Museum of Natural History. Nevertheless, this was not enough. Too many questions arose about the site that could only be settled by visiting the ruins. I had the good fortune of joining up with Edward Hueber, a patron of The University Museum, who is fluent in Spanish, has business contacts in Lima, and is a competent photographer, to form the Ray/Hueber Expedition of 1990 to Pachacamac.

With Max Uhle's work as our constant guide, Ed and I walked over the entire temple ruins several times, photographing, sketching, and measuring features and details. There is no substitute for being there. Uhle's drawings became more understandable and we also discovered some new features, such as the runway extension of terraces I and II of the NW face 75 meters to the west of wall 33, that were not indicated on his plan. In addition, since Max Uhle made his survey, the complex SW face of the temple has been excavated and partially restored by the Peruvian Government. At the new Museum of the Nation in Lima, we photographed for reference a scale model of the Sun Temple at Pachacamac on display (mine is different in several respects). Finally, we visited the reconstructed Incan site of Puruchucu, where we were able to study the reconstruction of rooves and windows presumably similar to those that once existed at Pachacamac.

Back at my studio in Swarthmore, I drew up scale plans and elevations for the model and submitted them to Dr. Reina and Kay Candler for approval. I also sent a set off to John Hyslop. Jack Murray, Exhibits Designer at The University Museum, approved the scale and configuration of the model, which cleared me to make it.

There are many leaps of faith and intuition on these plans. Sagging walls are leveled, buildings are imagined from their remnant wall bases, and various areas seem to work out logically into walls and courtyards, taking cues from Uhle's drawings and descriptions and our own field work. When it comes to considerations of accuracy, I have used the footprint of Max Uhle's plan at a scale of 1/200 (5 mm on the model equals 1 m on the temple). The basic lines are drawn with an error of ±1 mm or 20 cm to scale. The clearly identified hard-edged features like terraces edges are archaeologically accurate, but reconstructions of highly eroded structures are hypothetical and cannot be judged for accuracy. The model was built right over the blueprints where possible and measures taken off the plan with vernier calipers to 0.1 mm.

The model base is made of plywood braced with pine. The fine details are mainly done in basswood. Bits of landscape are done in very tough papier mâché over wire. All is sealed and spray painted. Decorations are made with a small brush or technical pen. One needs lots of time and patience to make this kind of model.

There are a few rather intriguing questions to be answered about this temple which should provide a rich area of investigation for archaeologists. First of all the geomancy of the temple is striking. The terraces on the NW, NE, and SE faces are quite skewed with respect to a rectangle and rise at different angles to the others on the same face. I purchased a large scale topographical map of Pachacamac at the Institute of Geography in Lima. If one sights along the NW and SE walls of level I they converge on a prominent hilltop 550 meters to the northeast, upon which there are ruins. Presumably, this was a sacred point from which the NW and SE walls of terrace I were plotted. The other levels remain cryptic. Perhaps some of them point at distant Andean peaks or notches and some are astronomically oriented. Secondly, how did the temple function in the worship of the sun god Inti? How was it organized and how administered? Finally, what ancient structure lies beneath the Incan temple?

I have thoroughly enjoyed researching, drawing, and building the Sun Temple of Pachacamac with research assistance from Kay Candler and guidance from Ruben Reina and John Hyslop. I owe much to Edward Hueber, who made the field expedition a success. I hope the model will grace the feathers exhibit and enlighten University Museum visitors for many years to come. Perhaps some bright student or scholar will be inspired by this model to unlock more mysteries of the great Sun Temple.

Christopher Ray
Ray Museum Studios
Swarthmore, PA

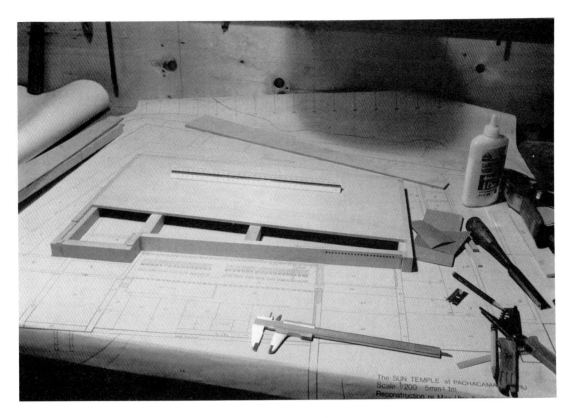

Plate 8. Upper plateau of model being built on blueprint.

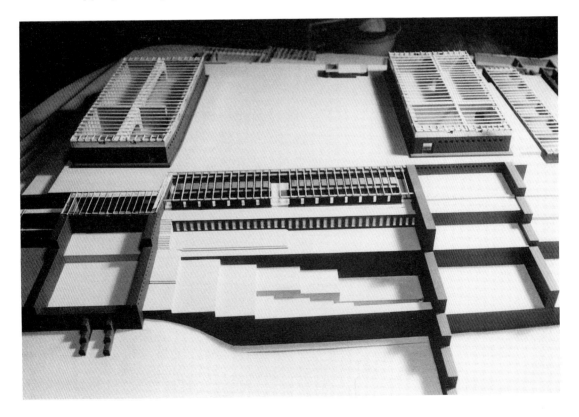

Plate 9. Partially complete model showing roof beams

Plate 10. View of completed model.

Plate 11. View of completed model from above.

UNIVERSITY OF PENNSYLVANIA

DEPARTMENT OF ARCHÆOLOGY

PACHACAMAC

REPORT OF THE WILLIAM PEPPER, M.D., LL.D.,

PERUVIAN EXPEDITION OF 1896

BY

Dr. MAX UHLE

PLAN OF THE CITY AND TWENTY-ONE PLATES IN PHOTOTYPE

PHILADELPHIA, PA.:

PUBLISHED BY

THE DEPARTMENT OF ARCHÆOLOGY OF THE
UNIVERSITY OF PENNSYLVANIA

1903

TRANSLATED

BY

C. GROSSE

———

PRINTED BY
MacCALLA & CO. Inc., 237-239 DOCK STREET, PHILADELPHIA
PHOTOTYPES BY E. MOEBIUS, CAMDEN, N. J.
1903

TABLE OF CONTENTS

LIST OF PLATES

LIST OF ILLUSTRATIONS IN THE TEXT

BIBLIOGRAPHY

SIXTEENTH CENTURY

MIGUEL ESTETE. La Relacion del Viaje que hizo el Señor Capitan Hernando Pizarro por mandado del Señor Gobernador su Hermano, desde el Pueblo de Caxamalca á parcama[1] y de allí á Jauja (1533). In Francisco de Xerez, Verdadera Relacion, pp. 119-149. Madrid, 1891.

Letter of HERNANDO PIZARRO to the Royal Audience of Santo Domingo, November, 1533, in Clements R. Markham, Reports on the Discovery, 1872, III, pp. 111–127.

FRANCISCO DE XEREZ. Verdadera relacion de la conquista del Peru y Provincia del Cuzco. Segun la primera edicion impresa en Sevilla, 1534. Madrid, 1891.

PEDRO DE CIEZA. La Chronica del Peru. Anvers, 1554.

PIETRO DI CIEZA. Crónica del gran Regno del Peru. Tradotta nella Italiana per Agostino de Cravaliz. Venetica, 1576.

PEDRO DE CIEZA. Segunda parte de la Crónica del Perú. La publica M. Jimenez de la Espada. Madrid, 1880 (Biblioteca Hispano-Ultramarina, Tomo V).

AUGUSTIN DE ZARATE. Histoire de la Découverte et de la conquête du Perou, traduite de l'Espagnol. Paris, 1742, tome I.

JUAN DE BETÁNZOS. Suma y Narracion de los Incas. Publícala M. Jimenez de la Espada. Madrid, 1880 (Biblioteca Ultramarina, Tomo V).

Informacion de las idolatrias de los Incas é indios y de cómo se enterraban, 1571. In Coleccion de Documentos Inéditos, Vol. 21, 1874, pp. 131–220.

MIGUEL BALBOA. Histoire du Pérou, traduite par H. Ternaux Compans. Paris, 1840.

Relaciones Geográficas de Indias. Publícalas el Ministerio del Fomento. Peru. Tomo I, II. Madrid, 1881, 1885.

    I, pp. 61–78. Descripcion y Relacion de la Provincia de los Yauyos hecha por Diego Davila Brizeño.

    I, pp. 197–216. Descripcion de la tierra del Repartimiento de los Rucanas Antamarcas. Año de 1586.

    II, pp. 29–37. Relacion fecha por el Corregidor de Chunbibilcas Don Francisco de Acuña.

JOSEPH DE ACOSTA. Historia Natural y Moral de las Indias. Sevilla, 1590.

F. HIERONYMO ROMAN. Republicas del Mundo. Salamanca, 1595. Especially Book I, chap. V: De los templos y lugares sagrados que tuvieron los del Reyno del Peru.

BLAS VALERA. Extracts from his lost work by Garcilaso de la Vega.

SEVENTEENTH CENTURY

FRANCISCO DE AVILA. A Narrative of the Errors, False Gods and Other Superstitions and Diabolical Rites in which the Indians of the Provinces of Huarochiri, Mama and Chaclla lived in Ancient Times, 1608. In Clements R. Markham, Narratives, pp. 121–147.

Inca GARCILASO DE LA VEGA. Primera Parte de los Comentarios Reales. Madrid, 1723.

Inca GARCILASO DE LA VEGA. Historia General del Perù. Segunda Parte de los Comentarios Reales. Madrid, 1722.

(ONDEGARDO.) Relacion de los fundamentos acerca del notable daño que resulta de no guardar á los Indios sus fueros.

(POLO DE ONDEGARDO.) Del órden que los indios tenian en dividir los tributos y distribuirlos entre sí ; both in Coleccion de Documentos Inéditos relativos al descubr. conqu. y organiz. de las antiguas posesiones españolas de América y Oceania. Madrid, 1872, Vol. 17, pp. 1–177.

POLO DE ONDEGARDO. Report in Clements R. Markham, Narratives of the Rites and Laws of the Yncas, translated from the original Spanish Manuscripts. London, Hakluyt Society, No. 48, 1873, pp. 149–171.[2]

Relacion de la Religion y Ritos del Peru hecha por los primeros Religiosos Agustinos. In Coleccion de Documentos Inéditos. Vol. 3, 1865, pp. 5–58.

FERNANDO DE SANTILLAN. Relacion del Orígen, Descendencia, Politica y Gobierno de los Incas. In Tres Relaciones de Antiguedades Peruanas. Publícalas el Ministerio del Fomento. Madrid, 1879, pp. 1–133.

CHRISTOVAL DE MOLINA. The Fables and Rites of the Yncas. Clements R. Markham, Narratives, pp. 1–64.

---

[1] That is Pachacama.

[2] The text here published corresponds to pp. 9–78 of the Spanish edition of the manuscript in the before-enumerated Documentos Inéditos. Madrid, 1872, Vol. 17.

Ludovico Bertonio. Vocabulario de la Lengua Aymara. Publicado de nuevo por Julio Platzmann. Segunda Parte Aymara-Español. Leipzig, 1879.

Joan de Santacruz Pachacuti Yamqui. Relacion de Antiguedades deste Reyno del Pirú. Tres Relaciones de Antiguedades, pp. 229–328.

Relacion Anónima de las Costumbres Antiguas de los Naturales del Pirú. Tres Relaciones de Antiguedades, pp. 135–227.

Bernabé Cobo. Historia del Nuevo Mundo. Publicada por M. Jimenez de la Espada. Sevilla, tom. IV, 1893. Especially chap. 17 : Del famoso templo de Pachacama.

Fernando Montesinos. Memorias Antiguas Historiales y politicas del Perú. Madrid, 1882.

Antonio de Calancha. Chronica Moralizada del orden de San Augustin en el Perú, 1638. Especially Vol. I, Book II, chap. 19 : Del celebrado adoratorio de Pachacamac.

EIGHTEENTH CENTURY

Jorge Juan Ulloa y Antonio Ulloa. Relacion historica del viage á la America Meridional. Madrid, 1748.

NINETEENTH CENTURY

W. B. Stevenson. A Historical and Descriptive Narrative of Twenty Years' Residence in South America. London, 1825, Vol. II.

Charles Wilkes. Narrative of the U. S. Exploring Expedition during the years 1838–1842. Philadelphia, 1845, I.

J. J. von Tschudi. Reiseskizzen aus den Jahren 1838–1842. St. Gallen, 1846, Vols. 1 and 2.

William H. Prescott. History of the Conquest of Peru. London, 1855, Vols. 1 and 2.

Francis de Castelnau. Antiquités des Incas et Autres peuples anciens, Recueillis pendant l'Expédition dans les Parties Centrales de l'Amérique du Sud. Paris, 1854.

Mar. Ed. de Rivero y J. D. de Tschudi. Antigüedades peruanas. Atlas. Vienna, 1851.

Mar. Edward Rivero y John James von Tschudi. Peruvian Antiquities, Translated into English by Francis L. Hawks. New York, 1855.

J. J. von Tschudi. Die Kechua Sprache. Part 3. Wörterbuch. Wien, 1853.

Thomas Ewbank. A Description of the Indian Antiquities brought from Chile and Peru in U. S. Naval Astronomical Expedition to the Southern Hemisphere, 1849–1852. Washington, 1855. Appendix E.

Clements R. Markham. The Travels of Pedro de Cieza de Leon, 1532–1550, contained in the first Part of his Chronicle of Peru. London, Hakluyt Society, No. 33, 1864.

Clements R. Markham. Reports on the Discovery of Peru, Translated and Edited with Notes and an Introduction. London, Hakluyt Society, No. 42, 1872.

Thomas J. Hutchinson. Two Years in Peru. London, 1873, Vols. 1 and 2.

Antonio Raimondi. El Perú. 3 volumes. Lima, 1874–1879.

Gustav Brühl. Die Culturvölker Alt-Amerikas. New York, Cincinnati and St. Louis, 1875–87.

Mariano Felipe Paz Soldan. Diccionario Geográfico Estadístico del Perú. Lima, 1877.

E. George Squier. Peru. Incidents of Travel and Exploration in the Land of the Incas. New York, 1877.

A. Bastian. Die Culturländer des Alten America. Vol. 1 : Ein Jahr auf Reisen. Berlin, 1878.
    Vol. 3, pt. 2 : Nachträge und Ergänzungen aus den Sammlungen des Ethnologischen Museums. Berlin, 1889.

Congrès International des Américanistes. Comptes Rendus de la III, VIII, X Session. Bruxelles, Berlin, Stockholm, 1879, 1888, 1894.

W. Reiss und A. Stübel. The Necropolis of Ancon in Peru. Translated by A. H. Keane. 3 volumes. Berlin, 1880–87.

Charles Wiener. Pérou et Bolivie, Récit du Voyage. Paris, 1880.

Daniel G. Brinton. American Hero-Myths. Philadelphia, 1882.

J. J. von Tschudi. Organismus der Khetšua Sprache. Leipzig, 1884.

A. Stübel, W. Reiss und B. Koppel. Kultur und Industrie südamerikanischer Völker. Berlin. Vol. 1 : Vorspanische Zeit, 1889.
    Vol. 2 : Neue Zeit. 1890.

E. W. Middendorf. Die Einheimischen Sprachen Perus. Vol. 2 : Wörterbuch des Runa Simi oder der Keshua Sprache. Leipzig, 1890.
    Vol. 3 : Ollanta, Ein Drama der Keshua Sprache.

J. J. von Tschudi. Culturhistorische und Sprachliche Beiträge zur Kenntniss des Alten Peru. In Denkschriften d. k. Akad. d. W., Wien. Philosophisch-Historische Classe. Vol. 39, 1891, I.

Daniel G. Brinton. The American Race. New York, 1891.

A. Stübel und M. Uhle. Die Ruinenstätte von Tiahuanaco im Hochlande des Alten Peru. Breslau, 1892.

E. W. Middendorf. Peru. Beobachtungen und Studien. Vol. 2, Das Küstenland von Peru. Berlin, 1894.

E. T. Hamy. Galerie Américaine du Musée d'Ethnographie du Trocadéro. Choix de Pièces Archéologiques et Ethnographiques. Paris, parts 1 and 2 (ab. 1897).

PREFACE

IN the course of early history in ancient Peru, several sanctuaries successively arose in importance above all others. Such were the unfinished temple of Tiahuanaco, the marvelous structures of which, erected near Lake Titicaca at an altitude of thirteen thousand feet, were so famous in myth and legend ; the sanctuary situated in the island of Titicaca in the lake of that name ; the Qorikancha, the magnificent temple of Cuzco, and, lastly, the temple of Pachakamaj, the creator god, at Pachacamac. Throughout the period immediately preceding the Spanish conquest, the three last-mentioned temples rivaled one another in importance. But of these, and in spite of the splendors of the Qorikancha, the "Golden Court" of Cuzco, or the well-established fame of the island temple of Titicaca, the shrine of the creator was looked upon with greatest awe. Reports of the glories of this temple had reached Francisco Pizarro when, at Cajamarca, on his expedition of conquest, Atahualpa informed him that at a ten days' journey on the road to Cuzco there was a wonderful "mosque," regarded by the entire people as the chief sanctuary of the land, and held in highest reverence by himself and by his father, Huaina Capac, before him. He added, that although each town had a special "mosque" for the worship of the local deity, the shrine of the chief divinity of the land, to which rich offerings of gold and silver were brought by the people of the entire country, possessed vast treasure.

According to Estete : " Pilgrims coming from all parts of Peru, three hundred leagues or more, flocked to this shrine, as the Turks and Moors flock to Mecca ".

For these reasons the writer, upon his arrival at Lima in January, 1896, decided to visit and explore the ruins of Pachacamac, which lie in the vicinity of Lima. He found the most hospitable welcome in the house of Don Vicente Silva, the proprietor of the hacienda San Pedro, on the territory of which the ruins are situated, and during his sojourn of many months he received the most friendly help in his labors, both from the proprietor and his son, Don Ricardo Silva.

The short visit planned at first was soon found to be inadequate, as it became more and more evident that the historical problem of the ancient city could not be solved in such a limited period. Some of the unforeseen difficulties met with may be mentioned here. The first graves opened, instead of clearing up former problems, presented new ones. Their contents could not be classified, and accordingly the cultural and historical position of the ancient sanctuary became more obscure than before. Scattered over the site of the ruined city were found numerous fragments of pottery of ancient date, corresponding to none of the vessels taken from the newly-opened graves. The search, therefore, had to be continued until burial-places could be discovered furnishing material dating of the same period as those fragments. By this method only might the history of the town ultimately be cleared up, and the objects recovered from the first graves be assigned to their proper period.

It may be added that no adequate plans or views of the city had ever been published, hence the first duty that presented itself was the preparation of a plan of the city, in addition to the taking of a number of photographic views.

The writer begs to express here sincere gratitude to the late Dr. William Pepper for his liberal support, and to his Peruvian friends, to whose kindness, indulgence and assistance he is indebted for much of his success in his undertaking.

PHILADELPHIA, 1898.   THE AUTHOR.

CHAPTER I.

GEOGRAPHICAL SITUATION.

THE peculiar character of the Peruvian coastland consists in a succession of vast, barren deserts and small, extremely fertile valleys. The former are the natural result of the almost entire absence of rains along this coast, while the fruitfulness of the valleys depends on the shallow coastal rivers, which run their short, rapid course down from the Cordillera to the ocean. By a wise provision of nature these rivers are filled to overflowing during the heat of the summer, when it is the rainy season in the highlands, and so the vegetation of the valleys is saved from drought. In winter the water-supply decreases with the end of the rainy season in the mountains, until there is barely enough to keep the arid interior of the valleys from parching. Wherever the water-supply is not sufficient for the purposes of irrigation, which is the case near the mouth of these valleys, there dense fogs from the ocean form a zone and protecting cover over ten miles wide, stretching along the entire Peruvian coast, and descending as rain upon the nearest headlands of the interior. The slopes of these foothills then clothe themselves with fresh verdure, and the Indian herdsmen with thousands of cattle come down to these 'lomas' and stay until the beginning of the hot season, when again they seek the higher altitudes.

A happy combination of human skill and the resources of nature have brought about the flourishing condition of these valleys. An admirable system of artificial irrigation, begun thousands of years ago, carries and distributes the water in numerous branches and side-arms, 'mother' and 'daughter' azequias, from points in the upper valley throughout the fields of the plain. The watered arable land may be seen contrasting in a distinct horizontal line of verdure against the yellow sand of the desert just above it. These irrigation works were as complicated and perfect as they are now before the coming of the Spaniards, who became the heirs and successors to all that the industry of the Indians had created.

The ruins of the ancient city of Pachacamac are situated in the valley of Lurin, the loveliest of these valleys, to the south of the valley of Lima and about seventeen or eighteen leagues[1] from the present capital. The stream which flows through the Lurin valley is smaller than the Rimac of the Lima valley, but its water-supply is abundant and steady, while the Rimac nearly runs dry in winter, since the latter

springs from the snow-fields of the Cordillera, and the Lurin has its headwaters only in the foothills of the Cordillera, near Huarochiri; yet even this small watercourse may become an impassable river during heavy rainfalls. The river is not known to have any name of its own. In early records, such as maps[2] and reports, it is indicated as the Rio de Pachacamac, and it was known under this designation in its upper course in the Huarochiri province.[3] The river, the sanctuary and the town bear their present common name of Pachacamac only since the period of the Inca conquest, about 170 years previous to the Spanish invasion, and so far it could not be learned what the older name may have been.

The Lurin valley, owing to its smaller river, is not as wide as the Lima valley. It forms a strip of land which near the coast is two miles and a half wide and stretches inland for a mile and a half, where it is narrowed in by projecting rocks from the south side to only one mile and a half. At ten miles from the coast it measures barely two-thirds of a mile; at sixteen miles, near Cieneguillas, it is about a quarter of a mile wide, and at twenty miles from the sea the Quebradas of the mountains begin. The valley of Lurin is most charming. Cieza[4] calls it "delightful and abounding in fruit," and it has probably not changed in that respect since the time of the ancient Peruvians. Lines of tall trees, mostly willows (salix), or thickets of cane (canillo) mark the courses of the canals which intersect the fields. Small groves of waranga (Leguminosa sp.) and other trees may be seen here and there; also fruit-trees, such as the Lucuma, Pakai, Palta and Chirimoya, are numerous.[5] Two small villages are situated in this valley at the present day, Lurin and Pachacamac, and several haciendas, the largest of which is San Pedro. A large number of the mestizos live in airy cane huts among the fields.[6] The modern village of Pachacamac must not be confounded with the ruins or the site of the ancient city of the same name;[7]

<hr />

[1] Latitude and longitude of Lima, according to Paz-Soldan, Diccionario, p. 513, are: Long. 77° 16' 20'', lat. 12° 2' 34''; latitude and longitude of the ruins of Pachacamac as given by A. Raimondi, III, p. 96: Long. 76° 59' 27'', lat. 12° 15' 19''. Assuming these figures to be approximately correct, the distance between Lima and the ruins would be from seventeen to eighteen miles or about six and a half Peruvian leagues, which nearly agrees with the seven leagues usually accepted in the neighborhood as the distance between the valley of Lurin and the city of Lima.

[2] Compare the map in Descripcion y Relacion de la Provincia de Yauyos, in the Relac. Geogr., I, p. 61.

[3] Francisco de Avila, p. 142.

[4] I, chap. 72.

[5] The early agricultural products must have been mainly maize, camote, cotton, etc. Seed-pods of the cotton plant are often found in graves. In modern times the cultivation of sugar-cane was carried on for some time, but had to be given up.

[6] See illustration in George Squier, Peru, p. 66.

[7] The word Pachacamac will be used in the present report in three different meanings, in each of which it is of general use:

1. For the ancient town on the right bank of the river.

2. For the modern village, founded in Spanish time, on the left bank of the river, three miles inland.

3. For the divinity which was specially worshiped at Pachacamac and which gave its name to the ancient city. Fernando de Santillan, p. 33: "The 'waka' said her name was Pachacamac." Cieza, I, chap. 72: "The name of this devil means 'Creator of the world.'"

Pachacamac in Kechua stands for 'the Creator of the world,' 'He who animates the universe,' 'the world-adjuster.'

The word Pachacamac is written in various spellings. The form now generally accepted for the geographical name is also found in the works of Garcilaso,

<hr />

it lies about three miles inland from the ruins on the opposite bank of the river, a mile away from it. The site of Lurin is, like that of the ancient city, on the road which skirts the coast, the 'camino real.' It is on the same side of the river as the ruins, but at a distance of a mile and a half from either. Between these lies the hacienda San Pedro, at about two-thirds of the distance from the river to the village. Lurin has 500 inhabitants and the entire parish about 2000; the modern village of Pachacamac has 300 and the entire parish about 3000 souls; the district of the hacienda Cieneguillas in the upper valley comprises circa 5000 persons. The inhabitants of these villages are poor and are nearly all economically dependent on the haciendas, mainly on San Pedro.

The ruins of the ancient town are situated on the northern limit of the valley, upon the right bank of the river, near its mouth and only 600 yards from the ocean.[1] The desert Tablada de Lurin lies between the valleys of Lima and of Lurin, the shallow beach and the towering mountain-range of the interior;[2] southward it slopes down to the valley and it is bordered by the green fields of the plain on its southeastern- and southwestern-, the valley- and the ocean-sides, while on the bluffs which rise above the valley it is from fifty to eighty feet higher than the plain; several hills[3] rise from 150 to 250 feet above the level of the desert. The territory between and around these hills comprised the site of the ancient city. On the other side the ocean rolls its mighty waves upon the sandy shore with an unceasing thundering roar, and two or three miles from shore the picturesque barren islands of Pachacamac may be seen with clouds of pelicans and other sea-fowl above them. To the south, the glance sweeps along the gently curving coastline as far as Cape Bubulusa, barely discernible in the blue haze at a distance of about twenty miles. Swept by the sea winds, the sand of the desert drifts over the ruins. A few Tillandsia plants, green only in winter, represent the scanty, almost invisible vegetation; a hooting owl, a lizard sunning himself,

or perhaps a small viper, are the only signs of animal life in this solitude. The sun burns fiercely upon the parched soil, still a cooling breeze from the near-by ocean moderates the heat, so that ninety and fifty-five degrees are the limits of temperature rarely exceeded in winter and summer.

There is a charming view across the valley from several points of the ruins. The church-spires of the modern villages of Pachacamac and of Lurin may be seen in the distance. The manor-houses of San Pedro and of the hacienda of Buena Vista stand out upon a picturesque bluff above the green groves of the plain. Farther beyond stretches the rolling desert to the southward in the direction of Chilca; to the left, at a distance of forty-five miles, the foothills of the Andes rise gradually to a height of 9000 feet and reflect at sunset the rays of the evening sun. In summer one may watch the course of the rainy season high up in the mountains from the valley here below, and in winter the snow-clad peaks may be seen looming up above this subtropical plain.

The presumable age of the present coastline is a question of some importance for Pachacamac. At one time these islands were doubtless connected with the mainland, as the ocean-channel is very shallow at this point. J. J. von Tschudi asserts that these islands were torn from the mainland as recently as the Spanish time by the earthquake of 1586,[4] which caused great changes along the Peruvian coast. Had this occurrence really taken place at that time, then it would have been impossible for Francisco de Avila to tell the myths of the province of Huarochiri in the year 1608, when he speaks of the beautiful Cavillaca, who fled out to sea with her child, where both were changed into rocks and were visited by another divinity.[5] The mother and child turned to stone must be the larger and one of the smaller islands of the Pachacamac group which can be seen from shore.[6]

It is claimed by Rivera and Tschudi that stone foundations of buildings may still be found on these islands,[7] which is denied by others; but even if this statement were founded upon truth, it would be but a slim proof for the existence of a connection with the mainland in the earlier period of the history of this valley.

It is another question to determine whether the coastline is now the same as it was at the time of the Spanish conquest, which seems doubtful. There is no tradition in the valley of any great disastrous flood,[8] still it is apparent that the ocean with its heavy surf is constantly washing into the shore. It is asserted that near the village of Lurin at very low tide the foundations of ancient buildings are to be seen on the shallow bottom of the sea. Señor Silva who is thoroughly familiar with that region states, moreover, that one of the islands which lies a little farther to the south, could formerly at low tide be reached by mules dry-shod, when hauling guano, which would be impossible to-day. In early legal documents, dating from the forties of the seventeenth century, which are to be found in the National Library at Lima and also in the deeds of the hacienda San Pedro, a place by the name of Quilcay is mentioned, which no longer exists in the valley and there is a legend that it has sunk to the bottom of the sea.

The coastline near the ancient town has undoubtedly

Santillan, p. 32, has 'Pachahccamahc.' Most authors (Cieza, Herrera, Zarate, Miguel Estete, p. 123, etc.) wrote Pachacama, dropping the final guttural, which is grammatically required. Secondary forms like Pacalcami, Hachacama, Pacama, which occur in Estete's printed report, must be attributed to errors in reading the author's manuscript. The editor of the Relacion de la Religion de los Indios del Peru, in the Col. de Doc. ined. III, p. 10, by mistake changed the correct spelling of Pachacamac in the author's MS. into Pachachaca.

According to the linguistic law of the Kechua, the accent lay originally on the penult of the word Pachacamac. Now, probably through the influence of the Spanish law of accentuation, the accent is on the ultimate and the word is at present pronounced Pachacamac'. This accent, therefore, is wrong, both historically and linguistically. In the form of Pachacama' in early editions of the works of Herrera and Zarate, the Spanish law of accent seems to have been followed, yet the ultimate guttural which caused its application was suppressed.

For scientific reasons it seems best to introduce a phonetic spelling of all ancient names, outside of names of places for which the Spanish spelling must be accepted. A phonetic spelling-system, to be of lasting value, must be easily read, therefore all modern designations have to be avoided. For this reason the phonetic spelling which Hr. Middendorf follows in his grammatical works on the Andine languages deserves the preference over that followed in the linguistic works of J. J. v. Tschudi, Pacheco, Zegara (Ollantai, Paris, 1878), C. F. Beltram, Ludovico Bertonio and others. The Middendorf system, however, needs some correction. He spells the palatal k sound before a, o and u with c; before e and i in the Spanish way with qu; the deep guttural with k. From reasons better discussed elsewhere, the higher k sound will always be rendered by k (k, kh, k'), the deeper by q (q, qh, q'); aspiration by h, the short mute (Middendorf 'c- Bertonio cc, kk, pp, tt) by —' (k', q', t', p'). J sounds here like ch in German, similar to the German ach; ll as in Spanish; w like the English w. For the Spanish and English ch it would be well to introduce the familiar sign č (also series: č, čh, č') if types were available. It must be admitted that the introduction of this system of spelling for designations not geographical involves an apparent inconsistency in writing the name Pachacamac in its different meanings. In its geographical sense, as the name of the ancient ruins and the modern village, it must be spelled according to the accepted Spanish form; as name of the divinity it is phonetically Pachakamaj (corresponding to this is the phonetic spelling in J. J. v. Tschudi, Beiträge, p. 121). The admission of this inconsistency seems to be of less harm than would be the avoidance of the phonetic spelling throughout.

[1] The relative distances of the ruins and of the village of Lurin from the river and that of the ruins from the sea are not quite correctly marked on the small map which accompanies the English translation of F. de Avila's Report on the Errors, etc., of Huarochiri, ed. by Markham.

[2] Compare panorama of the town, pl. 1.

[3] In the plan of the town, W, X, Y, Z.

[4] Peru, p. 245.

[5] P., p. 129.

[6] Cf. pl. 15, fig. 1, and pl. 16, fig. 3.

[7] P. 291. Waitz, Anthrop. der Naturw., N, p. 235, also erroneously attributes to Wilkes the statement that there are still some ruins to be found on these islands.

[8] If any destructive flood like those which occurred at Callao and in the Lima valley had visited this coast within the last two centuries, it would be impossible for the ruins of Mamacona to have escaped destruction (see plan), the base of which is only twenty-two feet above sea-level and the terraced chamber not more than thirty-three feet.

changed since the time before the Spaniards arrived, for the fields which extend between the town and the beach are sometimes inundated by heavy tides. Midway between these and the ocean, about 100 yards from it, the ruins of a strong dike or some primitive masonry may be seen, which date from the period of the Incas, as will be shown later. If this shore had been subject to occasional high tides at that early period, this dike would probably not have been built. Heavy spring tides are also washing away pieces of the bluff with which the desert, the Tablada de Lurin, abuts toward the coast, which at that point is only from two to three hundred yards wide.

If Estete's account of Hernando Pizarro's march from Cajamarca to Pachacamac may be credited, it must be assumed that at the time of his visit the connection between the two valleys, that of Lima and that of Pachacamac, was still unbroken. At the present day they are separated by a barren strip of land, which is three miles long at the nearest point. Miguel Estete writes that H. Pizarro proceeded from the Lima valley to the town of the god, "without ever leaving the cool shade of groves and villages." However inaccurate this statement may be, there remains enough ground for the supposition that since the time of the Incas the coastline has receded farther inland, although not the entire distance from the rocky islands.

CHAPTER II.

ETHNICAL AND POLITICAL CONDITIONS OF THE DISTRICT.

IT may be assumed that the geographical, climatic, ethnical and political limits between the coast-district and the Highland generally corresponded. In the geographical, climatic and political sense this was certainly the case. The province of Yauyos of Spanish time, which is the adjacent district in the mountains, must have existed, according to all sources, as a distinct conception at the earlier period. In Spanish time it extended down the slope of the mountain to the hot coastland, the Yuncas, and thus had its limits at the climatic dividing line;[1] and since former boundaries are usually accepted by the conquerors, it is almost certain that the older province of Yauyos had the same boundaries. It must, therefore, have included Sisicaya on the Pachacamac river and Chosica, with its altitude of 2800 feet as well as the neighboring Chechima, although the former lies but thirty-two miles and the latter forty miles from the coast. From this it may be seen that the political territory of Pachacamac was as small as its climatic district.

It is likely that the ethnical distinction was quite as sharply defined. Exhaustive anthropological investigations of this district have not been made so far, nor would it be advisable to select the neighborhood of the village of Lurin for studies of this kind, as the population of the district is a very mixed one.[2] The mestizos of the modern village of Pachacamac, who live further inland, may still possess some of the old blood of the ancient inhabitants of the town of pre-Spanish times. Among these people a type of face prevails, with a long narrow chin and a somewhat aquiline nose, similar to the type on the Chimu vase shown by Squier,[3] and which is still seen in modern Pachacamac.

It is not quite clear which language was spoken by the inhabitants of this valley, but it seems a mistake to classify it in the same linguistic group with the Chimu or their kindred, the Mochica, who lived southward from them, as was done by J. J. v. Tschudi.[4] They more properly may be said to belong to the Tallanes, who occupied a district between the Chimu and the Mochica.[5] P. Bernabé Cobo distinctly says[6] that the Chimu was spoken as far as Caraguaillo in the Chillon valley, while the language spoken in the valleys of the Rimac and of Pachacamac was different, and by some individuals the two languages were still used as late as 1630. Calancha also confirms the existence of a linguistic line of division in the neighborhood of Lima. The Mochica, living in the valleys of Cañete and Chincha, were the nearest neighbors of the inhabitants of Pachacamac to the south ; so there seems to be no doubt of the identity of the people of the Rimac and Pachacamac valleys with the Tallanes of Zarate. It was not possible, so far, to classify the language of the Tallanes, and it will need thorough local investigations to do so. It might be assumed as being of the same linguistic group as the tongue of the Chimu and the Mochica, since the Tallanes lived between the two, still, there is no proof for this supposition as no traces of the early language are to be found at present. The older names of places are mostly forgotten, which is different in the highland. Names of persons in the church registers might furnish one of the best sources, but studies of this nature require more time than may well be spared from the work of surveying and exploring of ruins. A few stray words only of the Kechua are still used by the people, although this tongue was generally spoken in all the provinces during the Inca period as well as in early Spanish times ; but not the least relationship can be traced in these words with the ancient language of the adjoining province of Yauyos, the Aimará, probably the basis of the Kauki.[7]

The political conditions are not as complicated as the linguistic. According to Garcilaso,[8] the valleys of Pachacamac, Lima, Chancay, Huacho, Supe and Huaman (Barranca), during the period preceding the conquest of this territory by the Incas, were ruled by a chief who had his seat at Pachacamac,[9] and who, like the Inca at Cuzco,[10] had the right to enter the temple of the chief deity, although not in the character of a high priest.[11] The dominion of this ruler of Pachacamac (if Garcilaso is correct and not Calancha, who gives the three northern valleys to the Chimu),[12] may be called quite extensive, as it is 120 miles long. But it must be remembered that this entire district comprised only a few narrow valleys between broad deserts. Also, if Garcilaso is right, the connection between the different parts of the realm was a very loose one for mere geographical reasons, even disregarding the very loose nature of ancient political systems. One fact points to closer political relations between the four

---

[1] Cf. the map in Descripcion de la Provincia de Yauyos, Rel. Geogr., I, p. 61.

[2] See below.

[3] P. 184.

[4] Organismus der Khetschua Sprache, p. 85 ; cf. also Brinton, The American Race, p. 225.

[5] Zarate, I, chap. 6. Also Cieza, I, chap. 61, speaks of "tres o cuatro linajes de generaciones," in which the Yuncas were divided.

[6] Extracts of his MS. work : Fundacion de Lima, by Jiminez de la Espada, Rel. Geogr., I, App. num. I, p. xxviii.

[7] The language of the province of Yauyos was, according to v. Tschudi, Beitr., p. 74, the Kauki, which he thinks an independent language now extinct. Other authors find in it relationship to the Aimará, such as Brinton, The American Race, p. 216, although here it is mentioned among the dialects of the Kechua families ; and Middendorf, Die Aimará Sprache, p. 15. Numerous names of places indicate close kinship with the Aimará, such as Ayaviri, Chosica, Omas (quoted by Middendorf), Huancané (in the district of the Mala river), Huaqui (Desc. de la Prov. de Yauyos, p. 66), Tanqui, Huanavi, Calahuaya ; names of places ending in co, like Surco, Chillaco (cf. Taraco, Tiahuanaco and many others) ; Parará (= millstone, see Bertonio, II, p. 250), name of a ruin near Chosica with a great many millstones near it (Hutchinson, II, p. 47).

[8] Book VI, chap. 30.

[9] Calancha states that the chiefs of the side valleys were dependent of the priests of Pachacamac.

[10] Garcilaso, VI, chap. 31.

[11] Jerez, p. 115.

[12] III, chap. 1.

northern valleys and the adjacent Chimu country, that is: the very peculiar language of this district which was spoken as far as Lima.[1] The sanctuary of Pachacamac must have enjoyed a certain political neutrality, according to Middendorf, who states that the Chimu had never touched it.[2] Even if this assertion is founded upon an ancient source, it may be erroneous, since the views on this subject varied greatly from the earliest times. Garcilaso tells of wars which the rulers of Pachacamac carried on with the Chimu previous to the Inca period and of defeats suffered by them.[3] Various other districts of the realm were at strife with their neighbors. So the Descripcion de la Provincia de Yauyos relates[4] that the inhabitants of the Lima valley had pushed forward as far as the Pariacaca mountains, and there had worshiped an idol; but there is no record that the people of Pachacamac were connected with this campaign.

The supremacy of the ruler of Pachacamac over the Lima valley still continued during the Inca period, since Francisco Pizarro, when he founded the city of Lima, enumerated the Rimac valley as a part of the Pachacamac district.[5] Only the names of four of these rulers are known at present: Kuismanqu, who surrendered to the Incas[6] and whose name appears to be of foreign origin; Taurichumbi,[7] who ruled Pachacamac at the time of Hernando Pizarro's advent, and whose name sounds Kechuan;[8] Saba, baptized by the Augustinian friars in the fifties, and Luyan, who soon succeeded him when the former did not prove subservient enough to the new masters.

The valley was very populous when the Spaniards came, a fact attested by numerous ruins and burial-grounds. A large number of ruined buildings surround the rocky headland of 'La Centinela.' Opposite the valley, in the Rinconada, on the sandy plain, are the ruins of large courts and halls, and across from Lurin, on a barren hill, extensive remains of buildings can be seen.[9] Even on the brow of La Centinela, 130 feet above the level of the valley, may be traced the foundations of a large building surrounded by a number of graves. Lines of masonry may be found all over the valley, which by the size of the adobe, 'tapia,' the kind made on the spot, betray their pre-Spanish origin. A long narrow strip of ground belonging to the hacienda

Huarangal, a part of San Pedro, is covered with graves bordering closely against the eastern side of the Centinela rock. Some ancient graves on the Venturosa hacienda show that the northern edge of the valley above Pachacamac also had its settlements. At a distance of from nine to twenty-three miles from the sea, on the right-hand edge of the valley, may be seen the ruins of four villages, and on the left the débris of two smaller ones, and in a narrow side-valley the ruins of the larger village, Huaycan, which stretch along a stony ravine (Kechua 'waiq'o') and for about half a mile up the side of the hill. The two small villages were built against the hillside, which in places is quite steep. This was done to utilize every spot of the arable ground for the raising of crops, since the valley at this place affords only a very narrow strip of fertile soil. The walls of these houses were built of stone, with adobe used as mortar, and tapered toward the top; owing to the dry climate they are in an almost perfect state of preservation.

This district possessed a number of good roads, one of which skirted the coast[10] in the early days. When Hernando Pizarro failed to obtain any information concerning the road to Pachacamac from the people of the coastland (which they were forbidden to give under penalty of death), he discovered soon that he had only to follow the southern road along the coast, from Paramonga, 10° 45' S. lat., and that the town must be situated on or near it.[11] Other roads followed the northern or the southern slope of the valley up the hill to Cienequillas. A bridle-path, now in a neglected state, but still known as the 'camino del Inca,' skirted the southern declivity and connected the ancient settlements along this line, one of which still bears the name of Tambuinqa.

Contrary to views held by others, the writer thinks that names which connect localities with Inca institutions were usually proved to be of such an origin after some archæological investigations. This path was probably laid out by the Incas, and a 'tambo,' a wayside refuge, was located on this spot. At Cienequillas the road from Lima strikes the road, which continues through the valley as far as Huarochiri; and in order to make a further connection between this part of the province and the highland, after the latter had been added to the realm, Tupak Inca had a bridle-path constructed from Huarochiri across the Pariacaca chain, one of the highest and wildest mountain ranges of Peru, 16,000' high, and extended it as far as Jauja. J. J. v. Tschudi[12] calls it a miserable road, while Cieza[13] thought it well worth seeing for the grandeur of the scenery in those regions.

[1] According to Calancha.
[2] Die Chimu Sprache, p. 21.
[3] Garcilaso, VI, chap. 32.
[4] P. 71.
[5] Order of Pizarro, issued at Pachacamac under date of January 8, 1535, extracts of the MS. work of the Padre Cobo, p. xi; cf. also Calancha, II, chap. 29: "ambos valles de un mesmo cazique."
[6] Garcilaso, VI, chap. 30.
[7] Chumpi, in Kechua = girdle, tarhui = lupine. Chumpi in some other combinations: Ahuachumbi and Ninachumbi, two islands under 14° southern lat. (letter of Pedro Sarmiento de Gamba, reprinted from M. Jiminez de la Espada, Tres Relac. de Antig. Introduction, p. xxiv), Suculacumbi (probably for Suculachumbi), name of Chancay (or of the cazique of that place; see below), Estete, p. 130. Tauri suggests: Tauriqui, title of a cazique in northern Peru (Sarmiento, l. c., p. xxv).
[8] Estete, p. 133.
[9] Wiener, p. 61, gives a vague plan of a ruin, said to be near Manchay; possibly he is referring to the ruins of the Rinconada.

[10] Traces of ancient roads, which may be known by their enclosures of tapia walls, can still be seen in the Lima valley and deserve to be more closely studied. Quite well preserved sections of roads are found along the northern coast of Peru, in the Santa valley and near Casma. The road there has a dividing wall in the centre (Hernando Pizarro, p. 121, tells of bridges so divided), one side being reserved for the ruler and his retinue, the other for the common people, each side is about sixteen feet wide. It might be of interest to trace the entire course of this road.
[11] Letter of Hernando Pizarro, p. 122.
[12] v. Tschudi, Beiträge, p. 75; p. 119.
[13] Cronica, II, chap. 58.

CHAPTER III.

RECENT HISTORY OF THE VALLEY.

THE modern history of the valley begins with the journey of Hernando Pizarro from Cajamarca to Pachacamac, where he was ordered by his brother Francisco to capture the temple treasure, early in the year 1533. From his own report, he started from Andamarca, circa thirty-two miles to the south of Cajamarca, about January 9, Julian cal.,[1] and arriving at Pachacamac on January 30, he must have traveled over the distance of 340 miles in twenty-two days, a daily average of about sixteen miles only. Considering the swiftness of Indian messengers,[2] it is small wonder that Pizarro on his arrival discovered that all the gold treasure had disappeared.[3] Including the contributions of gold and silver sent by the chieftains of Mala, Huarcu (Cañete), Chincha and others, his booty amounted only to 85,000 pesos of gold and 3000 marks of silver, 90,000 pesos altogether,[4] according to Miguel Estete.

If it is considered that the ransom which was amassed at Cajamarca for the delivery of Atahualpa amounted to more than 1,326,000 pesos of gold, the booty of Pachacamac seems quite insignificant,[5] being only one-fifteenth of the above amount.

At Pachacamac, Hernando Pizarro forced an entrance into the temple of Pachakamaj,[6] and first of all demolished the idol and the shrine in the presence of all the people.[7] A cross was raised upon the débris to symbolize the beginning of a new era.[8] From this day the decline of the city began, as its prosperity had mainly depended upon the prestige of the sanctuary.

Toward the close of the year 1534, Francisco Pizarro reached the town by way of Jauja after having taken Cuzco. He held wild orgies[9] here with Diego de Alvarado and made a treaty with him, according to which the latter waived all future claims in the Peruvian conquest. From this place Francisco Pizarro decreed, in January, 1535, the founding of a new capital, Lima, in the Rimac valley, a former plan of locating the capital in Jauja having been abandoned for climatic and economic reasons, while Pachacamac could not be taken into consideration for its want of a harbor.[10]

The Spaniards, on their arrival, found the city and the whole valley well populated,[11] and it is described as a desolate pile of ruins, as it appears to-day,[12] in the first part of the seventeenth century, with only a few Indians remaining in the valley. The depopulation of the city was hastened by the wars which ravaged Peru on the one hand and by the conversion of the population through the religious orders on the other, Franciscan and Augustinian friars and Jesuits appearing on the scene in succession. The beginning in this process of depopulation was made by the wars of Manco Inca, who, in the year 1535, gathered about him all the Indian forces for the death-struggle against the Spanish invasion; the next step was, that the Franciscan monks established a new settlement near the bridge in the valley and drew there the inhabi-

---

[1] P. 121. Estete gives the 14th of January as the day of starting. He incorrectly fixes the 9th of January for the departure from Huaman mayo (Barranca). The same day is given by Raimondi, II, p. 41, while apparently it was the 24th.
[2] The writer saw in La Paz, Bolivia, an old Indian who had once covered the distance of 190 miles from La Paz to Tacna in three days.
[3] Letter of Hernando Pizarro, p. 123 ; Miguel Estete, p. 134.
[4] The wealth of the Incas was without doubt grossly exaggerated in early accounts. Cieza, Cronica, II, chap. 65, tells of an offering of more than 100 'arrobas' of gold which one of the Incas had given to the temple in Pachacamac. 100 arrobas would have had a value in refined gold of $75,000,000 ; or in a strong alloy of half the weight only in pure gold, it would have represented a value of $38,000,000, which would be ten times the amount for Pachacamac alone more than the ransom of Atahualpa, to which the entire realm of the Inca at Cayamarca had contributed ; 85,000 or 90,000 castellanos or pesos de oro, according to Prescott, I, p. 305, amounted to between $261,000 and $276,000, or if the gold value of the dollar is estimated at 1.5406 grammes, this would have had a value of 402 to 416 pounds of fine gold ; 3000 marks of silver, a mark = 233 grammes, would have been worth 1550 pounds of silver, and by the former standard of value would be equal to $30,000, the present commercial value would be $1,116,000. For the transportation of this booty llamas were used, each of which can carry a load of 100 pounds. If the load of these animals depended merely on the weight, which was the case with gold in the form of gold-dust, twenty animals would have been sufficient. It is stated by Xerez, p. 118, that the spoils of Pachacamac consisted of twenty-seven loads of gold and 2000 marks of silver. Accepting this statement as correct, each llama carried $10,000 or thirty-three pounds in fine gold, or, if it was alloyed, about two arrobas.
[5] Raimondi, Peru, II, p. 29, carefully traces the march of Hernando Pizarro from Andamarca to Pachacamac, but without solving the difficulties in the description of the latter part of the road. Assuming the 30th of January as the day of the arrival in Pachacamac, Pizarro would have reached Supe on the 25th, Huaura on the 26th, while on the 27th he would only have traveled two leagues to Huachu. Here he spent the rest of the day carousing with the Indians. As the next day's march through a broad desert would have been too long for that day, forty miles, Estete, through some mistake, gives only five leagues as the distance. Pizarro, therefore, started early in the morning of the 28th of January and arrived at Chancay in the afternoon. This place is unmistakable from Estete's description, although he gives a different name (Suculacumbi). It is possible that this was the name of the chieftain of that locality, which is frequently given instead of the name of the place. From Estete's account it is clear that Pizarro and his men only stopped at Chancay for supper and continued their way to the south immediately after. Here Raimondi's misconstructions begin, p. 42. He cannot understand that the following night's camp of Pizarro's troop was in the Rimac valley, while the distance to that point was thirty-seven miles. It is evident that Pizarro undertook

a night's march, and the camp of which Estete speaks was only that of the next day, the 29th of January. Night marches through the desert are frequent during the hot season on the Peruvian coast, and there was another desert, twenty-eight miles wide, between Chancay and the Chillon valley. The inhabitants of Chancay supplied the travelers with provisions for a night's march, "dieron todo lo necesario de comida para aquel dia." When, therefore, Pizarro left Chancay on the 28th in the evening, intending to reach Pachacamac the next day, "por allegar otro dia al pueblo donde estaba lax mezquita," he meant the day following the next night's quarters, the 29th of January. On the 30th Pizarro made a short march only. But since he dined midway in an Indian village, and the road passed through groves of trees and villages, the last night's camp must have been within the Rimac valley, probably in the old village of Huatica, near the ancient Rimac temple ; and the interruption of the march for a repast must have been at the ancient Surco, the present ruins of Armatambo, near Chorillos, on the southern extremity of the Rimac valley. No matter how this rather obscure passage of Estete's is read, the length of the march on the last day, when Pizarro arrived at Pachacamac, cannot have been more than seven miles.
[6] Prescott, I, p. 292.
[7] Estete, p. 133.
[8] Prescott, p. 293.
[9] Garcilaso, pt. II, book II, chap. 17 ; Prescott, II, p. 13.
[10] Extracts of P. Bernabé Cobo's MS. work, Fundacion de Lima in Relac. Geogr., I, App., pp. vi–xv. A foundation of the new city at Pachacamac, toward the end of the year 1534, before the present site of Lima was chosen, of which Calancha writes, II, chap. 29, probably never occurred.
[11] Garcilaso, pt. II, book 2, chap. 17 ; Calancha, l. c.; Cobo, Historia, IV, chap. 17.
[12] Calancha and Cobo, l. c.

tants of the old town.[1] In 1553, Francisco Hernandez Giron, during his rebellion against the Spanish régime, sought refuge at Pachacamac,[2] and a garrison was quartered there by the Government to keep him in check. These circumstances were considerable factors in the decrease of the population of the town, so that at last only a few families remained.[3] When in the early fifties of the sixteenth century the Augustinian monks arrived, they transferred the town to its next site in the valley, abandoning the old place entirely. Thus in the Descripcion de la Provincia de Yauyos, 1586, it is described as being situated on the valley road upon the left bank of the river; but here the city was not allowed to remain either. When the Augustinian friars left the valley, their successors changed the site of the town once more to a point several miles inland, where it stands at the present day.[4] This succession of changes interrupted the connection with the original place.

A remnant of an Indian tribe ruled by a cazique and slightly differing from the surrounding people in appearance as well as in customs, seems to have led a separate existence in this valley almost down to our own time, from information gathered in that neighborhood; but no trace of these people can be found at present.

It is small wonder that so few indications of Spanish influence can be descried in the old town, if the rapidity of its depopulation is considered as well as that of its Christianization. A few changes of more recent date may be traced in the buildings of the ancient convent, due to the fact that the buildings were near the fields of the former hacienda Mama-cona, and therefore convenient for the use of the hacienda. Alterations of this kind were not found in any of the other buildings of the old town, and only a few insignificant finds indicate that the city was still inhabited when the Spaniards entered it. A sickle-shaped knife of rude workmanship, sharpened

Fig. 1. Copper knife, Spanish period. From an ancient house at Pachacamac.

on its outer edge (fig. 1), found in a house during our explorations, may be regarded as dating from the early Spanish time. A few sea-green glass beads in a jar of the Inca period were found in the ruins of a house of the outer city, and a cylindrical blue glass bead of older appearance was picked up in the inner town. These were the only signs noticed by the writer that the city was inhabited during early Spanish times.

One of the more important settlements in the valley is San Pedro, a Jesuit foundation. The ruins of a chapel dating from that period are still in existence. It is better not to mention here the village of Lurin in any historical connection with the other places, since it is barely 100 years old.[5] It was founded as a new station on the ' camino real,' after the transfer of the old city of Pachacamac to its last site farther up the valley. The name Lurin is of Kechua origin, a language which was introduced here by the Incas and gained a complete dominion in this locality during the early Spanish period.[6]

[1] Calancha, l. c.
[2] Col. de Doc. ined. III, p. 11.
[3] Calancha, i. c.
[4] Calancha.

[5] Middendorf, Die Chimu Sprache, p. 20.
[6] Lurin, or hurin = below, lowland. Comp. also the ancient classification of the village population in the highland into two groups, as it was made by the Incas, in Hanansaya and Hurinsaya.

CHAPTER IV.

FORMER EXPLORATIONS OF THE RUINS.

THE ruins of Pachacamac have been more frequently visited and described by travelers than any of the other monuments of ancient Peru, owing to their convenient situation so near the capital, yet few ruins of the importance of Pachacamac have been described so unsatisfactorily. Various reasons may be given for this neglect. The majority of the expeditions were undertaken for sightseeing rather than for serious scientific exploration, and the time spent on the ground was usually very limited. The ruins taken as a whole are more attractive than a study of the details would promise, for they seem more insignificant here than in many other ruins; the larger buildings are very much decayed and but few fairly well preserved ones remain. Prior to the expedition here reported only one is known to have made a stay here of two months, that of Bandelier in the year 1892 or 1893. This explorer took measurements of the more important buildings and determined the purposes for which they were constructed. He explored the eastern section of the vast cemetery which surrounds the temple of Pachakamaj.[1] The finds of these explorations are at present in the American Museum of Natural History at New York, and it is to be regretted that the report of Bandelier was not published; only a few notes on his discoveries in Peru are contained in an article of F. Webb Hodge.[2]

The earlier descriptions of the ruins vary in character and merit according to the time when they were written; those of the sixteenth century claim the value of documentary evidence, coming from the pen of contemporaries who saw the city in its glory, or who at least had heard of its wonders from the Indians who lived there in the old days. The reports of Miguel Estete and of Hernando Pizarro are of this character; they were the first Spaniards who entered the old town and destroyed the famous temple. Their reports, therefore, are those of eye-witnesses. Estete wrote two accounts, one of which in diary form was printed in Xerez Relacion de la Conquista, and with it was reprinted many times; the other copy is known from a few stray notes of William H. Prescott, who had the manuscript before him when writing his work.

Estete's report is one of the most valuable documents ever published on any ancient Peruvian town. Similarly important is the letter of Hernando Pizarro to the Royal Audience of Domingo, wherein this expedition to Pachacamac is described. The letter having been written ten months after the event, the description is more condensed in form, yet gives the impression that the writer had a clear remembrance of all the events. We owe to Markham the publication in English of this important document.

We possess descriptions dating from the sixteenth century by Pedro de Cieza, the great traveler and faithful chronicler, and by P. Hieronimus Roman. Cieza saw the town about one decade after the extinction of its religious life, when the inhabitants were converted to Christianity or, if not, they were at least quite intimidated by the invaders.[3] We find in the work of P. Hieronimus Roman, Las Republicas del Mundo,[4] an attractive description of the sun temples in the empire of the Incas, apparently founded upon a close study of the sun temple of Pachacamac, which he mentions in his account; he deserves the more to be credited as he gathered his information prior to 1595, the year of publication of his work, and from eye-witnesses who inhabited the town before its decline.

From the first quarter of the seventeenth century date the accounts of the two distinguished chroniclers, Bernabé Cobo and Antonio de Calancha; both knew the ruins well. The former, a Jesuit, gives an admirable description of the temple on the hill, which has the additional value of minutely describing important details, then existing but now lost. Calancha, an Augustinian friar, gives a splendid résumé of all the facts he could gather concerning the temple and its history. Unfortunately, when these men wrote their accounts, all original knowledge concerning the former use of the temple had died out; their information was from hearsay and local tradition, which in the course of a few decades distorted the facts; therefore their statements cannot be credited without reserve, in many cases they are entirely false. At the time when these men lived in this region, a vague local tradition, entirely unsupported by facts, had already begun to take the shape in which we find it at this day and whereby even in our nineteenth century many of the explorers were deceived. These false and misleading tales must therefore be entirely disposed of in order to establish a strictly historical account of the former conditions of the town.

The notes on these ruins, written by the two Señ. Ulloa, early in the eighteenth century, reveal only their ignorance and indifference concerning the history of the ancient temple. The only fact we get from them is that the appearance of the ruined city was just as desolate at the time of their writing as it is now.

It is true that early in the nineteenth century a new scientific interest in the ruins was awakened, but without leading to any immediate results. The ruins since then were visited and described by travelers as follows: In 1817 by W. B. Stevenson; on June 28, 1839, by Wilkes (of the U. S. Exploring expedition); by J. J. v. Tschudi, between 1838 and 1842; E. M. de Rivero and Clements R. Mark-

---

[1] See plan of the city.
[2] American Anthropologist, 1897, p. 393ff.

[3] Crónica, I, chap. 72.
[4] Quoted by Garcilaso, book II, chap. 2.

ham saw the ruins in 1853, 1854 and 1860; George Squier, in the sixties; Hutchinson, between 1871 and 1873; Bastian, July, 1875; Wiener, 1876; Middendorf, in the eighties, etc.

In the report of W. B. Stevenson we find no description of the ruins; he only gives a few general observations. Wilkes could, after his visit of a few hours at Pachacamac, not give more than a few superficial remarks and two indifferent views.[1] The notes of J. J. v. Tschudi are also too short to be of any real value.[2] The description of the ruins in the work of E. M. de Rivero and J. J. de Tschudi[3] is quite uncritical, although often quoted; nor are the plan and views of the town in the supplementary atlas to be relied upon.[4]

Markham often mentions the ruins in his works; he also prepared a ground plan of the sun temple,[5] which unfortunately was not published. George Squier visited this locality for a week;[6] but he gave only a very general description of the place; still his plans of the two principal monu-ments, the sun temple and the convent, are the best so far published and the only ones worthy of any scientific notice, although they need a few corrections. Hutchinson's notes[7] on the ruins give few details and are unreliable; the views are only partly true to nature. Bastian, in publishing his notes on the ruins,[8] merely wished to arouse an interest in them, and this present report may be considered as an attempt to meet his wishes. Wiener's[9] report on the ruins, together with the views, is of no value, although his observations were based on a visit of eleven days. Middendorf's[10] description of the ruins has the advantage over the notes of most of his predecessors in the great seriousness of observation and the careful attention to detail shown by him. The views given are reproductions from photographs, the first of the kind in this field.

That the present report can be offered in much greater detail than any of the foregoing, the writer owes mainly to the fortunate circumstance of having been able to spend at this one place a much longer period than former explorers, and devoting his time exclusively to the exploration of this one group of ruins.

[1] Wilkes, I, p. 278. On January 26, d'Osery passed the ruins of Pachacamac. In the book of travels of F. Castelnau, Expéd. dans le part. centr. de l'Amérique du Sud, Histoire du Voyage, Paris, 1851, IV, p. 179, there is only a short allusion made to this visit.

[2] J. J. v. Tschudi, Peru, I, pp. 289-291.

[3] Rivero y Tschudi, Peruvian Antiquities, pp. 288-291.

[4] Atlas, pl. LIV-LV.

[5] Reports of the Discovery, Introd., p. xxi.

[6] Squier, Peru, pp. 62-81.

[7] Hutchinson, Two Years in Peru, I, pp. 147-176.

[8] Bastian, Die Culturländer des Alten Amerika, I, pp. 51-53.

[9] Wiener, Pérou et Bolivie, pp. 56-70.

[10] Peru, II, pp. 110-126.

CHAPTER V.

THE RUINS.

GENERAL TOPOGRAPHY OF THE CITY.

FOUR hills may be noticed in the city plan, which partly encircle the town or are covered by it, W, X, Y, Z. The one at the extreme south, W, is the highest, about 250 feet above the level of the valley, and the most extensive of all;[1] its southern side projects into the valley like an outpost; surrounded by fields on three sides, it is on the fourth connected with a strip of land fifty to eighty feet high, upon which lies the ruined city, and on account of its commanding position it may be seen from great distances with the structures on its crest. From the northwest it is to be seen from the coast at a distance of six miles; from the inner valley at a range of four miles; from the south coast at a much greater distance. The second hill, X, and the third, Y, confine the city on the eastern side toward the valley. While the latter is insignificant, the former[2] extends in a long ridge in a southeastern direction into the valley and turns the river away from the southern part of the town from 600 to 800 feet out of its course.

The northeastern side of X slopes abruptly toward the valley. The summit in its northeastern section is broad and covered with innumerable craterlike hollows, which show that the stone was quarried here to be used in some of the buildings in the town. This stone is a sort of argillaceous slate, the fragments generally having a parallelepiped form.[3] Along the hillside toward the city traces of former terraces may be seen encircling the hill and following its curves. On the southwestern slope[4] small stall-like cells were found, three feet high and built of stones loosely laid; they were in groups and enclosed human remains, and in a few instances some broken pottery of a very crude kind. These burial-places do not resemble any others in the town, as they are far inferior to the degree of culture shown in the antiquities of the city in general, but it was impossible to determine their place in the cultural history of the town since no objects were found in them which could serve as guides.

The fourth hill, Z, stands in the centre of the town and is covered with buildings.[5] A narrow ridge branches off from here in an eastern direction and divides the southeastern section, B, from the northeastern, E. The city-plan shows the inner town mainly, that section which is covered by high adobe structures and which is a mile long from northeast to southwest and two-thirds of a mile from northwest to southeast. The entire area of the city within the outer walls measures two miles and a half in length to one mile and a third in width; a few more hills were included in the northeastern section.[6]

The structure which crowns the hill, W, in the centre of the town is the Sun temple, erected by the Incas after their conquest of this valley. The original sanctuary of the town, however, was the temple of Pachakamaj, the ruins of which lie at the foot of the hill, on the northern side, and on the level of the city.[7] Pl. 2, fig. 1, shows both these monuments in a perspective view, the latter surrounded by a vast cemetery, No. I of the plan.

Although the designation given here of these two buildings is quite beyond doubt, it has rarely been attempted.[8] It has become the custom to take the monument on the hill for the temple of Pachakamaj, and no attention was paid to the temple below or it was taken for the sun temple, as for instance by Rivero and Tschudi.[9]

---

[6] Wilkes erroneously gives the area of the town as one-fifth by one-third of a mile, which Brühl by a slip in writing changed to 800 + 500 feet (instead of meters).

[7] See plan.

[8] By Middendorf and Markham, 1872, in the Introduc. to the Reports of the Disc., p. xix.

[9] Balboa wrote his work on the Inca Empire at Quito, between 1576 and 1586; it was based upon an account written by Cristóbal de Molina, who lived at Cuzco, far from Pachacamac (see Markham, Narratives, Introd., p. vii); neither of these authors had seen Pachacamac, so the latter simply repeats the error of the former in stating that the temple on the hill, which had been newly erected by the Incas, gave its name to the city. There may have been certain relations between the cult of the Creator god Pachakamaj and that of the Sun temple on the hill, as according to Betanzos, chap. 11, there were between the cult of the Wiraqocha and the Sun temple at Cuzco; still it must be maintained from historical and other reasons that the temple on the hill W (see pl. 13 for ground plan) was the temple of the Sun, and the other at the foot of the hill was the old sanctuary of the Creator god, named Pachakamaj from the time of the Inca conquest. Fernando de Santillan, too, refers to the temple on the hill as the Pachakamaj temple. His account of the organization of the Inca empire dates from the time between 1651 and 1721 (Jimenez de la Espada, Introduc. to Tres Relaciones de antiqu, p. xlii), it is therefore to be assumed that he followed the inaccurate local tradition, which by that time had taken its present shape. PP. Bernabé and Calancha (about 1620) speak of the temple on the hill distinctly as the Pachakamaj temple. Their opinion does not bear much weight, however, as it is easily seen in their statements that neither of them knew exactly which of the buildings was Mamacona. The original meaning was quite unknown to P. Calancha, so that he identified the name Mamacona with the temple on the hill (plan, pl. 13). Cobo repeated the statements of Indians, that the temple on the hill antedated the Inca conquest of the valley, which is impossible from inward and outward reasons. The tradition that the upper temple was that of Pachakamaj could probably arise from the fact that the lower, the true Pachakamaj temple, was completely ruined. The worship of the Sun in the upper temple was introduced by the conquerors, not a native cult, and later tradition connected the cult of the ancient local deity with the imposing temple structure on the hill. This error was adopted among modern authors by Stevenson, Archibald Smith (Peru as it is, 1839, II, p. 308), Wilkes, de Castelnau, Rivero and Tschudi, Prescott and Squier. J. J. v. Tschudi's opinion is that the temple was dedicated to Pachakamaj and by the Incas turned into a Sun temple (Peru, I, p. 290; also Beitr., p. 126), which contradicts Estete's clear statement that both temples existed side by side. Rivero and Tschudi claim to have the testimony of contemporaneous authors on their side, especially that of Hernando Pizarro. How little this could refer to Estete and Cieza can be seen in the text above. Pizarro speaks of two courts of the sanctuary of Pachakamaj, an upper and a lower one; by the lower one he may have referred to the lower temple, by upper to the one upon the hill. Still, since the cell in which the god spoke to the priests in oracles was, according to Hernando Pizarro, "adjoining the upper court," and not in the temple upon the hill, it can only have been in the lower, the old temple; while the upper court could not have been any other

---

[1] It may be seen very distinctly, pl. 2, fig. 1; also pl. 9, fig. 2, its western declivity.

[2] Pl. 9, fig. 1, as seen from the town.

[3] Scherzer, Reise der Novara, III, p. 340, speaks of it as being cut in the form of bricks.

[4] Pl. 9, fig. 1.

[5] Comp. Panorama, pl. 1, to the right; pl. 11, fig. 1, western view, etc.

The testimony of several authors of the sixteenth century is sufficient for us, of men who saw the city at the time of its discovery, like Estete, or who got their information from persons acquainted with the city in its better days, as Cieza and Padre Roman. Estete tells us with convincing clearness: "The city has close to the mosque (i. e., the temple of Pachakamaj) a house of the Sun, which stands upon a hill and is well constructed with five terraces," and further on: "the image (of Pachakamaj) stood in a goodly house, which was well painted."[1] The only well painted house of the city was the temple of Pachakamaj,[2] the temple on the hill with its monochrome coat of paint could never have been so described.

Estete is corroborated by Cieza, who says: "The temple of Pachakamaj was built upon an artificial mound of adobes.[3] When the Incas realized that it would be difficult to supplant the cult of Pachakamaj, they made the agreement with the native caziques and the priests that in this temple of Pachakamaj the ancient cult should be continued with the condition that a larger temple for the Sun worship be built upon the most prominent place."[4] Also Padre Hieronymo Roman in his book refers to the upper temple as the temple of the Sun.

To the grounds of the temple of Pachakamaj also belonged the hill against which it was built, while the northeastern,[5] northwestern and southwestern sides of the grounds were occupied by the cemetery of the pilgrims.[6]

In the plan of the city a line of ruined masonry may be traced which encloses in a rectangle, and at an even distance of several hundred feet, the temple and the cemetery. Within its area stands one building to the northeast from the temple, which may have served some religious purpose, and the Sun temple upon the hill. The ancient convent lies on the outside of the older city wall opposite its western angle. The ruins may be seen on the panorama, pl. 1, to the left in the background.[7] The name, Mamacona, whereby this pile of ruins is still known, its secluded situation and its peculiar style of architecture, that of the Incas, seem strong proofs for the fact that this was the convent. Hernando Pizarro distinctly mentions the situation of the building in his letter: "This city of the mosque is very large and has vast edifices and courts. Outside of it is another large space enclosed by walls with gates opening into the mosque. In this enclosure are the houses of the women, who are the wives of the devil."

The ancient 'fields of the Sun,' 'inti chajra,' and in later days the hacienda Mamacona,[8] stretch toward the west, south and southeast to the foot of the hill upon which the Sun temple stands. These are the fields from which the inmates of the convent drew their sustenance. The plan shows that there was but one gate which might correspond to that mentioned by Hernando Pizarro, at the end of the western street; farther south seem to be no indications of other gates in the walls.

Thus the entire enclosed area south of entrance A is secured as the outer court of the temple of Pachakamaj.

Hernando Pizarro in his report continues: "Here are also the storehouses where the treasure of gold is hidden. There is none at the place where the women are kept." This seems to indicate that Pizarro thought the gold stores to be outside the city and at a distance from the convent. The buildings, the ruins of which lie to the southwest from the temple precinct, enclosed by the latter, the Sun temple and the hacienda Mamakona (the Inti chajra), must have had some religious character on account of their isolated position, among buildings of a religious nature only; here might be located the ancient gold magazines, of which Pizarro[9] speaks, although it seems unreasonable to seek them in these insignificant ruins. It would be more plausible to locate them on the square piece of ground to the north from the temple, which shows the ravages of unceasing digging for treasure.

The town (see panorama, pl. 1, taken from the temple of Pachakamaj) extended to the northeast, north and northwest from the temple precinct. The oldest quarter of the town presumably lay between the hills X, Y and Z, as this would be a likely position, sheltered by the hills and near the river, and our finds entirely confirmed this supposition; the built up part of the town situated within the horseshoe shaped inner city wall[10] is a later addition. It is still possible to distinguish a street crossing which divided the town into quarters.[11] The northwestern and northeastern parts of the city wall are similar to those which flank the northeastern and northwestern streets. These walls, the western one of which extends for 1000 yards in a straight line, seem to be parts of a well planned scheme of enlarging the city, the same plan was followed in the construction of the street crossings and of these walls, all at one period and previous to the erection of the buildings. This, however, happened at a later date than the laying out of the temple precincts, for the streets adjacent to these, the southeastern and the southwestern, are less regular than the others.

For a second time the city was enlarged, this extension taking in twice as much additional ground in the northwest and northeast than before, but only 500 yards more toward the sea.

It has been asserted that Pachacamac[12] at the time of the Spanish conquest was partly deserted. Miguel Estete speaks of ruined buildings and of the dilapidated condition of most of the walls. Still it must not be forgotten that Hernando Pizarro and Miguel Estete in every line of their accounts dwell on the size and importance of the town, and that the latter mentions the ruined condition of some buildings and walls only as a proof for the antiquity of the city. The dilapidated wall, of which Estete speaks, is the inner, older one, as the outer city wall is, even to this day, almost intact. All indications as well as the results of explorations tend to prove that the new territory which was added to the city at the time of its extension belongs exclusively to the Inca period. Our view, therefore, that the city at the time of the Spanish conquest was not a dilapidated place, but still a flourishing town, seems to be well supported.

---

place than the plateau of the lower temple, and a different interpretation must be found for the lower court. Markham (Cuzco, p. 15) changed his originally correct view concerning the designation of the temple. Hutchinson's theories on the purpose of the upper temple and the time of its destruction need not be discussed here.

[1] Estete, p. 133. "Este pueblo tiene junto á esta mezquita una casa del sol, puesto en un cerro bien labrada con cinco cercas." According to the way of counting, the terraces of the Sun temple may be numbered as 3 or 6.

[2] A few frescoed rooms, apparently chapels, cannot be mentioned for comparison.

[3] In some respects this description fits the lower temple more exactly than the upper, in others it applies to both.

[4] Cronica, I, chap. 72.

[5] See plan, pl. 2, fig. 1, and pl. 17, fig. 3.

[6] See plan and pl. 2, fig. 1.

[7] Pizarro speaks of "several houses," probably he meant the entire group with its several roofs.

[8] At present a dependency of the hacienda San Pedro.

[9] Pizarro probably expected to find storehouses of gold near the convent, since those buildings showed the Inca character in their architecture, and also otherwise bore a strong resemblance to the convent at Cuzco.

[10] This city wall has often been mistaken for the temple enclosure; by Rivero and Tschudi, p. 288 (and by others who quoted their statements, Brühl, p. 140, Bancroft, IV, p. 796, etc.).

[11] This division resembles that of the ancient city of Cuzco, where a street-cross divides the place into four quarters, which were a microcosmic repetition of the realm of Jawantinsuyu (Garcilaso, book VII, chaps. 8, 9), and it is possible that the division of the city of Pachacamac had a similar significance.

[12] Bandelier, in an article by F. Webb Hodge, American Anthrop., 1897, p. 303.

CHAPTER VI.

GENERAL SURVEY OF THE GRAVES IN THE CITY.

QUITE in proportion to the great antiquity of the city, in which all authors concur, is the enormous number of its graves. Skulls and bones are scattered all over the ground, as they were dug up and thrown aside.[1] The graves may be divided into three classes: those in open cemeteries, those in ancient dwellings[2] and those inside of temples; the first class are the most numerous, of the third there are but few. In the oldest section of the city, the southern, the number of graves is of course the largest. This part of the town, probably, passed through a long history before its enlargement. In the newer part of the town, there are likewise a large number of burial places scattered here and there under the desert sands, but they are not so overcrowded as some of the older cemeteries of the inner town.

On the city plan the sites of graves are indicated by crosses and some of the more important cemeteries are numbered, I to VI.[3] The writer explored most extensively graveyards No. I and No. VI; little work was done in Nos. II and III. Explorations were attempted in every part of the town, generally with small results, yet sufficient to ascertain the cultural periods to which each section belongs. These experimental spots are marked in the plan by red crosses and small letters. Judging from our experiences in exploring the cemeteries, we may estimate the graves at Pachacamac to have been between 60,000 and 80,000 in number. Operations in cemetery III were abandoned, the graves being much scattered and all articles in them of perishable nature poorly preserved; still it was ascertained that in this burial ground to a space of sixty square feet about three graves were untouched and ten ruined, disturbed by former explorations, yielding one body to five square feet of ground. Judging from the size of this cemetery of 250 by 100 feet, which is a low estimate, and the average closeness of graves as given above, this comparatively small cemetery must have held circa 5000 dead. Originally this cemetery extended 300 feet farther to the east with a width of 150 feet, but it was probably built over at a later period, therefore this one plot may have held 10,000 graves.

The cemetery at the foot of the Pachakamaj temple is about 750 feet long by a general width of 200 feet. Thousands of bleaching skulls and bones are scattered over its rifled surface. Estimating the average closeness of graves, the same as in cemetery III, there may have been 30,000 burials in this one place; the size of cemetery II is 230 by 100 feet, and it must have held at least 5000 dead; the two burial places IV and V, estimated in the same manner, would have held 10,000 bodies, and an estimate of 10,000 more for the rest of the city will surely be a low one.

Most of the graves were disturbed, especially those in dwelling houses, so that it was impossible to find any unopened ones there; cemetery II had been rifled to the utmost; cemeteries IV and V, after a cursory examination, yielded no results, likewise had graveyard I been rifled to its entire length and breadth. This fact is not surprising if it is remembered with what avidity the digging for treasure was continued ever since the Spaniards took possession of the country. Cieza, who visited Peru in the first decade after its discovery, says:[4] "Many of these graves have been opened and are still explored, for ever since the Spanish conquest of the empire much gold and silver was found in this way;" and, "the captains Rodrigo Ordoguez, Francisco de Godoy and others unearthed vast quantities of gold and silver[5] from graves at Pachacamac." Ulloa, who visited the place early in the eighteenth century, says:[6] "No idea can be formed of the topography of the ancient city and of its houses, as large mounds of adobe cover every part of it, débris of walls pulled down in the search for tombs and the treasures supposed to be concealed therein, since wild tales of some earlier finds spurred the people on to do this." It appears, therefore, that early in the eighteenth century the place was in about the same condition as it is now. A good deal remains yet to be accomplished for the explorer at Pachacamac, especially if systematic work is done in this field, as all former explorations here were carried on in a desultory manner.

The graves still remaining are, fortunately for us, entirely devoid of objects of gold or silver, or contain but few of these. If they were of richer yield they, too, would long since have fallen a prey to treasure hunters and none would be left now. Middendorf's view that the yield of graves decreases in proportion to the increase of exploration seems to be correct.[7] Our own experience may serve as an example, since the only burial plot which yielded a few silver vessels was the cemetery of Huarangal, which had not been explored quite so thoroughly, as it lies at some distance from Pachacamac. The Indians of old were not unacquainted with the custom of reopening the graves after some time and removing provisions and valuables.[8] It must be remembered, too, that many of the graves, especially older ones, which were as a rule the objects of our researches, entirely lacked utensils of metal. It appears, therefore, that the use of such implements for domestic purposes was not so general yet to find them largely represented in the graves of this period.

---

[1] Compare Hutchinson, I, p. 165.

[2] In ancient village ruins in the interior of the valley, at Huaycan, for instance, the houses are provided with cellars or vaults under the rooms or in the fore courts, which are lined and covered with stones and were used for the burial of the dead. They were not filled with sand in the course of the centuries like those at Pachacamac. Cieza, Cron., I, chap. 63, gives an interesting piece of information regarding these vaults: "In the province of Jauja and quite generally in Peru the dead for burial are wrapped into a fresh llama-skin, that is sewed together and a face attached to it with nose, mouth, etc. The bodies are kept in the houses, and those who in life were chieftains and caziques are on certain occasions during the year disinterred by their sons and with great ceremony carried about on open biers through the fields, and the customary sacrifices are made to them which consist in young llamas, even children and women." Doubtless the same customs obtained here in the Pachacamac valley.

[3] Wiener, p. 66, speaks of three principal cemeteries, which he erroneously assigns as belonging to the temple, the town and the pilgrims.

[4] I, chap. 63.
[5] Chap. 72.
[6] P. 301.
[7] Peru, II, p. 118.
[8] Cieza, I, chap. 13.

CHAPTER VII.

THE TEMPLE OF PACHAKAMAJ.

THE ancient temple (see plan, pl. 3), the most famous sanctuary of the city, was so entirely destroyed that its ruins are generally overlooked by visitors, and the imposing temple ruins on the hill are taken for those of the temple of Pachakamaj. Only Rivero and Tschudi,[1] Markham[2] and Middendorf[3] distinctly mention these ruins, and only the two last named assume them to be those of the Pachakamaj temple; Middendorf in his work attempts a description of these ruins.

This temple was built against the northwestern slope of the hill W (see city plan), on the summit of which, farther to the south, the ruins of the Sun temple are to be seen. The structure faced the northwest, probably an older part of the town, and looked toward the Peruvian coastland, while the valley extends back of the hill. The temple is 400 feet long by 180 feet wide and covers an area of two-thirds of an acre; by the projection of its northwest front, at h, in a western direction, an angle was formed in the centre of the façade, whereby the almost rectangular outline of the building was interrupted. Three sides of the temple were terraced, each of the grades being about twenty feet high, and the top of the temple formed a plateau, 330 by 130 feet, the nearly rectangular form of which closely followed the general outlines of the building. The fourth side or rear of the building, b, merged horizontally into the summit of the hill against which the temple was built.

Only on one side, i, the terraces are still distinguishable Five low and narrow grades, each three and one-third feet high by six and one-half feet wide, and covered with polychrome frescoing, formed the approaches to the temple on this side. The terraces on the other two sides are so deeply buried under sand and débris that the structure here looks like the natural hill, and only after excavating near h the former terraces were exposed to view. In this locality, near the northern angle, may have been the passageway up to the temple, but it is almost obliterated at present. Of the two galleries found here, k extends halfway up the temple, leading past its once richly frescoed northeastern and southeastern fronts, and here may have been the main entrance of the temple. On the plateau at the top of the structure only few details can now be traced. In the centre of the northwest front, near a, there is a deep trench, fifty by twenty feet, the earth and stones of which are heaped up in the mounds, b, as indicated on pl. 2, fig. 1. The shrine of the temple must have been at this place, the 'boveda,' as Estete calls it, which was torn down by Hernando Pizarro, and on this site many treasure hunters were at work in later days. The remaining area of the temple plateau was by a partition wall divided into an eastern and a western section; the former measured about 170 by 130 feet and must have been a large hall. A

few rooms, apparently sunk into the ground or excavated into the rock, but now completely ruined, were in the northeastern part. The walls of the large hall are ruined, but one small piece of masonry three feet high remaining of the southeastern wall, c, formerly eleven feet high. This may have been the hall where "the old 'bishop' stood and received the envoys of chieftains after they had gone through the prescribed fast of twelve months before being admitted to his presence, when he would receive them with his head covered, and after having heard the messages from their princes, praying for good harvests for the ensuing year, the devil's priest entered the adjoining cell, where he claimed to have speech with their devil," according to Pizarro.

The western section of the plateau appears to have been enclosed by a wall of inferior strength; along dividing wall d several rooms were sunk into the floor about six feet deep, while two terraces, g, g, from six to seven feet high, were built up against the rear wall. These grades are similar to those on the uppermost terrace of the Sun temple (pl. 13, No. 20) and were probably used for some sacrificial purpose.

At the time of the conquest the temple must have been as gorgeous an object to behold as it is now one of desolation. Smaller in all its dimensions than the younger Sun temple, it must have eclipsed it in splendor. Miguel Estete speaks of it as "well painted."[4] While the Sun temple was painted a monochrome red color, the former was frescoed with bird[5] and animal designs,[6] probably also with plant-ornaments,[7] to judge from finds and preserved fragments. On the small remnant of wall c on the south side of the eastern hall a yellow and red scroll pattern can still be seen. Miguel Estete in his second unpublished report says that the door of the cella was incrusted with "coral, turquoises, crystals and other stones." The truth of this statement is strengthened by the fact that in the Sun temple at Cuzco the frames of several large niches were set with emeralds and turquoises[8] in a similar manner. It is probable that the temple was decorated with ornaments of gold, presented to the sanctuary by the Inca Hvaina Qhapaj;[9] we do not find any reference to this, however, in the reports of the first discoverers, the Inca priests, warned of the approach of the Spaniards, having removed everything of value, while the incrustations upon the doors could not be taken off.[10] Thus it happened

[1] L. c., p. 290.
[2] Introduction to Reports, p. xix.
[3] Peru, II, p. 115.

[4] Cieza, I, chap. 72, tells that walls and doors were covered with designs of wild animals.
[5] See fig. 9.
[6] Fig. 8.
[7] Fig. 7.
[8] Garcilaso, book III, chap. 22.
[9] Cieza, II, chap. 65.
[10] The story that a pilot in the service of Hernando Pizarro begged to be given, for his share in the booty, the silver nails used to fasten the plates of hammered gold to the walls of the temple of Pachakamaj, and that this apparently small share in the spoils alone amounted to 4000 marks silver, was rejected by J. J. v. Tschudi, l. c., p. 87ff. In his opinion, which is secondary to the question itself, the gold plates were not fastened to the walls by metal nails but by wooden ones, an error on his part. In the Museum of La Paz the writer saw a

that no gold worth mentioning was found in the temple by Hernando Pizarro, only a small quantity of gold dust.[1] The great splendor and prestige of this place of worship, as well as the high reverence in which its deity was held by the Indians, made it the object of the most fanatic destruction by the Spaniards, therefore the ruins of this temple appear so much more desolate at present than those of the Sun temple.[2]

The wall in the rear of the temple, the southeastern, does not stand closely against the hillside, but it is connected with the latter by a sort of bridge, while the space between, m, is filled up with adobes to a height of two meters above the floor of the hall. An excavation near l did not result in finding the original soil at a depth of twenty feet. This filling up as well as the absence of any enclosing walls farther back, and the line of masonry, p, at a projected point from the southwestern edge of the temple plateau, suggest that these rear portions of the structure must have had some particularly close connection with the temple. These portions consist of the plateau of masonry, m; of the natural ridge of the hill with a northwestward slope, n, and the artificial mound continuing the latter, o, as is separately shown in view 3, pl. 17, and can also be seen on the extreme right-hand side of fig. 1, pl. 19. A peculiarity of these parts of the structure is the small amount of architectural detail in proportion to their massiveness, while the contrary must be said of the temple itself. The two sections m and n extend from northwest to southeast for about 360 feet, from southwest to northeast for 400 feet. The mound o, mainly an artificial one, is 450 feet long by 400 feet wide and 60 feet high. The ruined sides of this mound only show the construction of its nucleus, while no trace of an exterior finish can be found. These facts, together with a rude terrace grade, thirteen feet high, projecting on the northeastern side, give the impression that the structure was left in an unfinished state. However, it must be assumed that sections m, n, o were in use for a time. In section n foundations of buildings were struck; in section o, which slopes from n near r for about ten feet, a thick wall, s, was found; the remains of stone masonry and on the southeastern edge a large cremation ground were located near q, judging from the red color of the clay soil, which is caused by fire. In the entire section of n and o only one fragment of decorated pottery was found, while on the western slope of the mound in several spots large quantities of sea-shells (Concholepas peruvianus[3]) were brought to the surface.

The temple stood within the enclosure as described above, surrounded by an area extending to the northwest for 230 feet, to the southwest for about 260 feet and to the north, near the ruined building within the enclosure, for 210 feet. The enclosure itself is of a trapezoid form, its sides 1000 to 1370 feet in length seem to date from a very early period, as only a few yards of the former wall remain, and merely a sort of a dam enclosing a square space is all that is left.

Sections of its former course can be traced on pl. 2, fig. 1, on the northwestern slope of the hill W, below the Sun temple; likewise in pl. 15, fig. 1, on the southern declivity of the same hill; then again fragments of its eastern course can be seen in the plain, partly winding up the hill X in pl. 9, fig. 1, and traces of its northwestern line in the foreground of the panorama of the town on pl. 1. At this point the wall was not quite as thick as elsewhere, probably on account of the structures adjoining it. This ancient wall was doubtless the inner enclosure of the temple, as is clearly shown by the way the enclosed area was laid out, as well as by the structures outside of it. The dwelling house stood with its rear against this wall; the two walks encircling the square, at a small elevation, terminate abruptly before this enclosure and make a turn alongside of it. The western end winds about the structure in a semicircle and seems to terminate between the houses to which it may have been the approach; these being within the outer temple precincts, this walk must be considered as a second entrance to it.

Only one small terraced building stands closely against the inner wall, opposite the northwest front of the temple, and a winding path leads up to it from the inner temple. In the panorama of the town this structure stands in the foreground; its situation suggests a porter's lodge so clearly that Estete's words may be referring to it when he says:[4] "To this devil's house the Indian pilgrims resort from remote parts of the land, some of them coming 300 leagues or more with their offerings of gold, silver and garments, and upon their arrival they hand their gifts to the gatekeeper, who then goes into the shrine and has speech with the idol and hears his answers."

As before stated, the outer precinct of the temple extended as far as the western street of the town and to the gate near it. The larger part of this area, marked as fore courts 2 and 3, must for good reasons be regarded as outer courts of the temple. Court 3 is a peculiarly designed area near the temple gate, and can only be a part of a grand and original scheme; it forms a level sandy ground of 1050 by 235 feet, and where the structures, standing in front of the temple enclosure, have now disappeared, it is 350 feet wide; two long dam-like lines, much broken into, u (probably remains of a structure that was divided transversely on its eastern end), extend in an even distance of twenty-one feet along the entire north side of this large court. Two parallel lines, formed of small mounds of earth, n and x, run from the western side of the wall line through the entire length of the large court. These mounds terminate near the gatekeeper's lodge, the mounds x ending farther to the eastward. Near w the parallel rows are twenty-three feet apart; near x only eighteen feet nine inches, and all the mounds stand in pairs, facing each other. Examination of some of these mounds proved them to be remains of pillars of three feet three inches by three feet one inch thick and one foot high, perhaps originally a little more. These were set upon a path bordered at ten inches from the pillars with a single row of stones, and which near x was twenty-three feet six inches wide.[5] These seem to be the remains of two covered walks and the pillars may have served as pedestals or posts to support a roof[6] as a protection against the fierce rays of the sun. If this court 3 with its peculiar design is claimed as an outer fore court of the temple, the purpose of court 2, only indistinctly separated from the former, is likewise established. The significance of court 1, separated from court 2 by a thicker

stone from a wall at Tiahuanaco, which still held in drilled holes some copper nails that had held the gold plates. On the site of the ruins of Pumapunku (Tiahuanaco) are the ruins of a monolithic gateway with a relief frieze where the holes may be still seen in many spots like the ones above, and which have served a similar purpose. Photographic views of the gate-ruins can be seen in the Museum of Science and Art; also a fragment of a stone, ornamented with sculpture in relief, on which these holes are to be seen.

[1] Letter, p. 123.

[2] When Cieza came to Pachacamac, scarcely a decade after Hernando Pizarro, he found the temple partly ruined (I, chap. 72). The statement by Prescott, I, p. 293, that the Spanish colonists had destroyed the temple and used the adobe bricks as building material, seems to be unfounded and unlikely since the Spaniards did not build any houses in that neighborhood, and for buildings at a distance they could find material more conveniently in other ancient buildings.

[3] This sea-shell, from the Peruvian Sea, was found in several specimens in graves belonging to the earliest period of Pachacamac, and in a few instances the shells were colored on the inner side with a purple or an oxide green earthen pigment; from a communication of Pilsbury this shell yields a purple pigment, similar to the oriental color; it is probable that this color was used in Peru in early times.

[4] P. 131.

[5] Seen in panorama of the city, pl. 1, and in fig. 1 of pl. 17 from the distance.

[6] Stübel u. Uhle, Ruinenstätte, p. 2.

wall, but opening into it by a wide gateway, is thereby also guaranteed as the outer court of the temple. The houses, too, may have had some particular relation to the temple. In the court of the house near Z were found traces of large amphores of the regular type used by the Incas for 'chicha.' Hernando Pizarro speaks of these courts[1] as follows: "Before entering the first court of the mosque a man was obliged to fast for twenty days, but a fast of a whole year was imposed before a person had the privilege of ascending to the upper court." We may consider the inner enclosure of the temple or the outer court 2, or 2 and 3, as the first court in Pizarro's sense; since the latter saw the city in its old condition, it is likely that he took for the first court what in reality was but a fore court, and at that time must have been regarded as such. If this be the case, then it is true that to enter court 3 required a preliminary fast of twenty days, while the threshold of the inner court could only be crossed after a year's fasting. Among the buildings within the outer courts 2 and 3, we would therefore find the houses where the pilgrims were lodged. All these facts taken together lead us to surprising conclusions concerning the inaccessibility and the extraordinary sanctity of this place of worship.

---

[1] Letter, p. 123.

CHAPTER VIII.

THE CEMETERY IN THE TEMPLE GROUNDS.

THIS cemetery is one of the largest in the town and the most crowded. So many human beings were interred here that the soil is completely choked with remains of mummies, skulls, bones, fragments of stuffs, ropes, slings,[1] and still it is full of unbroken mummies, which were buried at some later period. In point of crowding this cemetery surpasses even burial ground No. II of the inner town, where the graves are exceedingly close together. This crowding of graves in the cemetery is explained by the great desire of the Indians of old to find their last resting place near the shrine of their deity. According to Cieza,[2] this was a privilege reserved to princes, priests and those pilgrims who could bring rich offerings to the sanctuary. Zarate also states that the chieftains of the entire community strove to get their sepulture in the hallowed ground near the temple at Pachacamac.

The ancient Peruvians had the custom of deforming the human skull from the time of birth on, the manner varying in the different provinces. It might be expected, therefore, that a great variety of types of cranial deformation could be found among the skulls of this burial place. This opinion was also entertained by Markham,[3] but it seems that it was the case to a very small degree only. The skulls taken from graves about the Sun temple in this respect differ greatly from the general class of skulls found at Pachacamac, for they really show a greater variety in the types of deformation than those of other cemeteries, such as No. I for instance There, in more or less pronounced form, prevails the common type of deforming which was practiced along the coast,[4] the Chincha type, as it is called by J. J. v. Tschudi; exceptions are few and generally limited to skulls taken from graves closely adjacent to the front terrace wall of the temple, which for various reasons must be considered as exceptional in the cemetery. This proves that the people interred here did not come from all parts of Peru, and not from such districts where the deformations were different from those in the Peruvian coast regions. Even the ancient provinces of the coast are not fully represented among these graves, since the well known ceramic type of the Chimu is entirely absent from among the specimens, although it is contemporaneous with this cemetery. If from these indications the graves do not represent as great a variety of provincial types as was expected, it is on the other hand surprising to see the difference among the graves in regard to the periods from which they date. The finds in the cemetery do not give much additional proof of the high reverence in which the sanctuary

was held and of its power to attract pilgrims from remote provinces, yet on the other hand we are surprised to discover in these finds proofs of an exceedingly extended use of this cemetery, accordingly of an equally long history of the sanctuary itself. With these finds as guides the history of the temple may now be traced back to the earliest periods of Peruvian civilization of which there is any knowledge at present and down to the point of the Spanish conquest.

The time has now come for a more serious and scholarly study and classification of Peruvian grave finds than that devoted to this subject formerly; it is no longer sufficient to merely explore in the old unsystematic way, without paying any attention to the various historical periods, and leaving all studies of this kind to future scholars in this field.

The extensive operations which are now undertaken in Peruvian exploration must have the aim of extending our knowledge of the great cultured types of Peru, of their development and successive periods. Only by methodical work and guided by scientific theories will these explorations lead to practical and instructive results. Sufficient material is now at hand and more will appear in time to enable the scholar to connect genetically all the main types of specimens of ancient Peruvian civilization in their historical relations to one another. Local peculiarities of style may thus gradually gain a typical importance in the general development of ancient Peruvian cultural forms, as they will present themselves interwoven with great historical movements or as derived therefrom, and so at some future time the history of all the various phases of Peruvian culture may be traced to its source. Types which were generally regarded as merely local now gain much greater importance. This may serve as a warning against the careless grouping of specimens of unknown extraction together with objects of similar appearance. On the other hand serious research will be rewarded, as these types may serve as guides in establishing the dates of certain periods, or even in settling the doubted identity of culture in localities far distant from each other. Great care must be observed not to consider rashly the finds of a single operation as representative for a certain locality.

All observations unite to show that the course of development of Peruvian civilization has been a very long one, passing through many different periods, the deposits of which we find side by side in the graves and cemeteries of all the valleys. The cultural and historical character of a locality may only be determined by examination of all the cemeteries to be found there. Occasionally graves of different periods are found intermingled. In such cases the contents of the graves must be carefully distinguished and separated from one another. It also happens that the graves are found lying in strata, as shall be seen in one example below, which

---

[1] Cronica, I, chap. 72.
[2] I, chap. 10.
[3] Markham, Engl. edition of Cieza, note to chap. 72.
[4] Virchow, Crania ethnica americana, 1892, p. 14.

is an especially fortunate circumstance whereby chronological classification is greatly facilitated. In these cases great care is needed to distinguish all the signs of such a stratification in territory outwardly identical.

One special ceramic type, a vase or flask with a long and thin neck and conical bottom (pl. 18, fig. 1), was named 'arybal' by Hamy, from its resemblance to certain ancient Greek types. This type is found all over Peru, Ecuador, Bolivia, in a part of Chile and Argentina, where it was carried by the conquest of the Incas.[1] The same may be said of some other ceramic types related to the former in form and decoration, such as plates,[2] jars,[3] various kinds of jugs,[4] of the Cuzco type, concerning which there has long been a general, if tacit, agreement.[5]

Another prominent decorative type of ancient Peru must be mentioned here, which is best known on account of its peculiarity and its great antiquity. Stübel and the present writer, in their work on The Ruins of Tiahuanaco, proved that those ancient monumental stone structures date from an early pre-Inca period, ignoring all legends of doubtful source, but entirely for serious historical reasons.[6] Numerous objects are found, possessing a surprisingly strong resemblance to

the style of these monuments in all their characteristics.[7] Some were shown in the above mentioned work, pl. 4,[8] with distinct reference to this similarity of style. The authors then ventured to suggest that one of the vases might serve as a proof of the occurrence of the same cultural forms on the Island of Titicaca;[9] moreover, its characteristic resemblance was pointed out to the much discussed sculptured stone slab from the distant Chavin de Huantar in the north of Peru.[10] At that period it seemed surprising that one particular decorative style, peculiar to a small district on the southern end of Lake Titicaca in Bolivia, should appear in an entirely different region of ancient Peru. New discoveries have since modified these views considerably. Rich collections of specimens in the Museum of Berlin prove that the decorative style, which, from lack of any other name, may as well be named after the ancient monuments of Tiahuanaco, is represented along all the shores of the big lake as well as on the islands. The writer found to his surprise that in Bolivia, to the south from the lake, the type abruptly ceased, its last traces were met with at Ancoaqui on the Desaguadero, ten miles south of the border town of Desaguadero. This important type must accordingly have been more closely connected with the north than with the south. The presence of objects belonging to this particular style all about the lake formed most convincing links between the ruins of Tiahuanaco and many objects in the museums from southern Peru which bore a striking resemblance to them.[11]

If this conjecture proves to be correct the great difficulty will be removed in establishing the connection of the stone-slab of Chavin de Huantar with the ancient monuments of Tiahuanaco and the resemblance in a richly ornamented poncho found at Ancon.[12] It becomes more and more evident that the type of the Tiahuanaco culture is not an isolated one, standing at the extreme southern border line of Peruvian civilization, but that it may have been a great type of historical importance for all Peru, which by some accident happened to come into our notice before any of the others at the extreme end of the Peruvian cultural territory. We have now two great starting points for the study of the cultural development of ancient Peru: the style of Cuzco, spread over a vast region of ancient Peru by the Inca conquests, and the style of the monuments of Tiahuanaco, the original seat of which cannot be determined for the present. The style was named after Tiahuanaco, as it found in these works its most pregnant expression, and since the works were created on the spot it is a proof that at some particular period this style belonged to that region.

The founding and growth of the Inca empire was one of the last great events in the pre-Spanish history of ancient America. No particular style was discovered, so far, from which the art of Tiahuanaco might have been derived; it therefore stands historically, and on account of its peculiar archaic character, quite isolated at the beginning of the cultural history of Peru, while the Cuzco style may be said to form the culmination of the same artistic development. So the task now presenting itself to us is, to fill in the wide gap

[1] Philippi, Verhand. d. Berl. Ges. f. Anthrop, 1885, p. 269. Bastian, l. c, 1888, p. 532. The writer: Kultur u. Ind. südam. Völker, pp. 24, 32 and 35. Hamy, Galérie américaine, text to Nos. 112, 113.

[2] Comp. pl. 18, fig. 6.

[3] Comp. pl. 18, fig. 3.

[4] Comp. pl. 18, fig. 2.

[5] Also the type of vases in cup-shape (pl. 18, fig. 4) is Cuzco and must not be classed with the ceramic products of the people around Lake Titicaca. Hamy, Galérie améric., suppl. to No. 108.

Below is given a list of some of the places of origin of ceramics belonging to the type of Cuzco, which will show the vast territory over which they were spread.

a. ARYBALS.
Ecuador: Quito, Kultur u. Ind., pl. 7, fig. 3.
    Achupallas, from Cañar: l. c, fig. 1.
    Quinjeo near Cuenca: Congrès des amér. Bruxelles, Atlas, pl. VI, fig. x.
    Chordeleg near Cuenca: l. c., pl. IV, fig. 4; VIII, fig. 6; XV, fig. 5; VIII; pl. XIV, figs. 1, 27.
    From Cuenca: l. c., pl. IV, fig. 6.
    Malachi, from Quito.
Peru: Huarmey: Kult. und Industr., I, pl. 10, fig. 9.
    Pueblo nuevo: l. c., I, fig. 10.
    Ancon and Trujillo: Hamy, Gal. amér., note to Nos. 112, 113; Reiss und Stübel, Necropolis of Ancon.
    Pacasmayo: Congrès des amér., l. c., I, p. 476, fig. 14; besides places about Lima and in the upper Rimac valley.
Bolivia: Corocoro: Kultur u. Ind., I, pl. 11, fig. 11.
    Tiahuanaco, Copacabana and all islands of Lake Titicaca: Collections at Leipsic, Philadelphia, Paris, etc.; comp. also Kult. u. Ind., I, pl. 12.
    Escoma: Collected by the writer, Mus. of Berlin.
    Truitu on the Desaguadero river: Specimens collected by the writer, Mus. of Philadelphia.
    San Andres de Machaca: The same.
    Turco and Chiriscalla, prov. of Carangas: Collected by the writer, Mus. of Berlin.
Argentine: Loma Rica, valley of the Calchaquis: Verh. der Berl. Ges. f. Anthrop., 1884, pl. 7, fig. 1.
    El Paso, valley of the Calchaquis: Coll. by the writer, Mus. of Berlin.
    Tinogasta, prov. of Catamarca, and neighborhood: Coll. by the writer, Mus. of Berlin.
    Ruins of an old town near Chilecito, prov. of Rioja: Fragments of large Cuzco arybals, coll. by the writer, Mus. of Berlin.
    Pucara, between Andalgala, prov. of Catam and Tucuman: Sample-specimens coll. by the writer, Mus. of Berlin.
Chile: Medina, Aborigenes de Chile, No. 211, and Philippi, see above.
b. PLATES.
Ecuador: Datacunga: Congr. des amér. Brux., pl. VI, fig. 6.
Peru: Zepita on Lake Titicaca: Coll. by the writer.
Bolivia: Tiahuanaco, all western, southern and eastern (Omasuqu) shores and all islands of Lake Titicaca: Coll. of Leipsic, Philadelphia, Berlin, etc.
    Truitu on Desaguadero river, Hachiri: Coll. by the writer, Mus. of Philadelphia.
    Prov. of Carangas: Coll. by the writer, Mus. of Berlin.
Chile: Vallenar: Medina, l. c., No. 162.
c. VASES AND JARS.
Bolivia: Tiahuanaco and all shores and islands of Lake Titicaca, Mus. of Philadelphia, Berlin.
    Desaguadero: Mus. of Philadelphia.
Chile: San Jose de Maipo: Medina, l. c., No. 183.
d. BOWLS.
Ecuador: Infantas: Congr. des amér. Brux., pl. VIII, fig. 2.
    Prov. of Imbabura: l. c., pl. XVI, fig. 5.
Bolivia: Shore of Lake Titicaca: Hamy, Galérie amér., No. 108.
Chile: Freirina: Medina, l. c., No. 182.

[6] p. 54.

[7] Larger series of these are to be seen in the Museums of Berlin, Leipsic, Philadelphia, Paris, etc.

[8] The stylistic identity of specimens preserved at Leipsic and shown in Kultur u. Industrie, I, pl. 11, figs. 1–10, 17–20; pl. 12, was pointed out, p. 34ff, ibid.

[9] L. c., pl. 41, fig. 6.

[10] L. c., p 48. A copy and a cast of the above mentioned stone-slab, brought over by Stübel, are in the Museums of Berlin and of Dresden. The first fairly good view of this object of so great an archæological importance was given by Middendorf in his work, Peru, I, p. 631.

[11] Several objects of this class from the region of Cuzco, Ollantaitambo, etc., are in the museum at Berlin. Among others the vase shown by Squier, p. 458, drawn by him at Cuzco at some earlier period.

[12] Reiss und Stübel, The Necropolis of Ancon, pl. 49; Stübel und Uhle, Die Ruinenstätte von Tiahuanaco, pl. 21, fig. 3.

between these two extremes and to write the history of the development of the Peruvian civilization into it.

Returning to the cemetery of the temple of Pachakamaj, it is apparent that it was used from the period of the Tiahuanaco style down to the Inca time. However, it seems to have been used mainly during the various periods preceding that of the Incas. Only a few of the graves belong to the last epoch, and these, judging from the manner of construction and their individual importance, show that the religious prestige of the temple had not suffered any decline during the rule of the Incas.

The extremely early date of the first use of this cemetery to which the finds must be assigned, and which are of such conspicuously pre-Inca character, are a remarkable confirmation of the conclusions drawn above from similar proofs, i. e., that this temple was beyond all doubt that of the Creator-god Pachakamaj, and had no connection with the Sun cult of the Incas, as was supposed by Rivero and Tschudi. The statements of the early historians concerning the great antiquity of the sanctuary of Pachakamaj are remarkably confirmed, a fact which has so much more significance in view of the ever growing tendency among archæologists to discredit the reports of early chroniclers and to consider them as more or less willful fabrications, although they are obliged to depend almost entirely upon their testimony, and are in this case, fortunately, quite safe in doing so.

CHAPTER IX.

DISCOVERY OF EARLIER GRAVES UNDER THE BASE OF THE TEMPLE.

THE open ground which surrounds the temple furnishes a vast field for exploration, and was made the object of research by many former explorers as well as by the writer of the present report. The terraces b,[1] dating from explorations in early Spanish times, covered a great many graves of

ground before it was so much disturbed. The cemetery was found to extend partly under the wall of the temple, and as this section must have been covered and built over a long time before the Spaniards came, explorations on this spot seemed to be promising of interesting results, since the covering up of this

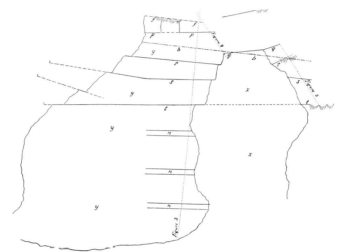

Fig. 2. Plan of cemetery at the foot and under the base of the temple. Sc. 1.240 (site of explorations).

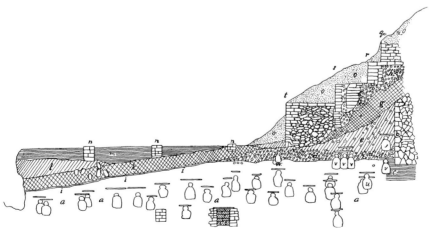

Figs. 3–5. Sectional views of the cemetery at the foot and under the base of the temple of Pachakamaj. Sc. 1.120.

the ancient cemetery, thereby saving them from the ravages of treasure-seekers. These graves date from the same period as the rest of the burial ground, since the soil was piled up above them long after this field had ceased to be used as a cemetery, and from them we may judge of the condition of this burial

territory at some early pre-Spanish period formed, to a certain degree, a preclusive time-limit for the construction of those graves, and it seemed probable that they would shed some light on the time of erection of those parts of the temple as well as give us some new clues concerning the relative age of the various classes of graves found here. The trenches made

[1] Plan, pl. 4.

for the exploration of this section were cut through several terraces and substructures of the temple, then continued in a horizontal line until a natural obstruction was reached in the front part. The local conditions are reproduced on the diagram of these explorations, fig. 2, and in a transverse section of the same, figs. 3–5.

Fig. 2; scale 1.240.

x, site of the former excavation of a treasure digger; *y,* territory of writer's explorations; *n, n, n,* foundations of pre-Spanish buildings in front of the temple façade; *f, p, q,*

thickness had apparently been spread over the soil underneath as a foundation for the building which was to be erected there. In addition to a wall, *f,* which seemed to rest upon some point above this stratum, there were built upon it the walls of terraces, *p, q, r, s, t,* see figs. 3–5, of various heights. During the centuries since the conquest these terraces were covered by sand, as indicated near *o* in fig. 3, while fig. 4 shows them in their present uncovered state. The wall *p,* fig. 4, was built against *f,* concealing it completely. During the progress of excavations in the direction

 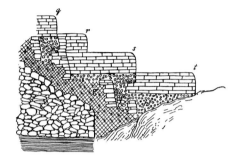

Fig. 4. Section of temple-terraces at the site of explorations, of fig. 2.

Fig. 5. Similar section. Sc. 1.120.

r, s, t, terrace walls; *b,* a covered stone wall in the interior of the temple.

Figs. 4–5; scale 1.120.

The outlines of the transverse section of figs. 3 to 5 are explained in the diagram, fig. 2. Figs. 3 to 5 have the same marking-letters as fig. 2. The original soil, *y,* figs. 2, 3, sloped down to the ancient stone wall *b,* in the interior of the temple, figs. 2–5. The latter, built of broken stones without mortar, was sunk about one foot deep into the original soil and rested upon a stratum of clay two feet in thickness, *c,* figs. 3–5, which extended a foot and a half beyond the wall. The exposed section of this wall decreased irregularly from the northern to the southern end from a height of ten feet to four feet. Also the filling of the wall in the rear had an irregular appearance, clearly it was not in its natural condition, but a ruin, and a very ancient one, too. In front of this

of the stone wall *b,* a fragment of masonry, *p,* fell and unexpectedly disclosed a section of wall which was covered with frescoing. The design was faint and barely traceable in its general outlines; it showed human figures in yellow, white or a greenish tint with black contours painted upon a background of red. The further uncovering of the wall, as far as it was still in tolerable preservation, exposed to view eight human figures, arranged as if walking in a procession, some of them connected by a line, as by a rope; there was also some oval object indicated (see fig. 6). This mural painting, in point of style, has no relation to any other find made at Pachacamac, nor to any object of Peruvian antiquity, except, perhaps, to the designs upon some of the most important of the Chimu vases from the region of Chimbote, Trujillo, etc., a number of interesting examples of which can be seen in the Museum of Berlin. It would be rash to insist upon any close

Fig. 6. Mural painting exposed by excavations. Ab. ⅓₂ n. s.

wall was found a stratum of adobe all broken and of irregular sizes, some of them decorated on their sides, *d,* figs. 2–5; this layer rested upon the natural soil of the burial-ground. A stratum of earth, *e,* figs. 3–4, in which only a few broken adobe bricks were found, extended to the upper edge of the ruined wall, *b.* A stratum of grave-soil, figs. 3–5, full of fragments of all kinds, was found above the former; it was intermingled with pieces of cane, llama bones, skulls, braids of human hair, pieces of rush ropes, scraps of cloth, a few fragments of crude pottery, etc. This layer of uneven

relation between these ceramic designs and the mural painting, especially since the latter is so very poorly preserved; still, in both of them there appears the processional arrangement of the figures and the same way of expressing motion, as, for instance, on the Chimu vase with the dance of the dead in the Berlin Museum. This mural painting, therefore, may bear some relation to the art of the Chimu.

The walls, figs. 7 and 8 and fig. 9, also showed some well preserved frescoing in bluish green, red and yellow.

The design of fig. 7 cannot be interpreted. Fig. 8 seems

to have figures somewhat resembling birds in the conventional style of the textile designs of the coastland.[1] Fig. 9 shows distinctly the form of fishes, probably sharks; there seems to be a striking similarity of design in the type of this pattern with that of a carved wooden bowl, fig. 95, of the time of the Incas.

The original soil in front of the temple terrace, figs. 2, 3, near *n, n, n*, was at some early period covered over in order to raise the grade of the ground about the terraces, where it was too sloping. A thin layer of leaves of the Pakai tree,[2]

mummies indicated near *u*, fig. 3, nearest the temple. These graves are marked by the objects found therein as belonging to the period of the style of Tiahuanaco and the one immediately following.

2. Graves of the oldest superposed soil, *d, e*, over the original cemetery, which were made previous to the construction of the temple terraces upon this ground; these graves are marked *v*, fig. 3. The cultural character belonging to these burials differs widely from that of the first stratum; a faint resemblance to the earlier style can be traced in these

Fig. 7. Fragments of painting on the wall of a temple terrace. Ab. $\frac{1}{15}$ n. s.

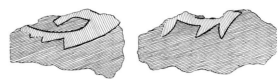

Fig. 8. Traces of mural painting on another spot of the same wall. Ab. $\frac{1}{15}$ n. s.

i, fig. 3, which may have been taken out of the fillings of old mummy packings, were the foundations; over this was an even stratum of one foot eight inches of grave soil, *k*, intermingled with scraps of cotton, cloth, pieces of straw-rope, slings, etc. A layer of common dirt was met near *l*, and the stratum *m* had finally been laid upon it for grading before the walls *n, n, n*, were set upon this soil. In this manner the section, *y*, fig. 2, immediately in front of the temple terrace, was in pre-Spanish time raised from two feet six inches to ten feet above its original level at the time of construction of

objects, but the technique, form and ornamentation show a new type, artistically inferior to the former.

3. A few graves situated in front of the temple, dating from a time after the erection of structures over the original cemetery, *y*, and of the graves, *v*, as well as the terraces, *q, r, s, t;* these graves are marked *w* on the cross section of this burial ground.

These graves are marked by objects of the Cuzco type or of that of the coastland, differing from the objects found in the open sections of cemetery *I*, which belong to an earlier

Fig. 9. Mural painting—Fishes, on another terrace wall. Ab. $\frac{1}{15}$ n. s

t, and this was the reason that no more burials were made in this locality.

It must be observed that to the three stages of soil, as it was demonstrated here, correspond three stages of burials, each of a different cultural character.

1. The graves in the original burial ground, *y*; the

type of the Peruvian coast-style. Below *n*, near *l* and *k*, fig. 3, some few unimportant mummies of children were found. It would be a mistake to speak of a regular and intentional stratification of these graves, since the relative depth of the graves entirely depends on the thickness of the soil-stratum in which they happen to be.[3]

[1] Cf. Reiss u. Stübel, The Necropolis of Ancon, pl. 64, fig. 2.
[2] Inga feuilli D. C. Cf. Wittmark, Congrès des amér., Berlin, 1888, p. 328. The fruit of this tree is often found in graves of this cemetery, together with its leaves, which were generally used as stuffing for the mummy bales.

[3] Squier, p. 72, speaks of strata in which the dead were buried, wherefrom it might appear that he observed stratifications of graves in the open parts of the cemetery, which would be erroneous, as there are none to be found there.

CHAPTER X.

GRAVE-FINDS.

GRAVES OF THE ANCIENT CEMETERY UNDER THE BASE OF THE TEMPLE AND IN FRONT OF IT UNDER THE NEW SOIL.

THESE graves were found at various depths below the original surface, but without any distinguishing marks whereby their respective ages might be established. The vertical plane of the uppermost graves was barely one foot six inches below the surface, while others were as deep as ten feet underground. These tombs generally were constructed in a very solid manner, built of stone or adobe in the form of chambers of a conical or cylindrical form, rarely square; a few were roofed over with stone, but the majority had a covering of cane, matting or some similar material. In some instances the roof was supported by a pole in the centre or it was covered with wood. The mummies generally are in the shape of bales or packages,[1] with a false human head attached,

the face of which is carved of wood or is merely painted upon a stuffed cushion, or occasionally made of burned clay and crudely tinted. The types were of the general class as given by Reiss u. Stübel in The Necropolis of Ancon, pls. 14–19.[2] The position of the mummies was found to be similar in most cases, facing east and the temple at the same time.[3]

---

[1] Although this type is quite rare among the mummies of the open cemetery it must not be regarded as exclusively ancient. The mummy, Reiss u. Stübel, l. c., pls. 12, 13, belongs to the Inca period, to judge by the stuffs with which it is covered; also, Cieza, Cron., I, chap. 62, states that in his time similar mummies were still prepared at Jauja. The mummy types as given by Squier, p. 73, and Middendorf, II, p. 117, in the description of Pachacamac, have no resemblance with any actually found there.

[2] Peru, I, 398.

[3] Tschudi's statement that the mummies faced west must therefore be corrected.

FINDS IN THE STYLE OF TIAHUANACO.

Only a small number of specimens were found and those intermingled with objects of younger, kindred or alien styles; objects shown in pl. 4, figs. 1 and 3, were taken from the same grave with pieces of pottery, pl. 5, figs. 1, 9, 10, 11. The association with articles of more recent date seems to prove that the specimens in the Tiahuanaco style were ancient ones at the time when these burials took place, since a grave must be dated by the youngest objects found in it. None of these graves, therefore, dated further back than the cultural period subsequent to and developing from the Tiahuanaco style. This conclusion is in harmony with another indication which points to the time when the temple was first built: a few decorated fragments of pottery were found during our operations near l, pl. 3, clearly belonging together, yet picked up at various depths. From their decoration they were assigned to the period described, p. 24, and seem to indicate that at least a part of the oldest temple structure was built during that period. The presence of articles in the style of Tiahuanaco in the graves is a proof that this period was still within the remembrance and feeling of the living when these graves were constructed. The graves containing objects of this class were the oldest in the cemetery and therefore most damaged by subsequent burials; for the older a grave is, the greater the danger of such a destruction. One object preserved of an ancient period must be regarded as a representative specimen of a larger number of similar ones, than would be one object of a relatively younger epoch. We

may, therefore, assume that originally this oldest period was far more numerously represented in these graves than it would appear at the present moment; many fragments of pottery, decorated in the Tiahuanaco style, dating from early graves and destroyed by later burials, were picked up during our explorations.

Pl. 4, figs. 1 a–1 c: Pieces of cloth painted with mythological figures; 26721, Mus. of Sc. and Art; $\frac{1}{10}$ n. s. This stuff was found, with the pieces of pottery above mentioned, near the mummy marked u, fig. 3. By its favorable position, being closely set against the stone wall b, fig. 3, this mummy escaped destruction. The stuff was folded double down the middle of the central figure, the painted surface turned outside, and was used to envelope a mummy bale and the back of its false head; in unwrapping the latter, the cloth was found to be in five pieces, three larger and two smaller ones, the edges of which were much rotten. The stuff may have been in fragments when the mummy bale was made; but it is also possible that the stuff, when folded, was in one piece, for the damaged spots which appeared, when unwrapped, were in each case symmetrical, figs. a, b and c, d and e;[1] some rents in the cloth had been mended before it was used to wrap the mummy. The original length of this piece of stuff cannot

---

[1] A few rotten fragments of the cloth dropped off since it was found, but fortunately the design had been copied previously, so of the lower parts of the central fig. a. The design of the latter in pl. 4 is completed with dotted lines. The texture of the cloth is still much firmer than it might be supposed from the decayed condition of the edges.

be estimated; it was woven in one width of three feet eleven inches; the material is a white cotton fabric, the warp of double threads and the woof thicker than the single warp-thread; it had twelve threads of woof to twenty-six of warp to the half inch.

The design upon this cloth is outlined in brown, filled in with a light yellowish brown, blue and red; the red color is of an ochrous substance, the others seem to be some organic pigments. Only a few colors were used, but each of these appears to have some special meaning; red possibly stood for gold, since the head ornaments are in that color; blue may have been used for silver; the yellowish brown for copper. In the three largest fragments of the fabric three figures may be traced, which stand full front, while two outer figures stand facing the central one. The grouping here is the same as in the sculptured relief upon the large gateway of Tiahuanaco.[1] There are some additional points of stylistic resemblance with the former design: the division of the space into squares, each of which is filled with one figure; also the hands,[2] the peculiar ring-shaped end of the noses[3] of some figures, and the heads of animals attached to various parts of these figures, to their feet, etc.[4]

The central figure is three feet eleven inches high, and if the same space were allowed for the two side figures, figs. 1 b and 1 c, the stuff would have been fully eleven feet six inches long; however, the three fragments, figs. 1 a–c, do not fit into one another in their details, and the two smallest pieces, figs. 1 d and e, show one right and one left hand with adhering parts which would not fit into the design anywhere if it had consisted of these three sections only. It seems, therefore, as if one section of each had disappeared between 1 a and 1 b and 1 c; at this rate the design may originally have had five sections and its full length may have been fully twenty feet. The central figure has an ornamental belt, armlets and anklets, ear and head-ornaments,[5] the latter with long-necked snakeheads drooping from it on both sides; hooked lines are indicated at the corners of the mouth. One hand of the figure holds a broad knife of the usual shape, while the other is grasping a human head by the hair. The figure is represented apparently after having decapitated a person; and more severed heads are suspended like trophies on the breast of the figure.

The awe- and terror-inspiring nature of the deity is further indicated by the snakeheads upon long necks which protrude from all parts of the body and from the headdress, from the hand, shoulder, elbow, breast, hips, etc., even from the knife-handle, from the topknot[6] and from the severed neck of the head held by the figure in its hands. Nearly all of them are stretching sideways and at the same time symmetrically filling the space about the figure. They are dotted all over with red, blue and brown spots, which are probably intended to indicate metals or precious stones. The snakeheads are crowned with a square ornament like the feathered serpent of Quetzalcoatl of Mexican myths;[7] and all of them appear in profile and have ears,[8] while the half-opened mouth shows its fangs; the end of the nose seems curved backward.

The heads of the side figures are in profile, while the rest

of the figure appears in full front; the lower parts are missing, also an arm of each and the greater part of the headdress; both have some ornament near the eye and the tongue is protruding, the same as with the trophy-heads; the nose is shaped differently, which shows an intentional mythological individualization; the objects which they hold in their hands are different; the right hand of the figure to the left holds only serpents, the left hand of the other figure a large knife; the missing figure, next to the central one, to the left, held a detached human head with its left hand, fig. 1 d. The filling of the remaining space with serpents' heads is the same as with the central fig. 1 a. The interesting design which covers the remaining space we owe, perhaps, to the accident that the entire right-hand side was left free. These figures therefore were added to cover the space, as if to indicate that they do not belong to the central figure and perhaps also to mark the terror which the serpents inspire, they are all turned away from the deity. There are four figures, the upper ones of which, for lack of space, are only indicated by their crowned heads. Nothing terrible can be noticed upon them, the only feature which might be called mythological is the ring-shaped nose of the lowest one. The latter resembles the two dwarf-like figures on the relief of the Gate at Tiahuanaco,[9] and the tufted crown, the head and the entire body, each occupy the same amount of space. A poncho and a girdle, anklets and armlets are the ornaments of the figure; on its breast is marked a crescent-shaped shield, the left hand is raised to the mouth, while the drooping right hand seems to hold a doll. The figure above is bent in a semicircle, while its feet are resting against the right-hand edge, probably for lack of another point of support in the space. It wears only a red garment, poncho, and an indented crown, similar to that worn by the severed heads and it may also be supposed to wear a girdle. This piece of cloth which, judging from its size and its peculiar ornamentation, probably came to be used as a mummy-wrapper in some accidental way, originally must have been used to decorate a temple wall, as an object of worship in itself.

Pl. 4, fig. 2: A figure with head and wings of a bird from a tapestry poncho. The present figure was completely reconstructed from several fragments of stuff, each of which showed the figure imperfectly. The original stuff was a black tapestry poncho, the pattern of which showed regular squares with the design of the above figure, repeated in rows, similar to the pattern in the tapestry poncho found at Ancon.[10] The rep-like fabric is of the finest wool, of 114 threads of the woolen woof to twenty threads of cotton warp to the half inch. The colors are bright, as in all stuffs of this period, green with white, red and yellow, blue with yellow, red and brown. The figure is an exact repetition of the sceptre-holding winged figures of the second row upon the Gate of Tiahuanaco,[11] with the only difference that the rectangular spaces are more closely filled and that the figures are stiffer. The heads of animals on the crown are also changed; the heads set upon the wings are simpler in form and a small head, like that of a fish, was added to fill the space near the sole of the hindfoot.[12]

The same figure as the above is shown on another fragment of a much finer material, which has 80 by 116 threads to the half inch and belongs also to a tapestry poncho. The figure here is on a yellow ground of brighter coloring and

[1] Stübel u. Uhle, Die Ruinenstätte von Tiahuanaco, pl. 5, fig. 2.
[2] L. c., pls. 8, 11, 15, 16, figs. 1–3.
[3] Comp. with heads of puma, l. c., pls. 8, 10, 15, 16, fig. 3, and notes to pl. 8, No. 2.
[4] Comp. l. c., pl. 16, figs. 1–3.
[5] For the band-like pendants of the headdress compare the head ornaments of various stone figures in the Ruins of Tiahuanaco, Stübel u. Uhle, pl. 31.
[6] Cf. Ruinenstätte of Tiahuanaco, pls. 8, 9.
[7] A feathered serpent of a different variety is on a vessel in the Berlin Museum.
[8] A serpent with ears appears on a stone sculpture of Tiahuanaco, also on serpents of gold of the Chilchas, Colombia, Kult. u. Indust., I, pl. 22.

[9] Stübel u. Uhle, l. c., pls. 17 and 21, figs. 1, 2.
[10] Reiss u. Stübel, l. c., pl. 49; cf. also Stübel u. Uhle, pl. 21, fig. 3.
[11] Stübel u. Uhle, l. c., pls. 13–15.
[12] Comp. the latter ornament to the heads and necks of animals attached to the points of the feet, fig. 1 a; also Stübel u. Uhle, pl. 21, figs. 1–3.

narrower. The poncho of which this piece is a fragment might have been a copy of the former, as the figures in both have the same height, six and five-eighths inches, and the design may originally have been of the same width, five and five-eighths instead of four and one-fourth inches, only it was more drawn in in weaving, the warp threads being contracted by the woof. The greater stiffness in the design of both these stuffs compared to the sculptured figures at Tiahuanaco was not caused by the weaving alone, as the figures of the poncho of Ancon show a much easier treatment of form, therefore it may be explained by a somewhat later date of origin. It is unlikely, too, that the very artistic arrangement of the bird in the square spaces of these stuffs could be older than the much easier arrangement of these figures in the stone sculpture. The exact repetition of the figures from the Gate of Tiahuanaco in these textiles is an interesting evidence of the great importance they must have had to the contemporaries. Even if the designs should have been entirely original with the makers, which is improbable, it would only show that the same ideas which caused the creation of the works of Tiahuanaco were at work in an entire people.

Pl. 4, fig. 3: Cup with two faces, of clay. 26707 Mus. of Sc. and Art. This cup was taken from the same grave, *u*, fig. 3, p. 19, as pl. 4, fig. 1. The object possesses all the technical perfections of the pottery of the Tiahuanaco style, and which was only matched, or in some respects excelled, by the art of the Chimu.

The design inside represented three figures facing front, like the central figure of the Gate in Tiahuanaco, each of them holding coiled serpents instead of a sceptre; they are clothed in a poncho with bands encircling wrists and ankles, the same as the figures on the right-hand side on pl. 4, fig. 1 *c*. The head may have been turned sideways as in the fragment of fig. 13, which, the same as fig. 12, belongs to a smaller vessel of a similar kind; this head resembles a dog's head[1] and wears a square headdress.[2] The linear design of pl. 4, fig. 4, is repeated on the rim; a ring-shaped animal's figure in outline runs around the outside of the vessel.

Pl. 4, fig. 5: Ear ornaments of wood, inlaid with pieces of shell. Mus. of Sc. and Art 26720. This object is in the shape of a pipe bent in an angle; it consists of a head with a piece attached to it like a stem, and which is also hollowed out like a pipe; but the vertical stem is so narrow that it may have been used as a holder of a small tuft of feathers.[3] The face shows the fine relief which is peculiar to this period and may be noticed on ceramics, stone sculptures, etc.[4] The natural form of the eye with the pupil is surprising for this early period.[5] A diadem encircles the forehead and triangular bits of shell were inlaid on the cheeks and above the diadem.[6]

Conclusions: The above described specimens in the style of Tiahuanaco are closely related to the objects known as coming from the ruins of Tiahuanaco; the flying and running bird on vessel, fig. 4, also harmonizes well with these designs, although nothing exactly similar has so far been

Figs. 10–13. Fragments of two or three vessels with a similar design, mythological figures, Tiahuanaco style. ¼ n. s.

The pottery of this period shows a greater variety of colors than any of the later styles; the same may be said of the textiles of this period. This cup, for instance, has red, yellow, gray, white and black in its decoration. The mouth shows four tusk-like teeth and scroll ornaments and wings are joined on to the eyes; lines of yellow scallops border the face above and below. The nose of one of the faces is gone, which helps to prove that these specimens of the Tiahuanaco style were old when put into these graves.

Pl. 4, fig. 4: Flask with bent neck, decorated with two birds. 26709 Mus. of Sc. and Art. The design on a red ground, as in fig. 3, is also bright in color; the two birds seem to be both in rapid flight and running; they must have some mythological significance, as each has a hand and a foot and some object hangs by a thread from their beaks, the meaning of which has not yet been guessed. The figures are separated by a linear design in black and white.

Among fragments of pottery belonging to this style worthy of notice are figs. 10–13, 26712 *a*, Mus. of Sc. and Art. These belonged to decorated vessels of a flaring shape, thick and well baked and not very porous, the decoration of the inside consisted of mythological figures and some had a simpler design on the outside. Figs. 10 and 11 must be parts of the same vessel, of about six inches in diameter at the bottom by fourteen inches at the rim and seven inches in height, with five-sixteenths of an inch in thickness.

found there; it is related to the kneeling winged figures in the relief of the large Gate, as well as to a seated monster with wings like fig. 14, and appeared also upon a vessel found at Tiahuanaco.

Then, on the other hand, there are features of less convincing nature. Bottle-shaped specimens, such as pl. 4, fig. 4, have, to our knowledge, not been found yet at Tiahuanaco, and although this object cannot be assigned to the northern Peruvian coast, yet forms similar to this one are rather frequent there; it may, therefore, be assumed that this flask was produced in Peru and not in Tiahuanaco, south of the Lake Titicaca. A decorative use of serpents, as seen in pl. 4, fig. 1, and in figs. 10–13 of the text, above, is foreign to the style of Tiahuanaco. It may be said to bear relation to the remains of the style of Chavin de Huantar, in the province of Ancacho,[7] although they cannot have been quite unknown in southern Peru.[8] Tusks in human faces, as in pl. 4, fig. 3, are not confirmed in Tiahuanaco, but seem sufficiently supported in the stone sculpture of Chavin. The dog's head

---

[1] Cf. fig. 11.
[2] Cf. thread ornament of main figure, pl. 4, fig. 1 *a*.
[3] Cf. besides pl. 4, fig. 3, Stübel u. Uhle, *l. c.*, pl. 4, fig. 4; pl. 8; etc.
[4] Cf. ear ornament, pl. 4. fig. 1 *a–c*.
[5] The eyes on cups, pl. 4, fig. 3, are indicated in a similar manner.
[6] Cf. pl. 90, fig. 13.
[7] The sculptured relief of Chavin, reproduced by Middendorf, Peru, I, p. 631, and a carved column, reproduced by Wiener, p. 575, and differently by Middendorf, *l. c.*, III, p. 99.
[8] From a stone sculpture from Cuzco, Mus. of Sc. and Art.

upon a human body, as well as the manner in which the detached human heads are held by the hair, have a strange appearance, as in pl. 4, fig. 1 *a*, this has a greater resemblance to the design upon the central vase, Squier, p. 458, which belongs to this style and was found near Cuzco, than to the suspended head trophies as seen on the main figure of the relief of the large Gate.[1] All these details taken together help to prove that, in addition to the district of Lake Titicaca, there must have been another important locality to which this style was peculiar. The specimens from Pachacamac seem to

come mainly from the latter, as they were not produced at Pachacamac and only a few of them might possibly have been brought from the shores of the Titicaca. The examples in pl.

Fig. 14. Mythological winged animal. Design on ancient cup from Tiahuanaco.
⅓ n. s.

4, figs. 2–3, sufficiently support the proof of a direct, inward and cultural connection with the most important monument of his style.

[1] Stübel u. Uhle, pl. 8.

CHAPTER XI.

FINDS IN THE EPIGONE STYLE.

FOR lack of a more fitting term, we designated as the Epigone style that cultural type which, although closely related to the style of Tiahuanaco, is inferior to its famous prototype in almost every respect. Objects of this class predominate in the graves under the covered section *a* of the original cemetery. Articles of utility are especially numerous among these; some classes of these specimens appear at all periods alike, workbaskets for instance, while others are peculiar to this particular period, among which are certain types of pottery, textiles, some carved sticks of wood, spinning whorls and ornaments of shell, bone or tooth.

A. POTTERY.

The shapes of the pottery of this period show in general the same types as those of the former period. 1. Cups, see pl. 5, figs. 1 to 4 and 7. 2. Bowls, see below, fig. 17; these resemble vessels of which fragments figs. 10–13 are parts. 3. Vases with bottle-necks, see pl. 5, fig. 5. 4. Vessels shaped like animals, having the opening in the back,

cat, pl. 5, figs. 6 *a* and *b*. 5. An important ornamental detail, derived from Tiahuanaco, where it occurs frequently, the triple, seldom quadruple, tufted headdress.

The decorative designs of numerous vessels doubtless have some religious significance. The sceptre-holding figure is identical with the image of the divinity pictured in the Gate relief and elsewhere; the condor has a mythological meaning in Peru and the running and flying condor much more so, as it is always pictured in connection with mythological figures, as in the design pl. 4, fig. 4; concerning the mythological nature of the cat, pl. 5, fig. 6, compare the description of the same. All this is easily explained, when it is remembered that these vessels were mostly used with the 'chicha' drinking at religious festivals, and were for that reason decorated with designs having some religious significance. During this Epigone period religious ideas still found expression in the typical mythological figures which the classic period of the Tiahuanaco style bequeathed to the following generations, and we are indebted to the religious customs of these Peruvians for many specimens which demon-

Fig. 15. Fragment of cup, Epigone period. ⅓ n. s.

Fig. 16. Complete design of cup, pl. 5, fig. 2.

such as pl. 5, figs. 6 *a* and *b;* all these ceramic types are familiar ones from Tiahuanaco. 5. A number of pieces of this period resemble the vessel, pl. 4, fig. 4.[1] These objects are technically inferior to the products of the earlier period, both in shape and color,[2] although the decorations upon the earlier specimens bear quite a strong resemblance to those of the classic epoch. The most important decorative types are these: 1. A figure bearing a sceptre and seen full front, like the central figure of the Tiahuanaco Gate or of the relief of Chavin.[3] 2. A condor's head, as it appears upon the Gate and upon many other objects from Tiahuanaco; compare pl. 5, fig. 3. 3. The condor in flying and running motion; compare the figures upon vessel, pl. 4, fig. 4; also fig. 19 below. 4. An animal type resembling a cat, apparently a mountain

strate the close connection between this period and the preceding one.[4]

Pl. 5, fig. 4: Cup with square face, imperfectly preserved. 26724, Mus.; ⅓ n. s. The face only with a headdress is to be seen here and with some decorations to indicate the clothing. The descent of this design from the type of Tiahuanaco is proved by many features; for instance, by the square shape of the face, its frontal position, the form of the eyes and the ornaments near them, the interlocking hooks in the headdress,[5] and the tufted effect similar to a feather crown.[6] Other cups of the same style and period have a more flaring rim and a design in red on a white ground, like fig. 15, 26723 *a*, Mus. The animal heads seem to be of

---

[1] See below, figs. 23-25. Vases with wide necks, as shown in Kultur u. Industrie, I, pl. 11, figs. 8-10, so typical for Tiahuanaco, were never found at Pachacamac.

[2] Many vessels, such as cups, bowls, flasks, are peculiarly dull in color; the cause of this may be that these articles served as drinking vessels for 'chicha.'

[3] Middendorf, Peru, I, p. 631.

[4] Therefore the local Wiracocha legend of Carabuco (Santacruz, p. 239) was reproduced upon wooden cups received by the writer at Carabuco and now in the Berlin Museum.

[5] Comp. the headdress of the figure on the Gate of Tiahuanaco, Stübel und Uhle, pl. 8; Kult. u. Ind., I, pl. 11, fig. 6.

[6] Comp. *l. c.*, pl. 11, fig. 6; also head ornaments of various sculptured figures in the Ruins of Tiahuanaco, pl. 31.

the type of foxes; the severed arms and legs in this design have a peculiarly savage appearance suggesting cannibalism.

Pl. 5, fig. 2: Cup with the figure of a divinity. 26726, Mus.; ⅓ n. s. The design represents a sceptre-holding god, as in fig. 16, and in its general outlines as well as in some minor points it is similar to the famous figure of the Gate relief. Among the analogous details are: the indented headdress, with a change of the centre to the form of rays; the vertical stripes in the poncho, and the girdle with tassels; likewise the geometrical division of the sceptres and the shape of the hands. From the close resemblance between the two designs it is supposed that both represent the same idol, and that the design upon the cup was derived from the older one. Four white teeth, distinctly visible in the mouth of the figure, bear a greater resemblance to the faces on cup, pl. 4, fig. 3, and to the figure in the stone relief of Chavin.

forms the centre; the headdress, with band ends terminating in condor heads and a plume set into it, has numerous parallels in the relief of the Gate;[3] the pendants at both sides of the head, ending in a scroll and a short plume, may be parts of a headdress.

The condor, running and flying, appears twice repeated as the decoration of a small cup, 26728, Mus., fig. 19.

Another cup, from cemetery III, 26733, Mus., is ornamented with several conventional animal heads, fig. 20, resembling those of fig. 15 above. Both are doubtless derived from the style of Tiahuanaco, judging from the hooked ornament on the neck.[4] A final interpretation of this head may be attempted only after some more specimens will be obtained, showing this figure in a more complete design.

Pl. 5, fig. 5: Vessel in the form of a figure playing upon a Pan's flute, two monkeys at its sides listening. 26747, Mus.

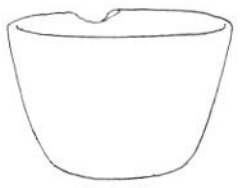

Fig. 17 *a*. Ca. 1/7 n. s.

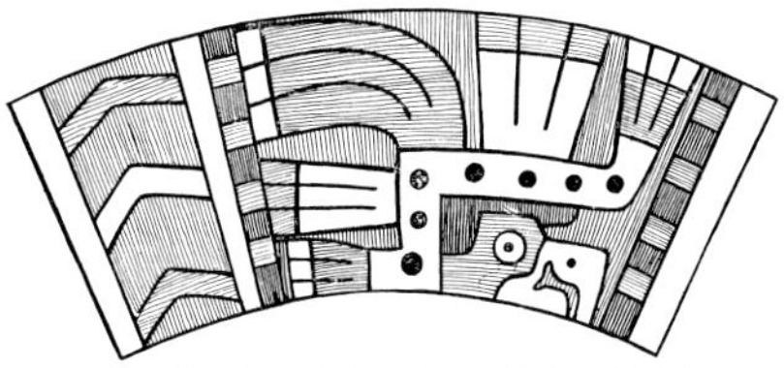

Fig. 17 *b*. Complete design of cup, pl. 5, fig. 3, Epigone period. ⅓ n. s.

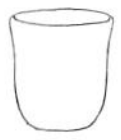

Fig. 18 *a*. Ca. 1/7 n. s.

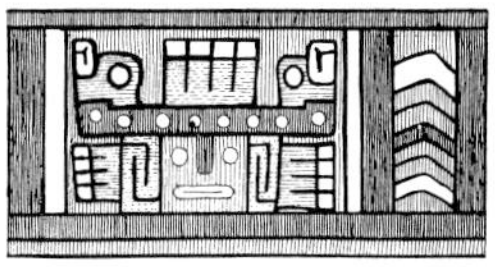

Fig. 18 *b*. Design of cup, Epigone period. ⅓ n. s.

Pl. 5, fig. 3: Cup with two condor heads. 26729, Mus. The stiffly conventionalized heads are quite in keeping with the general stylistic degeneration of this period; the head ornaments encircle the head like bands and end in feathery pendants (above, No. 5) which as a rule seem to be flying backward as if caused by the rapid motion of the creature.[1]

The bowl, fig. 17 *a*, with its decoration, fig. 17 *b* (26730 Mus.), resembles the foregoing specimen, but is of superior quality.

Pl. 5, fig. 1: Cup with two faces. 26734, Mus.; ⅓ n. s. This object was found in the same grave with the cloth, pl. 4, fig. 1, and the vessels, pl. 4, fig. 3, and pl. 5, figs. 9–11. The faces upon the cup[2] are similar to those of the cup, fig. 2, and of the famous Gate; the curved line indicating the chin must

⅓ n. s. The head and arms of the figure are modeled; the body of the vessel seems drawn in about the middle, and both the upper and the lower parts are indented like a melon; the face was painted red like the faces of mummies. The mythological nature of this figure is shown by the decoration on the body of the vessel, fig. 21; in the upper part of the design an animal is to be seen, with the head of a lizard; its tail is coiled upward and it is in rapid motion like the condor, pl. 4, fig. 4. The decoration on the lower part of the bowl consists of a crowned head, six times repeated. The pose of this figure and the hooked design of the border point to a close relation with the style of Tiahuanaco.

Pl. 5, fig. 6 *a* and *b*: Vessel shaped like a mountain cat, front and side views. Mus., 26745; ⅓ n. s. The animal is

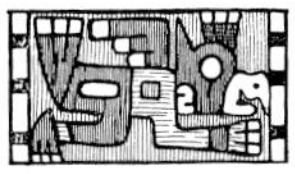

Fig. 19. Design of cup, Epigone period. ⅓ n. s.

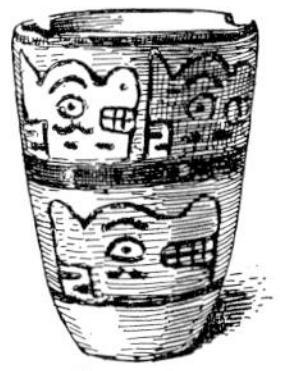

Fig. 20. Decorated cup, Epigone period. ⅓ n. s.

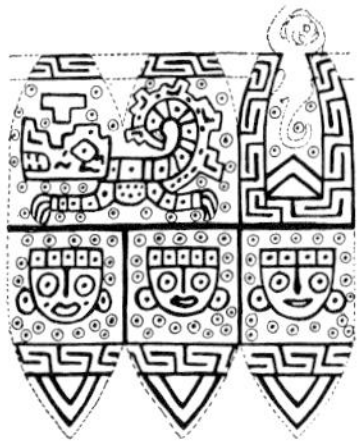

Fig. 21. Design of vase, pl. 5, fig. 5. ⅓ n. s.

be noticed; it suggests that the artist had in his mind a face in relief when he painted this, such as are shown in Kult. u. Ind., I, pl. 11, figs. 1, 2, from Tiahuanaco.

Another cup, 26710, Mus., found with the vessels above, is of a somewhat flaring shape, fig. 18 *a*. The design, like fig. 18 *b*, is twice repeated. The same head as that in fig. 16

quite realistic in modeling and coloring. The spots marked by curves and the two colors of the tail leave no doubt that the animal is meant for a mountain cat. Its name in Aimarà and in Kechua is 'titi'; and the island of Titicaca, 'Titi qaqa,' rock of the mountain cat, derives its name from this animal, which may to some extent explain its mythological importance. The coloring of this vessel presents several peculiarities: the pelt of the cat does not appear to be joined in the back, so that the tail was painted on each side of the animal, both sides meeting at the back; the animal stands on four legs of crude shape and has two arms in addition thereto

[1] Compare the rapid motion of the bird in pl. 4, fig. 4 and fig. 19 below; also the mantles of the side figures in the relief of the Gate, Stübel u. Uhle, pls. 11–15, which appear to be blown backward by the wind. It is characteristic for the divinity to be always pictured in repose, while its ministering servants are in violent motion. It must be assumed that the relief of Tiahuanaco formed the prototype for all these designs, or that the position of the divinity was represented according to a general conception entertained of it by the entire people alike; in this case the mythological significance of the relief on the Gate would gain considerably in historical perspective.

[2] A vessel of bowl shape of the same period with similar faces is shown by Reiss und Stübel, pl. 96, fig. 7.

[3] Comp. Stübel u. Uhle, pl. 8.

[4] Stübel u. Uhle, remarks pl. 8, No. 1; above, pl. 4, fig. 4.

on its forepart. The peculiarities of this object are to be explained thus: the maker had two models in his mind—one painted and the other modeled; the former, an animal resembling a cat, with hands at its forepart instead of feet, in accordance with its mythological character, and similar to the condor on vessel, pl. 4, fig. 4.[1] Among the objects from Tiahuanaco, too, are found some with the cat type in their

Fig. 22. Skull-shaped vessel from Chimbote. ⅓ n. s.

decorations, with hands instead of forefeet, where the maker had sought to express the mythological character of the animal by supplying it with human hands. The peculiar two-sided painting of the pelt with two tails originated from the attempt to make the flat painted picture of the animal distinct on both sides. Additional features clearly pointing to a dependence upon the Tiahuanaco style are to be seen in the indication of joints on the arms,[2] and in the scroll pattern

Pl. 5, fig. 11: Vessel in the form of a seated animal found like fig. 1. Mus. 26750; ⅓ n. s. The animal is represented in relief, all but the plastic head, and is colored dark red, wherever it is not engraved, as on the face, for instance, while the connecting parts on the body of the vessel show the undecorated surface of the clay. This specimen cannot be exactly placed in any of our rubrics, although it was found together with a number of objects of the Epigone style. It grows more and more apparent that contemporaneously with the development of the archaic style of Tiahuanaco in the highlands, another style may have developed elsewhere in Peru of which this present object may be a specimen. It may be said that the familiar Chimu pottery possesses some suggestive resemblances to this object, but at the same time in other respects very strong deviations.

Pl. 5, fig. 8: Vessel with conventional design.[3] Mus. 26755; ⅓ n. s. The design, divided into sections, shows a set pattern composed of rings. Objects with a similar design and with an additional decoration of some plastic small animal or human figure were numerous in the graves of this period; technically, these designs have some resemblance to those of the Epigone type. Although the character of this period is that of a general deterioration from the style of Tiahuanaco, there are some variations in the stylistic changes that may be defined specially: the figure designs in pottery

Fig. 23.　　　　　Fig. 24.　　　　　Fig. 25.

Three stages of degeneration of a bird design on objects of later period. ⅓ n. s.

bordering the rim of the vessel. This specimen was found in a grave, together with an exact counterpart.

Pl. 5, fig. 10: Vessel with two openings, a serpent; found with fig. 1, etc. Mus. 26571; ⅓ n. s. An object bent like a horn; its open mouth shows fangs, and its body is decorated with white dots upon dark lines on both sides of the creature. This characteristic pattern occurs on various plainer vessels of the period, and may be supposed in most cases to represent the design of the snake skin.

Pl. 5, fig. 9: Vessel in the shape of a cat. Found together with fig. 1, etc. Mus. 26752; ⅓ n. s. The head shaped like a ball has a shallow square mouth, a rather flat nose, and deep cavities for the eyes, which like the mouth have lines in them to indicate teeth and eyelashes. In its general character, and especially in the deep-set eyes, the vessel resembles those in the shape of skulls, one of which the writer found in fragments in a cemetery near Chimbote, fig. 22, Mus. 34334. The maker of the above vessel had probably a model of this kind before him, although the shape of mouth and ears shows that he intended to model a cat's head, and by the details of decoration the resemblance to a skull was lessened still more.

degenerate in various ways, mostly by shrinking into geometrical patterns. The style of Tiahuanaco, among others, uses the figure of a bird spreading about the neck of a vase.[4] This figure by progressive degeneration changed to patterns like those of pl. 4, fig. 4, or figs. 23–25. Objects with this decorative type were numerous in the above-mentioned graves.

Another class of vessels is decorated with textile patterns, wherein the variation of the figure pattern of an earlier period is still traceable in the main outlines. To this class belongs:

Pl. 5, fig. 7: Cup with polychrome decoration. Mus. 26792; ⅓ n. s. The clay of this object is granular and brittle, and the shape is inferior; the decoration is arranged in sections, each of which is filled with an irregular design and a textile pattern, the figures of which were changed into scrolls; the design is the same as that of pl. 6, fig. 9. Many vessels are decorated with typical textile patterns without any material change; meander borders are frequent; fig. 26 shows one of these which runs like a band around a plain vessel. A large number of objects decorated with textile patterns are only represented by many fragments, having been destroyed by later burials; among these are parts of bowls and vases with cylindrical necks, the lower parts of which had the shape of birds, and terminated in a point shaped like a bird's tail.

---

[1] Comp. heads resembling the puma in the Gate relief, the mythological significance of which may be similar to that of the mountain cat. Comp. Francisco de Avila, p. 128.
[2] Cf. Stübel u. Uhle, pl. 21, fig. 3; also pls. 11–15 and present report, pl. 4, fig. 2.

[3] Attached to this vessel is a thin string with which it was found.
[4] Kult. u. Ind., I, pl. 11, figs. 9 and 9 a.

Some of the fragments with these typical decorations are shown in figs. 27 to 29; another ornamental type to be found among these vessels is an inverted rhomboid figure, as in figs. 27 and 29, while fig. 30 shows the same design applied to textiles. The two vessels, pl. 5, figs. 12 and 13, were, for this cemetery, in a certain sense, the forerunners of the subsequent period. Their light ground, which allows of no coloring except in the three tints, white, light red, black, as in fig. 12, also the technique, justifies their classification with objects of the next period, yet certain points connect these vessels with the group found in the graves here described. The locality in which each object was found is a point of importance, and helps to interpret the same. Fig. 12 was found at a great depth; fig. 13 was taken from the same grave with the vessel of the Epigone period, pl. 5, fig. 5. The same degree of excellence of technique, as shown by figs. 12 and 13, was never seen in objects from graves of subsequent periods. Both these specimens show a textile design with a conventional animal motive, similar to that of pl. 5, fig. 7, which is quite general in the textiles of that period,[1] while only in a single instance did it appear upon an object of the later period.

Pl. 5, figs. 12 *a* and 12 *b* : Large object, a cat ready to jump. Mus. 26744; ¼ n. s. The head of the animal, showing mouth, teeth and tongue, is quite naturally formed, while the body is of pear shape; the position of the feet is characteristic, and the paws are very well formed. The ground color of this specimen is white, with a textile pattern in red and black upon it.

Pl. 5, fig. 13: Vase decorated with a human face upon

us the different technical procedures nor the treatment of the decorative elements. Even now we would know but little more, as the only specimen, a cotton cloth with a design painted upon it, gives little additional information; but as the pottery of the classical period gave clues for the interpretation of the pottery of the Epigone style, so we may interpret in a similar way, but in inverted order, the technique and decorative types of the textiles of the earlier period by that of the subsequent epoch, and we find that these fabrics are really the oldest existing specimens of the textile art of ancient Peru, of which we are able to fix the period, not including the tapestry poncho among woven fabrics. A number of stuffs were found at Ancon, all of the same class and period, but the circumstances of their discovery were not as favorable as those of Pachacamac to the determining of their age, which we now know as being that of the period of transition between the style of Tiahuanaco and that of the coast, and they were at first not valued as much as they are now that their high antiquity is recognized. The high degree of perfection of the textile art during the Epigone period, which is only equaled by that of the later period, the coast style, permits us to form conjectures as to the high qualities of the weaver's art of Tiahuanaco, the earliest cultural period of which we have any knowledge. Thus the textiles of this period help to support the theory expressed before: however remote the age of the Tiahuanaco style and however isolated its position at the beginning of the development of Peru, it must have been preceded by an immeasurably long period of cultural development, of which, as yet,

Fig. 26. Mus. 26748. ⅓ n. s.

Fig. 27. Mus. 27596 *g*.

Fig. 28. Mus. 27596 *f*.

Fig. 29. Mus. 26863 *a*.

its neck, and a rattle in its hollow base. Mus. 26807; ⅓ n. s. The plastic face wears a peculiarly grave expression, and a black decoration is painted upon its cheeks like a beard; the body of the vessel shows four conventional animal heads upon a light ground, similar to figs. 15 and 20 above, or upon vessels like pl. 7, fig. 1, belonging to the subsequent period and to be described below. The open work of the hollow base, which is filled with balls of clay, shows a textile pattern resembling those of fig. 7 and fig. 12 of pl. 6.

B. Textiles.

We possess but a small number of well preserved textiles of this epoch: some fragments of ponchos, a few forehead bands, a belt, etc., not enough to furnish a complete picture of the decorative designs of this period, but of great archæological importance. The ceramic art of the period of Tiahuanaco is sufficiently well known in its various types, but the knowledge of the textile fabrics of the same age was for a long time limited to a single specimen, the valuable tapestry poncho found at Ancon by Reiss and Stübel.[2] This piece of very fine quality testifies to the high degree of perfection reached by the weaver's art at that early period, which rivals that of contemporaneous ceramic art.

The peculiarities of the textile art of that period were not to be learned from this single specimen; it did not teach

we have no knowledge, although there may still be traces of it in existence.

We probably do not possess specimens of all the different technical types of the textile art of the Epigone style, but we can clearly define the following groups from the pieces now known to us:

1. Tapestries.
2. Plain stuffs.
3. Figured stuffs, the patterns of which are produced by coloring: *a*, the figures painted upon the stuff, pl. 4, fig. 1; *b*, the patterns obtained by dyeing in such manner that spots which were not to be touched by the liquid dye were drawn tightly together, fig. 31, below.
4. Figured stuffs, the patterns woven in the cloth: *a*, by warp threads of special colors, which were according to the pattern either woven in or left loose, pl. 6, fig. 14.
5. Stuffs with embroidered patterns, pl. 6, figs. 1–4.
6. Woven braids: *a*, flat braids, pl. 6, fig. 9; *b*, tubular braids, resembling the double stuff and having a round woof,[3] as in certain narrow head bands.
7. Various kinds of braided work, such as: *a*, a finishing edge for tapestries forming a band of braid, wherein at regular intervals the loose ends of the woof are caught together, pl. 6, fig. 7, this edge may be seen on several tapestries of this period; *b*, irregularly shaped braids, one of this class repeats the pattern of the stuff in its doubly edged outlines; *c*, tassels, pl. 6, fig. 9.

[1] See pl. 6, figs. 9 and 12.
[2] Reiss u. Stübel, pl. 49.

[3] The same technique is seen in the string of a wallet, pl. 18, fig. 13, but the design seems to be of an earlier type.

Certain types of vessels were described as presenting important features for the study of the ornament, and there are tapestries and embroidered stuffs which are valuable for the same reasons. Both classes of specimens are decorated with mythological figures, whereby the purpose of these articles is indicated. The tapestries are of a superior, more artistic type than the other stuffs, and seem to have been used for robes of ceremonial character. Embroidery appears upon many stuffs of a superior class and the designs are mostly of the mythological order. The dead were occasionally buried with small pieces of stuff which apparently possessed the character of a fetich. A small number of these pieces were found, some of them embroidered with simple mythological figures; the pieces were laid upon the head of the corpse or fastened to the shroud; pl. 6, figs. 1–4. These embroideries are square, or in strips, and seem to have been cut from larger pieces of stuff before being embroidered. The smallest specimens measure five and a half by three inches; the strips are as long as twelve and a half inches. The patterns consist of human or animal figures, double or single, or several figures all alike or different, and cover the pieces closely to the very edges, which in some examples are neatly trimmed off, so that one might be misled to take the piece for tapestry.[1] One or more additional pieces were found elsewhere in the mummy package, disposed in various ways, in workbaskets, in pouches, or

Fig. 30. Complete design of embroidered fragments of the cloth, pl. 6, fig. 1. ⅓ n. s.

as in some instances, used as coverings for the cushion of the false head of the mummybale. Several pieces were found with the same design on all, while similar figures also appeared upon larger cloths that had served as cerements for the dead. The small embroidered pieces may have been cut from these in order to be used as fetiches, or the significant symbols upon the larger cloths may explain their use as shrouds. The pieces in either case may be regarded as having the significance of fetiches. The designs of these embroideries are useful in throwing light upon the mythological ideas of those Indians who buried their dead with them. The figure of the design represented the divinity which protected them in life. These embroidered figures also mark the beginning of the development of decorative designs and are the key for their interpretation, as was shown before in the case of the decorated pottery used for ceremonial drinking at religious festivals. Thus we see that the designs of these embroideries were based upon religious ideas, expressed in the most primitive forms, deviations and changes from which caused their progressive development. In point of technique these embroideries form a class of stuffs entirely representative of this Epigone period. while in the same sense the embroidery

with loose threads covering larger surfaces belongs exclusively to the last pre-Spanish period. The foundation for these embroideries was a cotton cloth of grayish or natural brown color,[2] and the embroidery seems to be an imitation of tapestry. Two or three warp threads of the foundation are caught together in each stitch, and covered closely with colored woolen threads; the closeness of the stitches and the rep-like appearance of the surface make the resemblance to tapestry a very good one. The same effect was produced here in a similar way. While the tapestries remain the same through all the stages of cultural development, these peculiar embroideries belong to this period exclusively.

Pl. 6, figs. 1–4, reproduce a number of these embroidered specimens which were used as fetiches.

Pl. 6, fig. 1: Piece of stuff with a sceptre-bearing figure, all-over embroidery. Mus. 29647; ⅓ n. s. The figure in this piece (fig. 30) stands in the usual frontal position, and fills the square space evenly; this, in addition to the shape of the hands and the bearing of two sceptres, are strong points of resemblance to the figure on the Tiahuanaco Gate; also the two animal heads at the sides of the belt connect it with the same. The divinity here seems differently characterized by the branching, forked headdress, the two-toed, clawlike formation of the feet, and the ramified ends of the sceptres; the border around the figure shows birds with upstanding wings and long beaks.[3]

Pl. 6, fig. 2: Embroidered strip. Mus. 29654; ⅓ n. s. The strip measures twelve and a half by one and five-eighths inches. It shows four animal figures, which closely cover it; two condors in flying and running motion, and in opposite direction two winged figures, position, full front. These figures have a rhombic head, eyes and mouth, with ribbon pendants, triangular wings and tail; the claws of one are turned downward. At the first glance this creature resembles an owl, although it is strange that it should be represented flying, and in a full front position. Two rows of teeth can be seen in the beak, which might suggest some flying animal, a bat for instance.[4] That the animal here is represented with a tail is no reason to object to this interpretation, as this primitive art possessed only a few motives, of which the most daring combinations were made, and strange or fabulous animals produced.[5] The bat is frequently represented in the decorative art of northern Peru, and its presence in this design is quite plausible.[6]

Pl. 6, fig. 3: Animal with curled tail, figure upon an embroidered strip. Mus. 29653; ⅓ n. s. The same figure is repeated twice upon this strip of twelve and a half by three inches in size; one is in red and green, the other in black and yellow. The animal, pictured with realistic accuracy of detail, is seen in profile, in upright, sitting position, with raised forepaws, one of which only shows a large claw; the upper jaw is triangular, enlarged toward the front, and the open mouth shows the teeth; the ear on the back of the head is long, and curves upward; the long tail is laid upon the animal's back, and its tip has also an upward curl. This figure is repeated on several of the strips, but it is hard to find an interpretation for the creature in spite of its very distinct characteristics. The teeth prevent its interpretation as a native rabbit

[1] An embroidered piece from Ancon, Reiss und Stübel, pl. 53, fig. 1, is there described as tapestry; it resembles the specimens here described and belongs to the same period.

[2] Brown cotton is often found in graves; new cotton of a light reddish color the writer saw at Lambayeque.
[3] The figure of the small piece from Ancon, Reiss u. Stübel, pl. 53, fig. 1, is almost identical with the above, but for the knives in its hands, which lend it a greater resemblance to the Tiahuanaco figure.
[4] Teeth are indicated in the face of pl. 6, fig. 7, which was derived from the above figure.
[5] Comp. Stübel u. Uhle, p. 65, note 16, and the fishes in the relief of Tiahuanaco, l. c., pls. 9, 10.
[6] The Maya in Central America frequently made use of bats as ornamental figures.

(viscascha); the shape of the mouth and the position of the paw do not resemble those of a cat, nor is its general appearance that of a fox or a dog.

Pl. 6, fig. 4: Animal with a curled tail; design upon an embroidered strip. Mus. 29651; ⅓ n. s. The strip is eleven and a half inches long, and two and a half inches wide. The figure in the design is twice repeated in different colors, a simple textile ornament and repetitions of a conventional animal head separate the figures; only one of them is shown in the present view. This animal resembles closely that of fig. 3, but the face here is seen full front, and one forefoot and one hindfoot are turned upward. The forehead is divided by a line and the ears are also indicated. The animal must be of the same species as that of fig. 3; the curled tail here is less apparent, as this piece was cut out and sewed into another piece of the stuff; the wide mouth shows many teeth, whereby the possibility of its being a rabbit is strictly excluded.

Pl. 6, fig. 5: Sceptre-holding figure in tapestry; all-over design of a large piece of stuff. Mus. 29492; ⅓ n. s. The piece is eight feet four inches long, and consists of five strips, each of which is eight inches wide, joined together lengthwise, repeating the above figure as an all-over pattern; it has sixty-two woof threads by ten to twelve of the warp to the half inch. The white woof and warp-threads are cotton, the colored ones wool. The derivation of this design from the types of the Tiahuanaco style is shown by several features: by its adaptation to the square space, by the exact repetition of the figure,[1] which is seen full front, and by the staves which it holds sideways, instead of sceptres. The pronged crown resembles ornaments of the figures in the stuff, pl. 4, fig. 1 c; the ornament between the legs is a repetition of one on the main figure of pl. 4, fig. 1; the body seems to be clothed with a poncho. This stuff is a characteristic example of the deterioration in art since the period of Tiahuanaco; the color scheme is not good, the design of the figure lacks style; it is uncertain, changing from square to square and often appearing awkward in its details. The design does not cover the given space, as is shown by the shortening of the legs, the changing of the sceptres into staves, and by the wing-like additions.

Pl. 6, fig. 6: Square cloth, sixteen and a half inches, in double stuff with reversed animal figures. Mus. 29701; ⅓ n. s. The materials which form the design are one of red wool, the other of white cotton; the complete design being in three rows, each with four repetitions of the upright figure and of the same inverted. The design is finished like an all-over pattern on both sides, while at the lower edge appear the upper parts of the animal figures resembling bats.

Fig. 7: Round belt of tapestry, probably a young child's.[2] The little belt is seven inches wide, and four and a half inches high, closed by a seam. The colors are bright and pretty; the ground is red, the head of the principal figure blue. The blending of colors is soft; black outlines relieve the figures from the background, as if in imitation of a painted pattern. A meander in red and blue woven into the stuff forms the border. Besides the two repetitions of the principal figure, a bat, there are three rows of zigzag gradations; within the latter are the head and leg of a small figure in reclining position. The ground about the same is divided into strips resembling braid similar to that described above, No. 7 a. Two small human heads with a feather headdress stand facing the principal figure.

Fig. 8: Design of a fragment of tapestry, twelve and a half by seventeen inches in size. Mus. 29680; ⅓ n. s. To the upper edge of this piece was sewed a band of plain cotton one and three-eighths inches wide. This fragment seems to be the ornamental part of a loin-cloth.[3] The stuff is finished on the side with strips of tapestry showing a cross pattern in diagonal stripes regularly repeated. The ground color is purple, while the design is in various colors such as white, dark purple, green, light red. The figures are outlined with black or yellow.

Fig. 9: Woolen forehead band with patterns in various groups; found with the stuff, fig. 5. Mus. 29686; ⅓ n. s. The length of the band is five feet eleven inches, the width one and eleven-sixteenths inches; the tassels are six and a half inches long. Two inches of the length of the band are divided at each end, for the attachment of the four tassels with which they are ornamented. The band is scarlet, except in seven sections, where colored tapestry patterns, one and one-eighth to five and five-eighths inches in length, are inserted, and many cross-stripes, woven in a light pattern, serve as additional ornamentation. Each of the seven tapestry pieces is in a different pattern, a–f, and in various colors, such as green, light red, dark purple, yellow, blue and white.

Fig. 10: Design of a forehead band of tapestry. Mus. 29690; ⅓ n. s. The strip is two and a half inches wide and has a pattern with a figure resembling a star with eight points set into square sections, in the corners of which are small crosses, peculiar to this period.

Fig. 11: Part of a sleeve with narrow tapestry border. Mus. 29684; ⅓ n. s. The border is only one inch wide and closed in ring shape by a seam, the full length of the sleeve is fourteen inches. The pattern is formed by square sections with alternating colors, in each of which is the figure of a seated animal with curled tail, like the figure of pl. 6, fig. 3, but in its heavy foreparts it has no resemblance to any familiar American animal.

Fig. 12: Fragment of a small closed belt, like fig. 7, of tapestry. Mus. 29682; ⅓ n. s. The belt is only two and a half inches wide and six inches long. The ground colors are dark red and white, the pattern in red, light brown, green and black, blending softly with the ground colors.

Fig. 13: Design of a forehead band of tapestry. Mus. 29685; ⅓ n. s. The band is four feet five inches long and two and a quarter inches wide. Both ends are divided into three strands of three and three-quarter inches, and are finished with tassels five and a quarter inches long. The band is divided diagonally into twelve broad triangular sections, each half of which repeats a different design. The point where both patterns meet is shown in fig. 13. The colors are bright—white, green, purple, yellow and black.

Fig. 14: Embroidered design upon a plain cotton cloth, shroud. Mus. 29663; ⅓ n. s. The pattern is formed by figures nearly square, one and three-quarter inches each side, in chessboard design. The figures of each are the same, but the colors are different, each color being continued in a diagonal line.

Fig. 15: Short band or sash with wide ends of tapestry. Mus. 29668; ⅓ n. s. The connection of the pattern in this piece with those above described is quite apparent in the spur-shaped figure in the narrow cross-strip,[4] and in the slanting

---

[1] Comp. the figures of the three rows in the Relief of Tiahuanaco; also description of pl. 4, fig. 2, and Reiss und Stübel, l. c., pl. 49.

[2] In the belt, pl. 7, fig. 4, were found the skull and bones of a young child.

[3] These garments were identified as loin-cloths, the same still being worn by the mestizos in the valley of Lurin, who easily recognized those found at Pachacamac as similar to their own, which they wear when they go fishing. The ornamentation of a wide piece at one end of the cloth explains itself from the way in which the garment is adjusted upon the person of the wearer. The long gowns of the side figures in the relief of the Gate of Tiahuanaco were probably cloaks (yaqalla), like the supa yaqalla worn by the young men of Cuzco at their initiation into the nobility (Molina, p. 36), and which were fastened around their necks.

[4] Comp. pl. 6, fig. 7.

crosses which resemble the cross held by the bird in its beak in pl. 4, fig. 4. The conventional animal figure with hooks differs somewhat from the preceding, which shows that various stylistic tendencies might exist side by side, while so far we have little knowledge of their origin.

Fig. 16: A woven pouch for spindles, such as is usually found with all its contents standing beside the mummy.[1] Mus. 29733; ⅓ n. s. The pouch is twenty-six and a half inches long and three and seven-eighths inches wide, and consists of a piece of stuff closed along one side and at the lower end, the upper being open, tied with a cotton string. The cotton stuff of which this pouch is made has mostly red woolen warp-threads with a few white cotton ones and a woof of common brown cotton. While the two ends of the stuff are woven like plain linen, the central part shows a design which was produced by skipping the white threads of the warp in places and leaving them loose on the reverse side. Thus a complementary design of a diagonal meander was made to cover the entire space, in one part of which the red threads are mixed with the white, in the other unmixed. This design in the same color is seen in many textile fabrics of this period, on pouches like the above or on cloths which cover the false heads of mummies, and also on a poncho. The same design and technique appear also in different colors, in green and blue, on similar spindle pouches. The same method is sometimes applied to produce different designs, such as chessboard patterns, etc.

being joined together with the complementary sections and forming a new pattern in this combination; there are violet and yellow sections with red lines, light and dark blue sections with white ones. This design was produced by drawing the stuff tightly in before dyeing, first the red design on violet ground and then the blue; the red patterns on yellow were done by hand upon the plain ground.

Although the textiles here described present a great variety of typical features, the series is by no means a complete one, and many types are found side by side which have no relation whatever to each other. It is, therefore, not possible at this moment to furnish a complete survey of the textile art of this period, neither from the technical nor from the decorative point of view. However, it can be said, that the patterns of a majority of these stuffs have been interpreted. A number of ornaments, formerly unexplained, are now understood, and the certainty of their dependence upon the Epigone period established. The same is assured of numerous textile patterns found in graves along the coast, whereby also their descent from the Tiahuanaco style seems to be proved. The decorative designs of this period, both in textiles and pottery, are closely related; they continue ornamental features of the style of Tiahuanaco and have a number of these types in common, while both show the same tendency of conventionalizing figure patterns into simpler geometric patterns, which is a peculiarity of this period. This degeneration of the design occurs more frequently in textiles

Fig. 31. Stuff composed of pieces, woven and dyed separately. Epigone period. Mus. 29782. ⅔ n. s.

Fig. 32. Embroidered human figure. Epigone period. ⅔ n. s.

Fig 33. Design of a thick braid-like stuff. Epigone period. ⅝ n. s.

However plain the design and technique of these stuffs and numerous the articles made of them, they still belong exclusively to this oldest period, to judge from the objects with which they were found.

The stuffs that were dyed after being woven are represented by a special class of garments, one of which was found upon a mummy under a poncho of pure Tiahuanaco style. The rich and harmonious blending of colors, peculiar to these stuffs, proves that in style and technique they are closely related to the art of Tiahuanaco, while at the same time they seem to belong to a more advanced stage of development, to judge from the details of the pattern which among others shows rhombic figures, like figs. 25 and 27. This class of stuffs are composed of a number of small pieces, which were joined together after being dyed. The outlines of these pieces occasionally are in hooked shapes, so that two sections form one whole square. The joining together was done at the end of the warp by catching the end loops of adjoining pieces with a woof-thread, so as to give the appearance of having been woven in one, although the pieces were really sewed together along the edges. All of these procedures show that the makers of these stuffs had long passed the early stages of the weaver's art. The patterns upon these pieces are either lineal designs or rhombic figures, like fig. 31.

In this instance the pieces had a double design before

than in pottery, since the technique itself would prescribe it. The products of this ornamental development are taken from one technical department into the other. Thus certain patterns of importance for pottery are only to be interpreted after being found in textiles. The discussion has shown that in textile art four ornamental designs are most frequently met with:

1. The full front figure of the divinity, holding sceptres or staves.

2. The bird in running and flying motion.

3. The animal with curled tail.

4. A winged figure resembling a bat.

The two former are found identically the same in pottery.[2] The third explains some of the most important ornamental figures. The dog-head of the fourth class occasionally appears in ornamental derivations upon pottery. The figure of the first class also occurs without the sceptre, as in fig. 32, of which a copy exists also in an embroidered stuff. Figures resembling those in the textiles from Ancon, Reiss u. Stübel, pls. 50 and 69, fig. 1. Figures with staves in their hands on some small grave-tablets, copied l. c., pl. 33 a, are without doubt founded upon the same original design. The second typical figure can only be identified in designs derived from it, although it probably has not entirely disappeared during the subsequent cultural stages. The bird pattern

[1] Comp. also Reiss u. Stübel, l. c., pl. 86, fig. 2.

[2] Comp. figures pl. 6, figs. 1 and 5, with that of pl. 5, fig. 2; the bird in running motion of pl. 6, fig. 2, with that on vase, pl. 4, fig. 4, and fig. 19, above.

on the band of pl. 6, fig. 1, fig. 30 above, may be derived from it.

The animal with curled tail[1] is one of the commonest ornamental motives during the early periods of Pachacamac. Only in textiles it appears frequently in the entire figure. It may be said to resemble the skunk (Mephitis sp.) which was worshiped at Pachacamac in very early times,[2] but it is not possible to identify it distinctly as such. The head of this animal appears in a rather naturalistic treatment upon a small strip of brown and white double cloth, fig. 33.

The head of the ornamental creature in pl. 6, fig. 6, is similar. The animal may have been intended as being seated, as in pl. 6, fig. 3. It is strongly conventionalized, while two and two of these figures are interlocked in a complementary pattern. More advanced to a similar completion is the design in a, pl. 6, fig. 9, where the extended forepaw is still distinguishable. The heads with enlarged noses, above, fig. 15 and fig. 20, belong to the same creature; possibly also the heads of figures otherwise of human shape, fig. 13.[3] The triangular enlargement of the nose in the animal, pl. 6, fig. 3, developed from the former and has a parallel in the decorative figure of the vessel, pl. 5, fig. 13, but here the back part of the head is more developed into a symmetrical shape, beginnings of which were to be observed in fig. 15 and fig. 33 above. In this form the head continues as an ornamental type during the later pre-Inca period and appears on specimens of pottery.

In the Tiahuanaco style two animal types are familiar, both with similar tails, one representing the puma, while the

alized ears. The square head without any side attachments appears in b on the forehead band, pl. 6, fig. 9, between the bends of a meandering ribbon pattern.[5] It also forms cross patterns in many different combinations, as in the stuff from Ancon, copied by Reiss u. Stübel, pl. 55, fig. 3; stuffs with similar patterns were taken from graves at Pachacamac. Each of the two designs on the forehead band, pl. 6, fig. 15, shows one-half of the whole figure of the creature. The design a shows the head, as in fig. 37 b above; b shows the body formed like a stick, with its wings.[6] The design in fig. 8 was composed of the head in the original form, as in 37 a. It was further developed into a complementary design in f upon the forehead-band, pl. 6, fig. 9. By the combination of two heads of fig. 37 a and by interlocking the hooks of the two, the design a of the same band was formed. A further development is shown by g on the same plate and by the design upon the belt, pl. 6. fig. 12. The form b appears also at the ends of a meander joined on under c in pl. 6, fig. 9. A later conventional form of the design is seen in pl. 6, fig. 4, where the triangular head is used to fill a small square.

C. Woodcarvings.

The woodcarvings of this period are superior to those of the following epoch in artistic execution and in a greater variety of design. The objects upon which the carving appears are the same as in former periods, such as pointed staves, weaver's reeds, etc. The material is usually dark-

Fig. 34.
Decorative design of animal on cup. Tiahuanaco style. ⅓ n. s.

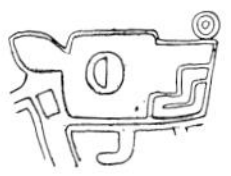

Fig. 35.

Fig. 36.
Decorative heads of animal (dog) on vessels. Tiahuanaco style. ⅓ n. s.

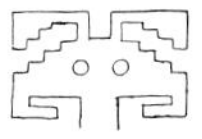

Fig. 37 a.   Fig. 37 b.
Typical forms of animal heads in textile patterns. Epigone period.

other has the head of a dog, figs. 34 to 36. Treatment and pose are different in both, while they must be regarded as typical ornamental figures of Tiahuanaco, even if we are unable to prove their identity. From the bat figure, as it is seen in pl. 6, fig. 2, developed a number of different ornaments, as may also be seen upon textiles from Ancon.[4]

A very good likeness of the creature, although conventionalized, is to be seen on the belt, pl. 6, fig. 7. The body here is represented by a straight line, and the mouth does not show the teeth. Five toes and a claw turned downward seem to be indicated at the ends of the wings; the tail also has feet with toes and claws, which strengthens the supposition that the animal is meant for a bat. The head and other parts of this figure were much used as ornamental types. The head developed into forms like the square head of fig. 7, and into others like figs. 37 a and b. The former differs from the original square one by its triangular shape and by the hooked attachments. Although these may be purely ornamental, it is possible that they are meant for the hooks at the ends of the wings in fig. 7. Fig. 37 b shows the addition of bands at both sides of the mouth, which, however, occurred before in pl. 6, fig. 2, and may be conventionalized

brown wood. If the excellent workmanship in all specimens of this period is an inheritance of the earlier epoch, this fact must above all be accepted for the woodcarvings, which are surprisingly realistic in form and pose. The highland probably was more productive in fine woodcarvings than the lowland. A pretty specimen is the wooden ear-ornament, pl. 4, fig. 5. Carved wooden vessels were common in the highland, and less so in the plain. Many carved objects were made in Pachacamac through the influence of the highland during the period of the Incas.[7] The derivation of the types of these carvings from the art of the highland, however, can only in a few cases be asserted. Owing to the perishable nature of the material few specimens have come to our knowledge, those of earlier periods having disappeared. The ornamental types of these objects reveal less of religious character than is shown in the pottery and the textiles. An Indian lying upon his stomach in a lazy attitude, as in pl. 5, fig. 14, and figures of captives with their hands tied behind their back, can surely not be considered as mythological subjects. Animal figures occur frequently— lizards, birds, etc. Often we find small scroll ornaments joined to their eyes, as in pl. 5, fig. 7; pl. 4, fig. 1, or as in the figures of the Gate of Tiahuanaco. These orna-

---

[1] Pl. 6, figs. 2, 3 and 11.
[2] Garcilaso, B, VI, chap. 31, speaks of the worship of the 'Zorra'; and J. J. v. Tschudi, Beitr., p. 127, points out that the Zorra was Mephitis sp. and not the fox. In the myths of Huarochiri the skunk is mentioned, however, among the animals cursed by the god Iraya (F. de Avila, p. 127).
[3] Comp. the figures in Reiss u. Stübel, pl. 69, fig. 3, and the second in fig. 1, l. c.
[4] Comp. also Reiss u. Stübel, pl. 44, fig. 3, 55 a; figs. 2, 65, etc.

[5] The type of a meandering band corresponds to that in the ornamental border of the frieze of the Tiahuanaco Gate, Stübel u. Uhle, pl. 17. In this case two ornaments were joined to the ribbon and detached faces were set between the bands.
[6] Comp. as the original form of this type the principal figure in pl. 6, fig. 7.
[7] Comp. the half-kneeling winged figure, Stübel u. Uhle, pls. 11–15.

ments may possess some religious meaning, while at the same time they form a certain link of connection with the art of the classic period.

Instead of numerous examples, only two typical ones may be mentioned here. Although these carvings are interesting in themselves they cannot furnish much information concerning the historical position of the period.

Pl. 5, fig. 14: Pointed staff with the figure of a man lying down. Hard brown wood. Mus. 27784; ½ n. s. The carved end of this staff shows the figure of a man, two and five-eighths inches long, resting upon his stomach with feet turned upward; the face is looking in a straight line and rests upon the right hand, while the left lies flatly extended. The man seems to be stretched upon a mat, the pattern of which can be seen on the under side. A flat oval object, possibly a coca pouch, fastened with a band, is indicated upon the

the religious element predominates in them, and three small objects may serve as examples.

Pl. 5, fig. 16: Animal, flat, carved in bone. Mus.; n. s. The animal is of the well-known type with the curled tail. The manner of suspension by the head shows that it is represented as if seated, with its legs extended in front, as in fig. 3, pl. 6. The tail may have been long, but is broken off. The ring pattern all over the animal's body might indicate that it was meant for a cat.

Pl. 5, fig. 17: Animal, winged and in running motion, carved in shell; n. s. The creature is of a mythological character, similar to those on pl. 4, fig. 4, and pl. 6, fig. 2, a bird with head and tail of a quadruped.

Pl. 5, fig. 18: Tooth of a mammal, carved at the root-end into an animal's head and engraved around the centre. It was suspended by the hole bored through the midst. Pieces

Figs. 38–48. Spinning Whorls.

head. Ornamental suggestions on the back may be intended for garments; curves on the thighs and shoulders are meant for the folds of the loin-cloth and the sleeve ends of the poncho.

Fig. 15: A head with open-work headdress upon a staff, similar to the preceding. Mus. 27782; ½ n. s. The face shows the well defined features of a man; the headdress is a circle with two prongs in front and an ornament above it, three and a half inches high, of a trellis-like open-work. Similar ornamentation is to be seen upon other carved pieces.

D. Ornaments of Shell, Bone and Teeth.

A number of small carved figures and kindred objects, which were worn as talismans upon the person, are typical of this period. They resemble a large number of such articles from the classic period of the Chimu. For obvious reasons

of this class are numerous in this section of the cemetery; in some specimens there is a head on each end.

Pl. 5, fig. 19: Small fish, carved in shell. Mus. 27852 c; n. s.

E. Spinning Whorls.

The types of these whorls change according to the periods, and they are numerously represented of all the epochs; they therefore form a very suitable material for the classification of graves.

Figs. 38–48 show several types of the spinning-whorls of this period; figs. 38–40 are of bone; fig. 41 of shell; figs. 42–44 of stone; figs. 45–48 of clay. These specimens are in the shapes of rings or balls or conical, occasionally they appear in the form of ornamented disks. The stone whorls are of a yellow or bluish-red stone, resembling soapstone. The only ornament upon all consists of circles or plain lineal engravings.

CHAPTER XII.

THE GRAVES IN THE NEW SOIL.

IT was demonstrated in the preceding chapter that the culture of the oldest and most untouched section of the cemetery depended upon that early period to which the stone monuments of Tiahuanaco owe their existence, while at the same time was shown its degeneration from the high degree of perfection of its prototype, both in technique and form.

The graves in the new soil represented the beginnings of another period, in which was continued the retrograde movement of the preceding epoch.[1] These graves were about one and a half to five feet below the surface, measured to the top of the light rush-roofing; each roof as a rule sheltered several mummies. When more soil was piled up above these graves, the roofs could not withstand the weight. This accounts for the finding of so few unbroken pieces of pottery in these graves.

A. POTTERY.

The pottery of this period is inferior in form to that of the preceding. The vessels are far less artistic, and consist mainly of a class of large jars with round bodies, flattened at the bottom, and having short cylindrical necks (see pl. 7, fig. 1). There is, too, a group of cups, flaring, conical, such as pl. 7, fig. 3; also vessels like fig. 2; plates having a rim underneath as a foot, fig. 6; jars like fig. 5, and lastly a few vases with small necks of which fig. 4 is a type. The shapes of all these vessels, especially of figs. 1 and 4 to 6, are entirely different from those of the earlier period. The technical character of the vessels is similar to that of pl. 5, fig. 12; they are made of porous clay, of crude shapes; the surface has little polish, and the color looks like whitewash with red and black figures. If there is any relation in some of the decorative features with those of the earlier period, it certainly is difficult to find, and the tradition seems to have faded.

Pl. 7, fig. 1: Vase decorated with a human face. Mus. 26811; ¼ n. s. The decoration on the upper part of the vessel and on the neck shows a human face surmounted by a headdress. The pattern upon the body of the object is in three sections, formed by vertical bands composed of interlocking hooks. The head of an animal appears in each section, in red or white, similar to those in pl. 5, fig. 14, having a tufted head ornament. This head resembles that of the animal with the curled tail of the Epigone period,[2] while the head ornament was described under No. 5, above, p. 26. The interlocked hook pattern resembles a design of that earlier period from which it was derived.[3]

Pl. 7, fig. 2: Vessel decorated with cats. Mus. 26815; ¼ n. s. Two vessels of this kind were found together in one grave; the design of one showed four cats, that of the other three. This motive was probably derived from designs of cats, such as in pl. 5, figs. 6 and 12.

Pl. 7, fig. 3: Cup, with crowned heads in its decorations Mus. 26845; ¼ n. s. The cup, of simple conical shape, of a very porous clay, is crudely ornamented; the colors are dull. The crowned heads seem to have a faint resemblance to heads of the Tiahuanaco and the Epigone period,[4] from which they may be derived.

Pl. 7, fig. 4: Vase, a seated human figure. Mus. 26906; ¼ n. s. The body of the object is round, with flattened base: the head, too, is flattened and has a small opening; the legs are marked in relief, while small handles represent arms. A wide molded feather ornament surmounts the face and is tinted in colors.

Pl. 7, fig. 5: Vase with decorations in white, red and black. Mus. 26832; ¼ n. s. The body is bowl-shaped, and surmounted by a thin tapering neck. Only the upper part is decorated, as in figs. 1–4. The design upon this specimen shows diagonal lines encircling the neck, and plain zigzag lines upon the body.

Pl. 7, fig. 6: Plate decorated with interlocked curved hooks, colored on the inner side. Mus. 26826; ¼ n. s. This plate was among the objects found in fragments, mentioned above.

B. TEXTILES.

The textiles of this period are represented only by a small fragment of tapestry with the design of an animal, the legs of which are turned into volutes, and by a large brown cotton cloth of a gauzy thinness, with a red and blue tapestry border. This cloth resembles the poncho from Ancon, (Reiss u. Stübel, pl. 40, fig. 1), both in color and in texture. The design of the border of pl. 7, fig. 7, shows a repetition of

Fig. 49. Design of tapestry border, garment of brown gauze. Later pre-Inca period; ⅓ n. s.

stiff animal forms. A gauze poncho, similar to the above, was found in another grave of about the same period; this had a border with a design like fig. 49. Both these figures are connected by certain stylistic analogies.

---

[1] See above, p. 19, fig. 3.
[2] See above, p. 33.
[3] See pl. 5, fig. 6, and figs 18 b and 21, above, p. 27. Its original use in the early period was probably limited to the suggestion of a crown-shaped headdress. Kultur u. Ind., I, pl. 11, fig. 6; Stübel u. Uhle, pl. 8.

[4] Comp. pronged crown in pl. 4, fig. 1 c; pl. 6, fig. 5.

C. Metal Implements.

The graves of this group yielded the first objects of metal of any importance.

Pl. 7, fig. 8: Pair of copper tweezers in the shape of a crowned human figure, seated. Mus. 28777; ½ n. s. The figure seems to hold a staff with both hands; the joint of the two parts of the tweezers is on this staff, while the edges on the back of the figure served as tweezers; the feet are damaged.

Pl. 7, fig. 9: Plain copper tweezers. Mus. 28779; ½ n. s. The most primitive tweezers in Peru were doubtless made of bivalve conches; they are still in use for this purpose with the Indians east of the Andes. Wherever metal tweezers are not represented among the objects in graves, it is safe to assume that natural sea shells were used instead. The derivation of the metal tweezers from bivalve shells may be seen by the rounded shape of the implement, where it appears in its earliest stage, while later the shape varied.

CHAPTER XIII.

GRAVES IN A SECOND STRATUM OF THE NEW SOIL IN FRONT OF THE TEMPLE.

SEVERAL graves were disclosed in the course of our operations, near the base, in front of terrace *t* (see view 3, above, p. 19), possessing specific features of interest in the peculiarities of their construction, and also in the types of the mummies and of the objects recovered. These graves were found in a stratum of adobe fragments extending underneath the front terrace of the temple. The depth of these graves was about six feet less than that of other graves, their base being only five feet below the surface. No special features of construction, such as cells, or of roofing were observed. The mummies formed bales of irregular shape, wrapped in large square cloths, five feet by six in size, and not sewed together along the edges. On a mummy bale from Ancon (Reiss u. Stübel, pl. 24, fig. 1), otherwise similar to the above, the edges were all sewed together on the outer cover. Only two mummies in a good state of preservation were secured at this spot, and with them a large number of textile fabrics. Small fragments of similar fabrics were found mingled with the soil in this locality, showing that originally there were more graves of this class here, but of different periods of construction. Some of the crania were of a more elongated shape than the usual type. The hair upon some of them was clipped on the top of the head as closely as three-sixteenths to three-eighths of an inch. The head ornaments were different from any previously discovered. Several heads were covered with spiral coils of black woolen cord of the thickness of a finger. One skull was found with a narrow white cotton bandage encircling the forehead. The hands, too, were of an unusual size and of a light yellow color. Among the bodies were some women; one, judging from the shoulder cloth, was that of a little girl; with the belt, pl. 7, fig. 14, were found the bones and skull of a small child. There were also fragments of girdles, ' chumpis,' and a pair of shoes of an unfamiliar type, pl. 7, fig. 12. In addition to the above mentioned there must have been three mummies of men.

To convey an idea of the variety and number of articles taken from these peculiar graves, a list of the contents of two of them may be given here. The cerements of the bodies are included in the number.

Grave a. A poncho with border of tapestry; design pl. 7, fig. 20.

A poncho with woven ornaments; fig. 50, below.

Seven large cotton cloths, one embroidered; fig. 52, below.

A quilt.

Two pouches, in fragments.

A plate; pl. 7, fig. 15.

A closed shell (spondylus pictorum).

A half shell of the same species.

A polished shell, bored for suspension; pl. 7, fig. 17.

Two pairs of ear ornaments; type of pl. 7, fig. 16.

Some seeds wrapped in wool.

A ball of fibre resembling reeds, used as twine.

A pair of sandals.

A long piece of black woolen braid, pl. 7, fig. 11.

A piece of round plaited braid, used as a binding on a shoe, like pl. 7, fig. 12.

The ear ornaments are duplicates; it is probable, therefore, that one pair came from another grave.

Grave b. A pair of shoes; pl. 7, fig. 12.

A loin-cloth; pl. 7, fig. 13.

A black poncho of vicuña wool; pl. 7, fig. 19.

A plain black woolen poncho with border of tapestry.

A fine cotton poncho.

A poncho with lineal pattern in openwork weaving.

Two common yellow cotton ponchos.

A brown cotton poncho.

Two large cotton cloths, one embroidered.

A woven belt; pl. 7, fig. 14.

A cotton cloth folded like a bandage.

Two small pouches with articles of food; pl. 7, fig. 18.

A pair of ear ornaments.

A shell (spondylus pictorum).

The contents of this grave may have been mixed with those of several others; the seven ponchos, however, were found together, between the arms of one mummy.

Description of objects taken from these graves :

1. The ponchos: most of the ponchos are of cotton, a few of wool, but all different from any found elsewhere in the cemetery; they are long and close-fitting, instead of short and wide. The measurements of some of the ponchos are as follows :

Length,	32½ inches ;		width,	25	inches.
"	33¾	"	"	28¾	"
"	32	"	"	27½	"
"	31¼	"	"	22½	"
"	32	"	"	22	"
"	26	" (imperf.)	"	27½	"
"	31	"	"	28½	"

The length varies from thirty-one to thirty-four inches, and the width from twenty-two to twenty-nine inches. The cotton ponchos are of various kinds, some thin, yellowish, of a plain cotton stuff, while others are ornamented with openwork weaving. One has a woven border, Mus. 27542; the design is in fig. 50. There are two horizontal stripes across the body of the ponchos, each four inches wide, and embroidered in a pattern similar to fig. 52, below. The cotton poncho, Mus. 27572, is of a very fine fabric. It consists of two different materials, one being used as a facing in a strip twelve inches wide under the other. The outside fabric is of orange color, the other shows vertical gray and brown stripes. The cloth is as fine as silk; it has sixty-four threads of warp to twenty-two of woof to the half inch.

Two ponchos, Mus. 27541 and 27543, found in fragments, are different from the former, being of a thick, brownish-white stuff, resembling felt; one has fifty-two warp-threads to sixteen woof; the second seventy-four warp to fourteen woof-threads to the half inch. The patterns upon these, which resemble that of pl. 7, fig. 19, appear in horizontal tapestry stripes as shown in pl. 7, figs. 20 and 21; one is black, yellow and red, the other blue, yellow and red.

Only two woolen ponchos were found, Mus. 27569 and 27570; one of very fine texture is shown, pl. 7, fig. 19, in $\frac{1}{3}$ n. s. Both these ponchos are black, a uniform line of embroidery stitching outlines the hem and side edges in black, red, dark and light yellow; a typical finishing edge for this period. 27570 is plain, while 27569 is soft and pliable, apparently of vicuña wool and of much closer weave than the former; it has seventy-seven warp by twenty woof-threads to the half inch; it is ornamented with a fine tapestry border in black, red, yellow and white. The pattern, enlarged, is shown in fig. 51. Alternating blocks show two different designs: the one with three pendent figures (fishes?), the other a peculiar design, repeated diagonally in an inverted order.

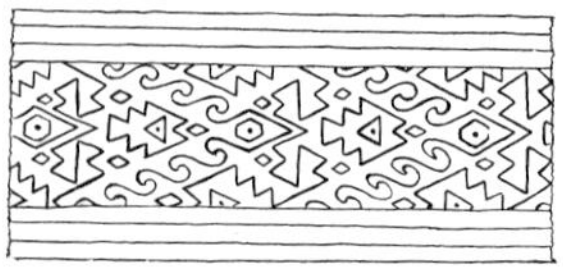

Fig. 50. Design of an embroidered border of a poncho, Inca period, coast style; $\frac{1}{3}$ n. s.

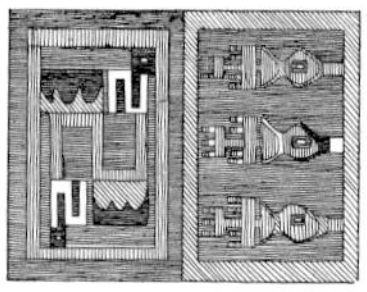

Fig. 51. Design of the border of a poncho, pl. 7, fig. 19, from Inca grave; $\frac{1}{3}$ n. s.

2. The large cloths: These cloths are of light cotton stuff, some plain, others figured. The former served as shrouds for the mummies and are brown, finished with a round edge of red wool; only one of the number is white, bound with a narrow black woolen braid. The size is approximately five feet eight inches by five feet, and nearly the same in all. Two other white cotton cloths, five and three-quarter feet by five feet one inch, and four feet five inches by four feet two inches, are decorated with light embroideries. One of these, Mus. 27563, is embroidered with three horizontal stripes in red and yellow, the pattern like fig. 52. The smaller cloth, 27535, is ornamented with a wide stripe across the centre, in brown and black cotton, the pattern being similar to the former; two narrower stripes run along the edges, the design as in fig. 53.

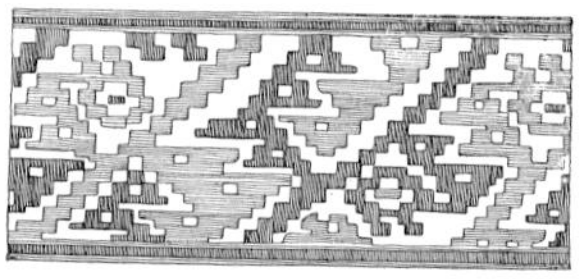

Fig. 52. Design of a border in raised embroidery on large cotton cloth, Inca grave, coast style; $\frac{1}{3}$ n. s.

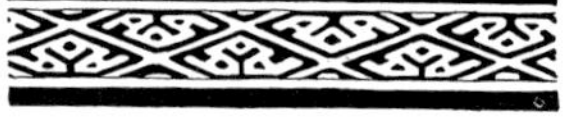

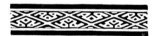

Fig. 53. Border like the preceding.

3. Small shoulder-cloth: Mus. 27544. The size of this cloth is twenty-five by nineteen and a half inches. The cotton fabric is thicker than that of the cloths described above. This article shows lengthwise stripes; the central one is black, bordered by yellow, red and green, all alternating with brown stripes of the same width as the central.

4. The quilt, Mus. 27533, is sixty-five by fifty-two inches in size. It has an interlining of cotton batting, the same as modern quilts.

5. The loin-cloth, pl. 7, fig. 13: Mus. 27573; $\frac{1}{3}$ n. s. It is woven of wool, black with red and yellow stripes along the edges; the bands of black and yellow are braided.

6. The small belt, pl. 7, fig. 14: Mus. 27574; $\frac{1}{4}$ n. s. It is woven of wool and closed in ring-shape. It is ornamented with five narrow figured stripes, bordered by red ones and alternating with yellowish-brown bands of the ground material. The figured stripes are woven in black and white, yellow and red alternately; the pattern consists of a diagonal line and two dots in sectional divisions and alternating in color.

7. The shoes, pl. 7, fig. 12: Mus. 27575; $\frac{1}{4}$ n. s. They are made of buckskin, the hair side turned out, sewed and bound with a knit braid. The inner length is eight and three-quarter inches.

8. The braided cords, pl. 7, fig. 10 *a* and 10 *b*: Mus. 26639; $\frac{1}{4}$ n. s. Figs. 11 *a* and *b* illustrate the manner in which this cord was coiled around the head. Beside the one preserved on this skull, there are two similar braids, twenty-one and a half and twenty-three and a half feet long. All three are of very soft black wool, probably vicuña; two are braided of thirty-two strands, flat, with four edges (see figs. 11 *a* and 11 *b*), eleven-thirty-seconds and seven-sixteenths of an inch wide by three-sixteenths of an inch thick. The ends are secured by sewing on one, and by tying the strands on the other. The third of these cords, twenty-three and one-third feet long, Mus. 27635, braided of sixteen strands, is almost round, but only one-quarter of an inch thick; on one end is a plaited loop three-eighths of an inch long.

9. The ear ornaments, pl. 7, fig. 16: Mus. 27548 *a*; $\frac{1}{3}$ n. s. They are made of strips of leaves, and are one and one-eighth to one and three-eighths inches wide, rolled into a spiral two and one-half to two and three-quarter inches thick; several sizes exist in pairs.

10. The plate, pl. 7, fig. 15: Mus. 27545; $\frac{1}{4}$ n. s. It is shallow of form, and instead of handles has small rim ornaments resembling loops; the color is red and yellow, and the pattern a familiar one, a diametrical stripe with lozenge-shaped figures in it, and a circular rim with small zigzags.

11. Small pouch with coca-leaves, pl. 7, fig. 18: This pouch, of plain linen, is nine inches high by five inches wide, and filled with coca-leaves; the top is closed by sewing; an exterior covering of rushes, held together by a light net-work, was put over the pouch as a protection against dampness.

This enumeration of objects may serve as an illustration of the correctness of the method of historical classification.

The plate, pl. 7, fig. 15, proves that the style of Cuzco, also, was represented here, since this type of plates with identical or similar decorative designs is seen in every collection brought from the region of Cuzco.[1] The pattern of the tapestry border, pl. 7, fig. 21, is typical, and is to be found everywhere, with more or less variation, on the Cuzco arybals;[2] the same may be said of the pattern upon the child's belt, pl. 7, fig. 14. The large plain cloths probably are the 'yaqolla'[3] cloaks, worn generally by the men of the highlands.

The forms or designs of numerous objects taken from these graves were represented among the specimens from the graves of the Sun temple, which also bear all the characteristics of the Cuzco civilization. This applies to the shoulder-cloth with triple stripes (above);[4] to the quilt[5] and the small pouch, pl. 7, fig. 18.[6] A binding braid, knit of wool, as on the shoe, pl. 7, fig. 12, was found in the Sun temple, and the typical stitching around the edges of the stuff, as in pl. 7, fig. 19, was repeated identically in manner and color.[7]

Fig. 54. Design of border of a large cloth, similar to the preceding number.

Besides the types of Cuzco,[8] those of the Coastland are represented among the objects in these graves. To this class belong, as regards technique and design, the woven braids of a poncho (fig. 50, above), and the various designs embroidered in the manner of fig. 52. The style of Cuzco and that of the last stage of the coast civilization go well together, as they are contemporaneous and often locally mixed.[9]

---

[1] Comp. also for form and general design : Medina, Aborijenes de Chile, No. 162, from Vallenar in Chile; for the design on the rim see, f. i., the fragments shown in Kultur u. Industrie, I, pl. 12, figs. 12, 13, 25.

[2] Comp. Kult. u. Industrie. I. pl. 12, fig. 16, from the Titicaca Island, the Cuzco arybal; Congr. des Amér. Bruxelles, Atlas, pl. iii, from the district of Cuenca in Ecuador; the design on stone pillars of Hatuncolla near Puno, Squier, pp. 385–386, in the style of Cuzco; designs on some garments and girdles of the portraits of Incas in oil colors, originals at Cuzco, copies in Museum at La Paz, Bolivia, and in private possession in the Hacienda Cusijata, near Copacabana. These portraits were often reproduced, f. i., by Hamy in Galérie améric., pl. 51, Nos. 145, 146; by J. Sahuaraura in Recuerdos de la Monarquia Peruana, 1850, and by Rivero and Tschudi on the title-page of the Antiguedades peruanas.

[3] Comp. Middendorf, Wörterbuch, p. 102.

[4] Comp. below, chap. xxi. Shoulder-cloths, 'llijlla,' figured with three stripes, are to this day a typical garment with the Indian women in the highlands. The colors, red, yellow and green, as well as the narrow stripes of this shoulder-cloth, are frequently seen in the ponchos of the Indians in Bolivia, where these are the national colors.

[5] The two peculiar quilts taken from these graves and from the graves of the Sun temple are the only ones found at Pachacamac.

[6] See bel., chap. xxi.

[7] Comp. pl. 19, fig. 7.

[8] The lower section of the design in fig. 51 of the vicuña poncho, pl. 7, fig. 19, which shows a conventional animal's face twice repeated, is derived from the style of Tiahuanaco. The white hooked figure is the same as that found upon the necks of animal heads (comp. above, p. 27, fig. 20; p. 33, fig. 35, and Stübel u. Uhle, Introductory remarks with pl. 8, No. 1); the dark square in the corners, the ring-shaped nose of the animal (see p. 33, figs. 34–36, and pl. 4, figs. 1 a and c); the small toothed figure, a form of the ear which is not uncommon (comp. the shape, fig. 54, on the face upon cup, pl. 5, fig. 4). The arrangement of the minor parts is, however, different, suggesting greater remoteness of time and loss of tradition. Another explanation might be given of the manner in which this design was brought into a poncho of the Inca time. It is possible that stylistic traditions of the period of Tiahuanaco survived in the region of Cuzco, or the poncho itself was made in Bolivia, where traditions of the earliest period may be supposed to have survived for a long time. It is certain that textiles (made by the 'mamaconas' of the provinces) were carried to Cuzco from the entire realm of the Incas.

[9] Comp. the finds of the cemetery of the northern town, below, chap. xvii, and of some of the graves on the Sun temple. In the poncho, also, where the patterns are of the style of the coast, see above, p. 38, the proportions corresponded to those of the highlander's poncho, p. 37.

MARKS OF THE INCA NOBILITY.

The interest claimed by these finds does not cease with their classification according to period and style. They possess another interesting aspect, for it can be proved from the objects discovered that the mummies buried in these graves were members of the nobility of the Inca realm. It is well known that in the land of the Incas the dwellers of the various provinces[1] were distinguished by the headdress, which also showed the degree of rank of the individual. One class of these ornaments, the llaut'u, made of braided cords,[2] was worn in a coil around the head as its only decoration[3] by the inhabitants of the province of Condesuyu.[4] In the empire of the Incas the color of the llaut'u was significant of rank, and therefore very important, certain colors conferring the highest distinctions and greatest marks of favor. Elsewhere the color had no special meaning, beyond designating the province to which the wearer belonged.[5] The llaut'u worn by the Inca himself was of crimson and blue, wound about the head in four or five coils,[6] with a fringe, 'masqua paicha,' in the same colors,[7] covering the forehead to the temples. The heir-apparent of the Inca, according to Garcilaso, wore the same ornament, except that the masqua paicha was yellow.[8] This forehead fringe was not a regular part of the llaut'u, but was reserved for the Inca and his successor. In confirmation of this statement the fact may be mentioned that the nearest relatives, probably the members of the Qhapaj aillu, wore two red and yellow tassels, paicha, on the right temple in place of the fringe.[9] The llaut'us of the nobles, the orejones, were black. Garcilaso informs us on this point as follows:[10] "The first privilege granted by the Inca to his followers was permission to wear the llaut'u like himself, provided it were black." It is therefore unlikely that any of his subjects except the nobility were permitted to wear black llaut'us. The fact that the Inca wore his coiled only four or five times about his head, while the one represented in pl. 7, fig. 11, appears in thirteen coils, is no obstacle to its identification as one of the llaut'us of the

---

[1] Zarate, I, chap. 6; Garcilaso, I, chap. 22.

[2] J. J. v. Tschudi, Wörterbuch, p. 351, and Middendorf, Wörterbuch, p. 514, give the inaccurate translation of "headband" for llaut'u. Congr. des Amér. Bruxelles, I, p. 608, pl. 2, fig. 6, has the still more incorrect designation of the same as "an ornament in the shape of a collar."

[3] Relac. por el Corregidor de Chunbivilcas, Rel. Geogr., II, p. 29: "las cabezas descubiertas con algunos llautos al rededor dellas."

[4] Rel. Geogr., l. c., p. 14 (Cotahuasi): "traen . . . . las cabezas con unas llautos blancos y negros en ella;" p. 18 (Alca): "las cabezas con unas sogas de lana al rededos de la media cabeza;" p. 22 (Llusco y Quinota): "las cabezas con unas sogas delgadas de lana;" p. 25 (Capamarca): "en las cabezas traen . . . . llautos, que llaman, de lana de colores."

[5] The inhabitants of Rucana, by order of the Inca, wore red and white coiled around their heads. Descripcion de la Tierra de Asunrucana, Rel. Geogr., I, pp. 204 and 207. The people of the province of Pacajes in Bolivia were recognized by yellow stripes in their knit caps.

[6] Montesinos, chap. 17; Garcilaso, I, chap. 22, says: "Of several colors." The statement of Garcilaso, V, chap. 20, and of Xerez, p. 82, that the fringe was only crimson, appears to be erroneous, unless the fringe differed in color from the llaut'u.

[7] Xerez, l. c. The translation of "tassel" for masqua paicha, used by v. Tschudi, l. c., p. 376, appears therefore to be incorrect.

[8] I, chap. 23.

[9] Garcilaso, IV, chap. 2.

[10] Garcilaso, I, chap. 22. Molina, p. 36, confirms the statement that the llaut'us worn by the young men of Cuzco on the day of their initiation into the rank of the nobles were black. The Inca Wiraqocha granted the privilege of wearing the llaut'u to the men of the kindred tribe of the Kechua, as a reward for their assistance in defeating the Chaucos. Garcilaso, V, chap. 23.

nobles, the color being the important point. The woolen braids in figs. 10 and 11 were llaut'us of the nobility, that of the Inca being described as of the thickness of one finger,[1] with four edges.[2] The short hair of these mummies is full of significance. The Incas had introduced strict regulations for the hair of their nobles, degrees of rank being marked by its varying length. "Some men wore their hair to the middle of the ears, others still shorter, only the Inca had his closely cropped."[3]

It is possible that haircutting as a mark of distinction was valued by the Inca nobility more even than the privilege of wearing the black llaut'u, as it represented a greater variety of degrees of rank. Judging from the shortness of their hair, the men buried in these graves must have been of very high station. Brühl, quoting from a source unknown to us,[4] states : "The orejones, the nobles, wore their hair partly long ; those who belonged to the Inca ayllus cut it quite short, as short as the Qhapaj Inca himself." The hair of these mummies[5] is from three-eighths to three-sixteenths of an inch long, therefore in life the men were certainly nobles and may have belonged to the ancient ayllus of the Inca at Cuzco.

Ear ornaments were badges of nobility and seem to have been granted to the nobles exclusively, according to the regulations of the Inca ;[6] for this reason the Spaniards called them 'orejones.' Their value was according to size and material. We are not distinctly informed as to the size, but those found in these graves, evidently belonging to the nobility, may perhaps be considered as the standard of those of the orejones of Cuzco. They are about as large as the foot of a goblet, and none might be worn by subjects larger than half the size of those of the Inca. Being made only of leaves, their value might appear insignificant, if it is considered that the chief of the orejones wore ear ornaments of gold ; but we are told that the Inca occasionally granted the wearing of 'totora' as a special favor,[8] from the resemblance which they bore to his own. The shoes, pl. 7, fig. 12, were possibly of some special significance, and perhaps indicated rank, although they may be women's shoes. Similar ones were found in the graves of the Sun temple where only women were buried. The style is that of the ordinary type of women's shoes,[9] and they may be compared to the llauki, which were adopted by young girls at the age of puberty.

A few points of resemblance between the textiles from the graves and some from graves in the Sun temple may be reserved for a later discussion. Some peculiarities appear in both classes alike, such as : a felt-like texture of the two cotton ponchos, a very unusual type of cloth ; also the fine stitching which binds the edges in exactly the same colors in each case, white, yellow, red and black. The same colors appear in the tapestry part of the fine poncho, pl. 7, fig. 19, and in the two stripes of the little child's belt. Even disregarding

these comparisons, there is sufficient proof of the superior rank of the persons buried in these graves.[10] This conclusion is in harmony with the favored situation of the graves, close against the wall of the temple ; and also with the statement made by Cieza,[11] that only princes, priests and pilgrims were buried around the temple. These graves would not be considered as belonging to persons of high rank if they were judged, as is usually done, by the presence or absence of precious metals, and if written testimony were disregarded. This fact proves that it is a great mistake to look merely for gold and silver objects in graves, in order to establish the rank of the bodies buried there. It is needless to conjecture whether the gold in these cases had been retained by the family, or whether it had been presented to the temple at the time of the owner's death. At all events it will be necessary to ascertain the rank of the persons by the objects actually found in the graves, especially by the textile fabrics in which the dead were buried. Possibly a statement coming from Garcilaso might be more considered when he says, in regard to the classification of the dead :[12] " As tribute they made three

Fig. 55. Colored braid, llaut'u. From a grave of Inca period. ⅓ n. s.

kinds of woolen garments, the first class, awaska,[13] being used only by the common people. The second, cumpi,[14] of fine wool, of several colors and well made, similar to tapestry, was reserved for the use of the nobles and of the Inca's retinue, also for captains and chiefs. The third class, compo, was made of the finest wool existing and worn by all persons of the blood of the Inca, both in war and in peace, by soldiers, captains and officers." The poncho, pl. 7, fig. 19, with its fine tapestry border, may be of the third class, and the two cotton ones, with plainer tapestry, of the second. Considering that the Incas as a rule only renewed old customs observed in Peru long before their rule began, the stuffs found in these graves may be classified according to this principle. We must bear in mind, however, that archæological research of the pre-Inca period is not advanced enough for us to accept without reservation the classification of textile fabrics as given by Garcilaso.[15]

[1] Garcilaso, V, chap. 2 ; I, chap. 22.
[2] The llaut'us as head ornaments pictured on the Inca portraits (described above, p. 39), dating from a later Spanish period, are incorrectly drawn. Instead of being wound closely about the head, and laid in a spiral decreasing towards the top of the crown, as described by Garcilaso, the llaut'u here is arranged in coils becoming wider towards the top and having the shape of a cap. An object in the shape of a cockade appears as a decoration, and the headdress looks almost like a helmet. In the face of these erroneous later-day representations it is an important fact to have the only authentic proof of the manner of wearing the llaut'u pictured upon the skull, pl. 7, fig. 10. As we see it here it was worn by the Inca nobles and the Qhapaj Inca himself. The masqua paicha was generally made too narrow and too short in those portraits.
[3] Garcilaso, I, chap. 22.
[4] P. 273.
[5] The hair is short, as if cut but lately. Garcilaso, l. c., too, states that the Inca and his nobles had their hair cut often, so as to have always the same appearance.
[6] The piercing of the ear was a privilege. Garcilaso, I, chap. 23 ; V, chap. 23.
[7] The Inca determined the exact size and measurement. Garcilaso, l. c.
[8] L. c., chap. 73.
[9] Shoes were generally alike for men and women.

[10] These men were probably natives of Cuzco, judging from their closely cut hair and the shape of their crania, which differ from the prevailing type of the coastland. They were not necessarily members of native chieftain families who, having adopted Cuzco civilization, had been received into the caste of the nobles ; but the fact of the two embroidered cloths and one of the embroidered ponchos having come from the coastland shows some certain connection with that locality.
[11] Cronica, I, chap. 73.
[12] B. V, chap. 6.
[13] Of 'alva,' to weave, v. Tschudi, Wörterbuch, p. 21, and 'awaska,' that which is woven.
[14] 'Qompi,' the costly garb, v. Tschudi, l. c., p. 166 ; 'qumpi,' fringes, l. c., is surely the same word.
[15] Near these graves a piece of colored cord was found (M. 32684), seventeen inches long, greatly resembling the llaut'us of black wool discussed above, fig. 55 ; ⅓ n. s. This cord, eleven-thirty-seconds of an inch in thickness, is braided of thirty-two strands, and almost square in its section. It resembles one of the black cords and is finished at one end by a loop one and a half inches in length. The colors are grayish-yellow and citron, crimson and dark blue, so intermingled as to form zigzag patterns. At the opposite end the strands are unraveled for two and a half and six inches, and the red and blue strands are tightly bound with a crimson thread while the yellow are hanging loose. This piece at first claimed a certain interest by its pretty colors and design, but there is a possibility that it may possess a still higher one. Red and blue were the colors of the Inca's headdress, while his nearest of kin, probably the whole 'gens qhapay aillu,' wore red and yellow. But as blue, beside red, is sometimes ignored in the description of the llaut'u of the Inca (Xerez, p. 82 ; Garcilaso, V, chap. 20), the same omission may have occurred in stating the colors of the clan of the Inca. We would thus have a combination of the Inca colors, red and blue, and of that of the adopted successor, yellow, the very colors shown by this piece of cord, besides a fourth one. We know furthermore that the chieftain of the town after the Inca conquest received the rank of an Inca of the "royal blood" (Garcilaso, IV, chap. 31). The colors yellow, brown, purple and blue are repeated in the embroidered figures of the cloth, pl. 7, fig. 21, described below.

CHAPTER XIV.

THE GRAVES IN THE UNCOVERED SECTION OF CEMETERY I.

THIS vast burial ground surrounds the Temple upon three sides, extending as far as the enclosure of the court, and embraces the much rifled area towards the north and the mound-like elevation towards the east. The finds of this field, with few exceptions, belong to the same period as the graves v of the upper stratum underneath the Temple. All the pottery found here is identical in shape, technique and decoration with that of the former graves, as will be seen on pl. 7, figs. 1 to 6.[1]

Not all the earlier types are entirely wanting, however. A ·conical grave built of stone was uncovered, wherein the mummy-bale was wrapped in textiles of the most ancient class, among which was found a tapestry poncho in the pure style of Tiahuanaco.[2] Such occurrences may be explained in this way: this section of the cemetery is of the same date as the ancient part y, and originally[3] both had the same class of graves. By being covered with strata of earth and débris, the old section was rendered impracticable for burial purposes, while the uncovered ground continued in use. Through gradual destruction of older graves in making new ones, the general character of the cemetery was continually modernized until it came to a standstill in the period of which the cemetery now bears the impress. The Inca period, as far as our observation goes, is not represented here.

This explanation throws light on other points of importance. It does not exclude the possibility of discovering older graves, which by accident or careful sealing escaped destruction. It explains the immense crowding of graves, and the condition of the soil itself, which is a conglomeration of remains of mummies of every kind—of bones, fragments of cloth, pieces of rope, human hair, etc. This was brought about by the long-continued use of the cemetery, extending through all periods of the history of the ancient Temple, until the time of the Inca period or soon after.

The graves, as to type, are similar to those described p. 35. Cane thatching covers grave structures of inferior durability, from two to seven feet below the surface. In some places, especially in close proximity to the Temple, there are found in this soil adobe-walls, which form rooms or narrow passages, into which the mummies are fitted, and in some instances closely packed,[4] one above another.

The majority of the mummies resembled the types from Ancon, shown by Reiss u. Stübel, pl. 20, figs. 1; 22; 25, fig. 1.[5] These are common mummy-bales, wrapped in pieces of cloth without false heads, and with or without ornament on the outside. Mummies with false heads were uncommon, but in many instances the material of the wrapping was found to be extended at the upper end like a handle, tied with pieces of cord and decorated with feathers, etc., as the real head might have been in life.

While a cultural decline is apparent, even in comparison with the preceding Epigone period, there is a certain progress corresponding to the general advancement of the age. In some cases earthen vessels have been made by the help of moulds; utensils of metal, such as tweezers, spinning-whorls of copper, etc., are more frequent; ornaments fashioned of hammered sheet-metal are seen in more developed forms; and scales appear for the first time in this period. Besides complete scales with nets, about a dozen wooden sticks, former scale-beams, were found in this cemetery.[6]

A. POTTERY.

Form and technique of these vessels were discussed p. 35 ff. Technically they are most nearly related to the well-known type of Chancay. The decoration of the surface by coloring without polishing is common along the entire coast of central Peru, at least as far north as Pativilca. Similar vessels have been found in the valleys of Rimac and Chillon, as well as in Ancon.[7] A large number of black vessels were recovered here, all of a plain local type, technically related to the more familiar Peruvian black pottery.

The ornamental features of this period at Pachacamac are inferior to the well-known type of Chancay. Figure vessels[8] are largely represented in this class of pottery, without any individuality of style, however, and of rather inferior, even crude workmanship. The vessels with white, red and black decorations show a great variety of patterns: figures of birds (pelicans), toads, fishes and others, possessing but little artistic merit. These figures are as simple as is probably their symbolism. The general character of the decoration may be seen on the vessels shown, pl. 7, figs. 1, 4, 5; pl. 8, figs. 2 and 3. Undecorated vessels are more numerous in this cemetery than in the others; the same may be said of vessels with primitive engravings, of the type shown, pl. 8, fig. 9, having very crude faces and decorations. There is a large series of this class of pottery; also of the figure-vessels and

---

[1] See above, p. 35 ff.

[2] These fabrics could not be preserved, as the fine warp-threads had decayed, owing to their great age.

[3] See above, p. 19, fig. 3.

[4] Graves as described by George Squier, p. 74, with all the details, and with exact determination of the different members of the family, we have not found.

[5] They may belong to the same period.

[6] The small sticks, Reiss u. Stübel, pl. 87, figs. 5, 14 and 15, were such scale-beams. These beams were made of wood or of bone. The cultural influence during this period, which came to Pachacamac from the north, is apparent in everything—pottery, textiles, copper spinning-whorls, which sometimes show human faces with lip-ornament, etc. From there, probably, was imported the use of the scales, which could not be traced in earlier graves. Waitz, Anthropologie der Naturvölker, 1872, III, p. 381, mentions several tribes of the northern coast of South America who used scales for testing gold.

[7] Reiss u. Stübel, pl. 96, fig. 3.

[8] Comp. pl. 8, figs. 1–3 and 5.

those in red, white and black, none of which give evidence of much artistic taste.

Among the ornamental types preserved and continued from the Epigone period, are the animal's head with enlarged ends and the tufted headdress (comp. both, pl. 7, fig. 1). Some vessels shown on pl. 8 are intended to illustrate more clearly the character of the period as generally indicated in pl. 7, figs. 1–5.

Pl. 8, fig. 1: Vase, formed like a human figure. Mus. 26895; ¼ n. s. Only the face of this figure, with large head ornament, and the arms, are formed in detail, the legs being merely indicated in relief. The figure is painted in the ordinary manner. It represents an Indian with a high crown of feathers in gradations, the head ornament for one of the numerous festivals which the Indians celebrated in all parts of Peru. The figure is seated and playing a Pan's flute, such as is customary at festivals, while one hand is shaking a rattle, suspended from its neck.

Pl. 8, fig. 2: Vessel in the shape of a cat-like animal. Mus. 26916; ¼ n. s. The head, in proportion to the body, is very large, especially the ears. The face of the animal is exceedingly unnatural, while the claws are quite realistic and the tail is curved over the back. The vessel is colored.

Pl. 8, fig. 3: Vessel in the shape of a bird. Mus. 26917; ¼ n. s. The bird is seated, so that the vessel rests on the feet and on the back part of the body. The tail ends with a broad flat line.

Pl. 8, fig. 4: Clay doll. Mus. 26960; ¼ n. s. The figure is hollow, the head is quite large and out of proportion with the body. The hands are extended and resemble the type of many clay dolls of the same or later periods on the northern coast. These figures are usually painted.

Pl. 8, fig. 5: Black double vessel with human figure. Mus. 26879; ¼ n. s. This vessel consists of two barrel-shaped parts with separate feet. The small cylindrical neck is attached to one of these parts, while the other is surmounted by a seated human figure, about the head of which is coiled a spiral band.

Pl. 8, fig. 6: Double vessel with bird's head and whistle. Mus. 26885; ¼ n. s. The two bodies of this vessel are rounded, one of them bearing a large parrot's head, in the hollow of which the whistle is concealed. On some similar specimens the wings are indicated on the bowl. These vessels are usually colored.

Pl. 8, figs. 7–9, reproduce a peculiar kind of vessel. Fig. 10 comes from the region of Lambayeque. Mus. 34760; ¼ n. s. Vessels of this type are also represented among those from Pachacamac.

Pl. 8, fig. 7: Black vessel in the shape of a woman, nursing a young animal. Mus. 31796; ¼ n. s. The woman is seated on a square support and presses the animal with her right hand against the left breast. A second animal, which is awaiting its nourishment, lies at her right side.[1] This vessel is well polished and of attractive workmanship. It belongs to the same class as fig. 10, as may be seen by the two human figures on the handle, which resemble those on the side of the vessel, fig. 10. This object is evidently an imported one. Vessels of the same class occur at Ancon, as shown by Reiss u. Stübel, pl. 93, figs. 11 and 12; and in the Santa valley. There is no indication as to the locality from which were brought pieces of this type, but it may be the northern part of Peru. None of them are to be regarded as native to Pachacamac.[2]

---

[1] The nursing of young animals by women was observed by the writer in the highland of Bolivia.
[2] On ancient trade connections along the coast of Peru, see above, p. 5.

B. Textiles.

The textile art of this period is represented by a large number of specimens. There are examples of all the different techniques known at that time: tapestries, plain textures, figured material, in which the figure is produced by warp-threads in two or three colors (see pl. 8, fig. 14); double stuffs, open-work materials with interchanged warp-threads, gauzy fabrics and embroidered ones, besides a great variety of braids, etc. The same class of objects repeated here is illustrated by Reiss u. Stübel in their book on Ancon; but grave tablets, like those on pl. 32, l. c., are wanting. In design and technique these stuffs resemble many of those shown in the before-mentioned work, with the exception of some of either an earlier or a more recent date than this period.

The following designs may be specially mentioned as being characteristic of Ancon, according to Reiss u. Stübel, and of the open section of this cemetery, at the last pre-Inca period: rhombic (or rather hectangular) ponchos represented in pl. 44, fig. 1. The patterns are always the same. Ponchos identical in texture and design with those in pl. 35, figs. 2 and 4. Braids such as those on the mummy, pl. 22. Figure designs in tapestry, as pl. 51, fig. 1; pl. 52, fig. 1; pl. 69, fig. 1. Separate ornamental figures, mostly indistinct in detail, but of the general character as those in pl. 67 b, figs. 3 and 4; pl. 53, fig. 2. Bird designs, pl. 56, fig. 1. Lineal ornaments developed from figures, pl. 63, fig. 3. All-over designs, pl. 67, figs. 1 and 6; pl. 63, fig. 4; pl. 62 a, fig. 3; 35 a, fig. 1; 59 a, fig. 4. Patterns like that of pl. 67 a, fig. 1, are often seen in fewer colors and in a different technique, the pattern threads running through the design. Subdued coloring is characteristic of this period. One very important category of all-over patterns, found in this cemetery, seems to be entirely wanting at Ancon; therefore a few typical specimens are shown, pl. 8, figs. 11–13, 15 and 16. Gauze-ponchos, of the class shown by Bastian, l. c., pl. 5, are not represented in the Ancon plates. These ponchos are white, colored, or with mythological figures painted upon them; the material is a very fine cotton, with a strip of tapestry down the front, and a border around the edges and sides to strengthen the stuff. The ground color of these borders is nearly always green, rarely blue. The ornaments are typical and designed from plants. In some cases small pieces of tapestry are attached to the gauzy material, as may be seen on the poncho shown by Bastian. A large number of ponchos with similar borders were found in this section of the cemetery, and it is possible that the poncho shown by Bastian, the origin of which is not known, may have come from here.[3]

Comparing the designs and technique of the weaver's art of this period with that of the earlier, some great differences are to be noted.

1. The figures in the tapestry designs show a tendency to curtailment in details, which is evident in various ways. a. The figures become more rigid and inartistic, as pl. 7, fig. 7; above, fig. 49; they are set side by side, or sporadically, without any connection, pl. 8, fig. 14. b. The figures repeat the main forms of the design in a characteristic, even natural

---

To commercial relations point: the beads which were numerous in the graves of the central Peruvian coast and in Pachacamac, probably coming from the island of Lobos; also the fishing-boat, made of a tree from the forests of Equador, still in use in that region (comp. Reiss u. Stübel, pl. 3), the type of which is a very ancient one.

[3] Wiener shows, p. 514, a strip of border of the same width and design as the central strip of the poncho mentioned above. He calls it 'the central part of a cloth' (linceuil); it is shorter in the reproduction, but probably by faulty reconstruction, and it is evidently the central strip of one of these gauze ponchos. As to its origin, Wiener states: "Trouvé dans la 'huaca' nord du Gran-Chimu, non loin du groupe des grands palais"(?). This again seems to be one of those conscious and systematic falsifications of locality (see Stübel u. Uhle, l. c., p. 49, note 2), whereby Wiener's book loses all scientific value.

and animated way, but lack beauty of style and finish in detail. Examples of this class from Ancon are the figures in the stuffs by Reiss u. Stübel, pl. 51, fig. 1 ; pl. 52, fig. 1. A fine and characteristic example from Pachacamac is shown in fig. 56.[1]

2. The all-over patterns of the earlier periods followed the principle of the rectangular outlines, corresponding to the figures from which these were developed. The edge therefore followed the warp and woof.[2] In the present period the principle of the diagonal arrangement and outline of the design become typical. This new principle has an influence on the figure design, comp. pl. 8, fig. 14.

In the fabrics, pl. 8, figs. 11–13, 16 and 17, it is apparent that the edges of the designs were adapted diagonally, so as to follow the direction of the warp. The slits occurring in tapestry patterns were thus avoided. The specimen, pl. 8,

Fig. 56. Tapestry with mythological design. From later pre-Inca period.
⅔ n. s.

fig. 15, however, shows that occasionally the outlines of the design might follow the direction of the woof, and were thus

changed into a diagonal arrangement.[3] There are several examples of this class, bearing certain marks which may date them from a transitional period, when the diagonal outlines were only being introduced.

3. Tapestries of earlier periods, as Reiss u. Stübel show, pl. 49 ; 55 ; 69, fig. 6, here pl. 6, figs. 5 and 9, etc., are of the 'basse-lisse' technique or mainly so. The stuffs of the present period on the contrary, such as Reiss u. Stübel show, pl. 51 ; 52 ; 69, figs. 1 and 3, are of the 'haute-lisse' order. That the choice of a special principle is intentional is, perhaps, proved by the design of the pouch, pl. 8, fig. 14, where the figures are set side by side, although the effect would have been better if standing vertically.

4. The ornamental types of the earlier period are developed more and more into numerous all-over designs, gradually losing their symbolical meaning. The design, pl. 8, fig. 16, seems to be a reminiscence of figures like pl. 6, fig. 9 a; it also is in a state of transition into a mere all-over pattern, similar to that of fig. 11. In the design of the type of fig. 13 the process of transition has come to a close.

DESCRIPTION OF OBJECTS.

Pl. 8, fig. 11 : Forehead-band with ends of tapestry. Mus. 29506 ; ¼ n. s. This band is six feet ten inches in length and consists of a plain cotton band six feet long by one and a quarter inches wide, with end pieces of tapestry five inches long and three and a quarter inches wide. Two-thirds of the length of these tapestry pieces are divided into three strips, joined together at the ends and finished with a long brown fringe. The tapestry shows the colors white, red, yellow, blue, in a diagonal all-over pattern with many gradations.

Pl. 8, fig. 12 : A forehead-band resembling the former. Mus. 29517 ; ¼ n. s. The length of this band is five feet eight inches, without the fringe. It consists of a plain cotton band of five feet two inches by one and seven-eighths inches. Tapestry ends are woven on to it and terminate in a long fringe, which has been joined on after weaving. The band proper is loosely woven, with partly double, partly single warp threads. It widens out near the tapestry ends, which are three inches long by three and a quarter inches wide, woven in two sections of coarse yellow, red, brown and black woolen threads. One section at each end has a red and black ground. The design, however, is different on all four strips, consisting partly of an all-over pattern with many gradations, partly of rhombic, triangular, spurred and inverted rhombic figures. Forehead-bands of this class, all very similar in their general type, in color and design, were found in large numbers in this cemetery.

Pl. 8, fig. 13 : Strip with tapestry. Mus. 29924 ; ¼ n. s. This strip, fourteen and three-eighths inches long, consists of a loop three inches long by three and five-eighths inches wide, showing a faint design and a tapestry piece attached to it. At the joint a piece of cane has been inserted to keep the stuff stretched flat. The tapestry piece is eleven and a quarter inches long and four and a quarter inches wide; the edges are stitched all around. The design shows in white, green, blue, red and three shades of yellow, a complicated all-over pattern, with many gradations, in which birds and cat-like faces are repeated. Red, white, black and yellow strands ten inches long form a fringe. This fabric may have served in some ornamental way, attached to a wooden staff.

[1] This interesting piece of stuff is decorated in the centre with a design showing a staff or tree with crosses and figures about it ; fruit with grain-like contents streaming from the staff like rain. A number of human figures, standing, kneeling or running towards the tree, seem to receive gratefully, with outstretched hands, the gifts poured down upon them. They seem to be chieftains, judging from the ornaments on their heads, and each one is marked by several tablets bearing arms or signs. A similar tablet, a seal of clay with a condor's head on it, is to be seen among the acquisitions from Tiahuanaco. These signs resemble the figures in Mexican picture-writing. The occurrence in Peru of these shields or tablets, bearing marks explanatory of the figures, should be more closely investigated.

This important design is imperfect in its upper part. Two figures, probably similar to each other, stood on both sides of the pole in the centre. One is still visible ; it stands in a frontal position, different from the lower. Its headdress is high, blue and ornamented with something like an axe ; the almost square face is red, and the left hand is extended, as if bestowing gifts. It is clear that the two upper figures were the sources of the gifts which the human beings below received gratefully. The square face is a reminiscence of the figure on the Gateway of Tiahuanaco, and of the cloth, pl. 4, fig. 1. It appears that the color of the Huacas was red (comp. the description of the vessel, pl. 5). The pole in the centre formed at the same time a continuation of the slit of the garment of which this piece of stuff was a part, and of the design itself, serving as the medium, whereby the gifts of heaven were poured down upon humanity. For the first time, perhaps, we see here a distinct religious significance connected with the cross in Peru, outside of a vague statement made by Garcilaso, that the Incas possessed and worshiped a cross of stone. The Chilcha erected a cross of stone upon the grave of persons killed by snake bites. This reminds us of the cult of the cross among the Mayas and the Mexicans, where, too, it is connected with beneficent powers.

The ground of the stuff is white, the figures being mainly yellow with red outlines ; the loin cloths are blue, a few additional colors are grey, blue, brown, green, all rather faint.
[2] Comp. pl. 6, fig. 6, p. 31.

[3] The same is the case with the tapestry : Reiss u. Stübel, pl. 66 a, fig. 1, from Ancon, but in that instance the slits had been dexterously closed by the tapestry. A very similar piece of stuff was found in a peculiar grave at Pachacamac.

Pl. 8, fig. 14: Pouch with design in colors, part tapestry, part plain. Mus. 29900; ¼ n. s. The pouch is seven and a quarter inches long by six and a quarter inches wide. It consists of woolen vertical and cotton horizontal threads. The inside and outside are alike; the sides and upper edges are stitched. A thick band serves as a strap; it is woven with a round woof as a double band. The pattern upon it is reciprocal;[1] it is one and three-sixteenths inches wide; the colors are dull white, red and green. The ground color of the pouch is purple; the pattern consists of two sets of figures in alternate colors, blue, green, light-red, yellow and white. The woven stripes are black and white, and show a sort of animal figure and an all-over design. The texture of the plain parts looks like fig. 57, which gives the ground a dotted

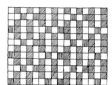

Fig. 57. Three-ply weaving of pouch, pl. 8, fig. 14.

appearance. The ends of the pouch are finished off with tassels.

Pl. 8, fig. 15: Belt of tapestry. Mus. 29878; ¼ n. s. The belt is ten and a half inches long by five and a quarter inches wide. It is closed and consists of two thicknesses of material of the same design, which are joined at both ends by means of a round knit seam; a similar one secures the edges. The pattern shows many colors and vivid contrasts—white, two shades of red, also brown, yellow, blue, green and black. There are seven stripes of uneven width, the four narrower ones of which repeat a meander design, and the three wider ones show an all-over pattern in mostly rectangular gradations. The original figure design of this pattern may be seen in eyelet ornaments. A red woolen tassel finishes each of the two lower corners.

Pl. 8, fig. 16: Border of a cotton poncho. Mus. 29934; ¼ n. s. The poncho is of a grayish-brown color, of a thin gauzy tissue; its dimensions are twenty-five and a quarter inches in length by forty-one and a quarter inches in width. The opening for the neck and armholes, three and three-quar-

ters inches long, were bound with colored knit borders. The lower edge, two and fifteen-sixteenths inches wide, consists of a wider border and a narrow sort of braid binding, with a short fringe formed at intervals by the woof. The wider border shows, in sections, interlaced figures. The figures of each color cover four of these sections, two of them on both sides being interlocked with the adjoining figures of contrasting colors.

Pl. 8, figs. 17 and 18, show figures of two central strips of gauze ponchos. Mus. 29576 and 77; ¼ n. s. The two figures, 17 and 18, appear in several repetitions in both strips. The design of both is the same. Two figures clothed like men and facing each other, are holding on to a staff, which is broad at the upper end and pointed at the lower. In fig. 18 a flat object is noticeable under the point of the staff, which appears to be resting on a support with two points or feet, in such a manner that the centre lies hollow. Judging from the pointed shape of the staff in both reproductions, and the manner in which it is held, the two figures seem to be engaged in piercing the object beneath it, and it may be assumed that the figures are keeping a drill in motion. The drill as seen in pl. 8, figs. 17 and 18, is being applied to some object, the nature of which is not clear. It rests upon a foundation having two prongs or supports, and is evidently not a fire-drill; it may have been used for the boring of pearls. The procedure as here represented is not an ordinary one, as the figures are pictured with high festive headdresses, similar if not identical in both plates. The headdresses in fig. 17 are of the same shape as the support upon which the object for drilling rests in fig. 18. The faces of the men resemble those of animals. Square objects at the back of the neck seem characteristic, as they are reproduced in both plates. This scene evidently pictures some ceremonial act. Such representations and mythological figures are of frequent occurrence upon ponchos, but no interpretation can be attempted until the ancient customs shall be better known and more specimens brought together depicting similar scenes.

Pl. 8, fig. 19: Central strip of a gauze poncho like the preceding. Mus. 29578; ¼ n. s. The ground in this strip is dark blue, and upon it are two figures in a frontal position with high headdresses. The staves in their right hands resemble those in figs. 17 and 18, being wide at the top and pointed at the lower end. Some object, such as a flag or an axe, seems to be attached to one of these staves. This strip is duplicated, and a mythological meaning suggests itself, on account of the heads which decorate the ground and the border.

[1] Throughout this report we use the term reciprocal for patterns which are alike on both sides, only in opposite colors, and complementary such designs which are continued in the same outlines through colored stripes, etc., reflexive for stripes of a different color which cross designs, only partly changing their color, but not the outline (as in woven baskets, comp. Kultur u. Industrie, II, pl. 8, figs. 6, 8, 11, 12).

GENERAL REVIEW OF THE PERIOD.

The characteristics of this last period are in marked contrast with those of the preceding. Only a few slender threads connect them, in the form of ornamental types, such as the head of an animal symmetrically developed (pl. 7, fig. 1) and the tufted ornament, resembling a staff broadened towards the top. A few additional resemblances might be traced in the elements of ornamental design, but differences and departures from older designs are much more numerous. The strong contrast between the older forms and technique of the pottery and those of the present period is very evident, quite apart from difference in artistic skill. A new decorative type appears, and entirely new principles of technique arise in textiles, such as the tendency toward diagonal outlines of the patterns, together with a complete transformation

of design. It has been suggested that during this period a distinct transition had been accomplished in the technique of tapestry from 'basse-lisse' to 'haut-lisse.' This sudden and abrupt change[1] must have been brought about by unknown circumstances, strong enough to cause a revolution in the cultural forms of Pachacamac. The difference in the headbands from those in older graves[2] may serve as a proof of this. In the lands of the Incas each tribe or province was distinguished by the headband. Doubtless this custom was an old one, and merely confirmed by law through the Incas. The uncivilized tribes of eastern South America are now dis-

[1] See above, p. 29.
[2] Comp. pl. 6, figs. 9 and 15.

tinguished from one another by the peculiarities of the feather ornaments in their headdresses. Headbands of plain white cotton with two colored tapestry ends (pl. 8, figs. 11 and 12) are entirely wanting in the older section of the cemetery, while they are so characteristic of the graves in the uncovered section. Such change in cultural form might suggest a difference in the predominating population. The nature of the new elements which came to rule at Pachacamac seems to be proved by the technical types of pottery and textiles, which correspond to those extending along the coast of central Peru as far as Pativilca, or even farther north. Gauze ponchos,[1] so characteristic of this period, point to the coast, especially its northern part, as their climatic home and natural place of origin. It appears, therefore, that previous to the conquest by the Incas two forms of civilization had met upon the soil of Pachacamac; the older, that of the earlier graves, depending upon the culture of the highland, the more recent being introduced from neighbors on the coast and, although inferior, abruptly supplanting the earlier.

[1] Comp. also p. 37.

CHAPTER XV.

REMARKS ON THE HISTORY OF THE TEMPLE.

A TOPOGRAPHICAL description was previously given, p. 19, ff. (with fig. 3), of the site of the Temple and of the different strata of soil found under and in front of the Temple terraces. We shall have to draw conclusions concerning the history of the sanctuary from the character of those different strata in relation to the graves found in them. The graves of the original cemetery, *a* (graves No. 1 above), extended to the wall, *b*,[1] as has already been shown, and the characteristic objects found there belonged mainly to the style of Tiahuanaco or to that immediately following. The wall, doubtless, formed part of the original building and was in existence before the foundation of the cemetery. The Temple structure, therefore, if not older, must be at least contemporaneous with the period illustrated by these graves, and must have been built at a period and by a people holding the same religious views which found their most artistic embodiment in the ancient monuments of Tiahuanaco. Some fragments of pottery found near *l* in section *m*, in the rear of the Temple, were identified as being the same period. They were discovered at various depths, five to fifteen feet, among adobe fragments, and were classified with vessels of that period decorated with textile patterns.[2] After the cemetery at the foot of the Temple had been in use for a long time, events took place during the course of which the building was destroyed. This destruction is shown by the leveling of the stone front wall, and by the stratum of fragments of ruined adobe walls above the soil of the original cemetery. The adobe fragments are from the old Temple, judging from their position and from the style of their decoration, one which in this ancient city was used only on buildings devoted to the cult. The débris of the ruined walls piled up in front of the structure and formed a slope (*d*, *e*). The destruction of the sanctuary corresponded to a complete change in the dominant form of civilization in the town, as is shown by the graves *v*, found in the débris of the Temple. These graves, made since the destruction of the original Temple, not only reveal a different form of civilization, but even a different nationality, a people by whom probably the ruin was effected. This people possessed close cultural relations with the northern part of the coast, which always had an ascendency over the cultural forms of the highlands. It is a difficult matter to fix the date of the wall with mural paintings in the manner of the Chimu, since it was untouched by the destruction and by the rebuilding of the Temple. If older than the first event, it seems strange that it escaped unharmed. The character of the painting would be more in harmony with the later period, that revealing the supremacy of the tribes which possessed the general culture of the coastland. On the other hand, the wall does not belong to the plan of the terraces of the new Temple, since it was concealed by one of them built in front of it, and its height, four and a quarter feet, compared to three to three and one-quarter feet of terraces, *p*, *q*, also points to a different date of erection. No mention is made by any of the early writers of temple walls frescoed with human figures. These paintings, therefore, at the time of the discovery, belonged to a past era, and that they had been in existence a long time is shown by the fact that the figures have been renewed, the older ones still being visible under the more recent. The date might be assigned to three different periods of the Temple, two of them after its destruction. As, however, the wall was not destroyed, but only concealed by another, it may be assumed that the two last periods were not separated by any great convulsions.

When the Temple was enlarged by the addition of terraces certain sections of the ancient cemetery were built over. The extension included more than one side of the Temple, as there are graves of the same period underneath the terraces of the northeast front.[3] The people to whom the destruction of the Temple must be ascribed evidently made their appearance prior to its reconstruction, as several graves, very characteristic of that period, were found in the ruins under the later temple terraces (the graves *v*). Graves bearing marks of the Cuzco type, however, are situated only outside the Temple, in no case under its terraces. The graves *v*[4] also seem to reflect only the first part of the period to which they belong; various earlier forms peculiar to the same, and which might be expected in these graves, are wanting. There are only a small number of graves of this class. They are entirely wanting in the section of the cemetery which was covered over with stratum *i* at the time of the rebuilding of the Temple.[5] A more complete representation of the characteristics of the period was prevented by the rebuilding of the Temple during the period of the graves *v*, at least in all those sections upon which the terraces were set, *p* to *t*, and under stratum *i*.

Numerous types of specimens are found only in the open section of the cemetery, never duplicated in the part which was built over, and all of them quite free from any admixture of Cuzco types. The existence of these objects in the later graves, which were made after the rebuilding of the Temple, mark that period as a far earlier one than that of the appearance of the Incas in the valley. It seems, therefore, difficult to assume that the rebuilding of the Temple should have taken place as late as the Inca period.

---

[1] See above, p. 19, fig. 3.
[2] Comp. above, p. 29.

[3] See above, p. 19.
[4] See above, p. 19.
[5] See above, p. 21.

There is no doubt that the nature of the tutelar deity of the ancient city is not yet fully known and interpreted. We learn from early accounts no more than that Pachakamaj was the supreme deity of the Incas, and Garcilaso states that the worship accorded to him was of a spiritual nature. We also know that the ancient Indians said prayers to the god Pachakamaj on certain spots upon the roads, as do some of their descendants in the highland to this day, and that his sanctuary was in the lowland near the coast. In the highland the cult of Pachakamaj was an ancient one, while early records show that the Incas in the lowland adopted it shortly before the arrival of the Spaniards. The name Pachakamaj, 'Creator of the world,' is of Kechua origin,[1] and cannot, therefore, be of more recent date than the Inca conquest of the valley. During earlier times the divinity must have had a different name, which would agree with a statement of Fernando de Santillan, that he had formerly been called Irma. It is difficult to understand why the Incas should have given him a name in their language, signifying the highest conception of their own religion, if it were true, as historians will have it, that they became familiar with the god and his shrine only after their conquest of the region.

If Dr. Brinton is correct in identifying the name of Pachakamaj with Wiraqocha,[2] on the strength of the testimony of Acosta, and of an old song preserved by Garcilaso, it rather complicates the individuality of the divinity in the ancient sanctuary on the coast. At once the questions arise, What relation had the ancient god Irma to the later name of Pachakamaj? Was there any historical reason for the change of name? If so, what was its nature and what caused the Incas to make the identification?

All we really know about the Temple is that the building is of great antiquity, and that in the early part of its history it was known by a different name. Cieza makes several references to it in his writings;[3] also Garcilaso,[4] when he tells how the ruler of Pachacamac, in his negotiations with the Inca, proudly mentions his forefathers from whom he had inherited customs and laws. Montesinos gives the sanctuary a very great age, dating it back to an early period of Peruvian history, 2000 before Christ,[5] but as a rule his chronology is not trustworthy. Garcilaso states that the Inca had spread the cult of the supreme creator and preserver of all things, Pachakamaj, through the entire realm, and that those who adopted this faith were the ancestors of Cuismancu, who built a Temple to this deity. His account may be regarded as pure invention, intended to explain what otherwise seems so incomprehensible, the adoption of the divinity of the coastland by the Incas as if it had been originally their own. The testimony of the old chronicler cannot as yet be used for an historical examination of this question.

One of the most important points shown by the preceding discussion is this: that the style of Tiahuanaco, which, according to latest discoveries, extended over the entire shore country of Titicaca Lake, and probably included the southern section of the Peruvian highlands, spread from the highland to the coast country, and gained a deep influence over those regions, also becoming established in the valley of Pachacamac, situated farther to the north. We have thus acquired a very different point of view for the appreciation of the importance of ancient Tiahuanacoan culture on Peruvian soil, from that with which its historical discussion was introduced in an earlier work on the monuments of Tiahuanaco. It now seems certain that this ancient form of civilization was widely extended in oldest Peru. The entire coast of central Peru has been more or less influenced by it. The splendid poncho from Ancon is found to be in the pure style of Tiahuanaco, as well as numerous other specimens from graves in Ancon and in the Lima valley. Pieces of pottery of the class of pl. 5, figs. 1 and ff, are occasionally designated at Lima as 'type of Huacho,' which seems to indicate that the period of that style is represented a little farther to the north in the Huacho valley. The cultural relations between the ancient works at Tiahuanaco and the province of Ancacho, established by the discovery of the stone relief of Chavin de Huantar, at first so mysterious, now seem almost proved, and doubtless before long will be entirely understood. The De Ville collection at Brussels contains a vessel from Chordeleg, near Cuenca, in Ecuador, identical with the ceramic types of the Epigonal period of Pachacamac. A possible doubt as to its genuineness is removed by the fact that the collections of Berlin, Brussels and Philadelphia contain pieces of pottery from Ecuador of ancient Peruvian character, and bearing traces of the Tiahuanaco style. The vessel of Chordeleg must have been carried from northern Peru to Ecuador at some very early date. This points to a possible influence which the archaic forms of the Tiahuanaco civilization may have exercised as far as Ecuador. At the very beginning of the development of ancient Peruvian civilization we see the cultural form, which was only little inferior in the extent of its sphere of influence to the later one introduced by the Incas.

We are as yet unable to determine its relation to the Chimu culture, no investigations having been made in this direction; but it is possible that the latter either depended, proceeded from or was strongly influenced by it. If facts should be brought out to sustain this supposition, the culture of the Chimu would be the most brilliant outcome of the art of Tiahuanaco. In spreading this cultural form, its religious side especially was carried to the various parts of ancient Peru. The detailed description of the more important finds has shown that by them the same religious ideas are illustrated which caused the erection of the Tiahuanacoan monuments. We see there the same sceptre-bearing divinity, with winged and unwinged animals of mythological nature appearing as his servants. The figures of these mythological ministering spirits are, as a whole, almost identical with those upon the monuments and objects of art from Tiahuanaco; and the ancient forms of religion as revealed by the contents of the graves at Pachacamac must therefore have been similar in both places. Several features have been already specially noted. The custom of placing in the graves pieces of pottery or textiles, with religious figures of the nature of fetishes upon them, whereby the dead were recommended to the protection of the divinity at whose foot of whose sanctuary they were buried, shows that the occupants were adherents accordingly of the same religious faith. Doubtless the large cloth, bearing mythological decorations (pl. 4, fig. 1), had been chosen for this reason as a shroud for the dead. The grave where it was found (p. 19, fig. 3, u) was situated quite near the Temple, which might lead to additional conclusions in regard to

---

[1] J. v. Tschudi, Beitr., p. 121, discusses at length the meaning of Pachakamaj. 'Pacha' signifies 'time' or 'space, and 'world' means as much as 'earth' or 'soil.' The divine activity of Pachakamaj is therefore bestowed upon the universe in general, and the earth especially. 'Pachamama,' 'Earthmother,' seems to be the goddess of Earth. The worship of this goddess is still continued in the south as far as the valley of the Calchaqui in Argentina. Both she and Pachakamaj are said to dwell in the 'apachetas,' artificial stone-piles on the wayside.

[2] Hero Myths, p. 197.

[3] Crónica, I, chap. 72; II, chap. 58.

[4] VI, chap. 30.

[5] Chap. 9.

the special significance of the mythological group upon it, in itself an object of worship. The god pictured upon this cloth was presumably the same to whom the Temple was dedicated, and one of supreme rank, not inferior to the divinity of the Tiahuanacoan Gate-relief. Though he does not bear sceptres, he is still distinguished by similar attributes of greatness and power both to preserve and to destroy, such as the head-ornament surmounting serpents and trophies of human heads. The pose is similar to that of the figure of Tiahuanaco, and ministering spirits appear again in mythological figures waiting upon him. It may be assumed that in this picture we possess one of the oldest representations of the divinity of this Temple, which evidently was for the coastland the counterpart of the idol of Tiahuanaco.

In the earlier book on the Ruins of Tiahuanaco, the question concerning the principal figure of the relief was not conclusively settled; authors were inclined to regard this deity as a representation of Wiraqocha, the creator-god, and it did not seem impossible that he might be a personification of the sun.[1] All doubts on this subject are now removed; the figure does not represent the sun, but a creator-god. The Chimu had a powerful deity, the ruler of the skies, armed with club and arrows, and in Peru the god of thunder is generally shown with these weapons.[2] The attributes resembling sceptres of the main figure in the Gate-relief are symbols of the power of the god over thunder and lightning. It may be noticed that one of the sceptres,[3] the right-hand one, is short and broad, without ornament, while that in the left hand is half cloven in two. Both sceptres symbolize weapons; the short and broad one is the club which causes the thunder, the cloven one represents the three-armed bola, which, when swung and thrown at a goal, in flying resembles the form of a flash of lightning.[4] The bola takes the place of the arrows,[5] which symbolize lightning in the religious art of the lowlands.[6] This fact is another important proof that the art of the Tiahuanacoan style had its origin in the highland. The correctness of the interpretation of the two sceptres as club and bola, or thunder and lightning, is proved by a small circumstance not noted by others since the publication of 1892. There is a very small yet distinctly visible bird upon the top of the right-hand sceptre or club, the thunderbird, waiting for the waving of the sceptre, in order to fly off and carry the darkness and terrors of the thunder-storm over the land.[7] The power over thunder and lightning, attributed to the god of the Gate-relief,[8] entirely excludes his interpretation as a sun-god.

The sphere of power of this divinity is boundless. Judging from the legends, he appears to be almost identical[9] with Wiraqocha of the Titicaca Lake country,[10] and with the Peruvian Wiraqocha, whose nature was so ably described by Dr. Brinton. The apparently unimportant feature, alike in the Relief of the Gateway, in the legends of the Titicaca country and of the Peruvian Wiraqocha, that a host of mythical messengers are attending the god and sent out by him,[11] serving as mediums through whom he works, is exceedingly characteristic and definitely connects the three forms. The question as to the name of the god in whose honor those Tiahuanacoan monuments were reared, whether Wiraqocha, T'onapa or Tarapaka,[12] names which all appear for the same divinity, can only be of interest to us as far as it is connected with the question of the nationality of the builders of the ancient works of Tiahuanaco, which cannot yet be solved.

The sanctuary of Pachacamac originally was derived from the cult of this creator-god of the highland,[13] who appears in the Tiahuanaco relief, as well as in the legends and myths, as Wiraqocha, and sometimes as T'onapa or Tarapaka. By this conclusion various details of the ancient myths gain a greater importance.[14]

---

[1] L. c., p. 65.

[2] Relacion anónima, p. 139.

[3] Stübel u. Uhle, l. c., pl. 8.

[4] According to Ondegardo (v. Tschudi, Beitr., p. 58), the weather-god carries a club in one hand, a sling in the other. The god of the Gate-relief, however, must at the same time be a creator-god, since the sun is represented in the frieze in an inferior position, as if depending upon the main figures.

[5] Comp. also Brinton, Hero Myths, p. 49.

[6] The bola was used as a weapon in the highland of southern Peru and in Bolivia. It may still be found in use in the Puna of Bolivia for the hunting of vicuñas. The Uros on the Desaguadero use it for hunting water-fowl.

[7] A study of the thunder-bird upon pottery of the Chimu was published by Schurtz, Globus, 1897, No. 4.

[8] The power over thunder and lightning as well as over the lives of men, which is symbolized in the trophy-heads, go well together. According to the Relacion anónima, p. 139, the thunder-god is the originator of epidemics, of death, of famine. Similarly the Indians of Bolivia still believe that every flash of lightning kills a human being.

[9] The god causes fire to fall from the heavens; he flings flashes of lightning, burns up entire mountains, drowns whole nations in tidal waves, but also puts out conflagrations with his staff (Betanzos, chap. 2; Santacruz, p. 237 ff.; Calancha, according to Tschudi, Beitr., p. 182). In the account of Dr. Brinton, Hero Myths, p. 178, Ayar Cachi, the brother of Manqo Qhapaj, represents Wiraqocha. The Indians in northern Bolivia tell various animal and other fables. In one of these the Inca decides a quarrel as to the relative height of the mountains, Illimani and Mururata, by taking a sling and knocking off the summit of Mururata, which becomes the Sajama mountain, over 20,000 feet high, more than 130 miles distant. The Mururata appears flattened at the top, as if cut off. Similar stories are told of other mountains.

[10] Dr. Brinton, Hero Myths, p. 170 ff. Compare for the nature of Wiraqocha, Acosta, B. VI, chap. 21. 'Aticsi,' conqueror, is not a surname of Wiraqocha, as Markham states, Narratives, Introd., p. x, and Brinton, p. 170. A verbal form 'aticsi,' from 'atiy,' to be able, is impossible in Kechua. The participle would have to be atij. The surname is caused merely by the misinterpreted connection of the ejaculation 'ah'! with the name of the god: "Ticsi Wirakocha." The prayer begins (Molina, p. 33): "Aticsi (instead of Ah-tiksi) Viracocha," but in another, l. c., p. 31: "A Viracocha ticsi Viracocha," etc.

[11] Stübel u. Uhle, pls. 5, 11 and 16, pp. 55 and 60; Relacion anónima, p. 140; Garcilaso, V, chap. 18, and Acosta, 6, chap. 21.

[12] Santacruz, p. 236. Brinton takes the name Tarapaka for taripaka, from taripay, to judge (Hero Myths, pp. 174 and 184). This interpretation does not recommend itself. It is arbitrary to replace a by i (taripay); the derivation with ka is unusual; the conception of Wiraqocha as 'Judge of the universe' may have been caused by the corresponding Christian idea, but it is not to be found among the religious conceptions of the ancient Indians of Peru. The Relacion anónima also avoids (p. 154) reference to this side of Wiraqocha's character. Cieza has the form Tuapaca (II, chap. 5). Tarapaca is translated as 'eagle' by Santacruz. Compare paca—eagle, cocotaapaka and conturaapaka—very big eagle, similar to a condor (Bertonio, Diccionario Aimará-Cast., p. 241). The condor, eagle and falcon had many relations with Wiraqocha. Kon Traya Wiraqocha, in a legend of Huarochiri, blesses the condor and the falcon (Avila, p. 127 ff.). On the temple of Wiraqocha at Urcos an eagle and a falcon were cut into the stone (Molina, p. 29). After having won the victory over the Chaucas with Wiraqocha's help, the Inca had two condors carved in stone at Muyna (Garcilaso, IV, chap. 23).
As a special emblem of distinction the Inca wore two feathers of two different birds of the Coraquenque species, which were considered as symbols of Manco Chapaj and of Mama Ojllo. Garcilaso, VI, chap. 28, describes the bird as resembling the falcon. According to Bertonio, Dicc. Aim. Cast., p. 241, and Cast.-Aim., p. 29, Kurikenke or Kurikanke is a small eagle, "speckled black and white, and with white throat."
The Indians in Bolivia call the condor the Supreme God and a number of pretty fables are connected with it. They avoid killing a condor. A friend of ours in Bolivia who had a stuffed specimen of this bird in his country house, for that reason alone enjoyed the highest respect of the Indians.

[13] Very different and more unreliable is the tradition as Montesinos gives it. According to him, a nation arrived in the plains, one part of whom built the temple of Pachakamaj, the others moved to the interior and founded Huaitara and Quinoa. Huaitara, with ancient stone monuments, is situated in the mountains above Pisco (Paz Soldan, Dicc. Geogr., p. 443). Not far from there, in another valley, lies Ica, which possesses similar traditions (comp. v. Tschudi, Beitr., p. 193).

[14] According to Betanzos and Molina, the creator sends messengers from Tiahuanaco to Condesuyu and Andesuyu, along the coast and the wooded slopes in the east, all over Peru, as far as Guayaquil (comp. Stübel u. Uhle, p. 55).
The existence of a huge stone image at Jauja is confirmed in Spanish times (Descripcion de la provincia de Jauja, Rel. Geogr., I, p. 80): "and in Jauja were monuments of the highest antiquity, which Tupaj Inca went to see." Santacruz, p. 263, speaks of ancient stone figures at Jauja, Pachacamac and Chincha Yungas, and connects them with T'onapa. According to Molina, the creator-god turned men into stone at Tiahuanaco, at Pucana (north of Lake Titicaca), at Pachacamac and at Cajamarca. Santacruz states that the Guancas at Jauja and the Chinchaisuyus believe that T'onapa had been in their country; he even identifies the divinity of the Guancas, Wariwillka, with T'onapa. This shows that the myths point to a direct dependence of some of the ancient places of worship of pre-Spanish Peru upon the creator-god of Tiahuanaco. The old stone images mentioned by Molina and Santacruz as standing at Pachacamac have disappeared.

The peculiar nature of the god of the coastland is well illustrated by myths connected with him. Antonio de Calancha (II, chap. 29) writes as follows: " I will here relate the labors and achievements of the god [Pachakamaj] : The remembrance of Adam and Eve had been lost among these people, as among the Greeks and Romans ; they ascribed the creation of the world to various agents and gave different names to the first creatures or first men. It has already been told from whom the dwellers of the mountains considered themselves descended, and we will now consider the god whom the people worshiped—the people of the coast, the Yungas, the dwellers of the plain and of the sandy desert, over all the district from Piura to Arica, three hundred leagues in length and from twelve to fifteen in breadth, according to the width of the coastland. One particular legend was firmly believed in by all, up to the time of the general visitations to exterminate idolatry, which were extended as far as Huarmey. This legend was found to be about the same in all villages and districts, and even at the present day the people believe in it more than in the articles of the Church. They did not acknowledge that Adam and Eve were the first parents of mankind, but at six hearings, in which more than a thousand persons were examined, all agreed in their beliefs concerning those beings whom they worshiped."

P. Luis Turruel, the companion of P. Joseph de Arriago, gives the following narrative: " They say that the origin of the Indians of the plain, and of their ' wakas ' and their food, is this : In the beginning of the world there was no food for a man and a woman whom the god Pachakamaj had created. The man starved to death, but the woman survived. One day she walked abroad to seek roots among the thornbushes, in order to sustain life. She lifted up her eyes to the Sun, and with abundant tears and lamentations and sighs she said : ' Beloved creator of all things ! Why hast thou brought me into the light of this world, if I am to die of hunger and want ? Oh, that thou hadst not created me out of nothing, or that thou hadst suffered me to die immediately upon entering this world, instead of leaving me alone in it without any children to succeed me, poor, cast down and sorrowful ! Why, O Sun, having created us, why wilt thou let us perish ? And if thou art the giver of light, why art thou so niggardly as to refuse me my nourishment ? Thou hast no pity, and heedest not the sorrow of those whom thou hast created only to their misery. Cause heaven to slay me with lightning, or earth to swallow me, or give me food, for thou, almighty one, hast made me.' These and other prayers and lamentations she poured forth to the Sun, in such outbreaks of frenzy as the sting of hunger will cause. The Sun was touched with pity and descended to her. Pretending ignorance, he inquired into the cause of her complaints. She told him of her distressing life, and of having to find her nourishment in so painful a manner as digging roots. While he listened to her lamentations he pitied her in her sorrow, and spoke kind words and bade her give up her fears and hope for comfort, for she would soon be delivered from the cause of her trouble. He bade her to continue digging roots, and while she was doing so he impregnated her with his rays, so that to her great joy she bore a son after four days. She believed that the life of anxiety had come to an end for ever, and that abundance of food would be given her. It was not to be so, however, for the god Pachakamaj was displeased with her for having given worship to the Sun, his father, and for having borne him a son in defiance of himself. He seized the new-

born demi-god, not caring for the cries of the mother, who implored the Sun to help her child, his son equally with Pachakamaj. But the latter killed the new-born infant, his half-brother, and cut him to pieces. The mother cried to the Sun to revenge this fratricide. Pachakamaj did not intend the woman to suffer through the lack of foresight of his father, the Sun, in not producing food for her, and in order that she should not worship any one but himself, he sowed the dismembered parts of the murdered boy. From the teeth grew corn, which resembles teeth in form ; from the ribs and bones yuccas, a root which resembles bones in shape and whiteness, and other roots as well. From the flesh came cucumbers, pakais and all the other vegetables and fruits. Since that time men have known no more want, and there has been no more weeping on account of it. This abundance of food they owe to Pachakamaj, and the earth has ever since continued to be fruitful. The mother, however, was not comforted, for every fruit reminded her of her child. Moved by her sorrowing love for the dead son, and by her thirst for revenge, she again dared to appeal to the Sun to punish the murderer and to heal her sorrow. The Sun was powerless against Pachakamaj, still he pitied the woman and descended to her, asking for the umbilical cord of her murdered child. The woman showed it to him and the Sun put life into it, thus giving her another son, and bidding her clothe the weeping child and to name it Wichama, or Willamo according to others. She brought the child up until he grew into a fair and strong youth. Desiring to travel all over the world like his father, the Sun, he set out on his journey, having obtained his mother's permission, but had hardly left when Pachakamaj, finding her old and feeble, slew her. Cutting her to pieces, he caused the gallinazos and the condors to devour her. Only the hair and bones he saved, concealing them near the shore. Then he created men and women, who were to take possession of the earth, and set curacas and caziques to rule over them. Wichama, the demi-god, then returned to his native valley, Vegueta, about a league from Huaura, and found it abounding with trees and plants and beautiful with many flowers. Anxious to see his mother, he looked for her, but found her no more. He learned from a chieftain of her cruel death, and his eyes blazed with rage and his heart burned with sorrow. Calling the inhabitants of the valley together, he made inquiries for the bones of his mother, and learning where they were concealed he found them, joined them together and brought his mother back to life. Then he planned with her for revenge and decided to murder Pachakamaj, the god. The latter, to avoid killing this second brother also, and enraged against all mankind, threw himself into the sea, on the spot where now stands the temple and the city which bear his name. When Wichama saw that Pachakamaj had escaped from his wrath, with the breath of his nostrils he set fire to the air and scorched all the fields. He then turned his wrath against the inhabitants of Vegueta and accused them of participation in the murder by not preventing it, and even of rejoicing in the deed. In his blind rage he disregarded their prayers and pleadings and besought his father to turn them all into stone. After having turned into stone all the creatures of Pachakamaj, who was invisible and could not see or help them, the Sun and Wichama repented of their deed. They could not undo their cruel act, but to atone for it somewhat they resolved to have the curacas and the caziques accorded divine honor, also the nobles and braves. They brought them all to the coast, setting up some there to be worshiped as Guacos ; others they set in the sea, where they now stand as rocks and reefs. They were all to receive divine honor, with annual offerings and sacrifices of silver-plates, chicha and espinco, thus to be propitiated for having been changed into stone. The highest place was accorded to Anat, the chief—a rock surrounded by the waves of the sea, one league from shore. He was formerly the greatest among men, and is now worshiped by the Indians as their supreme deity." In this legend concerning the origin of the human race, all the Indians of Huaura, Cupi Barranca, Ancallama, Huacho, Vegueta and the dwellers of the coast believed as firmly as we do the articles of the Creed, as was ascertained by the missionaries, Fernando de Avendaño and the PP. Josef de Arriago and Luis Teruel. The same belief was held by the Indians of Caraguaillo, five leagues to the north from Lima, and at Pachacamac, five leagues to the south ; also by the inhabitants of all the villages on the coast southward as far as Arica, who worship their rocks and reefs. They believe, however, that Pachakamaj created the people who later filled the earth, and who were to worship the gods and the huacas, and that he accomplished it in this manner: he sent four stars down to the earth, two male and two female, from whom the chieftains, nobles, the great, as well as the poor common people and serfs are descended. This is the legend in which they believed, and still do believe to this day, as firmly as we believe in the Creed, and that is the reason why they worship this god and the wakas.

Zárate, I, chap. 10, gives a shorter and slightly different version of the myth : " They relate that a man came from the north who had no bones and no joints, and when on a march he could lengthen or shorten the distance at will, also decrease or increase the height of mountains. This man created the first Indians. When the dwellers of the coast caused his displeasure, he changed the country into a desert, such as it now is, and ordered that rain should fall there no more for ever. He sent them some rivers, however, which flow through their land, so that they may at least drink and refresh themselves. The name of this man was Con, a son of the Sun and of the Moon. He was looked upon as a god and worshiped as such. It is said that he also provided the people whom he had created with wild herbs and fruits for their nourishment. After that another man came from the south, so it is said, who was stronger than the former. He was called Pachakamaj, which means ' Creator,' and he also was a son of the Sun and the Moon. On his arrival Con disappeared and left the people he had created without a protector. So Pachakamaj turned them into birds, apes, cats, bears, pumas, parrots and many other creatures which are to be seen in the land. Then the same Pachakamaj created the Indians of to-day and gave them for their occupation the cultivation of fields and the growing of fruit. They worship him, and all the chieftains of the land desire after death to be buried in the province of Pachacamac, which bears his name, since he has his shrine there. The valley is situated at four leagues from Lima. They also say that their Pachakamaj lived during several centuries, until the appearance of the Christians in Peru, and that since that time he has disappeared."

It may be seen from these two forms of the myth that the god personified the creative powers of the earth by giving to men as their nourishment the fruits of the soil, which before had not existed. He is the god who gave to man the fruitfulness of the valleys in the plains, and as this can only be obtained by the most careful husbandry, besides being a god of nature, he is also a god of cultural significance. In this he resembles Wiraqocha Pachayachachij, a ' world-

instructor' of the lowland, who drives out the savage and uncultured Con. The myth, as related by Antonio de Calancha, therefore, is a myth of the seasons, describing in mythical form the phenomena of nature as they are annually repeated in the clime of the coastland. The description of the climatical conditions, p. 1 ff, shows, as the most characteristic feature, the annually repeated struggle of the vegetation of the valley, which depends entirely on artificial irrigation against the scorching heat of the sun.[1] The former is personified in the myth in the god Pachakamaj. The Sun, with whom Pachakamaj carries on his struggle, represents the solar year, the first solar son, whom Pachakamaj kills, possibly the spring-sun, before the beginning of the rising of the rivers in the highland, when the season of fruitfulness begins. The scattering of the teeth and bones of the murdered son produces at once the fertility of the soil. The woman who bears a son to the Sun-god is the year. From a needy but toil-free life in the natural wilderness,[2] Pachakamaj leads her into a life full of care and toil, such as the cultivation of fields will require. Dissatisfied and still grieving at the death of her first-born son, she implores the Sun for another son to be the avenger of the slain one. This is Wichama, who personifies the autumn and winter sun, with whom Pachakamaj soon enters upon a struggle. The woman grows old, as does the year. Pachakamaj kills her, as the course of the year is ended with the harvest, and there is rejoicing over the death of the woman as over the harvesting. After the ingathering of the harvest and the autumnal decrease of the rivers, Pachakamaj is unable to resume the struggle, and the myth explains this from the gentleness of his nature, which refuses to kill the second son.

The flight of Pachakamaj into the ocean to escape the wrath of Wichama corresponds to the protecting cover of dense fogs which every winter for a time of six to eight months overspread the parched fields of the plain. Wichama, the Sun-hero, seeing himself deprived of the object of his revenge, wreaks his anger upon these fields, " his eyes ablaze, his heart kindled into flame and setting the air on fire." All the fields within reach of his eyes are those of the fog region, stretching inland about ten miles from the sea, and which are even in winter exposed to the arid sun, although they are still partly watered. For the climatic significance of the myth may also speak the fact, stated by Calancha, that all inhabitants of the narrow coastland between Arica and Huarmey believe in this myth as firmly as in their creed, for this strip of land is principally distinguished by the climatic phenomena which served the legend as a foundation. The climatic form of the myth of the god is related in its origin to the primitive myth of Wiraqocha, from whom the principle of the god Pachakamaj has been derived. Even the name, Wiraqocha, ' foaming sea,' points to a relation with the sea.[3]

---

[1] Cuismanku, the chieftain of Pachacamac, was right in telling the leader of the Inca army that his people did not need the Sun for a god, as he only caused them trouble. In Santillan's report, p. 32, Pachakamaj tells Tupaj Inka 'that he gave being to all creatures here below and to the Sun above.' This is ambiguous and may refer as much to the difference between the creative powers of the earth and those of the heavenly bodies as to the different forms of cult of both in the highland and the lowland.

[2] J. v. Tschudi, Beitr., p. 126, thinks it surprising that the Sun should have so unwisely neglected to supply mankind with food, and concludes that the myth was invented by a people of a different mode of thought, based upon a racial difference. This difference in the conception of the Sun, however, was caused by the difference in its climatic importance in the lowland.

[3] This interpretation, which we owe to Pacheco Zegarra, seems to have much to recommend it. Brinton, Hero Myths, p. 19 ff, mentions several facts in support of the same. Others of similar tenor are as follows : Ondegardo, Doc. ined., XVII, p. 80, says : " The name of the creator is Pachayachachij, which is a general name, and when they speak of the sea they say : 'Tiksi Wiraqocha,' that is 'the foaming sea, the origin of the world.' The vast market place of Cuzco was covered with sand from the coast to the height of two spans and a half, in honor of Wiraqocha " (l. c.), and "the ashes of the sacrifices which were offered up to Wiraqocha were scattered into the two rivers running through Cuzco, probably in order to let them flow into the sea " (comp. also Molina,

According to the oldest myths the god has risen out of the sea, whither he returns at the end of his labors.[1] It would not have been easy to find elsewhere in Peru climatic conditions which could more readily have been referred to the continually repeated rising out of the sea of Wiraqocha and return into it as on that coast of central Peru, and it may be possible that this added to the high degree of reverence in which the sanctuary was held all over the country.[2]

We may go still further. The god Irma of Pachacamac is the same as the god Iraya of the myths of the province of Huarochiri, in the upland of the river of Pachacamac. Francisco de Avila gives the following account:[3] "In ancient times Kon Iraya Wiraqocha came to Huarochiri in very ragged attire. By his word he created terraces and fields along the steep slopes of the ravines. By wielding a simple wand of cane he opened channels for irrigation. In the shape of a bird he descended from a tree upon the fair Kawillaka ('Sweetmouth'), who bore him a son as a virgin. Ignorant of the paternity of her son, she called the gods together and identified Iraya as the father when the boy ran to him laughingly. With shame and humiliation at his ragged appearance she fled into the sea. Iraya, however, who was the highest of the gods in spite of his poor attire, desired to win the favor of the goddess. He, therefore, clothed himself

The god Iraya evidently signifies productiveness of the soil as the result of cultivation. The staff with which he opens channels suggests the sceptre wielded by the thunderer Wiraqocha of the highland.[6] In the mountainous upland, with its narrow valleys of inferior fertility from climatic causes, the otherwise powerful god appears in beggar's attire. But while following the fair Kawillaka downstream, he dons splendid robes and " by his splendor lighted up the whole country," just as the golden cornfields in the plain are shining brightly between barren strips of desert. Thus he transforms himself again into the resplendent and powerful god Irma of Pachacamac. To him it is not difficult to pacify the serpent who is guarding the daughters of Pachakamaj. His wrath at the absence of Urpi Wachaj is natural, since she is his wife. By filling the sea with fish he renders a cultural service to mankind, one that would become Pachakamaj himself. As the personification of the fertility of the soil, Pachakamaj marries women[7] who represent rivers. The fish-pond of Urpi Wachaj, Pachakamaj's wife, seems a sufficient proof of this relation. The 'mother of the doves,' Urpi Wachaj herself, may denote the river of this valley. The season of the year when the god shows himself in the valley in his resplendent robes is the time when the rivers are swollen by the rains in the highland. Then Urpi

Fig. 58. Ruins on the Mama river, above Chosica.

in splendid golden robes, and ' by his splendor lighted up the whole country' and followed her, begging her to turn back and look upon him, but she refused. When he reached the shore, she had turned to stone in the ocean. The wife of Pachakamaj, Urpi Wachaj, 'mother of doves,' was visiting the goddess Kawillaka in the sea, and he found only her two daughters, guarded by a large serpent.[4] While he was trying to pacify the latter one of the daughters made her escape in the shape of a dove.[5] Angered by the absence of Urpi Wachaj, he emptied her fish-pond into the sea, whereby the sea became stocked with fish, while originally it had contained none.

Wachaj is absent in the sea; the waters of the river flow in a current of a different color far out into the sea toward the Pachacamac Islands, the rocks into which Kavillaca and her child were changed. The ponds of the legend are always numerous in winter. They are formed by the power of the surf, which is stronger than that of the river, and so the water is backed up in pools along the coast, diked in by the sand washed into the mouth of the river. Upon the appearance of the rising waters these dikes are broken and the ponds are emptied out into the sea, which in the myth is ascribed to the wrath of the god. The water-course of the Lima valley is also regarded as Pachakamaj's wife. At San Pedro de Mama, in the neighborhood of which is the confluence of the headwaters of the Rimac of the Lima valley, there stood a famous temple dedicated to the wife of Pachakamaj. These two rivers were her breasts.[8] The fertility of

p. 49). The sea, therefore, seems to have been considered as the origin of the world.

[1] Wiraqocha came out of the sea, according to different legends (Betánzos, chap. 1; Garcilaso, I, chap. 18; Oliva in v. Tschudi, Beitr., p. 130), and returned into it (Cieza, II, chap. 5; Santacruz, pp. 239, 240; Betánzos, chap. 2). The disappearance of Pachakamaj over the sea at Pachacamac is told by P. Maestro (Lima, 1602). According to S. Jimenez de la Espada, Congr. des Amér., Bruxelles, I, p. 593, in the same manner as that of Wiraqocha in the myths on Lake Titicaca.

[2] From all these sources it is clear that Pachakamaj should not be regarded as originally "a simple tribal deity of the Yunka," as Bruehl, p. 465, calls him.

[3] Markham, Narratives, p. 124 ff.

[4] Compare the piece of fabric, pl. 4, fig. 1, and figs. 10 to 12, in the text, p. 24.

[5] Doves, which live on grain and are only to be found in richer countries, go well with Pachakamaj as the god of fertility of the soil.

[6] In the central figure of the design, fig. 1, pl. 4, interpreted as the divinity of Pachacamac, the sceptres seem to be replaced by the knife and the severed human head, that of the murdered solar son. Thunder-storms being entirely unknown in the coastland, the omission of the staves symbolizing them in the highland seems to explain itself.

[7] Comp. Santillan, p. 32.

[8] Descripcion y relacion de la provincia de Yauyos; Rel. Geogr., I, p. 75. Mama is synonymous for 'breast' and 'mother.'

the valley of Lima was apparently the child of this divine pair, nourished by the breasts of the goddess. Starting from Lima in the company of a friend, the writer visited a ruin on the left bank of the Mama river, the left arm of the headwaters of the Rimac, close above its confluence with the right arm. The ruin is an extensive though plain building of broken stone, with doors and windows, and having several terraces in front which slope down toward the river, Fig. 58. As this building is distinguished above all others in that neighborhood by its size and importance, it may be the ruin of the temple dedicated to the wife of the divinity, which is the subject of the preceding chapter.

THE GOD AS THE CENTRE OF AN ORGANIZED NATURE CULT.

One of the most important clues to the interpretation of the ancient god Pachakamaj is the account of the Inca realm by Fernando de Santillan.[1] From this alone may be gained sufficient information concerning his significance as the creator-god throughout this coastland. According to this account Pachakamaj formed the centre of the 'waka' cult, which possessed a fundamental importance among the Peruvian religions. With the acceptance of the cult of Pachakamaj, that of the 'waka' came to be generally adopted in the land of the Incas. The original meaning of 'waka' is not known. It corresponds in a general sense to the Latin 'sacer.'[2] This word designates all idols, temples, all extraordinary products of nature, either attractive or repellent, especially monstrosities, graves, sacrificial offerings; all such localities or objects in nature which seem to reveal the creative power or a mysterious presence of the divinity, such as high mountains, springs, caves, etc.[3]

In many of these places the god had an oracle. This idea seems to have been attached especially to stone images.[4] Santillan, therefore, interprets the word waka as "certain stones through which the devil spoke." The real meaning, however, is not so simple. As we are surprised to learn in the Relacion anónima that the images of gods were called 'willka' and not 'waka,' we are furthermore obliged from other statements to distinguish between images which were 'waka' and those which were not. Thus Santillan distinguishes the cult of the sun, the moon and the earth from that of the wakas. He repeatedly speaks of "the wakas and the Sun," "neither the Sun nor the wakas."[5] Molina makes a distinction between the sacrifices offered to the creator and those to the wakas.[6] The Relacion de la Prov. de Vilcas Guaman, l. c., says also: "In ancient times they worshiped the wakas, and after the subjection under the Incas also the sun, the moon and the special idols of the Incas." From the foregoing quotations it appears that the images of the sun, the moon, the earth and the creator were not generally taken for 'waka,' being specially designated as 'villka.'[7] Thus Bertonio in his dictionary gives for 'villca' the meaning of "adoratorio dedicado al sol o atros idolos," and "villca el sol como antiguamente decian."[8] Some other idols of great importance or of special antiquity are termed 'villka'— so an idol mentioned by Santacruz, 'Guarivilca,' the chief idol of the province of Jauja,[9] and 'Aisavilca,' 'a great devil of the neighborhood of Lima.'[10]

Occasionally, however, images of the creator,[11] of the sun,[12] and the idol of the sanctuary on the mountain of Guanacaure near Cuzco are called wakas. Still this use of the word may be an erroneous one, as we know that the Incas were zealous persecutors of the wakas, while they worshiped the ancient idols, and before they acknowledged the sanctuary of Pachacamac.[13] The word waka may be supposed to designate the powers of nature, especially the productive force of the earth, in contrast to other and more independent powers. The wakas, generally speaking, were divinities of local character, dwelling in springs, mountains and caves, also mummies of the dead, who by their return to the creator had become mysterious powers. These powers of nature were grouped about the figure of the creator as emanations of the same. We do not know if all the wakas of the realm since the earliest centuries were thus connected with the creator-god of Pachacamac. Certainly something of this kind must have been the case in Pizarro's time, when Atawallpa told him that, although each village had its own 'mosque,' yet the common divinity of all the people together was at Pachacamac.

A people of the simple intelligence of the Peruvians could not have preserved this religious system in an abstract form. It was, therefore, by the priests adapted to the wants of the people and clothed in the garb of sensual relationship. Besides Pachakamaj, there were four principal shrines in the realm—Mala, Chincha,[14] Andahuailas and, since the conquest of the valley by the Inca, Cuzco—which were called the sons of Pachakamaj. "By these sons," says Santillan, "the wakas increased more and more, for the devil who spoke through them made the people believe that they could bear children, and caused them to build ever new temples and chapels for those who, according to their belief, were the descendants of the wakas, and as such considered to be their gods. Some they worshiped as men, others as women, and they laid their wishes before each of them according to his special nature. One they would implore to cause the rain to fall, another to make corn to grow and fruit to be abundant, others again to cause women to bear children and so forth.[15] In this manner the wakas were enormously multiplied, that at present there is a waka for nearly everything, and by their means the devil keeps the people so blindfolded that the greatest difficulty in that country is met in trying to teach the natives our holy Faith." Some of the wakas may have won their

---

[1] Santillan, p. 32 ff.

[2] The view of J. v. Tschudi, Beiträge, p. 152, that it meant 'cave,' lacks all foundation.

[3] Comp. J. v. Tschudi, Beitr., p. 150 ff.

[4] P. 34. Similarly the Descripcion de la Provincia de Vilcas Guaman, Rel. G., I, 149. "Wakas, which were images of stone, and which stood in certain places set aside for them." Molina, p. 7, speaks of wakas which had been turned into stone. Zarate, I, chap. 11: "Of certain stones which the Indians worship and call wakas."

[5] v. Tschudi, Beiträge, p. 171, doubts this statement (not in his Wörterbuch, p. 99).

[6] Pp. 30, 34, 35.

[7] Willka are also the highest classes of the priesthood (v. Tschudi, Beitr., p. 171).

[8] Diccionario Aimará-Cast., p. 386.

[9] P. 262, v. Tschudi, Wörterbuch; p. 315, Huari, god of strength.

[10] Santacruz, p. 275.

[11] Betánzos, chap. 5.

[12] Zárate, I, chap. 11: "Certain stones which represent the sun and are called waka."

[13] The mythical Manqo Qhapaj was looked upon as hostile to the waka (Santacruz, p. 244). The same is said of other Incas, such as Maita Qhapaj (p. 255), Pachakutij (p. 280), Tupaj Inca (p. 283), etc. v. Tschudi's statement, Beiträge, p. 158, that the ancient Peruvians had never distinguished between the waka and their anthropomorphized divinities, and had given them the same names, from their chief gods down to any kind of monstrosity or abnormal creation, does not seem to be quite accurate.

[14] Also Garcilaso, VI, chap. 18, terms the god Chinchaikamaj an early imitation of the god of Pachacamac. The chieftains of Chincha and Mala, among others, appeared at Pachacamac with presents during Hernando Pizarro's sojourn at that place (Estete, p. 133).

[15] "Provinces had special wakas as well as villages, owing to the general ramification of the sanctuaries" (J. v. Tschudi, Beiträge, p. 150).

fetish-like significance in that they derived their attributes indirectly from the great Creator and were appealed to independently for certain matters only, according to the division of power. The fear of the all-embracing creator-god was hereby enhanced, as in him was seen the comprehensible source of all those powers by which man is influenced every day of his life and which for that reason were objects of worship.[1] Only after all this is known is it possible to understand the extreme degree of awe with which the sanctuary of Irma was invested for believers. Hernando Pizarro[2] says in reference to this statement: " The temple is held in such fear by all the Indians that they believe, if any of the priests belonging to it should ask them for anything, it would mean instant death to them to refuse." This seems natural, as they were surrounded by the power of the god in innumerable sub-agents, each of which was specially feared and reverenced, even if the entire being of the creator-god remained incomprehensible to the people. In view of this, it is not so difficult to understand that pilgrims flocked to this sanctuary from great distances, even as far as eight hundred miles,[3] since every one of their own local sanctuaries was but a branch of the shrine of the supreme deity at Pachacamac, and that envoys were willing to fast a whole year before being permitted to invoke the deity for a good harvest for their chief and his country. This also explains the large number of wooden images standing, according to Estete,[4] in all the streets of Pachacamac, at the principal gates and all around the temple, which the people worshiped " as effigies of their devil." All the different powers emanating from the creator-god were embodied in these images, thousands of which surrounded the people in this city and formed the objects of their worship. It is, therefore, easy to understand that it would have been very difficult for the Incas to abolish the sanctuary, even had they desired to do so, on account of its powerful organization, as Cieza assumes.[5] Even before the Incas had reached Pachacamac in their conquest they had the hardest fights with the faithful adherents of the sanctuary. There are numerous

indications that the struggles of the Incas with the Chancas, and which nearly destroyed the flourishing empire of the Incas,[6] were not fought for political reasons only, but also on account of important religious differences between the adherents of Irma and those of Wiraqocha of Cuzco. The Chancas occupied the region of Andahuailas, whence they had at some early period driven the Kechuas.[7] At Andahuailas stood a minor shrine of Irma, according to Santillan. The priests had instigated the last decisive struggle and the last rebellion of the Chancas, previous to their final defeat, and the Chancas of Andahuailas were allied against the Incas with the Chinchas, who possessed another of the small sanctuaries of Irma.[8] Montesinos[9] points out the religious motive for these struggles, saying that the Chancas wished to " subjugate the son of the Sun." The god Wiraqocha was also said to have taken side with the adversaries, the Incas, in the most wonderful manner. He had given them warning of the outbreak of the rebellion long before it occurred.[10] In the greatest stress of the battle the Inca implored Wiraqocha for help,[11] which he granted by personally entering the fight with auxiliary troops.[12] All this indicates that the Incas in these struggles were actuated by religious motives. The outcome was an increase in the fervor of the worship accorded to the god, as well as various monuments erected in his honor in fulfillment of vows,[13] and the entire religious and political subjugation of the enemy. The cult of Wiraqocha was forced upon them by the victors,[14] a number of the priests of the idols were made prisoners, brought to Cuzco and deprived of their dignity forever, while a new sacerdotal order was introduced.[15] Henceforth the priests should always be poor and of lowly extraction, and in future rebellions they should be subject to the common law and to the death penalty. For this reason the Inca was surnamed Pachakutij, ' he who changes the world,' perhaps meaning as much as ' the great.' With minor sanctuaries the Incas could deal in this manner, but political and religious principles must necessarily be influenced and purified as soon as they came into closer relations with the chief sanctuary of Irma.

---

[1] Apparently we have to deal here with a transformation of the highland creator-cult to correspond with the religious views of the coast dwellers. In the highland we notice the worship of the powerful creator, together with a leaning toward the development of a waka-cult. Molina, p. 4, says: "The creator formed models of various nations and caused them to spring from the earth. Some came forth out of caves, others rose from springs, again others descended from trees. For that reason and according to the places from which they came they made wakas and places of worship of them." The Relacion anónima, p. 137, states: "The devil told them that the creator had invested various creatures with some of his power and divinity, and that these were attendants and ministering spirits of the supreme deity and had their dwelling in the heavens, as the sun, the moon and the planets." We are hereby reminded of the winged figures in the Relief of the Gateway. Compare with them also the interceders with Wiraqocha, mentioned in Coleccion de documentos ineditos, XXI, p. 142 ff. The changes which religions undergo with different races of men, and under different climatic conditions, are as a rule very great, as is shown by the difference between the Buddhism of Thibet and the original Hindostanic form of the same religion. A similar process may have taken place in Peru. It was a peculiarity with the Yunka peoples to have an exceedingly large number of religious observances, as may be seen by the numerous symbolical figures on the Chimu pottery. Under the influence of such a highly gifted people the cult of the creator-god of the highland might well have assumed the peculiar form of worship accorded to the same divinity under the name of Irma.
[2] Letter, p. 124.
[3] Pizarro, Letter, p. 124.
[4] P. 132.
[5] Crónica, I, chap. 72.

[6] Garcilaso, IV, chap. 15 ; V, chap. 17 ; Bétanzos, chaps. vi-x ; Cieza, II, chaps. 44, 45.
[7] Garcilaso, IV, chap. 15 ; Cieza, I, chap. 91.
[8] See above, p. 52. Stübel u. Uhle, p. 57ᵃ and 60ᵃ, note 1. The writer erroneously concluded from the fact that Wiraqocha was worshiped at Cuntisuyu, that he would also be adored at Andahuailas. Cuntisuyu is not the region about Andahuailas to the west from Cuzco, but to the south on the other side of the Cordillera, near Cotahuasi and Chumbivilcas.
[9] Relacion anónima, p. 172. Garcilaso, who pays less attention to the religious element, and whose historical interest in the Incas was more especially directed toward the Sun-cult than toward that of Wiraqocha, speaks nevertheless of an alliance of the Chancas with Chinchaisuyu in these struggles (Book IV, chap. 23). It must be mentioned that according to Balboa, a chieftain, Cusmanco of Conchucos, guarded the rear of the Chancas during their retreat, and later on was himself defeated and killed by the Incas. In the name of this chieftain we have a resemblance to that of the chieftain of Pachacamac. Cuismanco, who was defeated by the Incas.
[10] Garcilaso, IV, chap. 21.
[11] Bétanzos, chap. 8.
[12] Garcilaso, V, chap. 18 ; Bétanzos, l. c.; Acosta, VI, chap. 21.
[13] Garcilaso, Bétanzos, Acosta, Ondegardo in Col. de doc. ined., XVII, p. 15 ; also compare Stübel u. Uhle, p. 60.
[14] Montesinos, p. 175.
[15] The religious reforms are confirmed by Blas Valera, Garcilaso, IV, chap. 36.

CONQUEST OF THE SANCTUARY BY THE INCAS.

The chronology in Peru, up to the last decades before the conquest by the Spaniards, is at best very unreliable, in consequence of the entire lack of any kind of script and of the inadequate makeshift of knotted strings (kipus) as the only assistance to memory. The date of the incorporation of the

valley of Pachacamac into the Inca empire comes under this same chronological difficulty, although that occurrence was not a very remote one from the arrival of the Spaniards in Peru.

According to Garcilaso the last ruling Incas had the following dates:

7. Wiraqocha 1289–1340
6. Pachakutij 1340–1400
5. Yupanki............................... 1400–1439
4. Tupaj 1439–1475
3. Waina Qhapaj........................ 1475–1526
2. Waskar............................... 1526–1531
1. Atawallpa............................ 1531–1532

The statements of the various authors concerning the name of the conqueror vary between the four Incas:

7. Wiraqocha, according to Montesinos.
6. Pachakutij, according to Garcilaso.[1]
5. Yupanki, according to Balboa[2] and Santacruz.[3]
4. Tupaj, according to Cieza[4] and Santillan.[5]

Following the order of the names in the lists of the Qhapaj Incas, as given by the different authors, we find as the sixth Pachakutij, according to Garcilaso; Wiraqocha and Yupanki, according to Montesinos, Balboa and Santacruz, the fifth from the last. Tupaj was the fourth from the last according to all the lists.

The conquest of the valley would therefore fall between the years 1340 and 1400, according to Garcilaso, or, since it was one of the later achievements of the Inca (Pachakutij), probably not earlier than 1360, about one hundred and seventy years before the Spanish invasion. According to Balboa, Santacruz and Montesinos, the event took place between the years 1400 and 1440, ninety to one hundred and thirty years prior to the arrival of the Spaniards, and according to Cieza and Santillan it was even as late as 1440 to 1450, about eighty years before the Spanish conquest.[6] Whatever date between the years 1360 and 1450 may finally be accepted for the conquest of the valley, the fact remains that the Inca period of the valley and the sanctuary, in proportion to the age of the latter, must be considered a very short one, while the transformations which the city underwent in its appearance were relatively considerable.[7]

Garcilaso gives a detailed account of the political subjection of the sanctuary under the Inca rule. The Inca's army came from the south.[8] The Inca first sought to force the prince of Pachacamac to an unconditional surrender and renunciation of the original cult. The discussions held on this subject, however, convinced the Inca that the divinity worshiped under the name of Irma was really identical with his god Pachakamaj. He, therefore, felt induced to moderate his conditions, leaving the prince in possession of his lands and cult, and receiving him with full honors as an ally and near relative of his own family, incorporating his possessions into the Inca realm. However the prince was obliged to concede changes in his cult and to accept that of the Sun in his lands in addition. J. v. Tschudi thinks this account untrustworthy and partial to the Inca, since it represents him as reaping advantages without any apparent struggle. The details he considers incorrectly stated, since other chroniclers tell of a voluntary submission by the Inca to the foreign cult.[9] Garcilaso's account must, nevertheless, be considered the most complete and correct for several reasons. A voluntary submission by the Inca to the foreign cult did not take place, since the Sun-temple was erected on the finest and most prominent site in the ancient city of Pachacamac,[10] the Inca thus reaping advantages for his own religion. The details which Garcilaso is said to have incorrectly stated are under dispute,[11] and even if they should be proved to be false would not include the principal terms of peace as stated by Garcilaso. In his account of the recognition by the Inca of his own supreme deity in the divinity of Irma, J. v. Tschudi sees a palliation of the fact that the Inca had submitted to a strange god, and in order to conceal this and for the purpose of introducing the new cult among his own subjects he had given it a Kechua name. Tschudi, however, did not realize that such a superficial interpretation of the historical facts only renders much more inexplicable the renaming of the deity as Pachakamaj, 'world-ruler,' by the Inca. Garcilaso's account, therefore, corresponds in even a higher degree with the real facts, and is also in itself more harmonious and probable. It tallies, besides, with the account given in the preceding chapters of the derivation of the sanctuary at Irma from the creator-god Wiraqocha (T'onapa, Tarapaka) worshiped in the highland.[12] The course of events may have been as follows: The cult of the creator-god Irma was derived from that of the creator-god of the southern highland, who in different localities had different names, Wiraqocha, T'onapa, Tarapaka. This original cult of the highland was of pre-Inca date. The Inca realm grew up in it and retained it. In the course of time the two kindred cults of the highland and lowland became estranged, to be later reunited after the conquest of the valley of Irma by the Inca. Mindful of the religious kinship, the Incas reintroduced this cult, while it served their political purposes to adopt the sanctuary again as one of their own. In the kindred deity of Irma, the giver of all the fruits of the fields and the preserver of the powers that

---

[1] VI, chap. 30.

[2] Balboa relates in chap. 8 that Tupak visited the temple of Pachacamac and found it managed in accordance with the statutes of his father, Titu Yupanki Pachakutij. This would seem to indicate that the predecessor of Tupaj subjugated the valley of Irma.

[3] P. 275.

[4] II, chap. 58.

[5] P. 32, p. 172.

[6] A mean date of the conquest of the valley by the Inca is the most probable one. Garcilaso has two Incas by the name of Yupanki, the older of whom, immediately preceding the younger, was distinguished by the surname of Pachakutij, under which he is known in history; the other chroniclers only speak of one Yupanki having the same surname. Thereby the existence of another Inca Titu Yupanki Pachakutij, as distinguished from the former, becomes doubtful, being insufficiently supported. On the other hand the accounts of Cieza and Santillan of Tupaj's visit to Pachacamac admit that Pachacamac may have been conquered under the preceding ruler. The conquests in the highland were pushed as far as Jauja and Tarma under the preceding Inca Yupanki (Cieza, II, chap. 50).

[7] Concerning the great age of the sanctuary, compare above, p. 46. It is not possible at present to estimate correctly the age of the temple or to state the exact date of its foundation, nor even the century. The ancient monuments of Tiahuanaco were the outcome of a civilization which flourished in southern Peru prior to the beginnings of the development of the Inca realm, therefore at least as early as 1100 A.D. (see Stübel u. Uhle, pp. 52–54), and since the sanctuary of Irma (Pachacamac) may have been founded at the same time its approximate age would be the same. But we do not know as yet how long before the foundation of the Inca empire the works of Tiahuanaco were constructed. The highland of southern Peru having been but little explored, we are not in a position to know anything about the genetic relation of the Cuzco or Inca style to that of Tiahuanaco, from which it differs strongly. Nor can we tell if the derivation from the same was a direct one or transmitted by other intermediate types. The final settling of the question as to the relatively earlier or later date of the works of Tiahuanaco before 1100 A.D. approximately, will depend upon the determination of these doubtful matters.

[8] Garcilaso, VI, chap. 20. According to Montesinos, Cieza and Santillan, the Inca who conquered Irma came from the north. The first visits of the Incas seem to have been from an eastern direction, from accounts of Santillan and Balboa.

[9] J. v. Tschudi, Beiträge, p. 128.

[10] The erection of a temple of the Sun is mentioned as one of the conditions of the conclusion of peace in Garcilaso's book. Below, chap. xix, will be seen how the architecture of the Sun-temple on the one hand and that of the women's convent on the other was in keeping with the style of the people who, according to Garcilaso, were obliged to construct these two buildings in fulfillment of peace conditions.

[11] Garcilaso mentions idols which had been removed from the temple of the creator by order of the Inca. He made a mistake if he thought that this had included all the figures there, for Pizarro and his companions found an "ugly image" of the divinity in the building (Pizarro, Letter, p. 124; Estete, p. 131). However, no record in Spanish reports of the conquest of the idols of fish and fish-like character ('zorra') "which the Yunkas had set up in the temple previous to the times of the Incas." To connect with these the image of the god which Pizarro found and to call it fish-like ("the wooden fish-idol"), as Markham does (Reports of the Discovery, Introd., p. xvii, ff), is absolutely unsupported by facts; though there were fishes, etc., painted upon the walls of the terraces and temples (see above, p. 21).

[12] The statement made by Garcilaso that the cult of Pachakamaj had been spread to the coast in earlier times by the Incas rests evidently upon an excellent tradition, which claims that the original cult of Irma was derived from the highland, and it proves the value of the sources from which Garcilaso drew his material when he wrote his history. He, of course, ascribed the spread of the cult to the agency of the Incas themselves, since he, together with many early chroniclers, ignored the existence of a pre-Inca period.

slumber in the earth, they saw embodied principally those sides of their creator-god which correspond to his surname 'world-ruler.' Thereby the sanctuary came to be called by the name of Pachakamaj instead of that of Irma.[1] Only the recognition of this kinship of their religion to that of the worshipers of Irma can explain the unusual amount of honors with which, according to Garcilaso, the Inca received the prince of Pacha-camac into his realm, and the high veneration which the Incas bestowed henceforth upon the sanctuary throughout the days of their prosperity.

Each of the succeeding Incas either visited the sanctuary in person, consulted the oracle of the god and celebrated brilliant festivals with many sacrifices, or sent to consult the oracle on all the most important affairs of his empire.[2] Since the conquest, the god spoke through the oracle to princes and caziques only.[3] Tribute was partly paid at this shrine instead of being sent to Cuzco,[4] and some of the Incas bestowed great riches upon it. It was only with the overthrow of the empire and his own captivity at Cajamarca that Atawallpa became shaken in his faith in the ancient religion, and in the trustworthiness of the oracles of the god. As one of the last acts of authority before he himself was put in fetters he ordered the chief priest of the sanctuary to be thrown into prison, when he visited him at Cajamarca, "as the god had counciled him to wage war on the Christians, and had made the false promise that he would slay all of them."[5]

---

[1] Markham, *l. c.*, disputes the assumption that the divinity of this sanctuary had been a creator-god, and that he was himself called Pachakamaj. If the fish-form is not in keeping with the idea of a creator-god, the fact that the god was a creator-god and was called Pachakamaj forms a refutation of the fish-shape (comp. Cieza, Crónica, I, chap. 73; II, chap. 58; Santillan, p. 32; Estete, p. 132; further the proofs furnished by the objects found there—the historical derivation of the deity, the myths, the importance of the god as the centre of the waka cult). The Kechua name Pachakamaj being given to the god, also designated his sanctuary, and this in turn caused the city to be distinguished by the same appellation.

[2] Montesinos, chap. 26: Inca Wiraqocha sacrifices many llamas after the conquest. Garcilaso, VI, chap. 32: Pachakutij, the conqueror of Irma, visits the shrine and worships there before setting out on the campaign against the Chimu. Santillan, p. 32: Tupaj visits the temple, consults the oracle of the divinity and makes great sacrificial burnt offerings of llamas and garments. Similar, Balboa, chap. 8. Also, Cieza, II, chap. 58: Yet upon this occasion the god demands human sacrifices also. Santacruz, p. 302: When Waina Qhapaj visited his shrine, the god asked for "more buildings" and for riches. Cieza, II, chap. 65: Waina Qhapaj celebrates brilliant festivals at Pachacamac in honor of the god with dances and feasting, and makes rich presents to the temple; in return for which the god sends him favorable oracles. Similar, Montesinos, p. 229. Comp. also Xerez, p. 108. Santacruz, pp. 314, 315: During the war between Waskar and Atawallpa the leaders of both armies send offerings and cause the oracle to be consulted, whereupon victory is promised to both of them.

[3] Garcilaso, VI, chap. 31.

[4] Hernando Pizarro, Letter, p. 123; Estete, p. 132.

[5] Xerez, p. 115.

CHAPTER XVI.

THE CITY WITHIN THE INNER WALLS.

CROSS streets divide the ancient city into quarters or sections; one-fourth of its entire area being occupied by the temple district, there remain sections B, C and D, as will be seen on the map of the city. As the eastern street does not extend quite so far as the eastern limit, the dividing line between B and D is not distinct and the division of the city into sections has not been completely carried out. The eastern district, section E, appears to be different from the rest of the town by reason of its situation, being separated by hill Z and built upon slightly rising ground; the buildings, too, show some peculiarities. In comparison with section B, the sections C, D, E appear to be of more recent date, especially the parts situated in the plain. The division of the city's area by walls is upon a large scale, and the ground is not so closely cumbered with buildings. The graves in sections C, D, E are limited to some particular spots, such as the courts of the dwelling houses, while the ground of section B is filled with graves, which are, as a whole, of much greater age than those in the other three sections. The ground is full of ancient masonry, discovered unexpectedly during explorations; here and there traces of ruined buildings were found, covered by a thick stratum of apparently natural soil. Depressions in the ground seem to be ancient courts, a, a; mounds are found to be débris of buildings, b.[1] From all these indications there is no doubt that section B, situated between the hills X, Y, Z, is the oldest part of the city, situated nearest to the sanctuary of the god. There are no closely built-up rows of houses in Pachacamac, nor do we find such labyrinthine crowding of rooms and buildings as may be seen in the ruins of Cajamarquilla, about eleven miles above Lima,[2] and in the remains of the village in the valley above Pachacamac. The city for the most part consists of large detached buildings of palatial proportions, some situated with their courts toward the street, others lying within the sections. A considerable area has been cut into court-like sections by walls, devoid of any buildings; which are also wanting in another part of the city, B, the oldest section. The general ground plan of construction in parts B, C, D corresponds to that of the temple and follows the coastline, while that of the secluded section E is different, as is also the shape of its structures.[3] On the whole, the ground plan of the city resembles those of the ruins in the neighborhood of Lima, as, for instance, that of the ancient town of Huatica, and in a modern sense has more resemblance to a suburb than to a city. A group of closely crowded buildings is seen in the extreme eastern part, in one locality only, in E; here were also found several indications of the architectural influence of the highland, and to the same influence probably may be ascribed a divergence in the manner of building.

The city wall enclosed the town completely upon the most exposed northwestern side; an addition to it, two hundred and sixty feet long, is joined to it on the northern end, forming an imperfect enclosure of the northeastern side, leaving between the wall and a hill a strip of ground for a road, which may have served since early times for intercourse with the southern parts of the coast. The wall of the northwestern front and the northeastern section are eleven to thirteen feet high and about eight feet broad, while, judging from its foundations, the enclosure around C on the west side must have been about sixteen feet broad. This section at present is the most ruined, which accounts for the numerous gaps in it. The city wall is in a very dilapidated condition, and according to Estete[4] it must have been so for a long time. The northern and eastern streets have a width of sixteen and thirteen feet, and side walls similar to the city walls in breadth and height, so that the width of the streets was the same as the thickness of the two walls flanking them. A sort of open square appears on the point where the four streets cross each other, and various piles of small stones are to be seen there.[5] Another regular square is at the end of the southern street, and closely adjoins the temple enclosure. Both the city walls and the streets were of rather unusual appearance; the wall was more exposed to and the houses more secluded from the streets than is usually the case. Estete speaks of city gates, wherein idols were set up. It is doubtful, however, whether there were any means of closing the entrances to the city besides the guard-houses and the idol gates. Explorations in the extreme ends of the northern and western streets brought to light no traces of them. The city was almost open on the most important side, the northeast, where much traffic passed along the road. That the streets[6] were used by crowds of people is proved by the condition of the remaining well-preserved sections of the adobe walls along the eastern street, which are worn quite smooth by much use. The number of entrances from the streets into the palace courts are in no proportion to the size of the areas which they enclose, for it is still clearly to be seen, in spite of the ruined condition of the walls, that but few entrances existed and that some of the palaces could

---

[1] In certain places buildings have been superposed upon others, thus one wall near c extends over an ancient cemetery. The terraced house near d stands above older sunken rooms.

[2] The plan of a part of Cajamarquilla, Squier, p. 93, gives an idea of the crowding of buildings in that place.

[3] They are not rectangular, as they appear to be and as stated by Wilkes, p. 288.

---

[4] See above, p. 11.

[5] A similar arrangement may be noticed in the ancient city of Surco, near Chorillos.

[6] One of these is shown in pl. 10, fig. 1.

only be entered from the interior of the courts. It appears, therefore, that the different sections were much more difficult of access than the city itself, as may be seen in the 'barrios' or wards of the ruins of Trujillo, which, however, resemble these in no other respects.[1] The streets must have been used mostly by strangers, pilgrims, etc., and have served also to connect the different buildings.

[1] Squier, p. 159 ff.

TYPES OF BUILDINGS.

Among the foremost in number and prominence are the terraced houses which are scattered over various parts of the city. Some of these houses may be seen in pl. 9, fig. 2 and pl. 10, fig. 3. The characteristic feature of these buildings is that they are set upon massive terraces from ten to seventeen feet high, which they entirely cover. An inclined path leads up to them, seven to sixteen feet in width, furnished in some instances with side-rails.[1] Above the first terrace, and in the rear, rise similarly constructed grades of a lesser height, of from three to five feet each, approached by winding paths. The terraces reach to the top of the building, sometimes twenty-seven feet and more in height. The rooms within the houses are arranged in a semicircle along the three closed sides and enclosing the entrance-terraces. Deviations from this plan were noticed only in a few cases. The view, fig. 59, shows a section of one of these houses, and gives an idea of their construction. It must be observed, however, that the partitions of the rooms are not preserved, except in a few instances. The ruined condition of the buildings is caused not only by centuries of dilapidation, but also by the vandalism of treasure-hunters. In front of the houses, on the side of the entrance, there is invariably a more or less spacious court (comp. pl. 9, fig. 2). Buildings of this class, on

terraces, and portals thatched with mats." These houses in a measure resembled the mediæval castle, with cheerful activity inside and a sharp watch kept outside. Cieza, *l. c.*, says in regard to this subject: " Around the house lay a wide area where dances were held,[5] and whenever the chieftain dined, a crowd of people would assemble and drink of his chicha of maize or peanuts. There were gate-keepers in these palaces, who carefully watched all who came and went." The courts in front of the houses must, according to this statement, have served for the execution of popular festive dances, witnessed by the chieftains from the terraces of their houses. Constructions for the safety of the palaces are still to be seen in some places. There were gates, *g*, watch-towers, *t*, and a peculiar kind of entrance easily watched, *l*. Only in a few cases could any real gates be proved. There were two in the large palace, pl. 9, fig. 2. In front of the entrance of the court, on the side fronting the street, were two walls through which gates opened. One can be seen from the left in pl. 10, fig. 2, and from the right in pl. 10, fig. 1;[6] the other from the opposite side can be seen from the right in pl. 10, fig. 2, from the left in pl. 10, fig. 1. These two gates must have existed as, though there have been walks over both walls, the entrances may still be distinguished as doors, pl. 10,

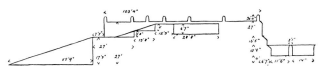

Fig. 59. Sectional view of a terraced house at Pachacamac.

account of the terrace construction, might, though erroneously, be taken for temples. The terrace is on one side of the house only, and, as a whole, differs considerably from that which surrounds a temple on all sides. Houses also lack the painting on the outside, so characteristic of temples, and they are all partitioned off into rooms, which can only have served for living purposes. The large number of graves found in them also mark the buildings as dwelling houses, as it was a very general custom to bury the dead in their own dwellings. The earliest writers specially speak of this form of houses as the dwellings of chieftains and nobles. Hernando Pizarro writes: " The houses of the common Indians are of reeds, those of the chieftains of adobe."[2] Estete, p. 133, speaking of Pachacamac, says: " There are houses with terraces, as in Spain," whereby he surely referred to private houses and not to temples. Finally the description of the houses of chiefs on the coast of Peru as given by Cieza[3] exactly fits these buildings: " Each chieftain had a large palace in his valley, with many brick pillars[4] and large

figs. 1 and 2. From the small terrace, *i* (see the plan on the right), it was easy to keep a watch over all those who passed in and out of the first gate. The entire building in pl. 10, fig. 2, in the foreground, may have served for the purpose of watching the palace, pl. 9, fig. 2; it is marked *t, t*, in the plan. Another watch-tower may be distinguished in pl. 11, fig. 2; to the right in pl. 11, fig. 1; to the left on the hill. This watch-tower, marked *t* on the plan, near entrance *l* of the house, overlooks the plain to quite a great distance. The long terraces into which the hill in pl. 11, fig. 2, is graded, doubtless served also as defenses. Other towers of similar character, *t*, are to be seen to the northeast from the house in section E, and on the side of a house near the city wall in D. The manner of watching the houses probably was the same in the platform buildings near *s*, although here a watch-tower cannot be traced so distinctly. To secure the approaches to the palaces there were also narrow winding lanes which led into angles, so that it was impossible for the enemy to cover them with their arrows, while the defenders were concealed. Of this nature are the approaches *l* near some of the palaces,[7] the first four of which at least could be overseen from the watch-towers

[1] An inclined path where both side-rails are still distinctly seen does not exist at Pachacamac, but may be observed in other ruins, such as those of the ancient Surco Chorillos.
[2] Letter, p. 122.
[3] Crónica, I, chap. 61.
[4] Similar ones may possibly have existed at Pachacamac, but have been destroyed.

[5] Cieza, *l. c.*, also tells that the chiefs of the coast land were always surrounded by troupes of dancers who executed dances, while others made music and sang for them.
[6] At this place only one jamb of a door is still preserved.
[7] Comp. pl. 10, fig. 2.

by which they were flanked. If it is remembered that several of these strictly guarded palace entrances were at the same time the only entrances to the interior of the city sections it will be seen how secluded the latter must have been on certain sides. Many of the terraced houses used as palaces were connected with artificial plateaus, ten feet or more in height and sometimes very extensive, on which in certain instances there have been rooms.[1] The construction of these plateaus seems to be the same as of those found near Lima by Bandelier and in the neighborhood of Trujillo, of which he has given a good description.[2] In making cross cuts through terraces adobe walls were found, forming the skeleton of the terrace, which were worn so smooth that it might be supposed that they had served as rooms before being filled in and covered to form the terrace. However, many of these rooms or sections are far too small for such use; in some cases they are only seven feet in length by ten to twelve feet in height. Several were found together at Pachacamac in one house in an unfinished condition, in various stages of construction, so that an intermediate use as rooms seems entirely out of the question. In Pachacamac they were mainly filled with driftsand, together with refuse from the houses. The covering on the top of the terraces consists mostly of sand or of large flags of adobe. Fragments of big earthen vessels were found upon several of these terraces which could have held as much as fifty gallons and may have served for domestic purposes. There is another type of dwellings which is in close relation to these castle houses. These consist of rooms, square or rectangular in shape, formed of plain walls from eight to thirteen feet high, without any mode of entrance whatever except from above.[3] These rooms are mostly arranged in groups of two or four, or simply in rows of six or in double rows of eight, ten, twelve or twenty, or they are in three rows in a network arrangement. The different rooms are thirteen to twenty feet square on the average, but larger as well as smaller ones are found. Near one palace a room of this class is seventy-two by sixty-five feet in size. The rooms or groups of rooms are either accessible directly from the walls above, or they are enclosed in other walls five and one-half to ten feet higher, and in each case very thick, from which descent has to be made to the top of the room walls, and from there still further down into the room itself. In this case the lower walls are built against the upper ones as retaining walls, of two to five feet in thickness, forming a walk around the rooms, which may be as low as sixteen feet or more below its upper edge, and which has quite the appearance of a dungeon. Niches in the walls of these sunken rooms are not uncommon. We have found but one instance, however, where two of these rooms were connected by a door opening through the lower dividing wall. The means of descent into these rooms were most difficult, consisting of small grooves in the wall down one corner of the room into which the point of the foot would fit, as may be seen in pl. 11, fig. 4. These steps may be seen in nearly all the rooms of this class. Other means of descent, such as beams, notched like ladders, may possibly have existed, but only exceptionally. The descent from the higher enclosing walls down to the lower walk around the top of the rooms was usually made in the same way, although in a few instances use was made of an inclined plane, such as is indicated in fig. 60 or in pl. 11, fig. 4.

The close relation of these structures to the castle-houses

is quite evident. They are generally connected either on the sides or in the rear,[4] and the occupants of both buildings evidently had intercourse with each other. In one instance these closed rooms[5] are joined to the house on the court-side and connected with the main building by a wall. In another case a high walk, covered on the south side by a parapet, u, conceals the connection with the closed rooms belonging to this palace. It is easy to see that there was a great difference, however, between these rooms and the living apartments of the palace proper. The closed rooms are situated with their base as low as sixteen feet, sometimes twenty-six feet, even forty-two feet, below the level of the palace rooms. They were much more secluded than the main building; although grouped together in honey-combed fashion, they formed dwellings for large numbers of occupants. They were perhaps used by the retainers and servants of the chief, by his bands of dancers, by armed men for his protection, always ready at his call, and possibly may have formed the rear defence of the palace.

The peculiar formation of these dwellings entered only from above has its parallel in other parts of America; for instance, with the Pueblo Indians in New Mexico, also in Argentina in the extensive Ruins of Quilmes, the town of the Calchaquis.[6] In the latter are dwellings built against each other in honey-comb fashion, only separated by stone walls ten feet thick, which at the same time form connecting walks, from which inclined planes lead downward into the dwellings. These three examples of this mode of building also possess in common the peculiarity of the crowding

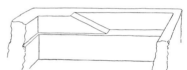

Fig. 60. Mode of entrance to rooms from above.

together of the groups. There is significance in the fact, as this and many other examples show, that close relations must have existed at one time among the peoples along the west coast of America and the Andes.

Large sections of districts B, C and D are cut into smaller courts by walls without any buildings. These courts were, like the above-described rooms, entirely closed, as may still be seen by the walls, although they are in a very dilapidated condition. It is not likely that these walls formed mere enclosures for fields, as suggested by Bandelier[7] in the Ruins of Trujillo, since within the entire ruined city not a trace of ancient water-channels was found. The courts are quite empty, except when in rare cases they contain an unimportant grave. Many graves, numerous enough for a cemetery, were discovered in a few fore-courts of buildings of palace-like dimensions.[8] When, in one of these otherwise empty courts a pile of household rubbish is found, it is safe to trace it back to some adjoining house. These court-like enclosures, devoid of any buildings, are to a certain degree still unsolved riddles. Their walls, however, served for roads. It is evident that intercourse within the sections of the city as far as possible was carried on by means of the walls. It has

[1] The plateau adjoining the palace in the western side is about one hundred yards in length by twenty-five in width.
[2] Hodge, Bandelier's Researches, Amer. Anthropologist, 1897, 306.
[3] Comp. pl. 11, figs. 3 and 4, and fig. 1 in the foreground.

[4] Comp. pl. 11, fig. 3.
[5] In pl. 11, fig. 1, in the foreground.
[6] Comp. also the good description given them by Sen. Ambrosetti, Bol. del. Inst. Geogr. Arg., 1897, XVIII, pp. 40, 41.
[7] Comp. Hodge, l. c., p. 305.
[8] For the signification of the massing of the graves in these courts in its bearings upon the ancient city communities, compare Cunow, Die sociale Verfassung des Inkareichs, p 45.

been previously shown how walks were laid above the walls of the gates, and how it was necessary to pass along these walls to reach the enclosed rooms and to descend into them. On the top of many walls were rooms and paths built of bricks, as their remains still show, m, also inclined planes for the descent, o, etc.[1] Some of these walls are worn down in the centre, by the traffic that must have passed over them, for the closed courts made roads over the walls a necessity. This manner of intercourse was evidently intentional and not due to accident. In the interior of section D of the city, eastward from the house near which the network of walls begins, and where the entrance is open from the east side across the plain, there is a peculiar construction for the guidance of travelers upon the walls, as may be seen in pl. 11, fig. 1, in a broad inclined plane near p. At first having a width of seventeen feet it gradually grows narrower, corresponding to the ramifications of the roadways over the walls, and in a width of nine or ten feet it runs around the net-work of the closed rooms which are located there, and to the terrace of a house, from which point more walls radiate as roads into other directions. The roadways over the walls were a very practical mode of connection, since the plane is deeply covered with driftsand, making communication across it very difficult. But as this system of roads forms a part of the peculiar architecture of the city, there must have been stronger reasons than mere local ones for its adoption. Even now the low tapia walls which enclose the fields are used as walks in preference to the dusty paths running alongside.

In addition to the castle-houses there is another class[2] of buildings to be found at Pachacamac, though only a few specimens exist, which to all appearance was derived from the former type, but lacking the character of the stronghold. The plan of apartments in this type of houses is similar to the former, but the court is generally smaller and the defences insignificant, especially wanting the high terraced understructure. The terrace consists of one grade only, three to five feet above ground. Some of the buildings of the type under consideration are still in a good state of preservation. This class of houses is not found in the district of the castle-houses and occurs more frequently in the northeastern part of the town, where there is less organization. This fact in itself speaks for the more recent date of the houses. Besides these two types of buildings, there is another class of a somewhat different order. A specimen of this, ninety yards long by seventy-six yards wide, and resembling a court, lies on the northern extremity of the town, in an isolated position, near the terminal point of the northeastern city wall. This court was cut into six parallel sections by walls of masonry, slightly raised one above another. The structure does not seem to have served for domestic purposes; judging from its location it might be taken for a tambo (Kechua: tampu, inn), and there are additional grounds for such a supposition. One building, with another adjoining, resembling a hall, is found in the eastern part of the town, leaning against the hill Y. This house shows the peculiarity of a simple mural painting in a checkerboard pattern, upon a wall in the main room, near the western entrance. The elongated hall structure is rounded off at its eastern end like an apsis. The inner side of the wall is pentagonal. The height of this room is only three feet three inches on the hillside by five feet nine inches on the other, and a view of its interior may be obtained from the hill, it must, therefore, have been used for purposes which would allow such conditions. Two buildings in the eastern town, in section B, and in the northern, E, have a very similar cross-shaped ground-plane, formed by two small side-terraces flanking a wider central one, simply graduated. The purpose of neither structure can be conjectured. One building in the northern part of the town, now a complete ruin, is worth noting, because it shows traces of a former complete circuit and a transept. This building is remarkable because it consists only of a court, graded in terraces, two and a half and five feet toward the west, and a line of six closed rooms, all enclosed together in broad and high walls. The few partitions of rooms in the court are not sufficient for dwelling purposes, and must therefore have been used in some other capacity, at present unknown. The palatial edifices constructed upon terraces at the northwest foot of hill X[3] are also unusual, but not strikingly so. Near q, q, q, in the eastern town B, are the remains of plain chambers, with polychrome mural paintings, which may have served as shrines for the cult of some idol. The three last-named buildings are situated in the neighborhood of the enclosure of the Pachacamaj temple, one in the centre of the square at the end of the southern street. They may have been shrines for the idols of which Estete speaks as existing in large numbers in the vicinity of the temple.

[1] Comp. pl. 9, fig, 2, and pl. 10, fig. 1.
[2] This type is found in the neighborhood of Lima in a few cases, as is proved by the dwelling house at Huatica, shown by Middendorf, Peru, II, p. 84. This ruin is at present so fallen into decay that the living-rooms proper have all disappeared.

[3] Visible from the distance in pl. 9, fig. 1.

CONSTRUCTIVE DETAILS.

The type of the buildings as well as that of the details of construction are those of the native style of the land. The roofs were flat throughout on account of the almost entire absence of rain. Although they are nowhere preserved, in many cases traces of such construction can be seen. It was easy to build a flat roof over the even walls of the rooms. Walls apparently designed to support others were often utilized to carry rafters on their upper edges, and a horizontal line of grooves is frequently met with (comp. pl. 10, fig. 2). These grooves are always on a level with the opposite wall, and served to hold the spars for the roof. This arrangement is found mostly in rooms of lesser width; in wider rooms the construction of the roof may have been different; possibly posts were used to support the rafters along the centre. There is no doubt as to the material employed for the roof, since Hernando Pizarro[1] states that it consisted of branches of trees; and to this day the roof of the natives is formed of poles, with cane, leaves and sand spread over them. The cell-like tombs for the dead, apparently an imitation of the huts of the living, show the same manner of roofing.

Doors.—These are preserved only in a small number, partly for the reason that the rooms in the principal buildings have been entirely destroyed, and that many, as shown above, were without doors. That a few are still remaining in perfect condition is owing to the good climate. The apertures for

[1] Letter, p. 122.

doors may be generally termed rectangular, for a decrease of width toward the top of one half inch, rarely an inch, cannot be considered as of material importance.[1] Height and width vary. There are doors of only three feet in height, and others of but one foot seven inches in width. Those of five feet three inches to five feet eight inches in height, and two feet four inches to two feet six inches in width, may be regarded as of average size. The upper sill, in accordance with material furnished by the coast land, is usually made of cane. Each sill was formed of three layers of cane sticks, the upper and lower closely laid, while the middle one, crossing the other two, consisted of three or more canes, laid at wide intervals. The three layers were closely interwoven with ropes, so as to form a stiff board (fig. 61), before being placed over the door as the upper lintel, and afterwards plastered with wet loam, overlaid by adobe bricks, as in ordinary walls. The excellent state of preservation may be owing to the mortar, which was packed into the cane-sticks and thoroughly dried.[2]

rooms are erected in tiers, one above another, as frequently seen in Inca buildings, for instance the houses on Titicaca Island and Coati in Lake Titicaca. From a pathway on the western side, several doors opened into upper rooms; other walks, situated at a lower level, led into rooms lying below these, with another entrance thirteen feet on the east side; unfortunately the rooms were filled with sand, so that no details could be ascertained. One of the two upper chambers shows two narrow apertures for light, seventeen and a half inches high by seven inches wide, on the south side, such as are frequently seen in Inca buildings, but not otherwise found at Pachacamac. There are no windows at all at Pachacamac, as the climate there renders them unnecessary.[3] The wall of one house, figs. 64 and 65, near the storied building, forms the only exception. It has in its lower part five niches, arranged in two rows, a cornice running above them, and over that a row of windows. Cornices were used to support floor-rafters for an upper story, while the wall above retreated and tapered toward the top. This is a special feature with Inca

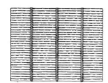

Fig. 61. Lintel of a door, made of cane.

Fig. 62. Same lintel, from below.

Fig. 63. Typical form of niches in the buildings of the town.

Niches.—Although niches are numerous at Pachacamac, the proportion of their number is small compared with that usually found in connection with the Incas. There are three types, all rather primitive: 1, more or less cubic in form; 2, shallow niches in walls; and 3, small, high and narrow (fig. 63 *a, b, c*). Class 1 is usually between sixteen and twenty-two inches in depth by the same in height, rarely varying more than two to four inches. Class 2 is insignificant, height, width and depth in proportion to 2 : 3 : 4 : for instance, 20 + 30 + 44. The width of Class 3 is usually two-thirds of the height, the depth about fifteen inches. The sides of the niches in Classes 1 and 3 are sometimes a little inclined, and in that case bear a stronger resemblance to the Inca type. Wide niches are roofed with cane, the same as doors, narrow ones with bricks. The ornamental use is not developed, they are only found in rows in certain cases exclusively upon houses of more recent date. Judging from various indications, their use may perhaps be traced to Cuzco influences. The same influences are seen in a few instances upon the buildings of the town, aside from the Sun temple and the Convent, but there they are very pronounced, though found only in the northern part. It is a characteristic feature of the architecture of the coast land to build a massive sub-structure under the living-rooms, but in section E, near *k, k, k*, one example is to be found, in which

buildings on the Islands of Titicaca and Coati.[4] The architectural influence of the highlands is very distinctly marked in these cornices. The wall is remarkable as being the only example known in Pachacamac in which two rows of niches were employed as ornament. The ornamental cornice, serving as base to a row of windows set immediately upon it, shows great similarity to the constructive principle of the western façade of the large Gateway of Tiahuanaco.[5] The analogy is, however, limited to this one particular, but the

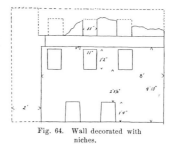

Fig. 64. Wall decorated with niches.

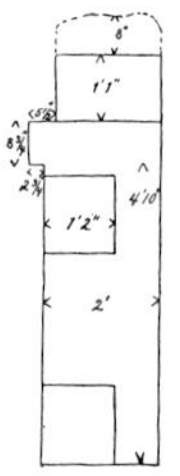

Fig. 65. Cross-section of the same wall.

single, ornamental characteristic, carried out in both buildings, may have been for centuries the distinctive feature of the highlands in the construction of windows.

---

[1] A variation in the width of even two inches, which was observed in a few instances, is insignificant.

[2] Wiener, p. 63, shows the upper sill of a door alleged to come from Pachacamac. Aside from the fact that in Mamacona, where he says this was found, there are no doors preserved intact, there is in all Pachacamac no construction of the kind, and it is altogether impossible for ancient Peru.

[3] Between the inner rooms of one house may be seen a door with the lower part closed like a window.

[4] In the ruins of the ancient convent on the Island of Coati, a wall is found with one window above and two niches below; compare also the ornamental portals (pictured by Wiener, p. 489, giving erroneously the Island of Titicaca as the locality).

[5] Stübel u. Uhle, pl. 5, fig. 1, and pl. 6.

Although no untouched graves were discovered in the houses of the town nor in the courtyards near them, some vessels were found intact, a great variety in fragments; very many pieces of fabric, some large, some small; various utensils, such as plates, cups and other implements of wood; a clay mould, some articles of copper, skulls, etc. These discoveries were sufficient to identify their period of chronology with the last era of the town, that of the Incas, during which objects of native manufacture were mingled with others, of Cuzco character. They were utterly different from those unearthed in the cemetery at the foot of the temple, as well as from those obtained in graveyards II and III, though both sets of graves belong to the same period. There is great resemblance, however, between them and the objects taken from cemetery VI, some examples of which are shown in pl. 13. In quality, articles found in graves in houses may have been superior to those of Cuzco characteristics in cemetery VI; arybals, plates, etc., are more numerous, but the fundamental attributes in both cases are those of the general culture of the coast land at that period.

CONCLUSIONS.

The description of the inner town has shown that at the time of discovery its characteristics were not purely those of the coast, but in the architecture of certain localities, as well as in the culture of its inhabitants, it had been influenced by the Inca conquest. In general, it appears that the inner town was a dwelling place for a number of chieftains, each of whom was surrounded by a large host of retainers. Against the assumption that the whole city was one palace,[1] speaks the fact of its division into sections and the existence of one or more important homes in each district. It is hardly probable that these houses were hostelries,[2] or family or county temples,[3] as indications point to their having been constantly inhabited, and their appearance is more that of castles or fortresses. Arrangements for the security of some of them are very noticeable, and many of the courts contain a large number of graves. The division of the older part of the town into B, C and D was probably according to the existing social order. The different sections or wards were occupied by people of various social grades. Intercourse between the members of each grade was much more active than that between different classes. The sections or wards corresponded to the 'Barrios,' and the different palaces with their courts bore some affinity to those which were found[4] in the Ruins of Chaucan, Trujillo; resembling also the 'Bandas' or 'Kanchas' (courts) which at Cuzco formed the subdivision of the 'Parcialidates' (aillus?).[5] The division of Pachacamac into four connecting wards was similar to the division of Cuzco by means of two intersecting streets into four quarters, corresponding to the four quarters of the empire, Cuntisuyu, etc.; also to the division into aillus, which still prevails in principle in the villages of the highlands, for instance, in Bolivia.

There are, as a rule, from three to eight aillus, generally four, all sharing in the plaza. In the case of four aillus, each represents one corner, together with half of each adjoining side, and the part of the village extending behind it.[6] Calancha states: "At the time of the Incas many nations settled near that sanctuary. Priests (ministros), together with their assistants, were sent there and supported by every town." In connection with this statement is probably his designation of the terraced houses as family, village, or provincial temples. Calancha is exceedingly unreliable in his interpretation of the ancient buildings, since he follows a posthumous and, as a rule, erroneous tradition. There may, however, be some truth in this particular, and that the terraced houses were, in a certain measure, occupied by religious communities, supported here by different parts of the coast. In that case the plan of the ancient town of Pachacamac represented in a microcosmic manner a religious macrocosm, corresponding to the political one at Cuzco.[7] We are not, however, in a position to further discuss such a possibility, since the objects gathered from houses in various sections of the town showed no cultural differences. If we are justified in supposing the largest palace of the ancient town to have been that of the ruler of the valleys of Lima and of Pachacamac, it can hardly be any other than that shown in pl. 9, fig. 2. Pizarro, when he came to Pachacamac, took quarters with his followers in a very large palace, situated on one side of the town.[8] This may have been the palace on the summit of hill Z,[9] which at the same time afforded the greatest degree of safety to the invaders.

---

[1] Ulloa, p. 301.
[2] Rivero y Tschudi, p. 288.
[3] Calancha, l. c.
[4] Squier, p. 159; Cunow, p. 47.
[5] Cunow, p, 48.

---

[6] The divisions known in upper and lower Cuzco as Hanan and Hurin have been preserved everywhere in the villages of the Bolivian highlands, under the following names, in Kechua: Hanansuyu and Hurinsuyu, or in Aimará: Alayajas and Manqhajas. Each of these divisions usually embraces several aillus, and the imaginary line of separation between Hanan and Hurin, or Alayajas and Manqhajas, always cuts through the centre of the plaza. At Cuzco two sections belonged to each of these, Hanan or Hurin (comp. Squier, p. 428).

[7] See above, p. 11, note 11; also Squier, l. c.
[8] Estete, p. 130.
[9] In the panorama, pl. 1, to the right on the hill.

CHAPTER XVII.

THE OUTSKIRTS OF THE TOWN.

AN apparently boundless desert stretches outside the city limits to the west, north, and northeast, in which may be noticed at a distance of half a mile from the city a dark line of masonry.[1] On closer inspection this wall[2] is found to measure twenty feet in breadth,[3] and to extend for four hundred and seventy-five yards, slightly curving over a depression in the ground. The extreme ends seem to disappear in the driftsand,[4] which is abundant everywhere, and sometimes as high as the level of the wall, in places entirely submerging it. Close investigation reveals that the masonry is not continued beyond its visible length. At the ridge, which almost touches the northeastern part of the inner wall, it is crossed by another, situated at about two-thirds to one mile distant from the inner town beyond the hills, and fronting the hacienda Las Palmas, still upon desert soil. This wall is almost fifteen feet broad and several hundred yards long, running from east to west. Again, when crossing the fields which separate the inner town from the sea, the ruins of a massive dam may be seen at about one hundred yards from the shore. Only small portions of it remain, but at one time it must have been an imposing structure. Its extreme end lies far to the northwest, near the hills which abut closely on the sea (comp. the panorama, pl. 1). Beginning with a sharp angle, the dam extended along the shore-line and ended somewhere in front of hill W, on the summit of which the Sun temple stands. It has been broken by the sea, which occasionally washes over it. The present dam may be the remains of an ancient wall. The construction of this work may, without doubt, be ascribed to the same people who erected the northwest and the northeast outer walls, and it must have formed a part of their general plan.[5] On closer examination of the territory between the inner city wall and those at the northeast and northwest, numerous lines of ancient buildings may be traced over the desert soil, only slightly noticeable upon the surface. Fragments of pottery are to be found everywhere. Cemeteries are numerous in various directions and at a considerable distance from the town, and although covered by the sands of the desert, have not escaped the ravages of treasure-hunters. The large area outside the inner city wall was occupied by extensive quarters of huts,

which have now disappeared, being merely cane shacks, and only their foundations of adobe bricks remain. The entire territory formed an outer zone lying around the town. All objects recovered from this zone, from graves, as well as from other sources explored in the desert on the site of ancient dwellings, belong to the Inca period of the city. In one instance a necklace was found inside a clay vessel, consisting of beads of shell and of sea-green glass, the workmanship of which showed that the occupants of this district of the town belonged to the Spanish period. Buildings were in process of erection here at the beginning of Spanish rule. On the northern extremity of the northern limit may be seen the beginnings of two streets, one in a northwestern direction, continuing older lines, and one running due north. Of the former one section only of its western enclosing wall had been finished; of the latter a section was formed by the construction of a building, the southeastern end of which, together with the inner city wall, enclosed a part of the street, the width of which was twenty-three feet. This leads to conclusions as to the scope of the builders' plans. Probably the new street was planned long after the old ones had been finished. To accommodate increased traffic, the new street was designed to be almost twice as wide as the older north street, and once and a half as wide as the east street of the town proper. One building at this point was in process of erection, as may be seen from the terrace adjoining it on its southern side. The retaining walls for the understructure had not all been erected, others were not quite finished, and interstices between others had not been completely filled in. The broad northwestern outer wall must also have been left in an unfinished state, and was probably intended to be connected with the northeastern one. In some places it has a height of twenty feet,[6] while in several others near its western extremity it is level with the ground, or has only an elevation of one and a half feet. Although the ground rises gently, the average level of the wall is the same everywhere, and such variations cannot be supposed to be part of the original plan. Its surface is exceedingly uneven in some places, in others projections occur of uneven length, in height varying from two to ten feet,[7] or terraced, rising above the general level of the wall. Since there is no other explanation to be found for the condition of this wall, it may be assumed that the city, at the time of the conquest, was just being extended.

---

[1] Compare the panorama; also pl. 20, fig. 1, in the background on the left.
[2] Comp. pl. 20, fig. 3.
[3] 6.10 m. The breadth of the wall was stated correctly by Bandelier (Hodge, p. 305), while Rivero and Tschudi's estimate of five 'varas' (thirteen and three-fourths feet) is erroneous.
[4] According to Rivero and Tschudi and to Middendorf, l. c.
[5] On the south edge of the valley, about three miles from the ancient city, the remains of another ancient dam are to be seen, which protected the district between the coast and the hills farther inland.

---

[6] Rivero and Tschudi estimate it ten feet below its actual height, which is varying and, owing to the drifting sand, can only be measured in a few places.
[7] See pl. 20, fig. 3.

Although the objects obtained in the outer zone of the town all belong to one cultural period, the specimens to be discussed here were found in one cemetery, situated about four hundred yards from the town proper, and from the outer northwestern wall just about two-fifths of the distance between the two. The cemetery was quite untouched. Numerous

Fig. 66. Large vessel from grave in an ancient house, outer zone of city. Inca period.

excavations in the neighborhood, in ancient house foundations, resulted in the recovery of various large vessels, two of which were added to the collection (fig. 66), also several arybals of the style of Cuzco and of large size, but imperfect, and therefore not preserved, and some ornamented cooking vessels, specimens of all of which abounded in the cemetery. The vessels shown in fig. 66 have sides five-eighths of an inch in

older graves, but there is a marked similarity to those from the castle-houses of the town, the occupants of which must be considered as natives. They also made use of numerous objects of Cuzco type, such as vessels of pottery, implements of wood and certain textile fabrics, which fact may be explained by the system used by the Incas in order to assimilate newly conquered provinces with their realm. Garcilaso[1] relates that the Inca carried the first cazique of the newly acquired province, together with all his children, to Cuzco, so that by intercourse with the people there they might acquire a knowledge of the laws, language and customs, as well as the religious cult of the realm; this accomplished, they were reinstated in their former dignities. Santillan has it[2] that the Incas caused the sons of all the Kuraka families to go as yanakonas[3] to Cuzco, and devote themselves to their service. After having become assimilated with the Inca people, they were sent back to their own provinces, in some cases invested with official dignities.[4] The common people went through a similar process of fusion; the Inca, following the well-known system of the mitimaes, would send inhabitants of newly conquered provinces to older assimilated districts,[5] "and citizens of Cuzco and other loyal towns" to the provinces as garrisons, as well as "for the purpose of teaching the natives the laws, customs, ceremonies and language of the realm."[6] This was the reason that in some of the villages on the coast most of the inhabitants spoke

Fig. 67.

Fig. 68.

Fig. 69.

Fig. 70.

Types of black pottery from graves of the outer city. Inca period of coast land.

thickness. Their decoration consists of white lines marking off sections, like a melon, a style typical of the period under discussion. In the cemetery perishable objects have mostly vanished; perhaps because the sand here possessed less preserving qualities than clay, or sand mixed with clay, as is found in cemeteries I, II, and elsewhere. On this account no mummies were found, only crania and bones, pottery, a few textiles in a somewhat better state of preservation, owing to some favoring circumstance, various implements and utensils of wood and metal. The discoveries were sufficiently numerous to establish the character of the period in every particular. They do not represent any distinct style; there are specimens of Cuzco type, as well as of the coast land, but between these two extremes are a number of objects which belong exclusively neither to the one nor to the other, but may be said to form a combination of both, and to create new types, as may be seen in the ceramics of the period. The specimens, although dating from the same period, do not correspond with those taken from graves in the Sun temple, which reflect Cuzco influence in such a striking manner; nor do they resemble those found in the ancient cemeteries of the inner town, I–III, which belong to another period of the style of the coast, and are entirely devoid of Cuzco objects, as well as of products of a mixture of both types. The contrast between the discoveries in cemetery VI and those of the older burial-places is in some respects very marked. In pottery, for instance, not one vessel resembles any of those from the

Kechua perfectly,[7] although originally three or four different languages had been employed in that district. The form in which the Cuzco tongue and that of the coast land became fused is, doubtless, due to the cultural change of the coast land, in consequence of the intermingling of peoples which the Incas effected after their conquest of new territory.[8] Certain types, such as pl. 12, fig. 6, show quite a local stamp, both in technique and ornamental details. It

[1] VI, chap. 12.
[2] P. 39.
[3] 'Yanakona' is really the plural of 'yana,' servant (see v. Tschudi, Wörterbuch, p. 82), as 'mamakona' of mama, but is used for the singular, in Peru, perhaps as much as 'vassal.' The usage must have taken root early, as Santillan employs it, making from it a further plural, 'yanakonas.'
[4] The chiefs are said to have lived always near the Inca. Even through the women the realm was kechuanized, as every year many good-looking ones were transported to Cuzco, some of them to be given in marriage to the vassals as a special favor (Santillan, p. 38).
[5] Santillan, p. 40, and many others.
[6] Garcilaso, l. c.
[7] Cronicá, I, chap. 62.
[8] Brinton, American Races, p. 203, says: "It is an error to suppose that the extension of the Kechua was the result of the victories of the Incas. These occurred but a few centuries before the arrival of the Spaniards, and their influence was not great on the native languages." This position is hardly tenable in view of the complete transformation of the culture on the coast, brought about by the Inca conquest, and of the effectual introduction of the Kechua. The rapid change in culture which the Incas worked wherever they extended their sphere must certainly be called remarkable. They introduced their speech with their culture. It is the same in the Argentine. The Calchaqui, according to the prevailing older names of places, were surely not Kechua. Objects of Cuzco character, nevertheless, are found everywhere, not only at Cuzco, but also throughout the provinces of Catamarca and Rioja (comp. collection of the Berlin Museum). Many are the 'Rios del Inca,' 'Fuertes del Inca,' 'Tambos del Inca,' although the conquest occurred at a very late date, and at the same time as the introduction of Kechua.

seems, therefore, that objects found in the graves of the suburban city must be considered as products of the coöperation of the Cuzco style with that of the native of the coast, the latter preserving its local peculiarities. The possibility that a certain proportion of the inhabitants of Pachacamac, during the Inca period, were colonists, transplanted there from other parts, cannot be disputed. The theory might lead to the expectation of finding the fact expressed in a great diversity of types of cranial deformation; but this is not the case. Outside the prevailing type, with broadened and flattened

colors. Among them only a small number show as highly developed decorative designs as those of purely Cuzco origin. A few examples of black vases of this class are decorated with human faces on the neck, as shown in pl. 18, fig. 2. Some small variations in shape or decoration may be noticed, as an evidence of outside influences, such as might be exercised by the style of the coast. A black arybal of this order is shown in pl. 13, fig. 1; it has two arm or ball-like attachments, from which protrude three thorns, and is represented by two specimens, while in Cuzco[2] it is unknown. Another specimen is

Fig. 71.   Fig. 72.   Fig. 73.

Types of black pottery from graves of the outer city. Inca period of coast land.

occiput, the common one of Pachacamac and other cemeteries on the coast, no additional types of deformation were noticed in cemetery VI and in the graves of dwelling-houses.

A. POTTERY.

In regard to the technique of the pottery of this cemetery, it must be observed that black vessels, or those of inferior make, yellow or red in color, with ordinary primitive decorations, form the principal contingent. The black specimens always show a good polish, at times even excellent, and occasionally with quite a metallic lustre. The shape in many cases is more artistic than even the finest arybals of Cuzco type. The sides are sometimes thin as porcelain, such as is seen in no object of purely Cuzco style. The yellow and red vessels, with primitive decorations, are of a coarser clay and in rare cases well polished. The colors are black and a sort of dull white. A careful treatment in both decoration and polish is seen only on articles of unmistakably Cuzco technique. The preponderance of black color in a large proportion of the pottery, and the fine finish of some of it, far surpassing anything of Cuzco workmanship, prove the influence of the very highly developed ceramic art of some parts

ornamented with a lizard in relief, the third has a flat base and only one horizontal handle, etc.[3]

2. Vessels, such as are represented in pl. 12, fig. 3, and small jugs, Cuzco style (pl. 18, fig. 7), have been found in several instances. The decoration is in good Cuzco manner. It is surprising that no plates were obtained nor any vessel like pl. 18, fig. 5.

3. Low flasks or vases with human faces, mostly black, rarely colored (pl. 13, figs. 3 and 4), are more numerous. Both black and colored are similar in the moulding of the face, and in the manner in which the arms are suggested on the bowl of the vessel, either painted (fig. 4) or engraved, or even moulded in relief. The partial influence of Cuzco is unmistakable in the contour of the neck (comp. the arybals), in the bowl-shape of the body of the vessel, which in general is the predominant fashion of Cuzco pottery (comp. pl. 18, figs. 1 and 7), and the type of the face (comp. pl. 18, fig. 2). The flask (pl. 13, fig. 4) also shows the coloring of the face, so often seen on vessels of Cuzco type (comp. pl. 18, fig. 2), while the arms are painted in the dull white color of the coast. Purely Cuzco ornaments decorate the handle.

[3] Philippi (Verh. der Berl. Ges. f. Anthr., 1885. XVII, p. 268) assumes that all vessels of Cuzco type, and all those found in remote parts of the Inca realm,

Fig. 74.   Fig. 75.   Fig. 76.   Fig. 77.

Types of black pottery from graves of the outer city. Inca period of coast land.

of the coast land. The red and yellow ware, on the other hand, represents in its technique a wide local branch of the art. The use of a dull white color is characteristic of some kinds of pottery from Pachacamac, and the valley of Lima, Ancon,[1] Huarmey, up to the northern parts of the country. The use of moulds can be seen in several specimens of this type, though they are not so extensively employed here as they were farther north (Trujillo, Chimbote, etc.).

1. The arybals are mainly black, a few of different

were made at Cuzco and introduced from there. This may be the case to a great extent with vessels of purely Cuzco workmanship, but the theory would be difficult to maintain in regard to vessels of the same size as the largest in the Centeno collection at Berlin. Many fragments of these were found on the site of an ancient city near Chilecito, in the province of Rioja, in the Argentine, and are now in the Museum of Berlin. There were local productions of vessels of Cuzco style, numerous specimens of which have been previously known, and which may be distinguished by peculiarities of technique or decoration; such as the corner-ornament in the inner design on the arybal from Huarmey (Kultur u. Industrie, I, pl. 10, fig. 9), which distinctly shows influences of the ornamentation of the coast. The spiral-winged decoration, however, does not belong to this class, as erroneously stated by the writer (l. c., p. 32 b). The arybal (l. c., pl. 10, fig. 10) from Pueblo Nuevo, on the Peruvian coast, is remarkable for its white coating; the arybal (l. c., pl. 11, fig. 11) from Corocoro, Bolivia, for its exceptional metallic red glaze; the plates from Freirina and Valdivia Medina (Aborij. de Chile, Nos. 165 and 173) for their shapes and decorations.

[3] Comp. also the vessel (Reiss u. Stübel, pl. 93, fig. 3) from Ancon.

[1] Reiss u. Stübel, pl. 97.

4. Simple flasks are also found of the greatest variety in the shape of bowl, neck or handle, many being perfect in form and technique. The majority are black, while some show the natural color of the clay, but none are painted. The connection between neck and bowl in many specimens is formed by a rim, mostly engraved in a simple pattern of the class often seen in Cuzco textiles, and the handle in some cases is engraved in a Cuzco pottery design. The shape of the vessel frequently represents a conical fruit, with an upright ape or a cat in the act of springing, in plastic mould-

collection, which comes from Quito;[5] another, from Cuenca,[6] is at Brussels. Vessels of the second type, fig. 9, show a difference in the proportion of the body, in the ornaments of the figures, and in the dots in relief, which are peculiar to the coast, as is also the face with indented brow—an indication of the deformation[7] of the skull. A similar[8] piece of pottery may be seen in the Æquatorian Collection at Brussels.[9] Vessels with four bodies were also used at Pachacamac. They consisted of four conical fruits, surmounted by a bow and neck. A specimen from Cuenca can be seen at Brussels.[10]

Fig. 78.

Typical flask of black pottery. From graves in the outer city. Inca period of coast land.

Fig. 79.

Flasks with flattened sides. From graves in the outer city. Inca period of the coast land.

Fig. 80.

ing, perched on the neck.[1] Pl. 13 shows in figs. 13 and 14 two types of this vessel, the first of which is very beautiful in outline. Similar specimens are often found in later cemeteries near Lima. Several vessels from Ancon belong to this class; also one discovered at Calpi, near Riobamba, in Ecuador,[2] which proves them to have been used over a large part of the Inca realm. These vessels resemble the Cuzco style in many particulars, while representing a more developed type. Points of similarity are to be seen in the bowl-shaped body, the tapering base,[3] the characteristics of the handle, and in the engraved ornaments upon it.

5. Flasks with curved neck, nearly all black, like fig. 78 in shape. The only red and white specimen is pl. 13, fig. 12. The type of these flasks belongs to the coast, and they occupy the same technical position as the former class.

6. Double-flasks; those in the collection are all black, and mostly 'silvadores,' that is, provided with pipes. Two

7. Oblated flasks; the majority of them are colored, a few black. Some specimens of this class are decorated with face and coloring in the Cuzco style; others are ornamented in the style of the coast, with raised figures and dots. A collection of pottery from Cuzco, described by Ewbank, contained a few oblated flasks.[11]

8. Jugs with small necks, representing the entire human figure, head and arms plastic, the lower parts indicated in relief only. They are black or colored, and represent a variety of types. On the specimen, pl. 12, fig. 2, a poncho is indicated, ornamented in the manner of tapestry-ponchos of the district of Cuzco. The pattern is indicated by engraving.[12] To this class belong some of the vessels from Ancon.[13] Another jug, resembling the preceding, colored, is shown by Bastian.[14]

9. Various plain flasks, or flasks representing animals or fruits with a bow. To this group belong pl. 12, figs. 11 and

Fig. 81.

Fig. 82.

Fig. 83.

Types of vases. From graves of the outer city. Inca period of the coast land.

main types of these exist, which are shown in pl. 13, figs. 8 and 9. The first belongs to the class of vessels described under No. 4, both as to form and workmanship. These double-flasks are generally very light in weight, and possess a metallic lustre. A bird or similar object decorates the closed neck.[4] To this type also belongs a specimen in the Leipzig

14. They are red or black, and show a large variety of

[1] Comp Reiss und Stübel, pl. 93, fig. 6; pl. 96, figs. 11, 13; also the ape, pl. 100, fig. 4.

[2] Kultur u. Ind., II, pl. 7, fig. 5.

[3] Comp. the vessel from Calpi, in Ecuador.

[4] The vessel, Rivero y Tschudi, Atlas, pl. 12, fig. 1, is of the same class.

[5] Kultur u. Industrie, I, pl. 7, fig. 4.

[6] Congrès des Améric. Bruxelles, Compt. Rend., II, p. 127, Atlas, pl. 19, fig. 1.

[7] Comp. Virchow, Crania ethnica, pl. 14, and fig. VI, p. 12.

[8] Comp. Rivero y Tschudi, l. c., pl. 17, fig. 1; pl. 18, fig. 2; pl. 20, fig. 1.

[9] Congrès des Améric., l. c., p. 126; Atlas, pl. XVII.

[10] l. c. with pl. XVIII. Another Rivero y Tschudi, l. c., pl. 20, fig. 2.

[11] Thom. Ewbank, A description of Indian antiquities, U. S. Naval Astron. Exped., App. E. p. 130, d and j.

[12] Even the seams of the poncho are indicated.

[13] Reiss u. Stübel, pl. 97, fig. 11; pl. 93, fig. 4. Comp. also Rivero y Tschudi, l. c., pl. 14, fig. 2.

[14] Die Culturländer Amerikas, III, 2, p. 68 and pl. 1, fig. 5.

objects, such as stags, cats, fishes, crabs, birds, fruits or vegetables, all in plastic reproduction, rarely in relief.[1] They doubtless belong to the style of the coast, but from the manner in which they were found they are proved to date from the last pre-Spanish period.

10. Red and black vessels with faces upon the neck, the hands moulded in relief, sometimes raised to the head or painted upon the bowl; the lower parts never indicated. The base is conical or flatly rounded. The black vessels have thick sides, the colored are of coarser clay, and mostly red, or decorated with black and white. Pl. 13, figs. 5–7, and fig. 79 in the text reproduce some of the types. The technique of this pottery is that of the coast, the conical base resembling the Cuzco arybals. Several similar objects with a pronounced local character come from Ancon,[2] others[3] with the same characteristics from Ecuador, and certain modern ones are produced in various places in Bolivia. They all, whether from Ancon or Pachacamac, have the hands in the same position, supporting the head.

11. Vessels with heads of birds on the neck or bowl, as in fig. 10. Objects of this class are found also in burial-places of later times in the vicinity of Lambayeque. The bird's head causes resemblance to objects like that in pl. 18, fig. 10, and similar bowls of wood, of the type of pl. 18, fig. 15.[4]

12. Cooking utensils, decorated, such as are shown in fig.

be confounded with the older specimens discovered near Chimbote; they are also met with in the vicinity of Lambayeque, in burial-grounds of more recent date. These vessels, so plain

Fig. 87. Clay figure. From a grave of the outer city. Inca period of the coast land.

in appearance, do not therefore represent a limited local type, although they belong exclusively to this one era. They form a proof of the cultural uniformity of the coast land throughout a vast region during the Inca period.

13. Various flasks with two handles, like fig. 86. Some of these are of plain red, with stripes of dull white, in melon-shape; others are well polished and decorated, after being baked, with a bird or other figure in the style of the coast. Many of these decorations have faded owing to the peculiar technique.

14. Among other objects a clay doll was found, made in a clay mould (fig. 87). The Berlin Museum possesses clay moulds from Peru for the making of similar figures.[8]

Fig. 84.
Types of cooking utensils. From graves of the outer city. Inca period of the coast land.

Fig. 85.

Fig. 86.
Typical flask of red clay. From graves of the outer city. Inca period of the coast land.

84. The vessels are found in great numbers in the outskirts of the town. One class shows ornamental bands in various designs in relief, below the rim; another group is decorated with undulating lines in relief upon the neck, or bowl, or both. Many specimens have a sort of embossed ornamentation, which was made by pressing the sides of the vessel into the desired shapes from the inside, before it was dried (see fig. 85).

Both types belong to the same period. Pottery resembling the second variety has been unearthed at Ancon.[5] The undulating lines in relief may be intended for serpents and can be compared to those on stone vessels of Cuzco type.[6] Such objects almost certainly originated at Cuzco. Vessels of the first-named description, with small local variations, are also found at Ancon,[7] in later burial-places, which must not

B. TEXTILES.

The textiles of this era do not show any marked difference from those of the last pre-Inca period. A practised eye may, however, in many cases easily distinguish whether a fabric belongs to the pre-Inca or Inca time, the difference consisting chiefly in a more advanced technical development. It is impossible to give a minute description of the textiles of this period in so small a space; only a general outline can be presented. Students are referred to the exhaustive work of Reiss and Stübel on their discoveries at Ancon, which goes minutely into the subject.

In many instances textiles of more recent date are distinguished by the brightness of their coloring, while earlier ones favored designs in dull tints.[9] The colors are also more harmoniously blended and softer, not showing such crude contrasts. Any fabric showing delicate color-blending will always, as a matter of course, belong to this period.[10] Red and yellow begin to appear together, a combination hardly ever before used;[11] while yellow as a ground color is much

[1] Of this class are also Rivero y Tschudi, l. c., lam. 10, fig. 2; lam. 11, fig. 1; 13, fig. 2; 16, fig. 2; 19, figs. 2 and 3. All these might readily have been found at Pachacamac, but whether they were so or not is unknown. Comp. Reiss u. Stübel, pl. 93, fig. 14, as belonging to this class and period.
[2] Reiss u. Stübel, pl. 97, figs. 1, 8 and 12.
[3] Congrès des Améric., l. c., II, pp. 117 and 122; Atlas, pl. 7, figs. 6 and 7; 13, fig. 2.
[4] Good examples are given in Kult. u. Indust., II, pl. 1, figs. 1, 3 and 8.
[5] Reiss u. Stübel, pl. 96, fig. 15.
[6] Comp. Rivero y Tschudi, l. c., pl. 31, fig. 1. A clay vessel of this kind was the first object found by the writer in the suburbs of the city, and was by him classified as of Cuzco type, on account of undulating lines, resembling the ornamentation on stone vessels. For this reason he assigned it to a recent date. The contents, among them a necklace with glass beads, confirmed him in this conjecture and helped to support the assumption that undulating lines indicate Cuzco influence.
[7] Reiss u. Stübel, l. c., fig. 13.

[8] Uhle, Ausgew. Stücke des Mus. f. Völkerk. Berl., Veröff. aus dem Museum, 1889, I, Taf. 6, fig. 1. Frogs of the kind reproduced, l. c., fig. 3, in the model, are often used as handles of vessels during the same period at Pachacamac.
[9] Comp. Reiss u. Stübel, pl. 66, fig. 3; 67 a, figs. 1 and 4; 57, fig. 1; 67, fig. 4; 68, figs. 3–6, etc.
[10] Comp. l. c., pl. 67, fig. 4; 68, figs. 5, 6.
[11] L. c., pl. 67 a, fig. 1; 59, figs. 1, 2; 67 b, fig. 1; 57, fig. 1; 66 a, fig. 4; 66, fig. 3; 68, fig. 6; 67, fig. 4.

favored,[1] having been rarely seen in earlier textiles. Many tapestries of this period are distinguishable from the earlier ones by the large size of the ornamental figures.[2] Designs on a large scale, similar to those shown by Reiss and Stübel, pl. 55, fig. 1, belong to this time. In figure designs the tendency is more and more toward large patterns. The technique is correspondingly treated. Texture, even in rich designs, is often

Fig. 88. Cross-shaped ornament of a necklace. From a grave
of Inca period. Outer city.

less close than in earlier textiles; long slits along the outlines of figures or colors are seen again,[3] similar to the tapestries of the earliest periods, when they were retained on purpose to mark the pattern. The tendency to replace oblique lines by graduated ones is often quite apparent, and the same general effect is thus produced.[4] The variety of ornamental designs seems infinitely greater at this period in the evolution of new figures, as well as in the continuation and development of earlier types. A pronounced tendency toward

belong to this period; also compare the braids of Ancon (l. c., pl. 68, fig. 3; 66, fig. 3).

All technical processes of textile art already known were continued, such as open-work weaving by interchanging warp threads, the weaving of small pieces of material to form patterns in combination,[6] as well as those produced by dyeing or painting or other similar treatment. In textiles, as well as in pottery, certain types appear to belong specially to the coast region and others to the highland, which is caused by the influences at work during the rule of the Incas. Compare, for example, a poncho with horizontal border in a pattern such as pl. 8, fig. 16; with fragments of ponchos resembling those found in the graves of the Sun temple, and the pieces of a woman's girdle (chumpi) (pl. 20, figs. 1–4, etc.). Certain attributes which modified the style of the coast may be referred indirectly to other agencies. As regards colors, gray appears at this epoch, sometimes in woolen materials, but generally in cotton. It may have been produced by some newly-discovered process. The same color is often seen in Cuzco textiles, taken from graves in the Sun temple. The frequent occurrence of textile designs in white and brown only, rarely found previous to this date, or in white and blue,[7] white, brown and blue,[8] brown and blue,[9] must be attributed to highland influences. In addition to the new color, gray, a number of combinations appear at this time[10] in striped

Fig. 89. Decorative design (trees) in a tapestry. From a grave of
the outer city. Inca period of the coast land.

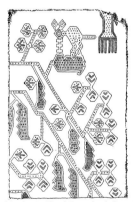

Fig. 90. Section of embroidered decorative design. From a grave
of outer city. Inca period of the coast land.

naturalistic reproductions may also be noticed. Variations and transformations of designs, such as may be seen in some of the discoveries of Reiss and Stübel, belong to this time. See, for instance, l. c., pl. 67, fig. 4 (design in the squares); 68, fig. 1; 66 a, fig. 1; 67 b, fig. 1; 59, fig. 2 (border). Cross-shaped figures, like l. c., pl. 68, figs. 5, 6, are frequently seen on textile fabrics, and are characteristic of this period. A small cross from a necklace, found in a house at Pachacamac, shows the same outlines as the figures above mentioned (fig. 88.) All kinds of animals are represented for the first time in the tapestries belonging to this era: spiders, scorpions, fishes, birds with a peculiar tuft on the head like that of a rooster, etc. Plants had already made their appearance in the preceding period, as tree-shaped figures,[5] with many variations, upon a certain class of fabrics. All these figures developed into richer designs (figs. 89 and 90) or were embellished by the addition of a leaf-pattern (fig. 91), which is often seen on borders or braids. More naturalistic reproductions of common ornaments of earlier times, such as birds,

or figured materials, as well as in tapestries, clearly showing in every case the effect of highland industries.

Certain kinds of stripes are peculiar to this period, and may be traced to the same influences, for instance narrow stripes in two to four of the above colors;[11] also patterns in which wide stripes, frequently brown, are bordered by narrow ones in the same color, often repeated over the surface of the material. This pattern is very often found on the ponchos from graves in the Sun temple.[12]

Tapestries of the earlier era were either of pure woolen warp or part wool, part cotton; cotton being sometimes used for white in the pattern. Later, occasionally cotton is used for both white and brown, and wool for the other colors. Tapestries of pure cotton only exist from the last pre-Spanish period, and these are usually in the highland color combinations of brown, blue and white, though they occasionally vary.

The three-ply weave (as in fig. 92) is, in a certain degree,

[1] L. c., 59, fig. 2; 66, fig. 3; 68, figs. 5, 6; 67, fig. 4.
[2] Comp. l. c., pl. 55, fig. 1.
[3] Comp. l. c., pl., 55, fig. 1; 40, fig. 2.
[4] For instance like l. c., pl. 66, fig. 3.
[5] Bastian l. c., pl. 4 (on the central strip of the gauze poncho).

[6] Comp. l. c., pl. 15.
[7] Compare several modern cloths from the highland in the Stübel collection at Leipzig; also one in Kultur u. Ind., II., pl. 12, fig. 6 (from Chachapoyas).
[8] Comp. Reiss u. Stübel, pl. 24, fig. 1; 38, pl. 12, fig. 1.
[9] Comp. l. c., pl. 24, fig. 2.
[10] Compare the stuff, l. c., pl. 57, fig. 1; 24, fig. 3.
[11] L. c., pls. 24, 38 and 57.
[12] Also pl. 19, fig. 11.

typical of America. Almost, if not entirely, unknown in Europe, it is found generally in Peruvian textiles, also among the Pueblo Indians. The weave of fig. 92 produces a cloth with reciprocal colors on both sides. This class of textiles belonged to the earlier period, and is often represented at Pachacamac. Older fabrics show dots over the surface, the ply being doubled (as in fig. 57, above, p. 44). This weave allows only for two colors, therefore figures of a third color are embroidered into the cloth. Textures with a dotted surface are made to this day in the same weave in the highland of Bolivia.[1] Many designs in brown, gray and white are quite similar to those of the lowland during the last period, except that all three colors are evenly woven in. The texture is of this nature: On one side of the stuff, thread No. 1 covers thread No. 3, while No. 2 remains visible as a dot; on the reverse side, thread No. 3 covers thread No. 1, while No. 2 again appears as a dot. This weave is only exemplified in

3. Openwork patterns in textiles. The openwork weave produced by interchanging and drawing together the warp threads, appeared in earlier years, but the application of these methods of weaving to more complicated patterns in the cloth[6] seems to be of earlier date. This applies especially to the delicate embroideries with openwork ground. Of figures,[7] birds, puma-heads, etc., Pachacamac gives us a number of examples from this last period, and from this only. In shape the textiles generally correspond to those of the earlier periods, with one interesting exception.

In graves of the earliest times we find certain long shirts (fig. 94), with openings for the neck and arms.[8] They have as an ornament a square piece of plaited white cotton sewed on in front, on the breast. These garments are, perhaps, referred to by Cieza, I, chap. 62, when he describes the costume worn by the women of the coastland: "All were clothed in their ponchos and long cloaks; the women also, only that

Fig. 91. Leaf design. Tapestry border. From a grave of outer city. Inca period of the coast land.

Fig. 92. Three-ply weaving of ancient Peruvian textiles. From graves of outer city. Inca period of the coast land.

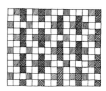

Fig. 93. More developed three-ply Peruvian textures. From graves of outer city. Inca period of the coast land.

cloth showing the color-scheme of brown, gray and white borrowed from the highland.

Patterns embroidered into woven cloths also belong to this period; they are of the same kind as the fabric from Ancon (pl. 59 a, fig. 3, Reiss u. Stübel).[2] There are, in addition, quite a number of different patterns, colorings and stitches

Besides the above, there are still three more technical methods apparently belonging exclusively to the Inca period of the coast, and which show no relation to imported cultural elements:

1. Woven borders or braids of the class shown by Reiss u. Stübel (pl. 67 a, fig. 1). In these braids threads of one color only run as woof through the whole piece, in the example cited, red or yellow, while other colors are worked in by embroidery. The texture has only one right side; on the wrong side the threads appear loose wherever not required in the pattern. This method was followed to a great extent in later times, especially for poncho borders, of which numerous examples are to be seen. A poncho taken from one of the Inca graves, and ornamented in the style of the coast, has such a border, the pattern of which was reproduced above (p. 38, fig. 51).

2. Surface embroidery upon cotton cloths with loose woolen threads. The embroidery threads cover the material quite loosely in large sections, being intended for wide spaces, and are laid side by side.[3] Of this class is the pattern of some modern scarfs (fajas) from Ecuador in the Stübel collection at Leipzig.[4] At Pachacamac, surface embroidery belongs as exclusively to latest Inca times as the method of embroidering upon cloth, giving a rep or tapestry-like appearance,[5] belongs strictly to the earliest period; it is extensively used at this time. The pattern of the garment from Pachacamac, pictured by Hamy in Gal. améric. du Trocadero, pl. 48, as well as many similar ones, have been produced in this manner.

their garment was ample and long, like a Spanish closed cape, open at the sides to allow the arms to pass through."[9] Garments as represented (fig. 94), or fragments of plaited fabric which may have served as ornaments upon similar articles of clothing, are of frequent occurrence in graves of women dating from this period; their pre-Spanish origin is thereby attested. This is, curiously enough, the first and only

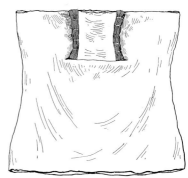

Fig. 94. Woman's garment with knife-plaited trimming. From graves of the outer city. Inca period of the coast land.

instance in all America during pre-Spanish times of the use of knife-plaiting as trimming for garments. The origin of the 'kuchma' is now also clear; this is a garment resembling a poncho, knife-plaited, worn at weddings by the Indians of Otavaló, in Ecuador,[10] and which could not be satisfactorily traced back to an imported Spanish custom.

[1] Comp. Kult. u. Indust., II, pl. 14, figs. 1–4.
[2] Textiles of the same class were repeatedly found at Pachacamac.
[3] Comp. Reiss u. Stübel, pl. 66 a, fig. 3.
[4] Kultur u. Industrie, II, pl. 11, figs. 4, 5; 12, fig. 5.
[5] Comp. pl. 6, figs. 1–4.

[6] Comp. W. H. Holmes, 6 Ann. Rep. of the Bureau of Ethnology, 1888, pp. 211, 309.
[7] Comp. l. c., p. 212, fig. 311.
[8] In some graves pieces of gauze are numerous, folded in a triangular way, or lengthwise into a band, and used as a sort of shawl. They were tightly sewed together lengthwise, with a border. It is not certain if these articles belonged exclusively to the earliest period.
[9] The two examples in the collection have such small openings that it is doubtful if they have ever been really used. Perhaps these garments had been purposely prepared to serve as covers for the mummy bales.
[10] Kultur u. Ind., II, pl. 13, fig. 2.

C. Implements of Metal.

A few objects made of copper from cemetery VI are shown in pl. 13, figs. 21–26. They represent an advanced stage in the use of metal, in regard to size, technique and purpose, when compared with the insignificant specimens found in earlier cemeteries.

Fig. 21. A knife, ornamented with a human face, made with a handle, showing that this tool was used by hand.

Fig. 22. An implement resembling a chisel, having a well-preserved handle of dark wood. A wide groove surrounds the handle at one end, which is flattened on one side to support the blade. A small fragment of thin cord, with which the latter was fastened, is still preserved.

Fig. 23. An ordinary flat chisel. To judge by another specimen, the chisel must have been fastened into a handle of stag horn.

Fig. 24. A necklet of a narrow strip of copper, the ends of which are bent so as to form hooks.

Fig. 25. Earpick, the upper end of which forms a well-executed figure of a bird with long beak.

Fig. 26. Round object of two pieces of hammered copper, joined together on the rims. It is ring-shaped, with a hole in the centre. A similar object, both as to size and shape, made

attributed to Cuzco influences. The general shape of the plate in pl. 13, fig. 16, is the same as that of the clay plates of Cuzco style, with a round handle. Birds as ornaments for plates have not yet been traced, but the bird ornament

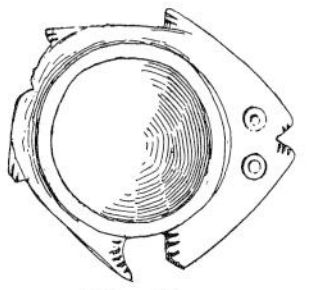

Fig. 95 *a.* 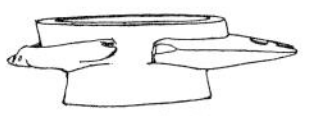   Fig. 95 *b.*

Bowl carved of wood. Shape of a fish. From the graves of the outer city.

upon this one may have been an imitation. Its general appearance is that of the Cuzco type, and it may have been carved by some denizen of the highland. Fragments of other wooden plates, good imitations of Cuzco plates, without handles, were frequently found in the houses of the inner town. Wooden bowls in the shape of birds or fishes of the type of pl. 18, fig. 15, were also occasionally discovered. In the bowl, figs. 95 *a* and *b,* the fish is formed differently and resembles the fishes upon a wall of the temple of Pachacamac.[3] This type is undoubtedly of Cuzco character.

Fig. 96. End pieces of a weaver's beam. From the graves of the outer city. Inca period of coast land.

Fig. 97. Small weaver's knife. Carved wood. From graves in the outer city. Inca period of coast land.

Fig. 98. Netting needle with carved ends (fish). From graves of outer city. Inca period of coast land.

of clay, serves as a rattle, and differs from the preceding only by being open in the centre and not perforated on the surface. It was probably filled with small pellets of clay, or with small stones, and fastened upon a stick. This same construction is to be seen in the magic rattles ('maraka') of eastern South America, which are made of vegetable shells. Several silver finger-rings[1] were found in the cemetery.

The tweezers in this burial-ground are of the usual well-known shape. One pair, possibly of later date, was found near a house in the northern part of the city.[2] The shape is a developed form of the original bivalve sea-shell.

D. Utensils of Wood.

These show highland influences, either in shape or ornamental detail. Three wooden cups were found, not in the cemetery, but in analogous spots in the town. Two, entirely alike, were taken from the grave of a young girl at the southern foot of the hill of the Sun temple; the third was picked up during excavations in the terrace of a house, where it had probably found its way during a libation while the house was being built. All three cups, from their decorations, must be

Wooden spoons, with a fish, a bird or a llama's claw upon the handle, were found occasionally. As spoons are very rare in earlier burial-places, it may be safe to infer that the use of this utensil was extended through the Inca conquest.

A small idol of wood, inlaid with pieces of shell, is shown (pl. 13, fig. 18); although of crude style it is carefully made. Wooden dolls of this period may easily be recognized by the triangular shape of the head.[4]

Weavers' beams, weavers' slays and netting needles, ornamented like figs. 96, 97 and 98, were found in cemetery VI, but not in older burial-places.[5] The same applies to the well-known variegated spinning-whorls made of clay.[6] In this burial-ground were also found two types of ear ornaments (pl. 13, figs. 19 *a* and *b* and fig. 20). One is a plain ring of dark wood, one and three-sixteenths to two and one-fourth inches in diameter, one-half to five-eighths of an inch thick—in a single instance only fifteen-sixteenths of an inch—and grooved along the outer rim, which is smooth. On one side are carved birds, repeated again and again, exactly alike on all specimens, embossed by a few incisions. In one case two rings of the

[1] Reiss u. Stübel, pl. 81, figs. 22, 23.
[2] Comp. *l. c.*, figs. 2, 4, 6, 8.

[3] See above, p. 21.
[4] Reiss u. Stübel, pl. 89, fig. 1.
[5] Comp. Reiss u. Stübel, pl. 86, figs. 3–17.
[6] Spindles and weavers' beams sometimes contain small clay pellets, neatly introduced into small cavities as rattles.

same kind are tightly fitted into one another. The second type, fig. 19 a and b, is represented by three specimens. It consists of a hollow wooden plug one and one-fourth inches high, the front side with a diameter of nine-sixteenths of an inch, and inlaid with shell fragments forming a man's head, surrounded by simple ornaments. Both types are wanting in the earlier burial-grounds. Cylindrical ear-plugs from the region of Lambayeque, belonging to the second type, had a diameter of one and one-sixteenth by one inch in height; they showed on the front side an inlaid figure of a fish, formed of bits of shell. Since all these ornaments were obtained from graves of earliest date, they were probably made in accordance with regulations imposed by the Incas, as to material, decoration and size, and were the ear-plugs worn as marks of distinction, of a special kind for each province.[1] To this class may belong the second type, being closely similar in all three specimens, although each is of a different pair. In the first type the general character is uniform, while the size varies.[2] The occurrence of two distinct types in one cemetery still requires future elucidation.

E. Gourds.

Vessels of this class are always quite plain in the earlier cemeteries, while those found in the outer zone of the city are decorated with burnt-in figure and scroll designs. These vessels, when found on the coast, must be regarded as dating from the last pre-Spanish period.[3] A gourd from the graves of the Sun temple shows ornaments burnt into it, although of a simpler Cuzco type.[4]

Flasks, represented in fig. 99, consist of three parts: the bowl, made of a gourd; a cylindrical piece in the centre, made of wood, and a small stick of wood or bone, extending through the cylindrical part into the bowl and finished at the top with

Fig 99. Lime-flask for coca-chewing. From graves of the outer city. Inca period of coast land.

a knob, prettily ornamented in some specimens. Flasks of this class are found in this burial-place exclusively. They still contain lime, which was used with the chewing of coca. Similar flasks for lime are still in use in the highland, and it must be noted that their occurrence on the coast is limited to the Inca period.

---

[1] Garcilaso, I, chap. 23.
[2] The width is generally uniform, except in the one instance. According to Garcilaso, the width was regulated by the Inca.

[3] All vessels made of gourds, Reiss u. Stübel, pl. 84, figs. 5–12, must be ascribed to the last pre-Inca period.
[4] Compare also the modern gourd with burnt decorations from Chachapoyas in the Stübel Collection at Leipzig, Kult. u. Ind., II, pl. 4, fig. 11.

CHAPTER XVIII.

DISCOVERIES IN OTHER PARTS OF THE VALLEY.

SUCCESSFUL operations in the ancient city naturally aroused an interest in the cultural conditions of other parts of the same valley. Lack of time forbidding extensive investigations, only two burial-places in the vicinity were examined, the one being situated to the east from the Centinela rocks in the hacienda Huarangal, on the southern side of the valley, about two miles from the ancient city;[1] the other, at a similar distance, in the vicinity of the hacienda Venturosa,[2] towards the northern limit of the valley.

---

[1] v. Tschudi, Peru, II, p. 301.
[2] See above, p. 5.

THE CEMETERY OF LA CENTINELA.

Specimens obtained in this burial-ground entirely correspond with those of cemetery VI of the outer city. They are of the last period of the coast style, as well as of the Cuzco type, together with blendings of both, and must be classed as belonging exclusively to the last era of the valley, that of the Incas. It was surprising to find here several graves containing silver vessels, and in one of these a pair of golden tweezers. There were three graves with such contents. The mummies were bale-shaped, bound with thick cotton cords, interwoven with straw-rope. The use of cotton cords, instead of ordinary straw-rope, is a distinct proof of wealth. From the shape of the bale, it is evident that persons buried here were natives of the valley, who practiced ancient methods of burial, side by side with the newly introduced customs of the highland—carrying on the forms of their own culture, besides adopting those imported from Cuzco. The false head on the mummy bale was ornamented with a face of hammered silver. The use of silver vessels, like that of ear ornaments, the length of the hair, and the style of headdress, was subject to regulations by the Inca. Only the Inca himself, the Sun maidens at Cuzco and at the temples had golden and silver vessels for ordinary use, while the kurakas and chiefs were only permitted such costly objects at grand ceremonies, their number being strictly regulated. Common people might use such vessels only as a special privilege, granted by the Inca. Gold and silver articles in graves are, therefore, a proof of the high rank of the persons buried there.[1]

Two objects obtained from these graves are shown on pl. 7. Figs. 22, 23 *a* and 23 *b* illustrate a trephined skull, found with a large silver cup, ornamented with a face, and remains of a feathered stuff. The cranium shows a slightly flattened occiput, and is that of an adult in the prime of life. Besides the trephining on the left side it shows the scar of a former operation on the right, a little further towards the frontal region, the inner bony part of which is one inch long and seven-eighths of an inch wide, covered by a circular cicatrice, forming a deep groove one half-inch in width. The second operation of trephining was made on the left side of the crown, removing an oval piece of bone (figs. 23 *a* and *b*) by a diagonal cut of one and one-fourth to one and one-sixteenth of an inch in diameter.[2] The cutting surfaces on the skull and the piece taken out are surprisingly even, still a loss of bone of three-sixteenths of an inch on the outside was caused by the diagonal incision, while on the inner side it was not one-thirty-second of an inch nor even in some spots one-sixty-fourth of an inch. The bone was not cut through, and was of the thickness of paper in one part, five-sixteenths of an inch in length in the line of the cut; here in removing the detached piece the bone had scaled off. The thickness of the bony structure at the spot of operation is one-fourth of an inch. The wound must have been of a very severe nature, judging from existing indications, and the preservation of such an instance of trephining is very unusual (figs. 23 *a* and 23 *b*). A flat object, probably an arrowhead, had entered the skull diagonally seven-sixteenths of an inch deep, with a point of the width of a pocket-knife, not piercing but splintering the bone radially on the inner side (fig. 23 *b*). The bone on this side seems to have become so loosened during the operation, that in one point it could not be cut any further and had to be broken through. The operation was begun probably by the removal of the foreign object which caused the wound, for which purpose all manner of introductory incisions were made to loosen it (fig. 23 *a*). Around the oval cut, the outside of the cranium in a strip of half an inch to an inch is darkly discolored by blood. It seems, therefore, that the scalp was loosened from the skull to this extent prior to the operation, so that the blood could color the exposed skull. This strengthens the supposition that the patient died during or very soon after the operation, as there is no cicatrization along the edge of the wound, nor was the blood cleaned away. The opening in the skull was closed by merely putting the detached piece of bone back into place for burial, and they were, therefore, found together.[3]

---

[2] In fig. 22 the detached piece of bone is shown in its original place.
[3] The Bureau of Ethnology at Washington owns an excellent and rare collection of trephined skulls from Peru, among which is one from Pachacamac, illustrated in the important publication on these skulls by Muñiz and McGee (Sixteenth Ann. Rep. of the Bur. of Ethnol., 1897, No. 11, p. 36, and pl. XXII). It has an oval incision like that above.

---

[1] Garcilaso, II, chap. 28; IV, chaps. 5 and 11; V, chaps. 11 and 12.

Fig. 21 shows an embroidered cotton cloth, taken from another grave containing silver vessels. It is forty-six by forty-three inches in size, well preserved and composed of two pieces. It is ornamented with all-over embroidery, described on p. 43, No. 2. Fig. 21 reproduces one-fourth of a section of the cloth. The figures embroidered upon it with woolen threads resemble birds, and are repeated all over the surface; the colors are purple, blue, yellow, and brown, alternating. The ends show only one-half of a narrow embroidered border in blue and purple, on account of having been composed of two sections. The cloth belonged to a chieftain, being found together with silver vessels. Owing to its colors, blue and purple, the colors of the Inca, and those of his nearest of kin, the Qhapay aillu, yellow and red, it gains a certain deeper significance. The brown color, which seems out of place, might have been intended to mark the province, as it does in the kipus.[1] It is possible that the lower grade took its own color, and added it to that of the higher, thereby making the color combination more significant. This would explain why the fewer colors of the Inca were so generally recognized and respected, that one thread of the frontal fringe of the Inca was sufficient to secure for its wearer the deepest submission to his orders. It is possible that the colors of the Inca may owe their origin to the synthesis. According to Oliva,[2] the god Wiraqocha emerged from the ocean in a violet tunic and a crimson cloak. Red and blue, accordingly, might be the colors of the universe. Crimson in the knotted strings signifies the Inca, and blue might be the color of the origin of the world, tiksi.[3] Blue is also among the colors which signify religion.[4] Blue, yellow and white might be the combination of the Creator, blue, the sun, white, and yellow instead of brown (?) for the wakas,[5] representing the three forms of cult.

[1] Uhle, A modern Kipu, Bulletin of the Mus. of Science and Art, Phil., 1898.
[2] In v. Tschudi, Beiträge, p. 130.
[3] Elsewhere it means 'nothing,' refusal or subtraction (see Uhle, l. c.).
[4] Uhle, l. c.
[5] Brown as the color of a province was at the same time that of the provincial waka cult. White signifies day, probably also sun. The sun-maidens and priests were clothed in white (see below, chap. xxi).

Another unusual cloth taken from the same grave is represented in fig. 100. The size is ten feet by five and three-quarters. It is made of cotton, of a thin brown texture, which has sixteen by sixteen threads to the half inch. Into this cloth are inserted at each end triangular pieces, woven separately, each of which is three feet deep and has nine gradations on both sides. A narrow dark stripe woven into the cloth extends from these white insertions to the ends of the piece. Simple as this cloth may appear, the manufacture

Fig. 100. Large cloth from the grave of a chieftain. Graves of La Centinela. Inca period of the coastland.

of a fabric ten feet long, and in which large triangular pieces had to be shaped in the weaving, requires a certain amount of skill. The size of this cloth precludes its use as a garment. As this grave, from all indications, is that of a chieftain, it is possible that the cloth is a mark of his rank, the brown color representing the province. Considering the character of the ornamentation, it must have been intended for distance effect, and the decoration of both ends gives ground for the supposition that it was used as a pall.[6]

[6] Comp. the ornaments on the fabrics shown by Bastian (l. c., pl. 5).

THE GRAVES OF VENTUROSA.

Two vessels only were secured from these graves, one of them being decorated. The design upon this object (pl. 7, fig. 10) consists of three birds in frontal view, their type being the same as those upon the arybals of the Inca time,[1] and clearly an imitation. This shows that during the period of the Incas some settlement must have been situated in the vicinity of the present hacienda Venturosa. The discovery of

graves dating from the Inca period wherever explorations were conducted in the valley outside the city, refutes the theory[2] that Pachacamac was abandoned during that time and left to fall into ruins. Whatever the Inca rule may have been in other parts of the coast, it was beneficial in the Pachacamac valley. Settlements were then extended outside the city, probably for the main reason that personal safety was guaranteed to the settlers in the valley.

[1] Rivero and Tschudi (pl. 36). The same vessel also Bastian (l. c., pl. 3, fig. 2).

[2] See above, p. 6.

Fig. 101. Decorated vessel from graves of La Venturosa. Inca period of coast land; ¼ n. s.

CHAPTER XIX.

THE SUN TEMPLE.

THE Sun temple, situated upon the hill, W, and the convent at the western end of the city are the only prominent buildings of the old town of Pachacamac which date from the Inca period. The Sun temple has been more frequently described than any building in the ancient town, still, so far only one plan exists of it, and four or five views by George Squier, which, however, give no adequate idea of the edifice. The writer here offers a more reliable plan (pl. 16[1]), elevations of the four fronts of the Temple (pl. 17) and a number of photographic views in reproductions, pl. 2, fig. 1, the Temple from the north; pls. 12, 14, 15, figs. 1, 2, which will assist in the study of its details.[2]

On the whole, the dimensions of the Temple have been so carefully established by the plan, the notes, and the measurements of elevations, that at any time it will be easy to make any number of cross-sections, twelve of which have been prepared and are in the collection.[3]

The hill W may be two hundred and fifty to three hundred feet high,[4] and is of a rocky nature.[5] Its base is broad, and slopes down in many curves;[6] at one point only, on the southeastern side, near the Temple, it is somewhat steeper. A narrow ridge, lower than the hill,[7] continues it in a northeastern direction, and at the foot of its northwestern slope[8] was the site of the ancient temple of the Creator as above described. Excluding the Temple, the circumference of the hill at this point may be one mile and a quarter.

---

[1] The plan of the Temple is especially difficult to obtain on account of its intricate construction and the ruined state of several terraces, therefore some glaring errors in Squier's plan (p. 69) must not be taken too seriously :
  1 The confounding of north and south, the same as on p. 275 in the plan, and the description of the Ruins of Tiahuanaco by the same author (see Stübel u. Uhle, p. 15 b, note 5).
  2. The rectangular shape of the structure.
  3. The complete misconstruction of the plateau, absence of structures on the southern part of the plateau of the entire fourth terrace of the southeast front, the misplacement of the centre of the western front too far south, whereby the rooms adjoining it on the north become detached from it, and those on the south side too much crowded.
  4. Misdrawing and misinterpretation of the third northern terrace.
  5. Misinterpretation of the displacement of the terraces between northeast and southeast on the eastern angle.
  6. Removal of the ascent of the second terrace from the inside to the front.
[2] Among earlier views those of Hutchinson (p. 159) and of Wiener (p. 484) are intended for reproductions of the west front of the Temple, shown in pl. 15, fig. 2. Those by Wiener (p. 62), Rivero and Tschudi (Atlas, pl. 54), show the Temple from the northwest. The view given by Squier (p. 68) and one by Wilkes are intended to show the north angle of the Temple, but are not exact ; better views of the same point may be seen in the collection.

[3] It might be suggested that a perfect model in clay could be made of the Temple in its present condition (1 : 100 or 1 : 200) from photographs and exact measurements. In some respects it would be more instructive than the original, as its small dimensions would facilitate the study of the structure, while at the same time it would preserve the memory of the famous monument which seems doomed to destruction at no distant period.
[4] Wilkes and Hutchinson (p. 158) estimate the height as above ; Markham and Middendorf, 400 feet ; Rivero and Tschudi (p. 288), with remarkable correctness, 458 feet ; Cobo and Squier (p. 68), 500 feet ; v. Tschudi, Peru, I, p. 291, 558 feet ; Bancroft, Native Races of the Pacific States, V, p. 796, 600 feet. In some of these estimates the difference of the original hill from the summit of the building is too high, so that of Wilkes.
[5] Hutchinson, I, pp. 160, 172 and 176, regarded the hill, with a remarkable lack of judgment, as being artificial and piled up above a large cemetery. Santillan is doubtful on this subject (p. 32). Wiener addresses an unscientific public ; as in nearly all his work, so in his erroneous explanation (p. 711), when he describes this hill as being of breast-shape, representing in a figurative sense the 'creating Earth' under the Pachakamaj temple (elsewhere he calls it the Sun temple).
[6] See plan of the city, and pl. 2, fig. 1.
[7] See plan of the city, pl. 1.
[8] Compare pl. 2, fig. 1 ; 9, fig. 2 ; 13, fig. 1.

SITUATION AND GENERAL REMARKS.

The distance from the base of the hill to the sea may be estimated at about one-third of a mile. As the Temple lies from six hundred to one thousand feet away from the southwestern foot of the hill, the present distance of the Temple plateau from the sea would be about one-half mile, as estimated by Markham. From the prominence of its site, the Temple gives the impression, as Squier says,[1] "that it reaches close to the shore, so that the ocean may be said to break at its feet." On the side facing the ocean the most delightful sea-breeze is felt all day long, making the crest of this hill a pleasant place, even on the hottest day. The Temple with its broad base has been built around the top of the hill and into a ravine, as Squier expresses it, facing toward southwest, as may be seen both on Squier's plans and in the views here shown (pl. 14, fig. 2). The edifice really is fitted into and around the hill, following its form closely. Although the section of the hill-crest with the Temple as given by Squier is quite imaginary,[2] it still serves to give a general idea of the manner in which this structure was built around the hill, and which accounts for the varying height of the masonry on the different sides. It is seventy-five feet[3] in the ravine in the centre of the southwestern front, and only forty-nine feet over the western base of the hill,[4] while at the extreme western end, within the terraces, the hill was left in its natural state near 69, 26 and 29, and rises there at a distance of seventy feet from the plateau to a height of only sixteen feet below it.

---

[1] P. 68.

[2] The natural hill may be seen on the entire lower terrace on the west side (comp. pl. 14, fig. 2 ; not so in Squier's plan). It is not known how deep the hill lies beneath the masonry, outside this one point. The summit, as given in Squier's cross-section, is also imaginary.
[3] See pl. 17, cross-section 1.
[4] See pls. 16 and 17, fig. 2.

The Temple is an imposing terraced structure, built of adobe. It has four fronts. The shape is trapezoid, conforming to the outlines of the hill, the longest front looking seaward in a southwestern direction. The northeastern and northwestern fronts are nearly parallel, the two others converge in a short angle toward northeast. The sides measuring 715 feet (southwest), 515 feet (northwest), 565 feet (northeast) and 347 feet (southeast),[1] it is safe to estimate its area at about twelve acres;[2] and as the height varies on the three last mentioned sides from forty-nine to sixty feet,[3] it may be seen that it is in a very small proportion to the size of the Temple about one-tenth to the length of the sides. The Sun temple of Pachacamac is one of the most prominent among the Peruvian terraced buildings, while it cannot compare in size with the largest Mexican structures. The pyramids of Teotihuacan surpass the Sun temple of Pachacamac in the length of the base on three sides (about 680 feet) as well as in height (about 180 feet); the pyramid of Cholula is twice as long in its base (about 1300 feet), and has more than three times the height of the Sun temple. The proportion of the length of base to the height is quite different in the Mexican pyramids; the proportion would be of $1 : 1\frac{1}{2}$ to $1 : 6$.

The Sun temple, nevertheless, is an imposing and magnificent structure, and must have been much more so when seen by Cobo early in the seventeenth century, from whose

description we are now able to reconstruct some parts no longer existing in its present state of ruin. The entire building was painted red. An imposing main front, decorated with niches, faces southwest, and presents a beautiful appearance.[4] The opposite front, facing northeast,[5] is noteworthy on account of the passageway[6] which winds up to the terraces and the plateau, and for the temple-cells on both extreme ends of the same, rising above it symmetrically for more than twenty feet.[7] A vast plaza extended over the summit of the structure, facing northeast and southwest, and bordered by temple-cells on the other two sides. Here the great festivals in honor of the divinity were held. The view from this point is superb, commanding a panorama embracing the town, the desert back of it, the convent with the adjoining fields, the ocean and the islands near the shore,[8] the valley in its perennial verdure against the background of the desert, and to the left the towering peaks of the Andes. Even the terraces of the northwest, northeast and southeast sides were by no means monotonous. Their grouping was peculiarly varied; they had different details and formations, while various superstructures broke the straight lines, and the pious and initiated native may have attached special ideas to each part of the structure, always in his full view from the town.

---

[1] Former measurements, Wilkes: length of the Temple, 500 feet, width, 400 feet.

[2] Comp. pl. 17, fig. 4.

[3] Squier gave 54 feet, Cobo 74 feet (Span.) as the height of the Temple, a difference which may be explained from the different sides where the measurements were taken.

---

[4] Pl. 14, figs. 1 and 2. From the existence of a main front of this order, around which three terraced sides of less importance were grouped, Squier (p. 68) and v. Tschudi (Peru, I, p. 291) derived the rather unfortunate description of the structure as "crescent-shaped" or as "resembling an amphitheatre."

[5] Pl. 13, fig. 1.

[6] Pl. 15, fig. 1.

[7] See the reconstruction as marked in pl. 17, figs. 2 and 3.

[8] Comp. pl. 13, fig. 1; pl. 14, fig. 3.

THE NORTHWEST, NORTHEAST AND SOUTHEAST FRONTS OF THE TEMPLE.

It is fortunate that the main lines of the front were so simple and regular that an adequate idea may be formed of many details of the original construction without making many excavations, simply by studying the existing parts of the building.[1] So far the descriptions of the terraces were misleading in regard to their number and form, as well as their height, width and relative position, which accordingly were assumed to be far too uniform. Instead of measuring each terrace separately, travelers were satisfied to take measurements at random, at any spot, often not even typical ones. The results were the most varying descriptions, frequently giving no remote idea of the size and individual character of buildings.

The system of terracing on the northwest, northeast and southeast sides, compared to that on the fourth, the southwest side, is, as a whole, quite uniform. The foot of the Temple is

correspondingly regulated in a symmetrical plan on these three sides[2] and different from the southwest sides, where it is formed by the natural slope of the hill. Its height and width both vary about ten feet.[3] In this it differs from the terraces. It is also graded and distinguishes itself from the surroundings by artificial slopes, so that P. Bernabé Cobo described it as the lowest terrace. Kitchen refuse, containing chips of pottery, fragments of fabric, parts of shells (mytilus) cast out from the Temple (near 75), were thrown down the northeast and southeast slopes.

The system of terracing turns at the southern angle, near 41, toward the southwest front of the Temple, in such a manner that the second terrace, southeast, lies on the same level with the southern part, 23, of the second southwest terrace. But here was a dividing wall, and this piece, 23, of the second terrace, southwest, extended without connection along the third and fourth terraces, near 40 and 39. Near the corner, the terraces of the southwest front and that of the northwest are in no wise connected, on account of the hill which separates them. The walls divided near 26, 28 and 29, only three areas of various sizes, like courts. The second and third terraces of the northwest front terminate near 65 and 64 with walls.[4] The formation of the hill did not prevent the continuation of the lowest first terrace farther toward the west; this latter therefore terminated only below 69, near a former wall, 68, in the line (33) of the northern continuation of the second terrace of the southwest front. But since the hill rose above the first terrace and, near 67, above the foot of the Tem-

---

[1] Very mistaken views concerning the period of the destruction of the Temple were given by v. Tschudi and Hutchinson, which originated from their failure to see the Sun temple in this building. The Temple was not in such a state of decay at the time of the Incas (v. Tschudi, Beitr., p. 127), or at the time of H. Pizarro's visit, as it was when Stevenson saw it in this century (Hutchinson, I, p. 167), for Estete describes it as being beautifully ornamented with niches ('bien labrada'), and at that date, evidently, the building was as good as new. It doubtless suffered much during the conquest, but probably less than the temple of Pachakamaj, the destruction of which alone by Hern. Pizarro is reported (Estete). Cieza does not specially mention it as being in an advanced state of ruin. When Cobo saw it in the seventeenth century it was indeed 'desportillado,' but the temple of Pachacamac must have been much more so. He could still see in an almost complete state of preservation the winding passageways up to the terraces, the height of the walls of the cells on the plateau—then twice their present height—and the roof of the uppermost terrace of the southwest front. It is probable that Roman, before the close of the sixteenth century, saw carved ceilings in the Temple cells of the plateau, as may be assumed from his words. Under these circumstances there is no need to resort to earthquakes as causes of the early decay, as is done for instance by v. Tschudi. Adobe walls crumble to pieces during the course of a few centuries without any additional destructive agent. In what degree earthquakes may have contributed to the ruin cannot be conjectured.

[2] See the diagrams 2–4 in pl. 17.

[3] Comp. plan, pl. 16.

[4] See pl. 17, fig. 2.

ple, probably from æsthetic reasons, the hillside west of the second terrace end, near 63, was built over with another second terrace, and west from the end of the first terrace, near 66, with still another first and second terrace, which gradually merged into the hillside. As a whole, four terraces may be distinguished, including that of the plateau, on the northeast and northwest sides, while there are five on the southeastern side.[1] At the eastern angle, 52, of the first terrace, the system of the two former sides is interrupted. The southeast side is divided into terraces of different degree, branching out into a fifth terrace. During the transition into this altered arrangement of the front, the first, second and third terraces of the northeast side are raised in a sort of half-story, three and a half to nine feet, and then form the second, third and fourth terraces, while a new first terrace is constructed outside of these; the latter is only about four feet lower than the first of the northeastern side, but is separated from the former by the masonry of the second southeast terrace. But, as if asserting its claim to be a part of the Temple, its eastern angle (44) lies in the direction of the first northeastern terrace front, while the terrace itself, with its superstructures of rooms (45, 46), projects farther toward northeast.

Although the terraces vary in width, they are generally laid in parallel lines and symmetrical with the outlines of the plateau. This regular arrangement has been reversed in the terraces of the northwestern front, and in the lowest of the northeast front; the frontal lines of the second and third terraces northwest converging with the edge of the plateau above them on the north, while that of the lowest terrace again pursues the contrary direction of the former. In a symmetrical way the lowest terrace, northeast, joins closely at the eastern end (52) the second terrace, but leaves it again to follow a northern direction, thereby becoming united with the first terrace, northwest, at almost a right angle (60), resembling that of the northern angle of the plateau just above it, but facing differently. This creates an open plaza, near 60, more free and open than any spot on all the other terraces, and having the peculiarity that the terrace near 66 has the edge of the plateau above it in a perpendicular line, which occurs at no other place.

The terraces of the northwest front are the best preserved of all the three sides, but even here the second is almost entirely ruined.[2] The same is the case with nearly the whole of the second terrace and the fourth (the plateau) on the northeast side;[3] also the terraces on the east corner and along the entire southeast side.[4] Nevertheless it was possible to ascertain from these remains the entire plan, and to prepare diagrams of the fronts in minute detail, as shown by pls. 16 and 17, figs. 2–4. The height of the terraces on these sides varies between twenty and ten feet; it is mostly about thirteen feet, and generally decreases in the upper stories.[5] The width varies from five and a half feet in the third terrace of the northwest front, in some parts, to fifty-nine feet in the first terrace near the northern angle (60). The general width is between thirty-three and forty-six feet.[6] The grading of the

terraces seems to have been perfect, although at present in their state of ruin this is no longer the case. The explorations by treasure hunters had a great share in the devastation, especially upon the first southeast terrace on the southern end. In many instances the terraces were subdivided into lesser grades, and occupied by a number of smaller buildings.

The most varied gradations were found in the southeast side, which now unfortunately is the most ruined. Thus the second terrace to the east sloped in one grade, the third in two, the fourth in one; on the west side the second was in one grade, the third in two, the fourth in three.[7] While the terraces of the northeast front were all on the same level, those of the northwest front have in the third terrace a remarkable and quite well preserved subdivision.[8] Its eastern part formed a ledge between the third terrace northeast and its western part (62). On the western end of the ledge, however, another piece of the terrace (63) projected above the original level like a half-story, and that continued westward in its divided form. One grade (48) extended as a half-terrace on the inside of the third terrace northeast across the front, as far as it may still be traced in its present ruined condition. Indications of similar small terraces are to be seen near 53 and 55, on the northeast foot of the structure. A short projection adjoined the half-terrace (48) at the back near 49, on the third terrace northeast. A retaining wall (72), which probably supported a roof, was built against the wall of the fourth terrace near 61. On the third terrace[9] there is a slight elevation like a bank along the rear wall of the second northwest terrace, near 73.[10] Rooms were built upon the different terraces, the remains of which are to be traced in the plan (pl. 16) at the following points: 45, 67, 43, 42, 47, 50, 54, 56, upon the first terrace northwest, the first terrace northeast, and at the foot of the Temple northeast and northwest, on the first, second and third terraces southeast.

The superstructures were of varied nature, as shown by the plan, with regard to extent, division and the manner in which they were set upon the terraces. Rooms (67) were built against the front edge of the terrace, and the passageway lay behind them; those at 50 were set against the rear of the terraces, leaving an open walk in front four feet wide. Rooms (43) apparently occupied the entire depth of the terrace,[11] one wall being set upon the front, while the others were built against the rear.

Very curious are rooms 45, 46 and 47; the first two are on the first terrace southeast, and 47 is built up against them at the foot of the Temple.[12] In the adjoining building (56) a connecting passageway (58) may be traced, apparently continuing over (57) to the first terrace southeast, and forming another side entrance to the temple terraces. Numerous evidences of room partitions are also noticeable on the first terrace northeast near 51, and on the third terrace southeast, west from 42. Remains of small square rooms, partly fallen down the slope, may be seen near 70 on the

---

[1] It is somewhat difficult to count the terraces, as may be seen from the fact that Squier in his plan has partly overlooked one on the southeastern front (the third), and another (also the third) on the northwestern front. But when the number of the terraces is given as three (Ulloa, Markham, Reports of the Discov. Intro., p. xix) and elsewhere as six, the difference is caused by the manner of counting, either by taking on the northeast and northwest sides the terraces only, without the plateau, or by counting all half-terraces, and also the foot of the Temple (Padre Cobo). Miquel Estete numbered five terraces, which may easily be done, if his manner of counting is followed.

[2] See pl. 2, fig. 1.

[3] Comp. pl. 13, fig. 1.

[4] Comp. pl. 13, fig. 2.

[5] Comp. pl. 17, figs. 2–4. The decrease in the height of the terraces in the upper grades was noticed by Middendorf, II, p. 114.

[6] Earlier measurements reversed the proportions between height and width

and gave general extreme measurements of all the terraces, which are so varied in their relative size. The general height was given by Rivero and Tschudi as thirty-two feet; the same by Markham following Cieza; Bancroft (probably on the authority of Rivero and Tschudi) gave it as thirty feet; Markham, Cuzco, twenty feet; Hutchinson, six to eight feet; Middendorf, lower terraces, seven to eight and one-third m. = 25–30 feet. The width was stated to be seven to eight feet by Rivero and Tschudi; five to eight feet by Bancroft.

[7] Comp. pl. 17, fig. 4, and pl. 13, fig. 2.

[8] Comp. pls. 16 and 17, fig. 2.

[9] Comp. pls. 16 and 17, figs. 2 and 3.

[10] Comp. pls. 16 and 17, fig. 2.

[11] Similar near 42 on third terrace, southeast.

[12] Comp. pl. 17, figs. 3 and 4.

[13] Comp. pl. 13, fig. 1.

northwest foot of the Temple. Plain as these room structures upon the terraces are, they still show by the variety of niches constructed upon them that they dated from various periods. The niches in chambers 43 and 47 are of the type described above (p. 60, No. 1). In rooms 50 and 54 are niches of the type No. 3, *l. c.*, and an attempt was made to claim for this type a later date.[1] The impression is strengthened here, where it is apparent that the rooms form a later addition, since near 54 the red paint of the original terrace wall was continued on the parts covered by the more recent buildings.

[1] Niches of a similar shape are also to be seen in the rooms of the convent, built by the Incas.

THE TEMPLE ENTRANCES.

The plan of the city shows that the Temple with its north angle, the whole of the northeast front, and half of the northwest front lie within the enclosure surrounding the sanctuary of the Creator god. As the entrances of the Sun temple, which face northeast, are situated within the wall, it is clear that the Temple as a whole was enclosed in it. This serves as a proof of the amicable relations between the two sanctuaries, which may be compared with the circumstance related by Betánzos, that an image of the god Wiraqocha at Cuzco stood in a temple dedicated to the Sun. Similar relations, however, cannot be assumed to have existed at Pachacamac, as Estete and others make a local separation of the Sun temple and of that of Pachakamaj. The women of the convent were, according to Garcilaso, consecrated to the Sun, although H. Pizarro calls them the 'wives of the devil,' thus referring to the god Pachakamaj. It is possible that they served both divinities. Certainly it is an additional proof of the good relations between the two sanctuaries that the women had to pass through the outer and the inner courts of the temple of Pachakamaj in order to reach the Sun temple. The wall of the enclosure must be of a much earlier date than the Sun temple, judging from its advanced state of decay, and the Sun temple was evidently built into its area. The irregular way in which the enclosure runs into a point on the northwest front of the Temple favors this theory. Apparently the Temple had two entrances, both opening within the enclosure, and both situated on its northeast side. The first (35) of these was in the centre of the northeast front, and continued as a winding passageway, cutting through the various terraces, up to the plateau of the Temple. The second entrance seems to have been near 56, as stated above, and after passing through the passageway it led into minor rooms, primarily to the first terrace of the southeast front. The former was the main passageway up to the Temple. The plan shows that the passageway leading to the three lower terraces are still to be traced in some of their principal lines, while that of the fourth terrace is completely obliterated or choked with débris. It probably turned an angle, similar to that of the lower passageways, over 38, about half way up to the front of the plateau. Pl. 15, fig. 1, and pl. 14, fig. 4, show to what degree the passageways of the three lower terraces are yet discernible. The lower passageways (35, 36, 37) were inside the terraces, and to make the ascent easy they were not constructed radially up to the top, but were cut into the terraces in a slowly ascending grade, with one angle each. It must also be mentioned that none of these passages run parallel with the section of the terrace in which they are located; that in the lowest terrace is turned too far to the outside, those in the two following run within the general line of the terrace, but with an inward incline. This may have been the case in a more marked degree with the fourth terrace, and it seems not merely by accident that the passage inclined more and more toward the plateau the nearer the shrine of the divinity upon it was approached. The width of the passages varies between five feet ten inches and six feet six inches. In several places, as for instance half way up to the second terrace and in the centre of the third, the width was reduced by pillar-shaped projections on one or both sides to only four feet. To these points P. Cobo probably referred when he spoke of gates. What he calls 'resting places' may have been only landings on a level with the terraces, or possibly other places specially prepared. A peculiarity of the passageways was that the lowest one in the centre of the first terrace (35) was cut into the terrace, while the upper one apparently projected from the middle of the topmost terrace (near 9); that the different openings were not placed one above another, and that after reaching the first terrace the passage made a backward turn to the entrance into the second passageway (36). With the rest (37, 38) the progress was always in a forward ascending direction, as far as the second backward turn (to 9). This peculiarity might suggest that access to the first terrace was a special privilege, and ascension to terraces two, three and four possibly was denied to many who might have obtained the right of entrance to the first terrace of the Temple. By the angles in the passageways through the terraces the line of the actual ascent was increased to 150 and 200 feet. With an altitude of fifty-four feet to climb, the average grade would have been as low as 1 : 3, 6. This figure agrees with the statement of P. Cobo, who saw one part of the original passageway. He describes it as being built of quarried stone, without mortar. "The grades were so low that one could ascend without fatigue, although it was a long way up." In one part of the stairway he counted twenty steps, estimating from these the entire number to the top as 150, or more, originally. Therefore with fifty-four feet of altitude, and 150 to 200 feet of length, each step must have been on an average four inches high and one foot to one foot four inches wide, a proportion justifying P. Cobo's remark as to the ease of ascent. Middendorf[1] supposes the passageway to have been only a supplementary one, on account of its narrowness, and believes the main ascent to have been a spiral, leading over the terraces up to the Temple, as is often seen in Mexico. However, considering the usual proportions of Peruvian architecture, the stairway is really unusually wide and luxurious, and the plan of the Temple, together with the sections of the fronts, show that a spiral ascent would have been impossible. It is not likely that under original conditions it would have been easy to reach the southeast terraces from the northeast.[2] The graded ascent on the northwest front, looking seaward, which Middendorf claims to have seen from the town, does not in reality exist. Superstructures barred a convenient passage on the terraces, and wherever graded steps are actually preserved, as between 62, 61 and 63 on the third terrace northwest, the gradations are three and one-fourth to four feet high, and so disconnected that they could not possibly have been used for processions. There is absolutely no trace to be

[1] The stairs mentioned by Middendorf, II, p. 114, are no longer in existence.
[2] Comp. pl. 17, fig. 3.

discovered of an additional entrance to the Temple, the former existence of which Middendorf supposed. The architectural construction forms the strongest argument against the theory that a spiral ascent, as in the Mexican temples, could have existed here.[1] However, in consideration of the graduated slope of the terraces on the southeast front,[2] it is not impossible that over these, or at least over some of them, a side passageway led to the top of the Temple, a point which it would be hard to determine in the present state of the ruins.

[1] P. Roman, in his description of the newer Sun temples of the Inca realm, probably had in mind the Temple at Pachacamac, mentioned by him together with that of Cuzco. All the details of his description apply to this structure, but in addition he mentions two large temple-gates, perhaps rooms on the plateau,

reached by two stairways of thirty steps each. These stairs are not to be found at all, and the number of steps, each of which would have been two feet high, excludes the possibility of a double ascent. Roman either took this detail from another temple, or meant a double stairway in the upper part of the ascent only, the existence of which might be proved by exploration.

[2] Comp. pl. 17, fig. 4.

THE SOUTHWEST FRONT OF THE TEMPLE.

The southwest front is apparently the main façade of the Temple, its elevation exceeding that of all the others by seventeen feet. The effect of height is increased by the horizontal and vertical divisions of the façade and by ornamental niches forming a frieze.[1] Another notable feature is its close connection with the plateau, the rooms of which are situated toward the southwest side. Judging from the termination of the terrace on the southeast front near 39, 40 and 41, the rooms 14, 16, 19, 22 and 24 may be considered as belonging to the plateau, although situated on the southwest slope of the structure. For this reason, and on account of their share in the general effectiveness of the building, they were included in this discussion, hence the irregular outline of the rear. It embraces on the south end only one outer grade of the terrace, situated in front of those of the southeast front (23), and including farther north 14, 22, 19, 16, 24, 26, 28 and 29. While all other fronts are divided by horizontal lines only, the southwest façade was divided by radial walls into four principal sections, marked 30, 31, 32, but now partly destroyed. They seem to be closely connected with the rooms upon the plateau, being simply continuations westward of lines of masonry dividing it in the same direction. The two northern of the four sections, with courts 26, 28 and 29, are situated mainly upon the natural soil of the hill. A small room, now ruined (27), was built into 26. This with room 24 belonged to the second section, and in its ruined state still shows the peculiarity of a transverse division by four parallel dams from north to south. They stand near together, but vary in height, so that a cross-cut through all would show a waved line, decreasing toward the southwest. The two outside dams, 11 and 25, were the walls of the room. It may be supposed that here three narrow and short passageways ran parallel to each other at different heights, and that the dividing walls between have crumbled into their present state, presenting the appearance of dams. The two southern sections are subdivided into terraces. The third, the most beautiful of all, is situated above the southwestern ravine or depression of the hill, exactly in the centre of the front. The entire elevation of the Temple at this point is about seventy-seven feet from the base. As the foundations are sunk deeply between the spurs of the hill, the lowest terrace grade fitted into the ravine (34), lying outside the limiting line (33), and curving inward along the entire southwest façade, which is more than six hundred and fifty feet in length. The transverse wall (32) extended over 34, or was intended to do so; its line may still be traced upon the ground. A graded elevation of the hill, requiring only the addition of a frontal wall to form a terrace, seems to have been utilized in constructing the lowest plateau (34). In pl. 14, fig. 2, the natural soil of the hill is still visible in the terrace. The third, near 21,

and fourth sections, near 14, of the southwest front are similarly divided by vertical lines. Apart from the almost identical measurements of height and width of the terraces, they differ from the other fronts in the very small variation in the height of the topmost grade (16 and 14) and that of the plateau, and the rapidly increasing distances downward. The variations in the height of the terraces from the plateau here measure eight, eighteen and thirty-three feet. In other respects the third and fourth sections are different from the first and second. On account of the southern limiting wall, 13 to 22, the lower terrace (23) was continued farther to the south to 41. There were probably no niches along the front of grade (14), now entirely ruined, but some may be seen along the front line of 16, with its continuation northward. P. Cobo, who saw many of the more important parts of the structure while still in a fairly good condition, does not mention any niches at this point. It would have marred the general effect of the façade if the decoration of the central section had been continued too far to the south. The superstructures of the highest terrace (16) are wanting near 14. Decorative niches were used sparingly, judging by their absence from the southern side of the wall (32). In the third section of the southwest façade, 16 to 34, the principle of increasing both height and width toward the top was carried out to a greater degree by the construction of the high and broad grade (31) in front of it. The measurements of the grades, taken from the top downward, are as follows: Eight, eighteen, thirty-three and fifty-eight feet, the terrace grades increasing in height approximately in the proportion of 1 : 2. The widths of the grades, taken from the top, were approximately fourteen, sixteen, fifty-nine and seventy-three feet. The second terrace grade of the centre (21) now almost entirely merges into the third (19; comp. pl. 14, fig. 1), which appears to have been much disturbed by treasure hunters. It is impossible now to see how the connection between 19 and 21 was constructed. It appears that passage 19 must have been faced with stone coping along the front edge, extending as far as wall 31, passing it northward in an angle and enclosing the area of 21.[2] In three wide grades of three feet each (20), the passage fell away from the northwest toward 21. The rear wall of 19 is decorated with large niches, visible from the sea at a great distance. This wall is a little over ten feet high. The niches, now open on top, stand with their base about one foot above the passage.[3] They are built of adobe of parallelopipedic shape and are nine feet high by two feet seven and one-half

[1] Comp. pl. 14, fig. 2, and pl. 17, fig. 1.

[2] Middendorf, Peru, II, p. 115, gives the height of the passage under the plateau as fifteen feet, which is approximately correct (comp. pl. 17, fig. 1).

[3] Markham, Engl. edition of Cieza, chap. 72, note 2, and Middendorf, l. c., misunderstood the ornamental purpose of the niches, taking them for buttresses. The presence of a cornice at base of the niches (comp. pl. 17, fig. 1) proves that they were not intended for supports. They were certainly roofed over. Ulloa, who took the Temple for a fort, interpreted (p. 301) the large niches as chambers for military guards.

inches wide and one foot nine inches deep. The distance between them equals their width. Architectural ornaments are lacking. Middendorf counted about fourteen of these niches; but it may be clearly seen from pl. 14, fig. 1, that they extended along the entire front from 19; their number may have been thirty-six. At the northern end, the pillars dividing the niches are either broken off or the niches are filled up. Originally they were painted red like the rest of the Temple, now they appear blackened by fire, similar to the rear walls of some of the superstructures. The discoloration must have occurred after the plaster and frescoes had in places scaled off, as both the injured and uninjured spots are scorched alike. From this fact it may be assumed that the blackening was not caused by the smoke of burnt offerings,[1] but simply by the burning of a wooden roof of some kind, occurring after the Temple had ceased to be used for the cult.

The topmost terrace grade (16) in its original form was not less remarkable than the one here described (see pl. 14, figs. 1 and 3). In the first view it may be seen near 20, above the large niches of grade 19; in the second, from the Temple plateau near 17, from the rear facing south. The plateau has a gentle slope down to the level of the terrace 16, in the rear near 18 (comp. pl. 14, fig. 3). A thick wall (17), standing like a slanting earthwork, and set with niches upon the inner side, divides a narrow passageway (18) from the outer side of terrace 16. It is lower than the plateau and one foot six inches lower than the piece of wall adjoining it on the south side (15). A number of mounds of refuse (comp. fig. 1), similar to those in the third forecourt of the Pachakamaj temple, extend along the full length of the terrace on the outer side. Digging near wall 17 resulted in the discovery that the cane roofs of the niches (pl. 14, fig. 3) observed in the rear extended through to a length of ten feet eight inches, and that this dam (17) originally had been a wall of that thickness, through which the niches were cut. The

mounds, judging from similar ones elsewhere, must be the remains of pillars for the support of a roof. A notice of P. Cobo may be mentioned in reference to this subject: "In the rear there was a lobby (18 in the plan), like a narrow corridor, running through the entire width of the building, its walls garnished with niches. The windows were toward the top. In front of this corridor was a gallery twelve feet wide, its walls likewise decorated with a row of niches (huecos de puertas), resembling closets in the wall (alacenas), with a row of pillars (danza) in front of them, rudely made (labrados) of adobe. The roof of this passage and gallery was like a white floor, and the construction could not be seen when walking across the court or plaza of the plateau, until, stepping upon its roof, it was found to be hollow and different from the rest of the plateau, the ground of which was solid." From this description it appears that P. Cobo saw a roof, covering gallery (16) and the lobby (18) with its supporting pillars, in a good state of preservation. The difference in height of one foot six inches of dam 17 and the piece of masonry 15 from that of the plateau, may have corresponded to the thickness of the roof resting upon it, and having the same level with the plateau. The lobby (18) at that time also had niches on the eastern side. An entrance to this lobby, nowhere to be seen now, must have been in the centre of 17, where the row of niches seems to be interrupted, or at the northern end, now covered up. There is no entrance at the southern end, near 15, but only a sort of bay-extension toward the southwest. The front gallery, with its pillars, must have been a beautiful sight from the distance, while it afforded a cool place for those under the shelter of its roof. The rear gallery (18) being covered, received but little light through the niches, as the space in front of them was itself obscured by the roof and the pillars. It is, therefore, a point of interest that Cobo mentions upper windows. Gallery 16 had an entrance from the south in wall 15. This aperture is partly preserved in the masonry, and it is at the same time the only door to be seen on the plateau.

[1] Comp. Hutchinson, I, p. 160. Concerning the use of burnt offerings in Peru, comp. Garcilaso, I, Book VI, chap. 22; Betanzos, chap. 11.

THE TEMPLE PLATEAU.

As shown in the preceding discussions, the area of the plateau was occupied by chambers 18 and 16, as far as the pillars, and probably also by 24, including the roof. The space 14 seems to have been uncovered, and might be considered part of the southwest front of the Temple, being situated about six and one-half feet below the level of the plateau, and opening in terraces facing southwest. Its floor, however, is on a level with the adjoining closed chambers (7), and it may, therefore, be included with the plateau, as was done by P. Cobo, who saw it in a much better state of preservation. The plateau is shaped like a large irregular trapeze, the southeast and northwest fronts being only approximately true, and the two other sides converging in similar angles. The roof over 18 and 16 has disappeared, probably also that of 24, which extended the plateau toward the southwest; the enclosing walls of the other three sides have fallen into ruin, and may be traced at a few spots only. The approximate measurements of the plateau were about two hundred and forty feet on the northwestern side, about two hundred and thirteen feet on the southeastern, while on the northeast and southwest the sides measured three hundred and fifty-four to three hundred and fifty-seven feet. Thus the trapeze on its smallest side faces southeast. The outlines of the Temple and of the plateau stand in the closest relation to one

another. The terraces of the southwest and southeast fronts, similar to the upper ones of the northeast front, run parallel with the outlines of the plateau above them. The reason for selecting the southwest front for the most ornamental façade of the Temple was given, on the one hand, by its situation in the ravine of the hillside, and on the other by the location of the open plaza of the plateau, the southwest extension of which it forms. The position of the decorated part of the southwest front in the centre of the façade was determined after fixing the south angle by the terrace of the southeast front, and the building thus extended westward as far as 66. From that point the northwest front was not built parallel with the line of the plateau above it, but sloped toward the east, in order to follow the shape of the hill as much as possible. While the plateau originally measured eighty thousand square feet, or one and four-fifths acres, it has but sixty-eight thousand square feet at present, or about one and one-half acres,[1] since the roofs extending it toward the southwest have disappeared. The entire area was divided into three sections. Bordering the northwest and southeast sides were buildings (2 to 7) enclosing the plaza (1), which opened southwest and northeast. The width of this plaza was about one hundred and sixty-five

[1] Hutchinson, I, p. 158, estimates the size of the plateau at ten acres, which would agree more exactly with the measurement of the base.

feet, by a length of two hundred and forty feet. Even now, after the disappearance of the extending roof, and with the width the same as formerly, the length is still about two hundred and twelve feet.[1] The original area was six-sevenths of an acre; it is one-half of an acre at present. On the northeastern edge, near 9, was the entrance of the passageway, now ruined; there is another depression near 4, which may be the remains of a second entrance to the plaza. At the point where presumably the main entrance was laid may be seen the remains of a chamber-like cavity, five feet deep (18), the inner walls of which still bear traces of frescoing. This is the only instance of mural painting in the entire building; it shows a pattern in yellow, ochre and green upon a red ground.[2] The room may from this fact be assumed to have been one of the more important upon the plateau. A deep cavity (10) in the soil of the plateau suggests an attempted exploration at this spot.

The buildings upon the plateau are described in detail by Cobo. According to him, they extended on both sides of the plaza to a length of one hundred and sixty feet, while not touching the edge of the plateau; there was a level circuit about sixteen feet wide around them on the outside. The distance between these buildings from the northeast edge of the plateau was thirty feet, from the southwest edge fifty-six feet.

walk may yet be seen. Near the north angle of the plateau the distance of the buildings from the edge was about

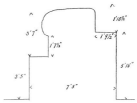

Fig. 103. Cross-section of same wall.

twenty-one and one-third feet toward the northeast, and twelve and one-third feet toward the northwest. The various chambers are almost completely ruined, as they were to a great extent at Cobo's time. He could still see some sections of the walls in their original height of twenty-four feet. At present only in one spot, near 2, the wall is still as high as ten feet. The measurements given by the conscientious Jesuit father may be considered approximately correct, hence they were accepted in the reconstruction of the original height of the buildings in the elevation shown (pl. 17, fig. 3). The room marked 2 is in the worst state of ruin from unceasing

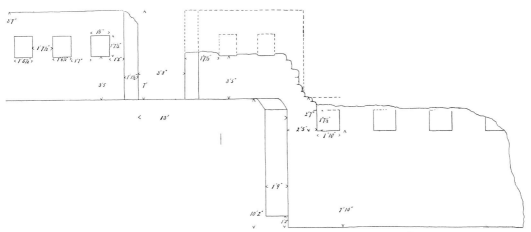

Fig. 102. Elevation of north wall adjoining the two upper terraces of the southwest front of the Sun temple.

In this estimate of the buildings must be included chambers 2 to 7, traces of which are still to be seen. Cobo remarks that the buildings on both sides of the plaza were of even length, extending toward the southwest; this applies to 2 to 3 and 4 to 7. Both groups measure one hundred and sixty-three feet, or one hundred and sixty feet according to Cobo's measurement. The chambers 14 and 24 were not included by him, being parts of the superstructures, and were measured with the section from the southwest end of the plateau. It may also be noticed that the length of both groups of buildings represents about the double of their width, about eighty-one feet (Cobo, seventy-five feet). A few traces of the circuit

explorations, and only a few fragments of walls and cornices were found during present operations. The entrance to this chamber could not be determined. No. 3 is in a similarly bad condition. It has an opening toward the northwest, which may have been an entrance, or only an aperture made by explorers. No. 4 is in the same state. In No. 5 a small room, painted red, was found, which still had niches in the wall; it had been disclosed during some recent exploration. In room 6 were two small elevations or platforms built of brick and facing each other, but now decayed into a mere dam. The cross-section from northeast to southwest and the frontal elevation are shown in figs. 102 and 103. The small platforms were on a level with the plaza, or possibly one and one-half to two and one-half feet below it. The chamber No. 7 has a level floor, but it is enclosed by walls of débris seven feet high, the remains of the ancient masonry.

[1] Middendorf measured the plaza by paces, and gave the result as being one hundred and seventy paces long by eighty-five wide (l. c., II, p. 114).

[2] A fragment of brick, with a piece of the frescoing upon it, from this room is now in the collection here.

It is surprising that no doorways are now to be seen, except the one mentioned in the description of the plateau (p. 79), the entrances to the passages, and a few remains in chambers or superstructures of the terraces. Rooms, such as 2, 6 and 7 upon the plateau, now appear as having been closed all around. There is no doubt, however, that once there were numerous doors. Passageway 18 has now no visible entrance, although there must have been one on the side where the roof covered it from above. We have, moreover, Cobo's testimony that he saw many doorways along the terraces and outer walls of the Temple, while there was but one gateway leading into it. It seems, therefore, that the learned observer was referring to the superstructures on the plateau when he spoke of outer walls. In that case the rooms would have opened by means of doors on their outer sides toward the circuit walk along the edge of the plateau; of these doors there are now no traces. It is still more difficult to determine the manner of communication between the various terraces on the southwest and southeast sides of the Temple. Further explorations may give a partial solution of this question, but it is doubtful if it will ever be fully known. The shapes of the roofs can be determined with some degree of certainty, as they possibly resembled the one which extended the area of the plateau over 18 and 16. Gable-shaped elevations of the walls for pointed roofs are nowhere to be seen, and the walls of chambers wherever preserved are of even height. The roofs must, therefore, have been flat in this city, and not pointed as at Cuzco.

Besides the trapezoid type of niches, only seen on more recent additions and discussed above (p. 60), there are only two other types, the square and the vertically elongated.[1] The former appear frequently in the city, the latter is found nowhere but in this immediate location. It may be seen in the Temple only on the fine main terrace of the west front, while the other type is generally used all over the building. Niches in rooms built up against the terraces, such as 43 and 47 on the southeast front, may be considered in this group; it is an important architectural characteristic of the Temple, used almost exclusively for wall decoration upon the plateau, and upon the third and fourth terraces of the southwest front. The niches are nearly all about the same size, being one foot eight inches to ten inches in height by one foot ten inches in width, and one foot seven inches to eight inches in depth; on wall 15 alone are some with a width of one foot four inches to six inches, the other measurements being the same as the preceding. This type of niches appears upon the west front on both sides of wall 15,[2] and on the northeast side of wall 17;[3] there are also traces on the eastern corner of chambers 2 and 6 of the plateau, proving that the fronts of the chambers upon the platform were decorated in this manner. Two visitors who saw the Temple in the sixteenth and seventeenth centuries bear out this observation, P. Cobo stating that " both groups of chambers on the Temple plateau were decorated with a row of niches all around them " ('un orden en torno') ; while P. Roman says that " the walls of the four temple cellas had many niches, in the manner of ancient Spanish churches, upon their outside walls, such as may be seen on Sancta Leocadia at Toledo." However simple and uniform the type of the niche appears in its proportions, it will be seen that its application always followed a certain regular scheme. This

is shown by the variety of the spaces between the niches, and in the various distances measured from below. P. Cobo states that " the niches surrounding the rows of chambers on the plateau stood only so far from one another as they measured in width." A space of nine feet ten inches, however, may be assumed for the inner side of room 2 facing the plateau. The intervening space on the exterior façade must have been six times less than that upon the interior, where the niches could not be seen from the outside. The space varies in the same proportions elsewhere; in the ruined wall 17 it is four feet two inches to four feet six inches; on wall 15, near 14 and 16, it is two feet five inches, but near passage 18 it is only one foot nine inches. On the chamber walls upon the plateau the height of the niches from the floor measured over eight feet, as may still be verified. This height was in proportion with that of the walls, and must have greatly added to the impressiveness of the building, judging by the reconstruction shown in pl. 17, fig. 3. On wall 15 the space from the floor in the direction of 16 and 18 was only three feet four inches, the roof above lowering the general height, while toward 14, where the wall was as much higher as the thickness of the roof, about one and two-thirds feet, it measured five feet six inches. The niches continued along terrace 19, and with it followed a downward line.[4] Here again their height above the ground is about eight feet. In this way were obtained the peculiar cross-sections of terraces 16 and 19 (shown in fig. 102). Similar niches probably decorated wall 31, terminating the terrace on the opposite side, but these have disappeared together with the wall.

The Temple was painted a uniform deep red, traces of which color may still be seen on all the terraces, on the interior of passageways, on the exterior of the chamber walls upon the plateau, on the inside of room 5, on wall 15 near the terrace of the large niches 19, etc. The paint had been applied not only once but several times, as in many spots a coat of the same color is seen underneath a thin layer of plaster, wherever the outer paint had scaled off. In some spots ochre yellow is found beneath the red paint, as in the corners of many of the niches, which may have been painted yellow at one time. Room 8 on the plateau with its mural painting proves[5] that occasionally the chambers of the Temple were decorated in this manner. P. Cobo speaks of " many rooms, terrace walls and doors, painted in many colors with animals," etc., which could be seen from the outside. The doors at every turn of the passageway had been much decorated,[6] not the faintest trace of which is now visible, and it would be unsafe to credit the statement had it not been made by so reliable an observer.[7]

From Garcilaso's description there is no doubt that the Temple at one time was richly ornamented with gold. " Each chieftain since then undertook to decorate with gold and silver the Sun temple of his own particular province, in proportion to his wealth. These temples hence were covered with gold

[1] Comp. pl. 15, figs. 1-3.
[2] Pl. 15, figs. 1-3, and pl. 14, fig. 2.
[3] Pl. 15, fig. 3.

[4] Comp. pl. 15, fig. 2.
[5] See above, p. 79.
[6] Calancha makes a similar statement.
[7] Of all the earlier statements concerning mural paintings upon the Temple, perhaps only those of P. Cobo, were founded upon careful observation. He describes them as " pintura de varios colores, con mucha laboras curiosas á su modo, si bien al nuestro toscas, y diversas figuras de animales mal formadas, como todo lo que estos indios pintaron." It is not likely that he should have confused this Temple with the painted Pachakamaj temple. J. J. v. Tschudi, Peru, I, p. 291, speaks of "several halls and niches," upon the walls of which might be observed half-faded, faint "frescoing" in brick-red and yellow ; Rivero and Tschudi, p. 290, mention "fragments of animals on the walls upon the whitewashed plaster." Their statements, however, regarding the details of the Temple are not always reliable.

incrustations, like the principal temple at Cuzco."[1] In the latter the interior of niches and the doorways were covered with gold and silver,[2] and animal figures made of gold; sacrificial offerings were suspended along the walls, possibly also on the roof.[3] Cieza writes that Waina Qhapaj, the Inca, had bestowed[4] costly gifts in gold, silver and precious stones upon the Sun temple at Pachacamac, of which at present every trace has vanished, even the fastenings having disappeared.

[1] Book III, chap. 24.
[2] L. c., chaps. 20 and 22.
[3] Roman, l. c.
[4] Crónica, II, chap. 65.

THE ARCHITECTURE OF THE TEMPLE AND ITS BUILDERS.

It has long been observed that the Temple is lacking in all the distinctive marks of Inca architecture, even if it may be considered at all as one of the Inca buildings. In its ruined state it presents few characteristic features, but to any one familiar with the ruins of the ancient convent the difference becomes at once apparent. There the niches belong to types peculiar to Inca style,[1] while here those of the third terrace of the southwest front, high and rectangular, correspond with no architecture of that period so far as it is known now. The plain, square niches[2] represent a more primitive type, probably local and native, differing from that of the convent, while quite common in buildings of the ancient town. The small trapezoid niches may have originated with the Incas, but are only to be seen in more recent additions,[3] and cannot be considered when judging of the original style of architecture.

In the convent at Mamacona the material and quality of the adobe bricks, their shape and mode of laying, the plastering of the walls with a colorless clay, all seem to be of superior order, distinguishing this one building of Cuzco style from all others in the town. The Temple, in all these features, has more in common with the town than with the convent, where the architectural details of ornamentation were quite profuse, and determined the entire effect of the structure. In the Sun temple, the expression of color surpassed that of architecture, while it undeniably shared the general marks of Inca influences with all the other buildings of the coast. No one, for instance, will fail to see that the order of ornamental niches of the third southwest terrace is out of keeping with the stylistic tendencies of the coast, while entirely agreeing with that of the Incas, verified on numerous edifices. They favored elevated points for their structures, so that the lofty terraced and niched buildings commanded the surrounding plains and valleys. A fine example is the large niched terrace structure at Ollantaytambo (Squier, Peru, pp. 496 and 497); of a similar character are the niched terraces of Colcampata at Cuzco,[4] and the ruins of ancient Inca monuments near Cañete.[5] In the plains, the Incas erected handsome buildings, garnished with airy niches, such as those now in ruins at Chinchero (pictured by Squier, p. 484), and the rows of beautiful niches upon several buildings situated close to the shore in the hacienda Yuumani on Titicaca Island. The type of the niches at Pachacamac, while not an exact repetition of that of Cuzco, represents in proportion of height and width that generally used by the Incas,[6] which is entirely absent from all buildings of the coast. The decoration of walls and enclosures on the plateau with long rows of small niches is only to be ascribed to Inca style, while elsewhere in the town, wherever timid attempts at rows of niches are found, they may safely be attributed to the influence of Cuzco[7] culture.[8] In no other building was the principle so perfectly carried out as in the Sun temple, described above (p. 80, and pl. 14, figs. 1 to 3). Two entirely different styles of architecture were clearly combined in it, that of the coast and that imported from Cuzco, the latter however being mainly limited to the superstructures upon the plateau, and possibly including the peculiar winding passageways leading up to the terraces, which were specifically destined for the cult. Even here, foreign influence could only determine the general character of the buildings and not the minor details. Therefore the local type of small niches was used decoratively, while for the high ones a new style was introduced, forming a transition between the technique of the coast and that of Cuzco.

If the question be raised why a Temple erected for the supreme deity of the Inca realm should have been built in a style different from that of the reigning cult, the answer can only be, that the Temple had more than one purpose in the minds of the ruling people. The Incas imposed Sun-worship upon newly-acquired provinces.[9] Garcilaso quotes one of the conditions of peace between the Inca and Cuismanku, to the effect[10] that the Yunkas should worship the Sun and erect a Temple for him, while apparently the Inca charged himself with the building of the convent, which to this day shows pure Cuzco style. We know besides that ministrations in the Sun temples of the provinces were performed by representatives of both nationalities, ruling and subjugated. Garcilaso tells repeatedly that the priests of the Sun temples in the provinces were members of the reigning chieftain's family of that locality (of the 'Aillu' of the prince), while the chief priest in every case had to be a relative of the Inca, the Qhapaj aillu.[11] He (l. c.) states also that all the Sun temples of the provinces were built after the model of that at Cuzco, and therefore he did not give special descriptions of them. Judging, however, from the ruins of some of them, they varied largely, according to the provinces. The following of the Cuzco model was probably limited to the arrangement of essential parts, on account of the similarity of the cult, while transition to the new worship was made easier for the people by having the Temple built in the style of the individual province, forming at the same time a monument of victory for the conquerors.

We possess information concerning the workmen by whom the Temple was built, given by Santacruz, p. 273: "At Vilcas Huaman Pachakutij Inca Yupanki met seven wakas, Aisawillka, Pariaqaqa, Chinchaqocha, Wallallo,

[1] See pl. 21, fig. 2.
[2] See pl. 15, figs. 1–3.
[3] See above, p. 60.
[4] Comp. Squier, p. 477, and plan; also view of the terrace, Wiener, p. 312.
[5] Middendorf, Peru, II, p. 128.
[6] Comp. Squier, pp. 477 and 484.

[7] The great preference of the Incas for the ornamentation of walls with long rows of niches is illustrated by all the Inca monuments of the Islands of Coati and Titicaca in the Lake of Titicaca; also views, Squier, pp. 499, 504, 515 [Ollantaytambo] and 527 [Pisac].
[8] Passages cut into the terrace are to be found only in one house at Pachacamac, situated in section D, and which distinguishes itself from other buildings by additional peculiarities. For Ollantaytambo compare the view, Wiener, p. 512.
[9] Compare, besides, many references in Garcilaso's works; also to Relaciones geograf., I, p. 149.
[10] B. IV, chap. 31.
[11] B. II, chap. 9; III, chap. 24.

Chukiwakra and two of the Cañares. He made them prisoners, and as a punishment for having tried to kill him he sent them to Cuzco, to build the fort Saksawaman. When this was finished they constructed another building, of the character of a summer palace, on the coast of Pachacamac or of Chincha, which rose directly from the sea." The waka Aisawillka was near Lima,[1] Wallallo and Pariaqaqa (of the same name as the mountain) was in the province of Yauyos,[2]

[1] Santacruz, p. 275.
[2] Descripcion de la provincia de Yauyos, Rel. Geogr., I, pp. 71 to 72.

Chinchaqocha was farther to the north.[3] The exact location of Chukiwakra is not known;[4] the two wakas of the Cañares were probably in a more distant part of the country. Four of the seven wakas were only twenty to one hundred miles distant from Pachacamac, and it is possible that the names of these wakas stand for the provinces where they were worshiped, and which had to share in the construction of the Sun temple.

[3] The lake between Cerro de Pasco and Tarma.
[4] Mentioned again by Santacruz, p. 255.

INTERPRETATION OF THE TEMPLE.

It is only possible, at this date, to make conjectures as to a satisfactory interpretation of the structure. Conclusions drawn from the building itself may serve as a basis for speculations, to which may be added information on the general construction of Sun temples in the Inca realm, supplied by P. Roman and Garcilaso in their descriptions of the one at Cuzco,[1] the supposed model for all those of the provinces. A comparison of the interior arrangement of the Sun temple at Cuzco and that at Pachacamac is unfortunately rendered impossible by the fact that the ruins at Cuzco[2] are in even worse condition than those at Pachacamac. It is almost impossible to verify Garcilaso's description from the scanty débris. All that can be ascertained is that he is not contradicted by anything in the actual condition of the ruins. It is still apparent that an open plaza lay in the centre, and was surrounded by temple cellas as he stated. The Cuzco Sun temple also had terraced sides. P. Roman asserts that in all the Inca Sun temples there were four halls, or 'cloister cells,' in a quadrangle. This probably refers to the rooms on the plateau described by P. Cobo. From Garcilaso we learn that in the Cuzco temple, on the side near the shrine of the sun image, there was a sort of cloister or court with five pavilions, dedicated to the moon, the morning star and other planets; also to the thunder and to the rainbow, besides one which the chief priest himself occupied, all these being comprised in the 'House of the Sun.' The Temple was accordingly a centre for the worship of astral bodies and other phenomena of the firmament, the sun cult being merely the chief. A comparison may be made between the pavilions mentioned by Garcilaso and the cella rooms surrounding the plaza of the plateau, to which a purpose would be difficult to assign. Garcilaso states that the altar of the sun faced east; room No. 2 on the north corner of the plateau facing, both northeast and northwest, may have been the shrine. This room is the most devastated of all upon the plateau, an indication in itself that it was from the first held to be of the greatest importance. Squier assigns to it the altar of the sun. The additional remarks by Father Roman, interesting in themselves, cannot now be connected with any visible parts of the Temple. He says: " The Temple had at one angle a room for worship, in the east, where the sun rises, having a high wall and a terrace six feet wide above it. In the wall there was an opening, into which the sun image of gold was set; at sunrise it was placed upon the altar so as to face the east, and from morning to noon the real sun and the sun image faced each other. Then the image was placed upon another altar or

stand (encaje) so that it faced the sun for the rest of the day the same as in the morning."

Cobo may be correct in surmising that the open plaza of the plateau served for sacrifices, feasts and dances. Calancha also is probably right in assuming that the grades of the large ornamental terrace of the southwest front were used for sacrifices. The platform upon the terrace near 20[3] may easily suggest a former use of that nature. We know that at Cuzco the sites for sacrifices varied according to the festivals.[4] Calancha supposes, and probably correctly, that the human sacrifices took place on the southwest side in front of the façade of the large niches, as from there an excellent view was to be had of the sun setting over the ocean. There is, however, no proof for these suppositions. Chamber No. 8, decorated with mural paintings, may have had some relation to the sacrifices. A reference to the sacrificial methods practiced at Huamachuco may serve as a key to the significance of that room. In the Documentos Ineditos, III, p. 14, is stated: " For the worship of this false trinity they had large courts, with a very high wall on one side, having apertures in which poles were erected for the festivals. A pole wrapped with straw stood in the centre. The sacrificing priest, clad in white robes, ascended this pole and killed a guinea pig, offering the blood to the divinity and eating the flesh. Other priests sacrificed llamas and sprinkled the poles with the blood, also eating the flesh, so that nothing was left. At the foot of the poles the chief priest sacrificed a large quantity of chicha and zaco, a concoction of cornmeal. Many niches along the walls were used for the disposal of the remains of sacrificed llamas." The practical use here ascribed to the niches is quite interesting. Roman furnishes an exceedingly clear description of the purpose served by the lowest terraces of the Temple, which may have a deeper foundation. " Within the two lower terraces," he says, " were the apartments of all the servants, priests and priestesses connected with the Temple. There were rooms for the manufacture of the Temple decorations, cellars and storerooms for the liquors (vinos), and living and slaughtered animals and birds were kept here for the sacrifices. There were sacristies where might be seen hangings of wool and cotton of the finest colors and texture, and so the entire edifice was excellently arranged (estava muy claro todo) and everything easily to be found." This account, if founded upon truth, would largely explain the disposition of the lower terraces of the Temple.

It was pointed out above that a large open space (60), situated at the northeast corner of the first terrace, seemed to

[1] B. III, chap. 20.
[2] Compare the excellent description of the ruins with plan by Squier, Peru, pp. 439-442.

[3] It resembles one of the western part of the plateau of the Pachakamaj temple (pl. 3).
[4] Garcilaso, III, chap. 23.

have been planned for a specific purpose. It was near the Sun image, which stood just above it, three terraces higher. It has also been shown that the only turn in the passageway to the plateau was upon the first terrace, forming a sort of stopping-place, and that this winding path was laid in a slightly outward inclination up to the first terrace, while the upper passages all leaned slightly toward the centre. These facts might suggest that the first terrace was a sort of vestibule, admission to which was granted to persons limited to this place alone, and not allowed to ascend higher. This assumption is supported by the fact that the plaza (near 60) seems to have served for assemblies and feasts. The wall of the second terrace, above the plaza, about seven feet from the ground, is the only instance in the entire structure in which stone takes the place of adobe. The reason for this may be that it was to serve as a protection for the wall from being worn away by the crowds of people passing here continually. Moreover, the ground of this plaza is strewn with chips of pottery, among which are numerous those of well-decorated arybals, used for chicha, and which were broken during feasts or similar occasions, when large crowds would congregate here.

The Temple was also used for a certain class of burials. Hutchinson observed three graves upon the plateau.[1] The occurrence of single graves at this spot is possible, but from the description of Hutchinson these were not of an unusual nature. Middendorf apparently thinks that all the terraces on the southeast front were used for burial purposes.[2] There were no signs of such a use upon the third and fourth terraces. A number of chips of pottery were found in the western part of the third terrace during an attempt at excavation, but no human remains. There may have been graves in this locality, but they must have been destroyed long ago. The lowest terrace only could be proved to have been a former cemetery, and it will be described in the following pages.

[1] I, p. 161.
[2] Peru, II, p. 14.

CHAPTER XX.

THE CEMETERY OF THE FIRST SOUTHEAST TERRACE OF THE SUN TEMPLE.

GENERAL REMARKS.

THE first terrace of the southeast front of the temple has a length of about three hundred and ten feet and a width of forty-seven to fifty feet. Rising abruptly above the base of the temple on its southwestern end at two sides, it was bordered at the eastern end by chambers 45 and 46, and by side-passageway 57, which from there passes 56 and so out of the temple. This terrace, which was filled in with earth, was an ancient burial-ground. In chamber 45 were found the fragments of a large decorated vessel. The cemetery closely adjoined the chamber on the outside, but was not continued underneath it. The western half of the burial-ground had been disturbed in the past. The devastation caused at that time is still noticeable, even the front wall of the terrace being completely destroyed,[1] and only a few scattered crania found in the ground, with no other objects. The eastern half of the terrace, however, was still intact. This section was now explored thoroughly and forty-six skulls collected from it. It is supposed that about twice that number of burials had originally been made here. Where the cemetery was undisturbed, it touched in its full width the thick foundation wall of the front which extends through the terrace. In parts of the rear, as well as at the base, it touched the rocky soil of the hillside around which the temple-structure is built. A few cross-walls supporting the front wall of the terrace divided it into sections. The burials had been made at various periods, and earlier graves had been occasionally disturbed or destroyed by the construction of later ones. As far as soil and climate alone were responsible for the preservation of objects, they were found to be in perfect condition. Numerous fabrics looked like new; the skin of the mummies had hardened to a leathery condition. Grains and vegetable substances were found in an excellent state of preservation, while even the ancient dried-meat preparation, 'charki,' seemed fresh enough to serve its original purpose.

---

[1] Comp. pl. 13, fig. 2; pl. 15, fig. 2.

CUZCO CHARACTER OF THE CEMETERY.

The objects found in this cemetery possess an unusual degree of importance as regards the cultural type represented by them. The cemeteries along the Peruvian coast as a rule reflect in different degrees the civilization of the coast, according to the period to which each belongs.[1] It is due to the favorable climatic conditions of this region that its type of civilization is so much better known in its details than that of the highland. There the annual rainy season, lasting six months, had naturally destroyed the contents of the ancient cemeteries.[2] Only a number of types of pottery, which are so characteristic of Cuzco culture, resisted this destruction, as clay withstands dampness more easily than textiles. Until now a complete and adequately exhaustive picture of Cuzco culture from a single cemetery was lacking. By slow degrees enough fragments might have accumulated from later burial-grounds along the coast to enable us to reconstruct a picture of Cuzco culture as a whole, but such a collection could never have had as great a value as the discovery of the entire culture united in one burial-place. The treasures unearthed upon the first terrace of the Sun temple offer the advantage of showing us the pure Cuzco forms of culture in the most favorably situated cemetery on the coast. The packing of the mummies is of the simple and yet peculiar class described in connection with those of the Incas found at the foot of the Pachakamaj temple. The pottery of this cemetery compares with the best specimens found near Cuzco in perfection of style and workmanship. The fabrics represent types so far unknown in our collections, both in regard to technique and ornament. We are able to recognize in these pieces the costume worn by the highland population of the sixteenth century, some of which may still be seen there in certain localities of Bolivia.[3] Their connection with Cuzco style is proved by a number of well-known patterns, and by the close stylistic resemblance of decorations upon Cuzco pottery. Simplicity of design, severity of form and a general absence of figure-patterns are the characteristic features of textiles and pottery of this period.

It was noticed that the common varieties of food of the coastland, such as yucca (Manihot sp.), camote (Convolvulus Batatas), lucuma (Lucuma obovata), pakai (Inga Feuillei), so frequently found in the graves of the town, were entirely absent from those of the Sun temple, while all kinds peculiar

---

[1] See above, p. 22 ff., p. 26 ff., p. 35 ff.
[2] Rüss, in Verh. d. Berl. Ges. f. Anthrop., 1879, p. 291, declares that the finds in Ancon do not represent the race of the Incas.

[3] As by the Indians in Torapalca, in the upper valley of Pilcomayo between Potosi and Tupiza, with the Uros on the river of Desajuadero, on various islands in Lake Titicaca, in some parts of the province of Carangas, etc.

to the highland were represented, such as chuño (black),[1] t'unt'a[2] (a preparation of white potatoes), uma- or wipi-kaya[3] (prepared of Oca, Oxalis tuberosa), apparently also ulluku[4] (so-called yellow potatoes), quinoa (Chenopodium Quinoa),[5] and the beans of aji (Capsicum sp. or cayenne pepper) strung on twine;[6] of coca and its various components (Llijta), prepared of vegetable ashes, many pieces were found; also a quantity of lime.[7] Beans only occur in the small round, black variety, not the black and yellow kind frequently seen elsewhere of a large, flat shape;[8] maize was found only in short ears, as it is grown in the highland.[9]

Under these circumstances there is no need to hesitate in regard to the 'bulldog-like Inca-dog' (Canis Ingæ molossoides Nehring),[10] of which two perfect specimens were discovered in this cemetery and nowhere else in the town below; they should be accepted as true Inca-dogs, brought here by the Incas from the highland.

It would be a mistake to assume that objects of a different type, belonging to the style of the coast, were entirely absent. The city with its distinctly different culture was too near for that, but such specimens amount to about two per cent. less than might be expected in a temple built jointly by the Incas and the people of the coast, and which, at the same time, is so well preserved. The purity in which the style of the Incas is represented here must be explained from specific causes. It would be impossible to find a more wonderful confirmation of the interpretation of the building as a Sun temple, founded upon the combined testimony of all the early chroniclers, such as Estete, Cieza and P. Roman, than is here represented in this group of Cuzco culture, found in a burial-ground of the Sun temple. The classification as Cuzco of certain types of pottery, such as are shown in pl. 18, figs. 1 to 7, up to now disputed by some explorers; the interpretation of the temple as an Inca Sun temple, the discovery of a cemetery in its precincts revealing the same type of culture represented by the pottery, together with the entire absence

of objects of earlier types—all these proofs support each other, each standing for itself as well. A solid basis has thus been gained for the elucidation of the early history of Peru according to strictly archæological principles, which this present work is intended to further. A closer examination of the objects recovered here will show the following facts:

1. All persons interred in this cemetery were women. The costume of women is represented in complete sets, not a single garment being found which might be considered as belonging to a man—no poncho,[11] no cloak (yaqolla), no loin cloth; no tweezers used by men for pulling out the hair, but instead numerous 'topos,' employed by women for fastening their clothes. In order to establish the details of men's clothing one would have to look elsewhere, a limited supply being furnished, for instance, by the Inca graves at the foot of the Temple of Pachakamaj.[12]

2. The persons buried here did not die a natural death, but were victims of strangulation. Proofs of this statement are to be seen in several specimens of the collection. In some may be noticed the unnatural thinness of the neck, which seems drawn into two inches in diameter. It may also be observed that the scalp in its dried state covers the lower opening of the skull, which is only possible when the neck has been dislocated before death. Again, in other cases, several vertebræ were found in a distorted position beneath the back of the lower jaw-bone, and the skin below was tightly drawn in. A summary illustration of these dislocations, as it occurs in many instances, is shown in the cranium of a woman, pictured in pl. 18, fig. 13. A plain white cotton cloth encircles the neck, which is drawn into one and five-eighths inches of thickness and two and three-fourths inches of width. The thick folded cloth fits the neck closely, so that drying is evidently not the cause of its reduction in thickness. The cloth is not tied in front, but closed in the back by a thick hard knot, the ends about one foot long, hanging down. If this cloth were a neckerchief, which it could not be on account of its tightness, it would have been closed in front. Neckerchiefs are never tied in the back, while it is quite plausible that the victims were strangled from behind. A most convincing proof that the cloth was used for the purpose of strangulation and not for neckerchief is, that in the front, immediately in the centre, is tied another hard knot, which would have closed the larynx mechanically, and thus increased and quickened the deadly effect. By the forceful pressure the lower jaw-bone is dislocated, and the skin has dried hard over it, so that it cannot be reduced. The manner of strangulation which we can here trace with the assurance of a coroner was the cause of death of all the persons buried in this cemetery. The above-mentioned analogous observations upon numerous other skulls are a proof of this statement. All were women, in the same strange town, buried in the same manner, together with objects of the same type. They were all buried after strangulation. They may have been maidens, but no children were found among them; all were adults; one of the skulls shows gray hair, nearly white. The hair is mostly parted in front, and hangs down loosely or is plaited in two braids. The eyes apparently dried up when closed. Faint traces of vermilion paint may still be seen on some faces, sometimes also traces of covering with cotton.

[1] Compare Hartmann and the writer in Verhandlungen der Berl. Ges. für Anthrop., 1890, p. 300 ff; v. Tschudi, Beiträge, p. 113. The manner of preparation is well known and varies but slightly. Those found by the writer at Pachacamac are possibly the first specimens from ancient graves. They are not represented at Ancon. Wittmack (Compt. Rend. du Congr. internat. des Amér., Berl., 1888, p. 340) correctly concludes from this circumstance that no highlanders were buried at Ancon.

[2] Their name in Aimará, and known elsewhere as chuño blanco, also called moray by v. Tschudi. The preparation varies slightly, probably according to the climate only. Besides the ways of preparation told by Hartmann and v. Tschudi, the writer learned of several more. The Indians not only prepare chuño blanco, as told by v. Tschudi, but also chuño negro (the real Chuñu) of lluq'i (bitter potatoes). This preparation is unpalatable to European taste; the Indians eat it thinking it strength giving. T'unt'a, white potatoes, have not yet been found in graves.

[3] Of Ocas three kinds of food preparations are made: qawi, by drying; umakaya, by the simple process which produces the t'unt'a from potatoes, and wipikaya (ripe kaya) by the process of the chuño negro. The writer learned these three ways of preparation on Titicaca Island, finding them quite palatable, contrary to v. Tschudi, l. c., p. 114, who describes kaya as a black paste cooked with tschuñied Ocas and very unpleasant to the taste. Tschudi also maintains that the Ocas preparation will not keep a year, but to our great satisfaction we found it in ancient graves.

[4] A yellow vegetable of a potato character, of glassy appearance, found in the graves, might be ulluku (Ullucus tuberosus), from its resemblance to the fresh variety. It seems to have been classified before from graves by Rochebrune (Wittmack, l. c.). It is much used as food in the highland.

[5] According to Wittmack, l. c., p. 333, the leaves of Quinoa were found at Ancon as packing material. Quinoa seeds were discovered in larger quantities in the graves of the Sun temple, some of them quite well preserved in their boxes of cane.

[6] Found in quantities. Rochebrune confirms their presence in graves (Wittmack, p. 346).

[7] Small chuños and coca were found also in the graves of the earliest period. As proofs of the use of coca on the coast during the Inca period may serve the above-mentioned gourd-flasks, used for lime.

[8] Wittmack discusses beans, l. c., p. 334 ff.

[9] On the coast maize grows in short ears only when imperfectly cultivated; since all the specimens of food are of highland character, the small size of the ears may be explained as being of that class.

[10] Nehring in Comptes Rendus du Congr. des Amér., Berlin, 1888, p. 312, with pl. III, fig. 3. One of these specimens is of a blackish color, the other spotted yellow and brown. A perfect specimen of the shepherd-dog species (Canis Ingæ pecuarius, l. c., fig. 1) was found in the graves of the Sun temple. It was light yellow and reddish-brown in color.

[11] Hamy, in Galérie Américaine du Musée d'Ethnographie du Trocadero, No. 157, pictures a poncho, described as the garment of a vestal found in the Temple of Pachakamaj, meaning the Sun temple. However, the garment is not that of a woman (comp. Cieza, chap. 61), and never belonged to a vestal virgin, because the Sun maidens wore the Cuzco garb described below, and not the costume of the coastland. At all events the garment never could have been found in the Sun temple, since it does not correspond to any of the styles represented in the graves there. It was brought to Paris in 1786, at such an early date when not much attention was paid to the locality where objects were discovered.

[12] See above, p. 37.

What could have been the reason for strangling all these women? First, the idea of punishment might suggest itself. Garcilaso[1] reports that women of the convents in the Inca realm were buried alive when they had sinned against the law of chastity. With burying alive, from analogies to be discussed later, might be understood burial after strangulation. In another place[2] Garcilaso speaks of a governor of the Inca empire who was hanged and strangled as a punishment for dishonesty in his administration. But the punishment of strangulation would not necessarily have been followed by burial in consecrated ground, as was considered every part of the temple precincts. It is more than probable, therefore, that the victims may have been strangled as sacrifices to the divinity. This conjecture necessitates a closer review of human sacrifices as practiced among the Incas. We find that they are explained in literature in a manner entirely satisfactory, and their prevalence at Pachacamac explicitly stated. Many peculiarities in the corpses, and in the objects buried with them, would be inexplicable without the assumption that they were human sacrifices offered by order of the Inca. The custom of offering human sacrifices by the Inca was obdurately disputed by Garcilaso,[3] although he was refuted by v. Tschudi with the enumeration of many proofs.[4] We gain from his words merely the impression that the Incas did not abolish human sacrifices, but restricted them by legislation. This view, however, does not bear close investigation. The difference between the customs of the various peoples before their subjugation by the Incas and after that event was only this: While formerly each of the tribes or peoples could kill their own human sacrifices, the right to do this afterwards passed over to the Inca exclusively, and he himself offered them, or caused them to be offered to the gods. Garcilaso is, therefore, correct, in a certain sense, in saying that the Incas forbade human sacrifices,[5] but he leaves unstated the fact that the right to offer them was thereafter vested in the Incas exclusively, and that they availed themselves of the privilege. The Descripcion de la Provincia de los Collahuas[6] says distinctly: "Whenever the Inca wished to make a high sacrifice in order to propitiate an offended waka, upon advice of the sorcerers, he would order a few human beings to be sacrificed to those wakas or mountains, and without his orders it was not permitted to sacrifice human beings." The Inca personally officiated at many of these sacrifices, sometimes offering several persons in succession to different gods.[7] The human sacrifices for all the places of worship in the empire were organized and directed from Cuzco on a large scale. The different modes of sacrifice in the empire were as follows:[8]

1. Strangulation and burial of the dead bodies. This mode of sacrifice is confirmed by Cieza, Crónica, II, chap. 28; Molina, p. 54; Ondegardo,[9] P. Ramos,[10] etc. The victims were buried in hallowed ground, in the precincts of the temple.[11] Betanzos, chap. 17, and Santacruz, p. 259, speak of

burying alive. But since they are apparently discussing the same class of sacrifices as Molina and Cieza, the term might merely signify that the victims were killed in some way without shedding blood.

2. Strangulation followed by cremation of the bodies; confirmed by Molina, p. 58.

3. Tearing the heart out of the body while living, using the heart and blood for sacrifice, followed by burial of the bodies; confirmed by Molina, p. 57.

4. Tearing out the heart, and afterwards burning the body; mentioned by Montesinos, p. 129.

5. Cutting the throat and using the blood for the sacrifice, according to the Relacion de la provincia de Vilcas Guaman, Relac. Geogr., I, p. 167, Xerez[12] and P. Ramos chap. xvii, p. 45.

The strangled bodies buried on the first terrace of the southeast front must have been sacrificed according to the first of the above enumerated methods. Children of both sexes were sacrificed, babies in arms[13] as well as older ones, especially those from seven to ten years of age.[14] Child-sacrifices were the most numerous, as many as two hundred being occasionally killed at one time,[15] but this was only in honor of chief wakas of the provinces,[16] or of Cuzco.[17] Adult were sacrificed after campaigns,[18] both men and women; in the provinces also at unusual events.[19] Outside of that our knowledge in regard to the sacrifice of adults is quite limited. In Cuzco maidens were set apart for sacrificial purposes;[20] also youths and men.[21] On the mountain of Guanacaure, one of the most important sanctuaries of the Inca, were sacrificed both men and women.[22] Besides these, there are other proofs of human sacrifices at Pachacamac.

Since the sacrifice of adults was not a common occurrence in the sanctuaries of the provinces, the fact that it took place at Pachacamac forms another proof of the great distinction of this temple among others of the empire. Garcilaso[23] states that up to the time of the conquest the Incas had sacrificed men, women and children at Pachacamac. Calancha also mentions the frequency of human sacrifices, and Cieza and Santillan suggest it in two passages.[24] Santillan observes: "Inca Tupaj asked Pachakamaj, the god, what kind of sacrifice would be acceptable to him." Cieza relates: "The Inca (Tupaj) prayed to the god, asking in what manner he could best serve him; whereupon the god sent him the reply that he should sacrifice to him a great quantity of blood of human beings and of llamas."[25] These quotations clearly show that human sacrifices were common at Pachacamac during the Inca period as well as before. The question where they took place and in which temple remains unanswered. The statement that men and children were sacrificed was not verified by our discoveries in the graves. Some light is thrown upon the subject by a notice of Santillan: "Occasionally at Cuzco, and at Pachacamac, they sacrificed adult young women (doncellas) and buried them alive, but this happened a few times only." This statement corresponds with the sex of the victims in

[1] Book IV, chap. 3.
[2] Crónica, II, chap. 28.
[3] Crónica, II, chap. 28.
[4] Beiträge, p. 46 ff.; also Stübel und Uhle, p. 60 a.
[5] B. II, chap. 8; III, chap. 24; comp. also I, chap. 11, and II, chap. 10.
[6] Rel. Geogr., I, p. 45.
[7] Descripcion de la Provincia de Vilcas Guaman, Rel. Geogr., I, p. 167.
[8] V. Tschudi, Beiträge, p. 49, assumed that killing for sacrifice had consisted merely in strangulation and shedding of the blood. This seems a mixture of several modes, ignoring the great variety of sacrificial customs. Molina, p. 55, and Santacruz, p. 259, discuss separately the methods of human sacrifices, with blood-shedding and without. Nowhere are both mentioned together. Strangulation, previous to the shedding of blood, would have represented a motive of humanity, of which the Incas were certainly not capable. V. Tschudi assumes that the human sacrifice in Peru was only carried out by bloodshedding, but sacrifices by strangulation in pursuance of other purposes exclude this one-sided view.
[9] Tschudi, l. c., p. 49.
[10] Ramos, chap. xvii, p. 45.
[11] Cieza, II, chap. 28: "á la redonda del oráculo."

[12] Barcia, Hist. primit., I, p. 190.
[13] Molina, p. 58.
[14] Santacruz, p. 249; Ondegardo in Tschudi, Beitr., p. 49.
[15] Tschudi, Beitr., p. 49.
[16] Molina, p. 58.
[17] Colecc. de Docum. inéd. del Archivo de Ind., XXI, pp. 141, 154, 183, 196, 208; Cieza, II, chap. 27.
[18] Molina, p. 59; Descripc. de la prov. de Vilcas Guaman; Rel. Geogr., I, p. 149; Montesinos, p. 129; Cieza, II, chap. 34.
[19] Rel. Geogr., II., p. 45.
[20] Ondegardo, p. 166.
[21] Betánzos, chap. 17; Cieza, chap. 27.
[22] Cieza, II, chap. 28.
[23] Book IV, chap. 30.
[24] P. 32.
[25] Crónica, II, chap. 58.

our graves. That they were maidens may also be assumed, since in a number of instances the hair was plaited after the manner of young girls. The fact that the two places, Cuzco and Pachacamac, are mentioned together points to a ceremony in the cult of the Incas, and consequently to the Sun temple; the "burying alive" would correspond with the mode of death[1] of the bodies found in the graves. Santillan, doubtless, referred to the class of sacrifices, which was verified by the exploration, and thus the remains found in the cemetery of the first terrace of the Temple confirm in a remarkable way the statement made by him so long previously.

The crania in this burial-place show a remarkable difference from the usual type found in the graves of the ancient city.[2] There the enlarged and flattened occiput predominates, while highland types of deformation, long and pointed heads, are exceptions.[3] The crania in the burial-place of the Sun temple present a variety of deformations, of a greater uniformity in the eastern section of the terrace, where highland types are chiefly in evidence.[4] A more careful study by anthropologists, which is to be desired, will surely serve to further elaborate the result here communicated. The difference in type, together with a few characteristics of objects buried with the victims, are to be explained from the manner in which human sacrifices were largely regulated in the empire.

In common with the requirements of other cults, inhabitants of the Inca realm sacrificed every year to their divinities a sort of tithes.[5] Human sacrifices were included in this tribute, each tribe furnishing one boy and one girl annually for the purpose. At a fixed period of each year, the victims from all the tribes of the realm were assembled together at Cuzco. There a division was made of them according to the four principal parts of the empire, and the chief wakas of the provinces. They were then sent to the points at which they were to be sacrificed. The management of this part of the service was admirable. One minister of the cult (willka kamayoj) for each of the four principal parts of the empire at Cuzco, kept a strict account in kipus of the number due to each waka in his special part of the country, while the chief priests of the sanctuaries correspondingly kept their own accounts of the number of victims received by them and duly sacrificed.[6] The mingling of natives of different provinces was not limited to children only. Ondegardo states that every year young girls from all provinces were taken to Cuzco. These were distributed among the different cults, that of the Sun, or of Pachamama, or of others, to become sun-maidens, etc., while a number were set aside for the sacrifices, "which occurred frequently in each year."[7] In this

manner young women could be sent as sacrificial victims to the prominent sanctuaries of the provinces, such as Pachacamac, and the result must have been that in the different sanctuaries of the country human beings were sacrificed whose cranial types did not generally correspond with those peculiar to that particular part of the realm.

The great uniformity in the Cuzco character exhibited by objects in these graves is remarkable, when we consider the very different cultural type of the town, the great diversity of cranial formations and the gathering of individuals from such a variety of provinces. This uniformity in the first point is explained beyond a doubt by the passage of the victims through Cuzco, where they received their uniform religious training and garb, and a good supply of necessaries for the long journey to the places of sacrifice.

The vessels found in these graves show a surprising purity of style, and appear to have been brought directly from Cuzco, to be used only for this ceremonial purpose, while many of the other articles were of an inferior and ordinary class. It is difficult to conjecture what purpose there was in burying at the same time with ceremonial objects, dogs, parrots, pieces of textiles in course of weaving, etc. Numerous specimens show signs of prolonged use, even of wear; the cooking vessels in particular are of this class. Besides girdles, apparently quite new, there are others which must have been worn for some time, and are even partly worn out; work-baskets showing long use, combs with hairs in them, a vessel and plate of pottery, and a wooden cup, bearing a mark such

Fig. 104. Engraved marks of ownership on vessels of Cuzco type. From graves on first terrace of Sun temple; n. s.

as was put upon articles of daily use by the owner (figs. 104, a, b, c). These things were not of a ceremonial character, but simply those in every-day use. Accordingly the objects in the graves in general had no religious significance; the persons had been interred "as they went and stood," and with them the articles which served them in their daily life. The vessels of pure Cuzco style were, no doubt, brought here from Cuzco by the victims themselves. If the objects in these graves do not bear a ceremonial character, the highland types of the articles of food seem so much more strange, in the midst of a valley abounding in more excellent and refined edibles. Their appearance here can only be explained by assuming that the victims came from a distance, moreover from regions in the mountains, and that they were seized and sacrificed immediately upon their arrival. Such dispatch in the sacrifice of the chosen victims is admitted by Molina.[8] The presence of specific highland articles of food proves the exclusively highland extraction of the victims, while their coming by way of Cuzco is convincingly proved by the character of the pottery. The purpose of these sacrificial rites must serve as explanation for the large quantity of pottery found in some of the graves, which would be still greater if the older graves had not been constantly disturbed by later burials. Persons who were strangled and buried in this manner, according to the belief of the Peruvians, went to serve

[1] Above, p. 86.
[2] Comp. O. C. Blake, On the Cranial Characters of the Peruvian Races, Transact. of the Ethnol. Soc., II, N. S., p. 227, on crania from Pachacamac in European museums, quoted by Markham, English edition of Cieza, Crónica, I, chap. 72, note 1.
[3] Virchow observed a constant mingling of various types of cranial deformations in one locality, in a number of crania collected by the writer in North Argentine, in separate territorial groups (Compt. Rendu du X Congrès des Amér. Stockholm, 1894, p. 38 ff.). The places of discovery referred to by Virchow were situated in the mountains, where various groups of people (aillus) lived more closely together, and buried their dead in certain places. This observation is at variance with a statement by v. Tschudi, Beiträge, p. 139, which must have been borrowed from an older source, that when a certain cranial shape had once been adopted by an aillu, no other might be used within that tribe. His accordance with Virchow in what he calls a well-known custom of the North American tribes, speaks for the accuracy of his observation in general. But however correct and important the conclusions may be which Virchow has drawn from these Argentinian crania, it would hardly be safe to apply them to the whole of ancient Peru. The populations of the Bolivian Puna and of the Peruvian coast seem to have shown a much greater uniformity of types of cranial deformation, which must have extended over a larger territory.
[4] In Peru four cranial types were known: Rumpu (round), p'allta (broad), wanka (long), and saitu uma (pointed head); V. Tschudi, Beitr., p. 139.
[5] The qhapaj qocha (rich lake), or qhapaj hucha qocha (rich lake of dues), of Cieza, II, chap. 29; of Santacruz, p. 259; of Molina, p. 54.
[6] Molina, l. c., p. 419.
[7] Ondegardo, p. 166.

[8] Molina, p. 58.

the deity in the next world, and for this reason were so abundantly provided with all household articles.[1] Although the outfit of the victims was a very rich and costly one in the neighborhood of Cuzco, and even seems to have comprised objects of gold and silver, the absence of such articles in graves here cannot upset our faith in the general character of the sacrifices. It must only be considered as a feature of secondary importance, just as the similar absence in those graves at the foot of the lower temple, identified as Inca graves. The course of the preceding investigation served to destroy the theory that sepulchres of distinguished persons may be recognized by the silver and gold articles found in them. There is no such rule, and future investigations will have to decide the question whether these valuables represent more than a very inferior means for the identification of tombs of illustrious dead. It might be inferred that the victims were sacrificed to the deity as a tithe, that is, in the very solemn rite of the qhapaj qocha.[2] Although Molina speaks only of children of about ten years being used for these rites, it is probable that in the most prominent sanctuaries adults were sacrificed as well. The sacrifice by strangulation and immediate burial was one of the most solemn modes of the qhapaj qocha. Santacruz seems even to identify that method of sacrificing with the offering up of the tithes.[3] But from Molina's[4] account it appears that the regular annual sacrifice of the tithes was always accompanied by shedding of blood, while on certain other occasions, such as the wedding of the Inca Wiraqocha,[5] the victims were offered by strangulation and burial. The idea of paying a tribute with persons who went to serve the deity rather than with others who continued to live, has probably always been the underlying one in these sacrifices. An example of this is shown in the offering, at the occasion of the marriage of an Inca, of a youth and maiden, who were buried together after having been strangled. This pair went to serve the deity as substitutes for the Inca, who hoped thereby to acquire the right to be spared for a long life, together with the 'Qoya,' his wife.

---

[1] Betánzos, chap. 17; Cieza, II, chap. 28; Santacruz, p. 259.
[2] "Those who had to escort the victims for the 'Qhapaj qocha' to the provinces avoided the regular roads of the empire; they sought with their charges a path in a direct line across mountains and valleys, running with unceasing crying and screaming, in order that the Creator might grant the Inca victory, health and peace. Natives meeting them upon their pilgrimage would silently prostrate themselves, not daring to look up while the procession passed, or they would hide in their houses in deepest awe" (Molina, p. 59).
[3] P. 259.
[4] Molina, pp. 54, 57, 58.
[5] Betánzos, chap. 17.

CHAPTER XXI.

OBJECTS FOUND IN THE CEMETERY OF THE SACRIFICED WOMEN.

CLOTHING.

GARMENTS taken from these graves are of different shapes from any others obtained in the city, or elsewhere on the coast. Their interpretation is facilitated by the fact that some articles of dress of the same shapes are still worn in the highland, and a number of accounts in the sixteenth century furnish minute descriptions of this garb. It was worn by all women in the highland and differed from the costume of the plain, as Zarate states.[1] Accidentally most descriptions refer to the garments of the province of Ayacucho.[2] Cieza, however, observed the same among the women of the highland of Ecuador, from Quito southward, and terms it "the costume of Cuzco, adopted with elegance by some of the women of Ecuador."[3] Since this same dress is still being worn by the women of some remote districts of Bolivia, there is no doubt that it had been spread all over these regions by the Incas, as well as among the Araucans in Chile, apparently also among the Chibchas in Cundinamarca (Colombia), and in every other place in which traces of it are found.

This ancient costume for a woman consisted of the following garments: One large square cloth,[4] 'ajsu,' worn for a skirt; two girdles, 'mamachumpi' and 'chumpi,' by means of which the cloth was held in place; one shoulder-cloth of the nature of a cloak, 'llijlla'; one forehead-band, 'wincha'; sandals, 'usuta'; occasionally also a cloth, 'ñañaka,' folded and worn upon the head. All these articles are represented in large numbers among our discoveries, except the ñañaka.[5] The ajsu was worn next to the skin;[6] beginning at the right side, it was wrapped about the whole body, covering it from the shoulders down, and from the hips to the feet,[7] leaving the arms free. It was held fast on both shoulders by clasps,[8] and the right breast could easily be bared by unfastening one of them.[9] It must not be supposed that this garment was

necessarily unattractive. Xerez states: "They trailed their garments on the ground like the ladies of Castile,"[10] and Zarate: "They girded them tightly in order to make their waist appear long." The same may still be seen among the Indian women of that region. The peculiar girdle consisted of two parts. Both were made of wool. One girdle, the mamachumpi, 'mother-belt,' short and wide and thickly woven, was worn next to the ajsu.[11] It was intended to confine the waist. The other, chumpi, more resembled a band. It was narrow, fine, of many colors, attractively woven and quite long.[12] Its length is given as five to six brazas.[13] It was wrapped many times around the waist, above the mamachumpi, and may have served mainly to give a trim appearance. The cloth, llijlla, square in shape, was worn around the ajsu above the shoulders and fastened over the breast with a clasp of smaller size than those on the ajsu. It reached from the head of the rather short Indian woman down to her knees;[14] although not of large size in itself, sometimes if hanging straight down it almost touched her feet.[15] The pins, topo, or thopu, were usually sharpened at their broad ends, so as to be used also as knives.[16] The forehead-band, wincha, was intended to confine the hair, and was made of wool, about two inches wide, and of gay colors.[17] Men wore winchas sometimes,[18] but of a different kind. In the sandals, usuta, there was, as a rule, no difference between those of men and women.[19] The mall cloth ñañaka (Aimará: iñaka) for the head was worn by women of a certain rank only. Thus it is mentioned in the Descripcion de la Provincia de Rucana. According to Bertonio, 'iñaka' in Aimará means 'palla,' married woman of Inca blood or another woman of high rank, and 'iñaka-chasiña' had the meaning of 'acting the great lady.'[20] The Indian women in Bolivia of to-day, when their husbands prepare a costly feast, spread their iñaka over the floor during the dances, and offer coca upon them to the dancers. The ñañaka or iñaka, therefore, was a characteristic garment for

[1] I, chap. 8.

[2] From Rucana, Sora and Vilcas Huaman, Rel. Geogr., I, pp. 149, 173, 189, 208.

[3] Crónica, I, chap. 41.

[4] Descripcion de la provincia de Vilcas Guaman, Rel. Geogr., I, p. 149.

[5] The types of an Indian woman from Sylvia and one from Pitayó (Colombia) in A. Stübel und W. Reiss, Indianertypen aus Ecuador und Colombia, 1888, pls. 23 and 24, give a general idea of the ancient costume of the Peruvian highland. There are a few important differences to be noted, as in the short and scant ajsu, which corresponds to the more primitive cultural condition of those Indians.

[6] Descripc. de la Tierra de los Rucanas Antamarcas, Rel. G., I, p. 208; Desc. de Vilcas Guaman, l. c.; Descr. de la Tierra de Atunsora, Rel. G., I, p. 173. J. J. v. Tschudi, Wörterbuch, p. 9, erroneously terms the ajsu an "upper garment."

[7] Cieza, I, chap. 41.

[8] Rel. Geogr., I, pp. 149 and 189; Desc. de la Tierra de San Francisco de Atunrucana y Laramati, Rel. G., I, p. 189. The ajsu is not a "chemise without sleeves and collar," as Middendorf describes it, Wörterb., p. 20. The statement that this garment was worn by men also is erroneous.

[9] The hip-cloth of the Araucan women is fastened over the hips by a girdle, then drawn underneath the latter up to the left shoulder, leaving the right arm and breast uncovered (Ochsenius, Chile, Land und Leute, 1884, p. 116). This garment suggests the ajsu of the ancient Peruvian women. But more suggestive still is the parallel to the shoulder-cloth or kerchief.

[10] Xerez in Barcia, Historiadores primit, I., p. 190.

[11] Rel. Geogr., I, pp. 149, 189, 208; Tour du Monde, 1883, p. 182.

[12] Rel. Geogr., I, pp. 173, 189, 208; Cieza, l. c.; Xerez, I., p. 80.

[13] Aimará: llimphi. Bertonio, Vocabulario Aim.-Cast., p. 204. There are also belts for men. Modern ones of this kind are pictured in Kultur u. Ind., II, pl. 11.

[14] Rel. Geogr., I, pp. 149, 189; Xerez, p. 80.

[15] Cieza, l. c. A resemblance to this shoulder-cloth may be seen in the icula, worn by the Araucanian women, wrapped around neck and shoulders, and secured at the throat by heavy silver pins; even the name is evidently derived from llijlla. The women of the Chibchas (Colombia) also wore a shoulder-cloth fastened with a topo. Restrepo, Los Chibchas antes de la conquista española, 1895, p. 135. The ancient author Piedrahita even gives its name 'liquida.'

[16] Zarate, l. c.

[17] Rel. Geogr., I, pp. 189, 208; Cieza, l. c.

[18] Montesinos, p. 135.

[19] Rel. Geogr., I, pp. 173, 189, 208.

[20] Bertonio, Vocabulario Aim.-Cast., p. 175.

the mistress of the house; though it is not represented among the graves its absence does not have much weight, as it would probably not have been appropriate as the dress of women who went to serve a divinity.

A. TEXTILES.

The material is sometimes wool, sometimes cotton; the latter is usually of medium thickness. Thin cotton fabrics, so numerous in the graves of the town, are absent here. Dark colors, such as brown and black, predominate, although all the principal ones are represented. Green is only found in a single specimen. Compared with the older textiles, gray appears as a new color—in wool as the natural shade; in cotton as an artificial dye. On page 67 it was stated that gray, which only appeared during the Inca period in textiles of the culture of the coast, seemed to have been introduced by contact with the Cuzco civilization.

In design as well as in technique these fabrics show great simplicity. Tapestries, so numerous in the graves of the town, and also appearing on men's ponchos of the Inca graves at the foot of the temple of Pachakamaj, are entirely absent. Larger cloths, with narrow woven stripes; show the plain linen texture. The pattern is generally produced by strips of one color, introduced among the multi-colored warp threads. In contrast to the great variety of textiles found in the ordinary burial-places of the coastland, but few technical processes are

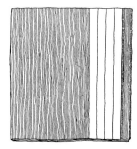

Fig. 105. Woman's garment, square ajsu, folded. From graves of Sun temple: $\frac{1}{10}$ n. s.

represented. These are: striped patterns, produced by warp threads of different colors, interwoven with each other; double-faced material, woven by a continued interchange of the warp threads throughout the piece; and cloth with designs embroidered upon it. The manufacture of textiles with a double face, and the weaving of entire pieces with continued interchange of warp threads are so peculiar to the thick mamachumpi, that they cannot be mistaken for the fabrics of a similarly produced class of textiles of the coastland.

1. The large cloths, 'ajsu,' of the costume: Fig. 105 shows one-fourth of one specimen. There are fourteen of these cloths, six of wool and eight of cotton. They are nearly square in shape, except one which will be described later, a white one, with an interwoven striped pattern; the rest are all of plain linen texture, generally numbering from fourteen warp threads to seven woof to the square inch, up to twenty-four warp to nine woof. The length is four feet three inches to six feet two inches, width three feet eight inches to five feet seven inches generally. The length of nine of them varies only between five feet and five feet ten inches; the width between four feet ten inches and five feet seven inches. There is no difference in size between the cotton and the woolen cloths. The color, except in two instances, is brown of various shades. A stripe, seven to ten inches wide, bor-

ders two of the edges. This stripe is either plain white or black, or as in some specimens composed of several narrow stripes of one or more colors—blue, white and some shades of brown.

2. The wide girdle, 'mamachumpi': There are twenty-nine specimens of these; four are pictured (pl. 19, figs. 1 to 4), representing the principal types. Among them the second type predominates, more than twenty belonging to this class, while there are four of the third, and only one each of the first and fourth. Characteristic peculiarities of these girdles are: their great width, which varies between three and three-fourths and six inches, and their thickness (pl. 19, fig. 4 is an exception), while the length is irregular, generally between four feet four inches and seven feet three inches. The short girdles of the third class (pl. 19, fig. 3) are exceptions, being exceedingly stiff; they cannot be tied, and have, therefore, thick cords at the ends, attached by several thinner ones, by means of which the belt is evenly drawn together.

The girdle (pl. 19, fig. 1) is very thick. Its length is four feet nine inches without the heavy cords ending with tassels. It is divided into three sections, two end-pieces twenty inches long and two and three-fourths inches wide, and a shorter piece for the centre, three and three-fourths inches wide and shield-shaped, covering the abdomen. While the end-pieces generally show the same technical character as fig. 2, that in the centre was made by weaving the running warp threads into a linen-like texture, and by the thickness of the woof, formed by heavy strands, the surface obtained a rep-like appearance. The warp, as it approached the centre, was distributed into thirteen strands, while in the end-pieces it formed only seven. The colors are red and yellow. On the two end-pieces the figures of llamas are red on yellow ground, and on the reverse yellow on red.

Pl. 19, fig. 2: A girdle typical of a group of more than twenty of the same kind. The girdles in this class vary in length from four feet four inches to six feet two inches, and in width from three and three-fourths inches to six inches. They are thick and stiff and of a peculiar technique. The woof runs double, in two layers, so that the material is woven double throughout. The two woofs change their position at the ends, running alternately on the surface, or on the reverse, and for each woof there are two threads used alternately. In this manner a thread of the woof of a first course is only repeated in the reverse in the third, that of the second below is above in the fourth; the thread of the first below is above in the third, and so forth. This makes the edges much stronger, while by the alternating of the woof the material has a firm substance of its own. The warp is woven in such a way that each thread crosses on the surface two threads of the woof, in an irregular manner, with no resemblance to the texture either of linen or of twill. The color of these girdles is always brown or black, and the design generally the same: narrow stripes with parallel lines in black and white, or in red, yellow and brown, etc. In some instances the design forms a zigzag pattern over the entire width.

Pl. 19, fig. 3: Girdle with bird design. This girdle represents the third type: a short and broad belt, the ends of which are stiffened by short pieces of cane woven into the material. The four specimens of this group are twenty-seven to thirty-three inches long and three and one-fourth to four and three-fourths inches wide. A zigzag pattern is on two of them; one is all black with red edges, closely woven with a constant alternating of the warp threads, giving the appearance of braid. The fourth girdle, here shown, is decorated with a bird design in the style of the coast; it is thirty inches long by four and three-fourths inches wide, the reverse showing the pattern of the right side in reversed coloring. It is one of the few examples of Cuzco objects showing influences of the style of the coast in the treatment of ornament. All four of these girdles are uniform in color, red and black.

Pl. 19, fig. 4: Thin band-like girdle; a section only is given here. It is seven feet one inch long by four and one-eighth inches wide, the woof is single, the design formed of white zigzag lines and conventionalized birds upon a background of black and brown stripes. On the reverse the coloring is of course in inverted order.

3. The narrow girdles, 'chumpi.' Five of these are complete; in one specimen the warp is finished, while the weaving is only partly done; there are a number of fragments

cloths are gray, one red, one white. The five specimens will be fully described later. One of these cloths, folded in eight lengthwise folds, is presented in pl. 19, fig. 7.

5. Forehead-bands, 'wincha' (pl. 19, fig. 9). They are of wool, in bright colors, in which red and yellow predominate. The length is seventeen to nineteen inches, in one specimen twenty-five and one-half by thirteen-sixteenths to one and three-eighths inches in width, finished off with plaited or corded ends, to be used for tying. The usual patterns are zigzag lines, small diamond patterns and small squares, such as the above (figs. 106 *a*, *b*). One band in red, yellow and white shows a design in stripes like pl. 7, fig. 14.

6. Pins, 'thopu.' The pins mostly resemble the speci-

a   b   c   d   e   f

Fig. 106 *a–f*. Various designs of women's girdles, chumpi, of the Cuzco costume. Graves of Sun temple; $\frac{2}{3}$ n. s.

of others besides. All these specimens are of wool, fine and like ribbons. They show a variety of rich designs. Figs. 106, *a* to *f*, reproduce some of the typical patterns; the colors are mostly dark, white, brown and black; red or yellow are rarely seen in them. The measurements of the present five girdles (pl. 19, figs. 1–5) are as follows: Thirteen feet four inches, fifteen feet eight inches, eighteen feet seven inches and nineteen feet eleven inches.

4. Shoulder-cloths, 'llijlla.' There are fourteen cotton and five woolen ones in our collection. They are square, except one which is thirty-seven to forty-eight inches long by twenty-eight to thirty-three inches wide; the edges are secured by fancy stitching in technique similar to figs. 6, 7 in pl. 19.

mens of pl. 19, fig. 10. Some have a small semi-lunar upper part which is thick and solid. The majority are made of silver, with a legation of copper, so that they are oxidized. Some are of copper only.

7. Shoes and sandals. Among the discoveries are sandals of leather, and others of fibres of Agave sp., both of the shape pictured (pl. 19, fig. 12); one sandal resembles pl. 19, fig. 13, and one braid, the binding of a shoe, plaited in a rhombic pattern in black, red, yellow and white, is shown (pl. 7, fig. 10). The sandals of the first type (pl. 19, fig. 12) have a leather sole, or one of braidwork, with four leather thongs, or with four loops made of Pita (Agave sp.). If of braid-work, through the loops runs a woolen or cotton string

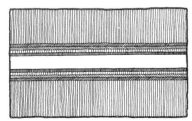

Fig. 107. Woman's shoulder-cloth, llijlla. Graves of Sun temple; $\frac{1}{20}$ n. s.

Fig. 108. Typical stripes on woven ponchos and other fabrics. Cuzco style. Graves of Sun temple; $\frac{1}{3}$ n. s.

The texture is plain, with the exception of a figured stripe in one of them, which will be discussed later. All these cloths are striped crosswise except two, where the lengthwise stripes are so arranged that two similar stripes enclose another of the same width, of different color. As a rule the two outside stripes are of one color, while the middle stripe is of another plain color or of several narrow lines of different colors (pl. 19, fig. 7); the opposite order is seen occasionally in cloths which, in various other points, possess peculiarities of their own. The two outer bands are in most specimens of a plain brown; white is also found sometimes. The central stripe is either white, brown or black; white, blue and brown; or red, green, yellow and brown. Three of these shoulder-

crossing the heel horizontally. The sandal is easily slipped on and is fastened by means of the string at the point of the foot, where it is drawn together in several loops across the toes. The leather soles consist of one layer of stronger leather, probably llama, or are made of three or more thicknesses of the skin of some other animal ('capybara'). The hair upon the latter is not yet worn off in some specimens; the different layers of leather are sewed together with thin leather strings to form the sole (pl. 19, fig. 12). The sandal (pl. 19, fig. 13) has only two thongs near the heel, while the sole at the point of the foot extends in two points with slits for eyelets. The strings on this sandal are fourfold, and crossing over the foot they are fastened into the two thongs at the back and the two eyelets at the point. The sandals of the former class are six and seven-eighths to eight and one-eighth inches long, that of pl. 19, fig. 13, measures on the inside eight and one-half inches, the average sizes for women's feet.

In addition to the above there are:

8. Pouches (pl. 19, fig. 11) in a large number, which should perhaps be regarded as part of the costume; they were apparently used mostly to hold coca and the ingredients for mixing it ('llijta,' etc.). Small bags with coca, like pl. 7, fig. 18, and sticks of the llijta were found in many of the graves, as before mentioned. The pouches are woven of wool or cotton, or of cotton with woolen stripes, generally narrow and vertical. Bird patterns and serge designs are also seen. The woolen pouches are as a rule of a dark color, the cotton ones light, many of them striped in red and yellow. The stripes shown here are the typical kind. Some varieties of stripe patterns are pictured in fig. 109.

Among the articles of clothing described above in a general way, there are three requiring special discussion.

1. A white cotton garment, ajsu: The length and width of this cloth are even (sixty-six to sixty-seven inches), and it differs from the other ajsus by its pure white tint and its peculiar and superior technique and ornamentation. The cloth was woven with an unusually fine warp in spite of its large size. The woof is thicker than the warp, as in many woolen fabrics; the threads are exceedingly close, thirty-six to forty-six of warp by eleven to thirteen of woof to one-half square

Fig. 109. Various designs on pouches. Cuzco style. Graves of Sun temple; ⅔ n. s.

inch. The material, therefore, has the appearance of rep, while it is as close, heavy and stiff as many woolen fabrics, and yet much finer. The threads are hardly visible on the surface, and it seems almost felt-like to the touch, similar to one of the ponchos with tapestry borders from the Inca graves at the foot of the temple of Pachakamaj, although much finer and of a purer white. On two sides, a red and yellow woolen stripe is woven in (pl. 19, fig. 8). The pattern in this stripe, a familiar one of the Inca style, resembles that of the stripes in pl. 7, fig. 14; it consists of a zigzag line, with thick jointed ends. In gradations it repeats alternately contrasting colors, red upon yellow and yellow upon red. The reverse also shows the pattern in reversed colors. The edges are secured by the familiar row of stitching (comp. pl. 7, fig. 20).

2. A white cotton shoulder-cloth, llijlla: The length of this cloth, which is not complete, now measures about fifty-two by forty-seven inches. It resembles the preceding specimen in its fine texture; it is of the same pure white and as closely woven (forty-four to forty-eight warp by sixteen to eighteen woof to the one-half square inch). A narrow blue band, with a black one above it, is near one edge. The edges are worked in the same manner as pl. 19, fig. 7—around the corners in white, red, yellow and black; on the shorter side simply in red; on the two long sides in red and yellow.

3. A red woolen shoulder-cloth in fragments: This cloth, the design of which in half its length is shown in pl. 19, fig. 6, is thirty-three inches wide and originally measured

forty-three inches in length. Compared with the others described above, it may be said to claim a place of its own, on account of its peculiar color and fine silky material (alpaca wool?), as well as its beautiful technique and ornamentation. The material is fine and closely woven, twenty-seven to twenty-nine warp threads by eight to nine woof to the half inch. It has a stripe like the white llijlla, No. 2; two bands, sixteen and one-half inches wide, of crimson border both sides of a white one, nine and one-half inches wide. A threefold band, two and one-fourth inches wide, repeats in three symmetrical lines a pattern similar to that of the white ajsu (fig. 8). The two outer lines show the pattern in yellow and red, while in the line in the centre it appears in black and red. The edges are worked in the same colors as in No. 2.

In a former report was pointed out the significance attached to certain colors in ancient Peru, each having a special meaning—for instance, in the knotted string, kipu, mentioned above, p. 72. These significations were not chosen arbitrarily, nor could their meaning have been limited only to the knotted strings. On a former occasion, when discussing a colored cord, which doubtless had been worn as a mark of distinction (p. 40), and a colored cloth from the grave of a chief (p. 72), an interpretation of the probable meaning of the colors was given. The principle of the significance of colors also extends into the province of woman's garb. The people, in a certain sense, were divided into classes by colors, and these colors corresponded with those of the kipu. White signifies silver, day, doubtless also sun; black, time, in the sense of night; scarlet or crimson means Inca; brown stands for the chief of the provinces. These color distinctions were followed by the Inca in the classification of the women of the realm. de Santillan,[1] in reference to this subject, says: "The Inca commanded that in each valley they should build houses for the women of the Sun, others for those of the wakas (the wakas are the provincial deities); also for those which he reserved for himself." From the rest, the common class, he selected the prettiest, and had a home built for them, where they would work in his service. This would represent a division of women according to four distinctive ideas: Sun, Inca, Province, Chieftain, common people. The same author (p. 18) says: "The Inca's governor of each province had to make the selection of women, to be sent by the province as a tribute to the Inca, both for himself and for the Sun. Others he distributed among the chiefs, and the rest he gave to the 'atunlunas' ('hatunrunas,' adult men), to the plebeians." This division elsewhere is carried out according to color—white, red, brown and black women—'yuraj ajlla,' 'wairuru ajlla,' 'p'aqo ajlla' and 'yana ajlla.' 'P'aqo' sometimes is translated as blonde, yellowish-red,[2] or as red, red-brown.[3] In the Aimará and Kechua of Bolivia 'pako' means alpaka;[4] in the Uro it means dog. Probably the above p'aqo is the same word, and designates the reddish color of these animals. 'Wairuru' is not clear in the dictionaries as a name for a color, although evidently used for one. Bertónio translates 'huayruru' as 'cosa muy hermosa.'[5] Middendorf takes it for a shrub, with red clusters of blossoms and red seeds[6] (Papilionaceæ). Accordingly the meaning of 'wairuru' may be the original or a derivative one of red. Santacruz, p. 284, says: "Inca Tupaj brought with him from his campaigns many young women, principally the chosen maidens (ajlla) for Tiksi Qhapaj Wiraqocha Pachayachachij, called Yuraj ajlla," etc.

[1] P. 37.
[2] Middendorf, Wörterbuch, p. 692.
[3] v. Tschudi, Wörterb., p. 417.
[4] Hon. Mossi, Diccion. Quich-Cast., p. 197.
[5] Diccion. Aim.-Cast., p. 157.
[6] L. c., p. 406.

P. 304 : " The Inca was unfortunate in the war, as he trusted too much in the promises of the Waka Pachakamaj, and was not satisfied with so many women wairur (u) ajllas." P. 253 : " He had houses built for the four classes, Yuraj ajlla, Wairuru ajlla, P'aqo ajlla and Yana ajlla. The first of these he destined for the Creator, Pachayachachij, the Wairuru ajlla for himself, the P'aqo ajlla for the chieftains (the apukurakas) and the Yana ajllas' for the common Indians." With this classification agrees that which, according to Balboa, the Inca Tupaj made in the convents, into Mama ajlla, the older ones, probably the Sun maidens, Guayor ajlla, that is, wairuru ajlla, about fifteen to twenty years old, who were being educated for future Inca wives, and the Sayapaya, " who stand still," the novices, twelve to fifteen years of age. The Descripcion de la provincia de Vilcas Guaman [1] must, however, be mistaken in mentioning for Vilcas Guaman a convent of Sun maidens, guayran calla, which might stand for wairuru ajlla,[2] and another next to it for Inca women.

This classification of the women of the empire according to colors corresponds entirely to the significance of the colors in the kipus, with the modification that black, besides night, also means the common class of people. It was carried out also in their clothing. Women dedicated to the Sun, or as Santacruz says, to the Creator, wore white garments. The accounts of Anonimus, so valuable in some respects, furnish this notice : [3] " When one of the maidens, after the three years of her probation, at the age of fifteen, decided to remain in the convent as ajlla, Sun maiden, she was clothed in white, a gold circlet, 'qoriwincha,' was placed upon her head, costly shoes upon her feet, and a white shoulder-cloth, 'pampakuna,' wrapped about her." The officiating priests also wore white garments.[4] The Willkaumu wore a sleeveless unbelted tunic, and over this a cloak, falling to his knees, of white wool, with red tassels and borders.[5] From this it may be assumed that the Sun maidens wore white clothing only, and the color being so characteristic of them, they were named after it as a class. It may be safe to say that no woman in the realm of the Inca had the right to wear white unless she belonged to this rank. Hereby we are led to the conclusion that the fine white ajsu and the white llijlla, described above, were worn by women of the order of Sun maidens. Doubtless also other classes of women wore the colors of their own station. Wherever in Bolivia the ancient ajsu costume is still worn it is uniformly black. The women corresponding to the black color, women of the people, probably wore black in ancient times just as they do now. Clothes of any other color therefore must theoretically designate a different class in the costume of the highland. For this reason the brown garments, ajsus and llijllas, cannot be regarded as having belonged to women of the lower class, but as having been worn by women of the rank of the chieftains. The fine red llijlla, described above, must have been that of a woman belonging to the station which is marked by this color, which would be a wairuru ajlla, one of the women selected for the Inca's special service. All these deductions show forcibly that the women here sacrificed to the glory of the divinity were not of the lower classes, which might otherwise be inferred from the simplicity of their garb.

P. Ramos [6] confirms distinctly the statement that wairuru, yuraj and paqo ajllas were sacrificed to the Sun. This fact is of so much consequence that small importance need be attached to the incident of his being acquainted with no other means of sacrificing than that of throat cutting. For we know that the manner of sacrificing was more subject to changes than the sacrifices themselves. In the white ajsu, the colors white, red and yellow appear ; in the red llijlla, red, yellow and black. It is also worth noting that white, red, yellow and black are combined in the row of stitching with which the edges of the red llijlla are secured, and also those of the white one.[7] The same stitching is repeated on the striped llijlla, the ground of which is gray (pl. 19, fig. 7). This might suggest that llijllas of such patterns and colors had a special significance; a note of Anonimus, p. 181, may serve here as an explanation : " The probationers in the convents were clothed in brown or gray llijllas (velo), and their garments were gray, very quiet." All these observations help to strengthen the supposition that the sacrificed women found in this peculiar manner were not of the lower classes, and Ondegardo's word may be accepted that " the victims were taken from among the maidens, either chosen to serve the god here in temples, as Sun maidens, or to whom fell the lot, not less coveted in some cases, of having to serve him in the other world by going to him as sacrificial victims."

Among the other textiles discovered in these graves are :

Two cotton cloths, sixty and sixty-three inches long and fifty-seven and one-half and fifty-nine inches wide, striped in white, blue and brown, similar to the ponchos (Reiss u. Stübel, pl. 38, fig. 1).

A cotton cloth, fifteen feet eight inches long by eight feet eight inches wide. This cloth shows wide brown and white stripes, and was pieced together across the width of four sections.

Woolen pouches with brown stripes and many small white cotton bags, similar to pl. 7, fig. 18 ; some filled with coca leaves, others with peanuts.

B. Pottery.

Pl. 18 shows a typical group of vessels taken from these graves. The types are mostly familiar ones, often seen in collections. Some of them were frequently reproduced, while others were never shown before. This may be said especially of the pottery of the style of Cuzco, no complete group of which had previously been in existence.[8] The specimens of pottery pictured in pl. 18 therefore may serve to emphasize the statements concerning the Cuzco character of the burial-ground, and to establish the types specifically characteristic of Cuzco for the benefit of future investigation. The objects (figs. 11 and 12 of pl. 18) are exceptions to this class. They belong to the style of the coast, and were here represented for chronological reasons, since they were discovered together with the other specimens in the same graves. The pottery of this burial-ground shows far more varieties of forms and ornament than can be indicated here. A summary report on explorations at Pachacamac, such as the present one, is not a suitable vehicle for the treatment of all the details of Cuzco pottery.

Fig. 1. Vessels of the shape of aryballos : [9] This type is

[1] Rel. Geogr., I, p. 168.
[2] It may be erroneous for 'ajlla huasi.'
[3] Tres. Rela., p. 184.
[4] Gomara, Historia de las Ind. in Barcia, Histor. primit., II, p. 112 ; Zarate I. chap. 11 ; Docum. inédit., III, p. 14.
[5] Anonimus, Tres. Relac., I, p. 159.
[6] Ramos, chap. ix, p. 23.

[7] White, red, yellow and black, when combined, possibly signified the 'people'; when variegated, as in the kipus, the color for 'government' (Uhle, p. 11). This combination of colors may have been the original one.
[8] The illustrations given by Ewbank (U. S. Naval Astron. Exp., App. E, in A Description of Indian Antiquities, p. 130), showing a number of pieces of Cuzco pottery, are inadequate ; there are even objects belonging to the Spanish colonial period. Hamy made the same error in presenting a vessel of Spanish times, of no style in particular, decorated with a cat's head (jaguar, African lion?), as " a very archaic " piece from the Peruvian highlands (in Galérie Américaine du Mus. d'Ethn. du Trocadero, pl. 35).
[9] A similar vessel, only larger, from San Sebastian, near Cuzco, is shown by Hamy (Gal. Amér., No. 110).

shown in fig. 1. There are about twenty specimens, from five and one-eighth to four and one-eighth inches in size. Some are black. The decoration is in the well-known Cuzco manner—rhombic figures, series of small triangles, a leaf-pattern as in fig. 7, hooked meanders, various kinds of insects, etc. All are of strictly Cuzco type. One of the vases is provided with a tube, to allow of its being carried upon a stick. Some of the smaller pieces are double-bottles.

Fig. 2. Jug with face: Its general shape is like that of fig. 1, but the handle is different and the base appears more flattened; the face may be compared to those upon arybals presented before.

Fig. 3. Decorated vessel: Vessels of this very common Cuzco type were possibly never before reproduced. There are fifteen pieces of this class in the collection, two to six inches high, with an upper diameter up to six and one-half inches. With most of these specimens the height is in a better proportion to the diameter than in these shown here. Several of the vessels are blackened by fire.

Figs. 4 and 5. Cup-shaped objects, fig. 4 with cover: As remarked by Hamy,[1] a large number of vessels of this general type are to be seen in the principal museums; but he is mistaken in asserting that the type is characteristic of the pottery of the shores of Lake Titicaca; the type is Cuzco. From the burial-ground under discussion ten of these cups were recovered, from three and one-half to eleven inches high. The partial type shown by Hamy is also represented in large numbers. About one-half of the vessels were used near the fire, but so that the foot did not come in contact with it. In one of them were crabs, in the foot of another was a rattle.

Covers of vessels, as of fig. 4, were found here, but in no other place in the town. They seem, therefore, to be more typical of the highland than the coast. The shape of covers shown in the Galérie Américaine is also represented in several specimens, besides some with bird heads for handles. A better shape is fig. 9.

5. Plates: One plate decorated on the inside in a peculiar manner is pictured in fig. 6, instead of the entire group, which presents many varieties, both in shape and decoration. There are forty plates, twenty of which are in pairs. Several pairs were spoiled by the breaking of one of them. These plates are either with handles or without.[2] Some of the handles terminate in a bird's head, or in a sort of knob.[3] Among the bird's-head handles all the different types of plates are represented.[4] This shows that no special shape of plate, with or without handles, is typical of any particular locality or period. The plates are black or colored. Many decorations appear upon them, fishes, toads, birds, llamas, insects, fruits, such as pepper-pods, etc. Geometrical patterns predominate, similar in design to one of the two plates shown by Rivero and Tschudi, pl. 36.[5] The plate, fig. 6, is decorated upon the inner side with frogs, cross-shaped figures and ornaments resembling arrow-heads, in white, yellow, red and black. Cross and toads combined also appear in the ornamental design in relief on a stone pillar of Inca character in

Hatuncolla, south of Peru,[6] and the repeated association of the two in one design may have some significance, as the cross has in itself.[7]

Fig. 6. Small jugs: The small jug stands for a larger number of vessels, which though of kindred type, still show many variations in the details, in size, in the position of the handle, in the proportions of height and width, and in the opening of the neck.

Pl. 18, fig. 8. Vessel with cylindrical neck and large bowl: This type is represented in one specimen only. Similar types are objects shown in figs. 74 and 86 above (pp. 64, 66); also the ring forming the connection between neck and bowl is here repeated, while the white design in pure Cuzco manner disposes of the doubt as to whether the shape of this vessel may be regarded as typically Cuzco. The ornamental squares resemble doors, reminding one of pottery decorated with pictured houses.

Pl. 18, fig. 9. Cover of vessel, with an animal resembling a cat upon it: The figure decorating this cover proves that plastic ornaments of a superior class are not entirely lacking in Cuzco style. A similar animal of the cat species was pictured by Ewbank (p. 138, R); the outstretched tongue is repeated in l. c., p. 136, K. The cover is grooved around the edge, and appears to have belonged to a vessel similar to fig. 4, since it has the same band-like decoration, interrupted on the rim, which is to be seen on many of these vessels.

Fig. 10. Bowl, representing a bird with spreading wings: Wings, neck and head are indicated on the rim of the bowl, which has some resemblance to the bird-shaped wooden bowls in pl. 18, fig. 15, also recovered at Pachacamac. A round bowl of pottery was found, the exact size and shape of the brain-pan of a human skull.

Fig. 11. Flask with small neck and gavel-shaped bow, representing a fish, called meru, coast style. The fish is black.

Fig. 12. A fine black double vessel, having the figure of a monkey upon the neck, coast style. The bodies of both bowls resemble fruits. The vertical bow connecting the two parts is broken off.

C. Vessels and Household Utensils of Wood.

It was shown previously (p. 69) that the richer development of wooden utensils, discovered in graves of the Inca

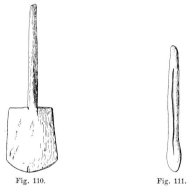

Fig. 110.   Fig. 111.

Figs. 110 and 111. Spade-like utensils of wood. From the graves of the Sun temple; ⅕ n. s.

period, must be attributed to the influence of Cuzco, which prevailed on the coast at that time. An abundant supply of

[1] Hamy, l. c., No. 113, shows one of this class from Copacabana in Bolivia, where a strong Inca colony was once established. Both in shape and design, this object seems identical with one (m) shown by Ewbank. Another reproduction of this type was given by D'Orbigny, Voyage dans l'Amérique méridion, Atlas of the historical part, Ser. 4, Antiquités, No. 10, fig. 6.

[2] A plate shown by Rivero y Tschudi, Atlas, lam. 36, is of that class.

[3] L. c., pl. 28.

[4] Only one type of this class is represented here in two plates, l. c., pls. 29 and 36.

[5] The transformation of a bird-design may be seen in this pattern. The painted central stripe of the plate may be the body running up to the handle, the head, and the sides with zigzag edge the wings. The as yet uninterpreted one-sided decoration on the arybals may be of similar origin. Birds appear elsewhere as decorative designs upon arybals (comp. Rivero y Tschudi, l. c.).

[6] Squier, p. 385.

[7] See above, p. 43.

all kinds from the graves of the Sun temple supports this fact. These are mostly cups and bowls.

Pl. 18, fig. 14. Small cup with engraved ornaments of blackish wood, which were originally filled in with white paint. They show distinct outlines of the human form, besides other designs. On the bottom of the cup appears the mark of the owner, one of those shown in figs. 104, *a–c*.

Wooden plates copying the shape of the pottery plates of Cuzco type were also found. Two are without handles,[1] one with a handle, the end of which is carved in the shape of a llama's claw.

A square wooden bowl with straight sides is seven and one-eighth inches long by five inches wide, and one and one-half inches high.

A small utensil of wood, composed of four compartments (pl. 18, fig. 16), resembles in its division a stone vessel from the neighborhood of Cuzco, pictured by Ewbank (p. 138, K).

Two small bowls, fish-shaped, similar to that of pl. 18, fig. 15, were also recovered. In one a small sediment of a red pigment was still visible.

Pl. 18, fig. 17, is a small square ornament, resembling a bell, with an eyelet on the upper part, and slightly engraved outside.

of a blue stone, lapis lazuli or sodalith, which has not yet been tested, but may be the same as that of a bead from a grave at Ancon, which was proved to be sodalith.[2] A similar bluish stone is found occasionally in workshop chips (to one and one-half inches in length) on the site of the ancient city, which might suggest the possibility that it was introduced by Cuzco civilization. It must, however, be observed that beads of this kind have been found in graves of the earliest Epigone period of Pachacamac, which might imply relations with the highland, as is inferred by the general style of the time, and by the presence of chuños, coca, etc. The writer collected many pounds of workshop chips on the site of the ruins of Tiahuanaco, some pieces being of the size of a hand, a proof of its extensive use in the locality. In the Museum of Science and Art, Philadelphia, a number of blue beads of the same stone are to be seen among the objects from Chulumani, in the Yungas of Bolivia, east from La Paz, but from whence it originally came has not yet been decided. A quarry of a blue stone, resembling lapis lazuli, seems to be near Cuzco;[3] another in the province of Ayopaya, in the interior of Bolivia. Specimens from both these sources are still untested.

Among the objects recovered in this cemetery are two

Fig. 112. Pendant ornament of shell beads. Cuzco. From graves of Sun temple; ⅓ n. s.

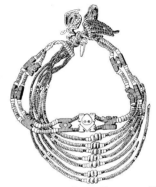

Fig. 113. Necklace. Cuzco. From graves of Sun temple; ⅔ n. s.

Spoons were unearthed in large numbers. Their length varies between four and one-half and fifteen and one-fourth inches. Many of them have carved ornaments upon the handles, such as llama claws, human figures, etc. One is decorated with the figure of a pelican, which suggests the coast (fig. 19). A few utensils of similar shape were also recovered, such as one spade-like object, thirteen inches long (fig. 110); another with spatula-shaped lower end, nine and one-half inches long (fig. 111).

Pl. 18, fig. 18. A bowl made of a calabash: The decorations in Cuzco manner are burnt into the shell.

D. Ornaments.

The persons buried here being women, a large quantity of personal ornaments were obtained, consisting largely of plain necklaces, bracelets and small pendants of shell (fig. 112). A certain typical significance belongs to one necklace (fig. 113), made of several rows of shell beads (wampum?), alternating with small squares of wood. Some are bored for the string, carved in animal form and inlaid with bits of mother-of-pearl. A frog carved in white shell, with one green and one red eye, is suspended from the chain. Certain trinkets are embellished with beads or small pendants

copper bells (figs. 114 and 115). Both types are numerous in graves of the highland, for instance in northern Bolivia, which is a proof of their Cuzco origin.

Fig. 114. Fig. 115.

Copper bells. From graves of Sun temple.

E. Combs.

A large number of combs rewarded the search of the explorer. Three types are represented (figs. 116 to 118), two of which have a handle. They are made of fine sticks of palm-wood, bound together and held in place by pieces of cane or, as in some specimens, by a fine plaiting of cotton, the patterns of which present a great variety. The combs of the

---

[1] Similar to one shown by Rivero y Tschudi, pl. 36.

[2] Stübel und Uhle, p. 43 *b*, note 4.
[3] To judge from a large block of that stone coming from there, and exhibited in Chicago in 1893.

Karaya in eastern Brazil correspond in their general form to the third type.[1] The combs of the earliest period of Pachacamac are different.

A sling: Of apparently ceremonial character was a sling taken from one of the graves. It is almost four feet long, not including the thick tassels of two feet two inches in length, one of which is brown, the other white. Each of the strings is three feet and a half long, the centre eight and one-half inches. The colors are white, red, yellow and black;

period. The whorls are of a triangular form in the half section (figs. 120 and 121), and are made of wood, bone or clay; the type is that of the clay implements shown by Reiss and Stübel (pl. 86). They are ornamented by means of stamps,[2] a technical process peculiar to this period. Several small black vessels recovered in the Sun temple were decorated in a similar manner.

The sewing needles are made of copper or of a thorn (of Agave sp.).

Fig. 116. Fig. 117. Fig. 118.

Figs. 116–118. Typical combs. Cuzco. Graves of Sun temple; ⅓ n. s.

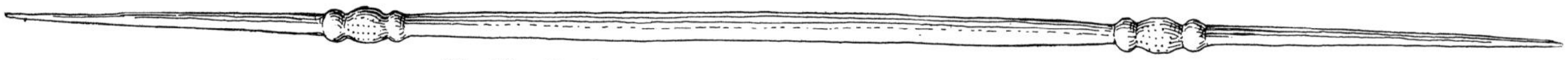

Fig. 119. Weaving staff. Cuzco type. Graves of the Sun temple; ⅛ n. s.

the symbolical and ceremonial significance of which was pointed out in the foregoing pages.

F. Implements for Spinning, Weaving, etc.

One weaving implement, which in its peculiar type was not found in older graves, is a small staff with knob-like swellings near the pointed ends (fig. 119). It is probable that articles of this class may be regarded as belonging to the last

Work baskets taken from these graves resemble those from older cemeteries.

Fig. 120. 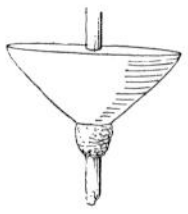 Fig. 121.

Figs. 120 and 121. Spinning whorls of wood. Cuzco type. Graves of Sun temple; ⅔ n. s.

---

[1] Ehrenreich, Beitr. zur Voelkerk. Brasiliens, p. 24, fig. 9.

[2] Comp. also l. c., figs. 3 to 7 and 17.

CHAPTER XXII.

THE CONVENT.

THE ruins of a building situated to the west from the western angle of the inner city wall, and away from the city proper, were (p. 11) identified as those of the convent. This structure (pls. 20 and 21) is marked as of special historical significance by its site, and by its distinct architecture, while the ancient name, Mamakona, still clinging to it, points to its former purpose. No other building at Pachacamac has a similar situation, standing, as it does, with its front to the edge of the green fields. The architecture cannot be classed with that of any other building in the town; it is neither a temple nor a dwelling-house. Small and attractive in design, it is built in three sections, each of which shows a distinct character, around three sides of a quadrangle. Niches, frame-like, and of a trapezoid form, decorate in long rows nearly all the walls visible from the outside. No other building in Pachacamac has niches like these, which, however, conform entirely to the familiar type of Inca architecture.[1]

The building, from these facts, was evidently erected by the Incas, and as such has been generally acknowledged by persons in a position to know.[2] It is the only one at Pachacamac still bearing its ancient name, Mamakona, which, however, does not belong to the edifice alone, but also to the adjoining fields belonging to it. 'Mamakona' means mothers, and was especially applied to the older nuns, both at Cuzco and in the provinces.[3] In this sense it is used by Cieza[4] and by Cobo for the women definitely appointed to the service in the temples at Pachacamac; Cobo even mentions "a house which the Mamakona possessed,"[5] and Pizarro distinctly specifies the locality as the site of the ancient convent. It seems, therefore, impossible to be uncertain on this point.[6] Garcilaso particularizes one of the conditions of the treaty of peace concluded between the Inca Pachakutij and the prince Cuismanku of Pachacamac,[7] in fulfillment of which this convent was built: "As a much finer monument of his greatness,

[probably that of Pachakamaj the god], they [the Incas] would build a house in the valley of Pachacamac for the chosen maidens, as the greatest distinction that could be bestowed upon this district, for in all other provinces these houses and the temples of the Sun were more admired than everything else, as they were really the finest buildings that existed at Cuzco."[8]

Squier's[9] carefully prepared plan of the convent is too much reconstructed in some parts and wrong in others. The main building, c in the plan, was photographed by Middendorf; his representation resembles ours (pl. 3, fig. 2).[10]

Some other views of this interesting building have been already published, but they are generally unsatisfactory in the details; such as one corresponding to pl. 21, fig. 2, by Hutchinson and Wiener; one of the southwest front by Hutchinson; another of a peculiar arch and the niche of a room by Squier, and one of the northwest of the convent by Wiener.[11]

In the present work the following views were given as indispensable for the interpretation of the building: One of the southwest main wing, taken from the south (pl. 3, fig. 2); one of the large niches of the northeast front, facing the court (pl. 21, fig. 2), and one of the central and eastern parts (pl. 21, fig. 1).[12] These views will show that the convent in its present condition is only a shadow of its former grandeur. Some parts could merely be traced along their foundation lines, such as the rear wall in nearly its entire length; others are covered several feet deep with débris, probably due to some elementary cause, such as inundations, etc.; others again are completely buried in driftsand. A careful exploration would, no doubt, uncover many important details of the original structure, which might be helpful in the study of the arrangement of women's convents under Inca rule. The convent is situated at a distance of seventy-six yards from the southwest side of the inner city wall, and about seven hundred and fifty yards from the Sun temple,[13] near the edge of the southwest slope of the desert. The fields, skirting it for about one mile in length and four hundred yards deep, stretch between the city and the beach, the hills in the northwest and the river in the southeast, and bear the same name as the

---

[1] Similar niches may be seen in the palace of the first Inca at Cuzco (Squier, p. 451); on the terraces of Colcampata, at Cuzco (l. c., p. 477); at Ollantaitambo (Wiener, pp. 335 and 491); Vilcas Huaman (l. c., pp. 266 and 267); in all the buildings of Coati and of the Titicaca Island; in a so-called Inca palace near Hervey, in the valley, of Cañete (Middendorf, Peru, II, p. 128; l. c., p. 139, etc.).
[2] P. Cobo, Squier, p. 69; Middendorf, l. c., p. 113.
[3] Kechua mama=mother, mamakona=mothers. Compare Garcilaso, B. IV, chaps. 1, 2, 5; also I, chap. 26; Relac. anónima, p. 184,-for Cuzco; Garcilaso, IV, chap. 4; Ondegardo, English edition by Markham, p. 165; Santillan, p. 38, and Relac. anónima, p. 180, for the provinces; also Balboa, chap. 9. Garcilaso and Balboa write the plural Mamakuna. most of the others Mamakona. Both forms are grammatically correct (comp. v. Tschudi, Organism. der Khetšua Sprache, p. 140). The frequent interchange of the vowels o and u is peculiar to the Kechua and Aimará. Compare also Yanakona.
[4] Crónica, II, chap. 58.
[5] "Las mamakonas tenian casa aparte junto a el" (el templo). Calancha, however, erroneously considers Mamacona as a later name of the temple, "el templo," that is, the Sun temple: "se llamava del Dios Pachacamac, que despues fue llamado Mamacona, nombre de las virgines dedicadas al Sol."
[6] Middendorf, Peru, II, pl. 112, is uncertain whether the building could be accepted as the convent, even with the name Mamakona and the apparent Inca architecture.
[7] Book VI, chap. 3.

[8] Hutchinson considered the building as some place of worship; Rivero and Tschudi (p. 154) equally erroneously saw in it a Sun temple, subsequently changed into a convent.
[9] Squier, p. 70. The plan of ruins given by Wiener, p. 69, judging from the niches, must be intended for Mamacona. This is the only ground for identification however. In the city plan by Rivero and Tschudi, lam. 55 of Pachacamac, the building was entirely omitted.
[10] Peru, II. pl. with p. 112.
[11] Hutchinson, I, pp. 161 and 163; Wiener, p. 71; Squier, p. 71.
[12] Pl. 21, fig. 1, shows also a glimpse of the desert stretching back of the convent, and to the right in the background a part of the ruined western section of the inner town wall, while to the left, in the distance, parts of the northwest outer city wall may be distinguished as a dark line against the desert.
[13] See plan of city, pl. 2.

13 (97)

buildings, Mamakona. A pond, thickly grown with rushes, the abode of many wild ducks, lies near. The green plain adjoins the city, reaching out to it with one arm six hundred feet wide by five hundred feet long.[1] Here stands the convent, facing the northwest corner of the city, and at a greater distance also the Sun temple. The site for the building was prepared by leveling the slope of the desert, originally twenty-three feet high at this eastern curve. The plot was cut into a rectangle, and graded to about eight feet above the general level of the plain. The convent was built with the rear against the slope of the desert, while the front overlooked the plain. Toward the east and west at the foot of the building, the desert was graded in a straight line toward the plain, with angles and corners, to a distance of seven hundred feet. Here and there traces of walls are yet to be seen, which formerly separated the plain from the desert. All these changes prove that the fields still bearing the name Mamakona were connected with the convent, and therefore represent the Inti chajra, a complex of arable land, set apart by the Incas for the cult of the Sun in newly conquered provinces,[2] to provide the women in the convents with all their sustenance.[3] A grove of date palms near the southern end of the building serves as a picturesque background to the ruins. The grove is of a later date, although it was mentioned as early as the oldest deeds of the hacienda, which proves that from early times the Spaniards began to change the character of the surroundings of the edifice.

The eastern wing, a, of the structure has the appearance of a terrace, open to southeast and southwest, adjoining in the north and northwest the more elevated plain. The terrace lies thirteen feet above the level of the surrounding ground, and is divided into three small cell-like rooms by partition walls, two of which still show along the rear walls the traces of decorative niches, of frame-like shape, set upon the floor, and flanked by smaller ones; the back wall of the third room was not decorated. The front walls, facing southeast and southwest, are so decayed that it is impossible to tell if they ever were garnished with niches or not. The building in the rear is adjoined by a wall with an opening like a gateway, near d; this gate served as an entrance from the northeast; its sides are much worn away, a proof of its extensive use. The gallery, b, must have been reached from d. It forms the rear terrace of the court, the back wall of which is now partly ruined. The gallery is eleven and one-half feet high by fourteen feet wide, and two hundred and eight feet long, while at the back it was originally over eight feet high, as may still be seen in one place, where the entire former height is preserved. Niches were used as decoration both in the front and back.[4] The eastern and western sections were divided by a wall, near k, which must have had a door through it; more walls may be seen to the west from this point, separating small cells, each containing a large niche, while to the east no such traces can be seen in the present ruined state of the building. The plan of Squier, showing the terrace as being cut into cells, is a reconstruction founded upon suppositions only.[5] The niches in the lower front of the terrace stood about ten feet eight inches apart and alternated with smaller ones. Whether the same order prevailed on the rear wall would depend upon the former presence of dividing

walls between the larger niches, as assumed by Squier, but in that case there would have been no room for smaller niches between the large ones.

The western wing, c, was the main part of the building, one hundred and twenty feet deep and one hundred and five feet wide, and arranged in a peculiar manner. It consisted of two platforms facing each other diagonally, e, f, one being connected with gallery b. An inner court, i, is formed by both platforms, together with the western part of the gallery, and a wall, g, which terminates in the northwest end of the east front of f. The platform, e, must have been accessible from the court, i, and perhaps from the western part of the gallery, b. It lies on the same level with b, about eighteen feet above the plain. Its floor space is divided up into rooms, the walls of which are still preserved in their full height, in one place of twelve and one-half feet. These rooms are planned so peculiarly that three oblong passage-like rooms, n, surround four smaller ones, o, in the centre on three sides, in such a manner that they touch the front wall of the terrace only with their fourth side, which faces the court, i. The terrace, f, is about three feet lower than e. The partition walls of rooms upon it have almost entirely disappeared, and even some of the lines as given by Squier in the plan can only be suppositional. Both terraces were separated by a passage, six and one-half feet wide, leading to the southwest end of the building, and apparently touching the wall g in the east. A room, p, was built into court i. The different walls of the court and the interior of the room were decorated with niches, and a gateway may have been cut through the wall g, separating the court i from the passage m. Several small rooms were added as a wing at the foot of the terrace, f, on the southeast front near r, and to the southwest from that point. The back walls of these formed a side of the passageway m. The condition of all these rooms now is so dilapidated that their original appearance cannot be guessed. All these buildings were decorated with a number of niches, large and small. Besides terrace a and gallery b, the building c on its northeast, southeast and southwest sides was entirely surrounded with niches. More large ones appear on the wall, separating platform e from the plain at the back of it; several additional niches were in the smaller rooms within platform e. The large niches are numbered from 1 to 28 in the plan. It will also be seen that a row of about ten handsome niches faces court h. Of these, those shown in pl. 21, fig. 2, are the only ones complete and fairly preserved, 6 to 8. The dividing pillars are worn smooth on their lower parts by the passing of people, similar to the gate-entrance d.[6] Five of the ten niches are on the wall in the rear, g, which continued the terrace front to northwest and separated courts h and i. A door seems to have been between the fourth and fifth niches, but the wall has disappeared and only a few traces of it are left.[7] Two niches, 11 and 12, ornamented the southeast wall of terrace f, but the walls of the rooms r concealed them from view; three more 13 to 15, may be distinguished on the southwest front of f; the traces of two, 16 to 17, on the southwest wall of the room s, built up against terrace f; five others, 18 to 22, on the southwest front of terrace e, while similar ones, 23 to 25, decorated the inner rooms of the terrace, and three more, 26 to 28, its posterior wall. Smaller ones were distributed over the rooms upon the platforms of the terrace. All these niches, including those of gallery b and of terrace a.

[1] The distance is given a mile and a half too high by Squier, p. 69.

[2] Comp. Santillan, p. 37, and others.

[3] Garcilaso, IV, chapter 1: "They were provided with all the necessaries, which they derived from the farm of the Sun, in whose service they stood."

[4] The plan of Squier shows niches also in this third eastern section of the terrace, which is erroneous.

[5] The number of cells as given by Squier must be incorrect, as he does not take any notice of wall k, and a bay-like curve in the hindmost wall, in pl. 22 near l, whereby the row of niches is interrupted.

[6] Wiener considers these pillars as being breast-shape and as the remains of caryatides.

[7] The front of the niches as given in the plan by Squier is based upon a reconstruction. The steps indicated by Squier at the eastern end of the building are in reality not to be distinguished with any degree of certainty; those indicated on the side of the front with the large niches are not existing.

were of nearly corresponding measurements. The inner depth was one foot eleven inches to two feet, and the upper width one foot eleven inches to two feet two inches (two feet nine inches in No. 12, two feet three inches in No. 23), and a lower width of two feet two inches to two feet four inches. The inner height varies; it is five feet in some, while in others it may be six feet seven inches to six feet eleven inches, as in those of the east front of c (pl. 21, fig. 2). An outer frame projected from this, one foot six inches to one foot nine inches deep, with an upper width of four feet seven inches to four feet eleven inches, and a lower of four feet eleven inches to five feet three inches. The difference of the height of the interior part of the niche was about one and two-thirds inches. The smaller niches, generally two feet four inches high and about one foot four inches deep, tapered toward the top from one foot to two and one-half inches.

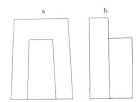

Fig. 122.   Cuzco types of large niches in the convent; $\frac{1}{60}$ n. s.

The roofing of all the niches was made of wooden boards, bound together with ropes, a mode which differed strongly from that of the niches in the ancient city. The boards are now nearly all torn out of the walls,[1] and thus the general effect of the niches has been destroyed.[2] Their former shape was like fig. 122.

---

[1] Hutchinson, I, p. 164, supposes the openings to have been used for fastening draperies to cover the niches.

[2] Squier pays too much attention to an arch to be seen in these ruins, near 29. It can be proved to date from the Spanish period, as was recognized by Middendorf (Peru, II, p. 113). It has been put into the place of a former niche, cutting it out, fitting the recess and closing it over the top with an arch. It may

The roofs were flat. They covered not only the rooms upon the terraces and those on the ground-floor, which may still be traced in their outlines, but other parts of the building as well, where indications of rooms are wanting. The grooves in the walls and over the large niches of the northeast front of c[3] and of the eastern wall of the court,[4] must have served for the support of rafters to carry the roofs. In this way the worn condition of the lower part of the pillars between the large niches of the northeast front of c is explained, as the space in front was in constant use, being under a roof. Similar roofs were probably constructed along the northwest rear wall of the court, the front wall of gallery b, and along the southwest front of c. The large number of roofs permits us to estimate the number of occupants of the buildings as much higher than could have been done otherwise.

In the surroundings of the convent are found a few remains of structures which must have had some relation to the buildings. In the plain, some low mound-like piles, of round or square shape, may be noticed; these are remains of former apartments. Another line, resembling a mound or dam, may be traced, extending like a road from the convent to the opposite end of the plain, in the direction of the Sun temple.

The area between the western end of the city wall and the plain lies at a level of forty feet above the latter; in this place ruined foundation walls and a number of small mounds may be seen, here as elsewhere representing the débris of a row of pillars, formerly supporting roofs. They must have had some relation to the convent, although situated outside of its precincts.

---

be seen that the quality of the more recent masonry and plastering are of an inferior order, compared with the ancient. These modern alterations are not the only ones in the building. Near 30 a deep recess in a wall has been closed by a shallow arch; the niches 23 have been altered by removing the pillars in the inner recess; similar changes took place in niches 26 to 28. The alterations prove that the buildings were in use in Spanish times and probably occupied by Spaniards. This may be connected with the former independent existence of Mamacona as a hacienda and the early appearance of the palm grove near it.

[3] Comp. pl. 21, fig. 2.

[4] Comp. fig. 2.

CHAPTER XXIII.

INTERPRETATION OF THE CONVENT.

THE description of the ruins is only one part of our task. The ruins themselves can only give a partial explanation of the peculiar purpose for which the building was intended, and as they are among the best preserved of the more prominent among the old convents of the Inca realm, it seems well worth the attempt to interpret them, as far as may be done with the help of the records at hand.

The institution of convents for women living in celibacy and consecrating[1] themselves to the service of the various deities was quite common in the land of the Incas.[2] They were to be found in all the larger provinces, and generally attached to a Sun temple[3] erected by the Incas. From all appearances, however, there were different classes of convents in the provinces, and it is necessary to distinguish between them from the beginning. H. Pizarro distinctly states that he found in all principal cities two classes of nuns—one consecrated to the cult of the Sun, or to that of the dead Inca; the members of the other destined to be presented to the Inca when he should pass through the town, besides having the office of brewing chicha, the Peruvian beer, made of maize, intended for any warriors who might enter the neighborhood. With this agrees the note in the description of the province of Vilcas Huaman, which mentions two large convents in connection with that locality, one for the Sun maidens and one for the women set apart for the Inca's service. Santillan even distinguishes between four different convents; but it is doubtful whether all four were always to be found side by side in the same place. Probably three classes might correspond to the first class as H. Pizarro assigns it, and the fourth would be the same as the second described by him. The convent of Pachacamac was of the first class, and the women occupying it were, like those of the convent Ajllawasi, "house of the chosen ones," at Cuzco,[4] set apart for the service of the Sun, as may be seen in the oldest records.[5] The pure Inca style of the building is also a proof that the women were destined for a cult of purely Inca origin. Therefore this convent very probably was an Ajllawasi, as Ondegardo calls the convents of the provinces, and the name Mamakona merely survived the former designation, as it may have been the popular name for the building.

The peculiar design clearly explains itself by the special purpose for which it was intended. This purpose was of the same nature in the convent of Cuzco and in the provincial institutions, except the slight difference that the occupants of the latter came from provincial families, and possibly also were presented to the Inca.[6] It is quite plausible that, as Garcilaso repeatedly tells, the convents in the provinces were all built after the model of the one at Cuzco. It should therefore be possible to find certain points of resemblance between the different convents of the realm and the description given by him of the Ajllawasi of Cuzco.[7]

Garcilaso emphasizes the fact that the Sun maidens lived secluded lives, separated from the world, and so far from the temple that they could not go there, nor could any man enter the convent.[8] The distance from Cuzco was only 200 yards.[9] However, it is of much more importance that Garcilaso lays more stress on the distance from the Sun temple than on its proximity. In the province of Pacajes, in Bolivia, the Sun maidens also lived outside the general settlements.[10]

On Coati Island, Lake Titicaca, are the ruins of an important structure, a very fair plan of which is given by Squier (Peru, pl., p. 360) remarking that this building was known as the palace of the Sun maidens, but that the better name would be Temple of the Moon. Here again the local tradition in connection with a monument proves of more value than later conjectures. The building shows striking points of resemblance to the convent of Pachacamac in its former state, and both resemble the convent of Cuzco in many of their details. "The Sun maidens saw neither men nor women; they lived in entire seclusion, and were never seen by anybody," according to Garcilaso. A passage extended through the large building, wide enough for two persons to walk abreast; on both sides were rooms, and at the end lay the apartments of the Sun maidens, never entered by any but themselves. The two convents of Coati and of Pachacamac show the same features, inasmuch as they are both secluded from the outer world upon three sides, while the front faces the fields or gardens, with a view over the vast plain or the sea. A definite principle seems to have been followed by the Incas in establishing the convents in this particular way, although in the populous city of Cuzco the feature could not be so pronounced. Both convents form a rectangle, similar to that of Cuzco, four times as long as it was wide,[11] according to Squier. In the ground-plan of the two buildings of Coat-

---

[1] To the service of the Sun, Pachamama (Ondegardo, p. 166), to the service of the dead Incas (H. Pizarro, Letter, p. 121), to the wakas of the provinces (Santillan, p. 38).

[2] Garcilaso, Book IV, chaps. 1 and 4.

[3] Cieza, Crónica, I, chap. 37, Caranqui, Rel. geogr., I, p. 168, Vilcas Huaman, Cieza, I, chap. 73, for Pachacamac. Comp. also Cuzco (Cieza, V, chap. 27), Coati in Lake Titicaca, etc.

[4] Garcilaso, Book IV, chap. 1. The translation in Garcilaso's text as 'house of stars' rests on some inexplicable error.

[5] Cieza, I, chap. 73 ; II, chap. 58 ; P. Cobo, H. Pizarro refers to them as the 'women of the devil.' He must therefore have connected them with the temple of Pachakamaj, the 'mosque.'

[6] Garcilaso, Book IV, chap. 4.

[7] Book IV, chap. 1 to 2.

[8] Garcilaso questions whether the Sun maidens had any duties in the temple, as is maintained by others (f. i. Relacion anónima, p. 184), perhaps not without cause.

[9] Compare the plan of the place (Squier, p. 428).

[10] Relacion de la provincia de los Pacajes, Rel. geogr., II, p. 59.

[11] Peru, p. 445.

and of Pachacamac there may be seen besides the long extended court, open at one side, a reminiscence of the long and narrow passage extending through the convent building in Cuzco. The subdivision into cells, in which the women worked, seems to have been copied at Coati, and must have been similar at Pachacamac; for this reason the reconstruction of the gallery of the cells, as seen in the plan of that building (Squier, Peru), may be considered a very good one. Finally, may be noticed in both buildings that one of the wings of the crescent-shaped construction is much larger and wider than the other. This was probably the most important apartment given up to the residence of the Sun maidens. The points of resemblance to the convent of Coati cannot be carried any further than this. Still the building of Pachacamac becomes more intelligible with the help of the description of the convent at Cuzco.

The terrace b, in its gallery-like appearance, was represented at Cuzco, by the long passage which Garcilaso calls a gallery. As in Cuzco, the apartments, "where no one might enter," were reached by the narrow passage-way, so also at Pachacamac gallery b and the line not to be crossed by any outsider lay near the gate in the wall k. The rooms a probably were the most secluded ones, in which the Sun maidens lived, while in the long front of the building, and near the door in wall g, was the main entrance, entered only by women of the highest rank, and through which new Sun maidens passed when about to be received into the circle of the chosen virgins. The rooms in the gallery were occupied by women working in the service of the Sun maidens, while the court and gallery served for the numerous novices who usually lived there.[1] The Relacion Anónima states,[2] in regard to the convent of Cuzco: "The novices lived apart from the real Sun maidens, and although there were no keys or doors, all doorways being closed with hangings, their obedience and discipline were so great that no one ever walked over to the novices from the Sun maidens' apartments, nor from those of the novices to their superiors', without the permission of the abbess or the chief directress."

There was a well regulated gate-service in these convents attended to by women.[3] Porters guarded the entrance at the door near d and kept up communication with the outer world. They allowed the visitor to go as far as the second door, probably near k, or they received the articles brought there and carried them so far, but they were forbidden under penalty of death to cross that threshold.[4] It is also likely that the convent was guarded from the outside,[5] and it is possible that the hall, of which the traces are to be seen on the higher eastern edge of the plain near t, had some such relation to the convent.[6] To judge from the small size of the building, the number of its occupants might be underestimated. But it may be assumed that the women lived very much crowded together in the apartments. The deeply worn sides of the gateway d, and of the pillars between the niches 5 to 9, may be considered as proofs of this, as well as the roofing over parts of the courts. Garcilaso may have exaggerated when he gave the number of the Sun maidens in the convent at Cuzco as 1500, with 500 women servants. It is probable that all over the country the convents were crowded with women. We always hear of high estimates given for the numbers in each of them. Two hundred is mentioned for the convent in Caranqui, Ecuador; five hundred each for the two convents in Vilcas Huaman, and Ondegardo states that in each Ajllawasi of a province little girls from eight to nine years of age were chosen to be trained for novices and lived together with one hundred Mamakonas.[7]

The convent in Cuzco was 800 feet long by 200 feet wide,[8] and occupied about four acres of ground. The number of inmates being estimated at 2000 persons, and not allowing any space for walls, etc., this would give eighty square feet to each person. If it is assumed that the convent at Pachacamac, which occupied only about one acre of ground, housed 200 persons, the above figure does not seem too high.

---

[1] Ondegardo, p. 165; Garcilaso, Book IV, chap. 4; Relacion Anónima, p. 180, for the provinces.
[2] P. 182.

[3] Garcilaso, Book IV, chap. 1.
[4] L. c. chap. 2.
[5] In connection with the convents the early chroniclers always mention the large number of guards and doorkeepers; comp. Cieza, II, chap. 27; Ondegardo, p. 166; Santillan, p. 38; Rel. geogr. I, p. 168; H Pizarro, Letter, p. 121; Doc. inéditos, III, p. 41; Relacion Anónima, p. 180; Gomara, Hist. de las Ind in Barcia, Hist. prim., II, p. 113. The three latter speak of eunuchs, whose existence in Peru is disputed by J. J. v. Tschudi, Beitr., p. 94.
[6] See the plan of the city, pl. 2.
[7] The Spanish text, which is full of errors, gives here 'ciertas Mamakonas,' instead of ciento. The text of the English translation by Markham (p. 165) gives more correctly 'hundred'.
[8] Squier, p. 445.

CHAPTER XXIV.

TECHNICAL POINTS OF BUILDINGS.

THREE different kinds of material have been used in the buildings of Pachacamac : sun-dried adobe bricks, stone and plain adobe clay used as a sort of plaster upon walls and simply dried in place, 'tapia.' The stone was quarried in the neighborhood of the ancient city. The yellow clay for the adobe and tapia is found near the river, which washes it down from the mountains. In some terraces of the temple of Pachakamaj a blackish kind of adobe has been used for more important purposes, a kind not found elsewhere in Pachacamac, and seemingly baked of the mud from the bottoms of canals or ponds. Residents of the neighborhood who distinguish the adobe bricks by their quality assured us that those used for the buildings of the town are of the best quality. Difference in quality does not consist in the material used but in the method of preparation—whether the adobe bricks have been baked immediately after taking the clay from its bed, or whether it has been allowed to "rot" in water for one week or longer.[1]

The buildings of Pachacamac are nearly all constructed of brick. Nevertheless Bandelier's statement is correct, to the effect that there is hardly one large pile of ruins to be found along the coast entirely without stone. The foundations of buildings especially are built of stone. As above stated, an ancient wall in the interior of the temple of Pachakamaj,[2] disclosed during the excavations, and certain terraces and structures along the hill were constructed entirely of stone;[3] this is also true of the high substructures of the original enclosure of the Pachakamaj temple. In the Sun temple stone has been used in the construction of the foundations, for sections of the interior masonry, previous to a facing with adobe, in the construction of the northern angle of the second terrace, also for the terrace in front of the large niches of the southwest façade,[4] and in some other places. The foundations of houses and also the side walls of many grave cells of the earlier times (in Cemetery I) were built of stone. Nevertheless, the use of stone as building material is so secondary in Pachacamac to that of adobe that in a general survey of all the buildings in the town it is not at all noticed.[5]

Tapia has been still more sparingly used in buildings. We only noticed it in five buildings of the town, where it occurred in a secondary way, such as in the platform f in Mamakona, in some of the houses, in the ruins to the north from the inner city wall and the road skirting it. In these cases the tapia had been used in some partition walls and in some of the terrace walls.

The almost exclusive use of adobe in buildings at Pachamac is peculiar, for the reason that in all other ruins of the neighborhood tapia constructions are in the majority or exclude all other material : thus in the ruins of the Lima valley in Cajamarquilla ; also the other ruins in the valley of Pachacamac,[6] in the Rinconada, are built entirely of tapia ; likewise those on the rock and at the foot of La Centinela, as well as numerous field enclosures in the lower valley.[7] Adobe constructions, however, are not exclusive to Pachacamac. In the valley of Lima, near Maranga, numerous mounds are to be seen, of the same nature as that situated above the temple of Pachakamaj, m, in the plan. In the ruins of the ancient Surco, near Chorillos, tapia is more extensively used, while adobe is also represented. Judging from a view, the buildings in Paramonga also seem to have consisted of adobe. Farther up the coast to the north, adobe constructions are to be found, for instance in the valley of Santa.

Middendorf raises the question as to whether all of the city of Pachacamac does not date from the time of the Incas, since it is built of adobe ;[8] but it is much more likely that adobe represents the earlier form of building. Very ancient portions of the temple of Pachakamaj, dating before the Inca period, are built of it. The mound at Pachacamac and those of a similar nature in the valley of Lima impress one with their great antiquity. The occasional use of tapia at Pachacamac is found to be in buildings of the Inca times, also in Mamacona and the walls in some of the more recent buildings, whereby an increased use of tapia is proved during the period of the Incas, while in all buildings of apparently greater age tapia is not to be found. It would seem correct, as seen from former discussions, to classify the other ruins in the lower valley, which are built of tapia, as belonging to the last Inca period. If the adobe construction was the older mode of building in the lower valley of Pachacamac, it would by no means prove that all those buildings must have a higher antiquity than those built of tapia in the valleys of Pachacamac and Lima. An originally older form of construction may be retained longer in one place than in another. Several kinds of building material rarely exclude each other in the same periods, as several may be used at the same time, and this use mostly depends on local conditions. Therefore it is possible that at Pachacamac adobe was still used for building long after other places had changed to the use of tapia. Although the adobe bricks at Pachacamac have about the

---

[1] Mixing grass into clay ('tchu') is quite general in the highland ; we never found grass mixed with the clay of the adobes at Pachacamac (Bandelier, Amer. Anthrop., l. c., p. 305).

[2] Above, p. 20, fig. 4.

[3] Above, p. 51.

[4] Comp. pl. 15, fig. 1.

[5] Prescott, I, p. 291, erroneously speaks of the temple as built entirely of stone ; Hutchinson, I, p. 173, states that the main portion of the material in it is stone.

[6] However, the ancient walls of the hacienda Las Palmas, ½-1½ miles from Pachacamac towards northeast, consist also of adobes.

[7] Wiener, p. 494.

[8] Peru, II, p. 121.

same proportions as baked ones, they are generally larger in size and their measurements are of endless variety. The smallest bricks are those of the mound, about eight inches long, seven inches wide and four inches thick. The largest seen by us at Pachacamac are two feet long, one foot two inches wide and about six inches thick.[1] The size varies according to the purpose, if used as fillings of terraces or platforms (mound, terrace in the rear of the Pachakamaj temple, Sun temple), or for ordinary masonry and front walls of terraces, or for the floors of terraces and plateaus. The former class are the smaller everywhere, the latter the larger. In the Sun temple, for the filling of terraces bricks of the smallest size were used, little larger than those of the mound; a larger size served for the fronts of walls, but the largest of all for the flooring. It can not, therefore, be said that buildings of a certain given period at Pachacamac, such as the Sun temple, consisted entirely of one even size of bricks,[2] nor may the bricks of one building, even in their peculiar use, be compared to their use in another; indeed the size of bricks varies within the same building for the same purposes. The bricks in the flooring of one terrace were found to measure one foot eight inches and one foot two inches in length. Five different sizes were observed among the bricks in one of the younger terraces of the temple of Pachakamaj, the length of which varied from one foot one inch to one foot six inches, the width from eight inches to one foot three inches, the thickness from three to six inches. From this may be seen the difficulty in fixing the age of a building by the size of the bricks. No safe distinction may be drawn between the sizes of adobes of apparently pre-Inca buildings and of those dating from Inca times. It may be said, however, in accordance with the view expressed by Middendorf, that the bricks of the most recent period seem as a whole somewhat larger than those of earlier times. Future explorers will have to decide how far it is possible under these obvious difficulties to draw conclusions concerning the relative ages of the various buildings. The bricks were laid in mortar composed of the same kind of clay as the bricks themselves. A glance at the plates will show that the walls of buildings incline inward, which gives increased strength. In a wall twenty feet high the inclination may be between four and eight inches. Partition walls did not taper towards the top, while this is frequent with tapia walls, such as may be seen in the ruins of the Lima valley and in the walls built of stone in the ruins of the upper part of Pachacamac valley. Terrace walls more than twenty feet high are, as a rule, strengthened by a lower retaining wall. This class of walls is found up to twenty-three feet high. The highest point of elevation of terraces is to be seen in the houses of the town, forty-three feet above the city level. Partition walls occur in all degrees of thickness, ranging from one foot six inches to twenty feet (the northwestern outer city wall), as the city plan will generally show. The walls were formerly coated with a smooth layer of plaster, still adhering in some spots on the walls of the convent.[3] In the town this coat of plaster is preserved upon walls inside of terraces, which were filled in with sand and overlaid with flagstone, while from exposed walls nearly all traces of plastering have disappeared. Mural painting was uncommon and is only found upon sacred edifices. The peculiar mode of decoration upon walls with large grooved ornaments, seen on the buildings of the Lima valley, cannot be proved to have been in use at Pachacamac, while it is not impossible that it was once known here, but may have disappeared in the course of the centuries.

[1] Pl. 16, fig. 1. They were set on their long and narrow sides, corresponding to the different purposes for which they were used.
[2] Middendorf, Ollanta, 1890, p. 21.

[3] Pl. 21, fig. 2.

ERRATA.

On p. 63, line 2 from below; on p. 64, line 13, and on p. 65, lines 20 and 26 from above, read pl. 13 instead of pl. 12.

Uhle, Pachacamac

PANORAMA OF PACHACAMAC

SEEN FROM THE TEMPLE OF PACHAKAMAJ

1

THE SUN TEMPLE AND THE TEMPLE OF PACHAKAMAJ

FROM THE NORTH

2

Uhle, Pachacamac

THE CONVENT, MAMACONA

SEEN FROM THE SUNFIELDS

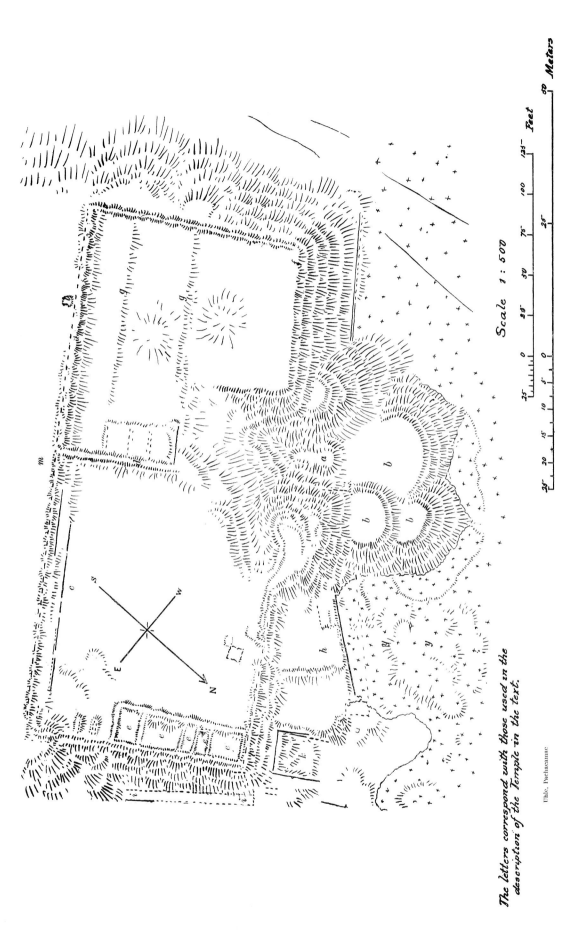

The letters correspond with those used in the
description of the Temple in the text.

Scale 1 : 500

Uhle, Pachacamac

PLAN OF THE TEMPLE OF PACHAKAMAJ

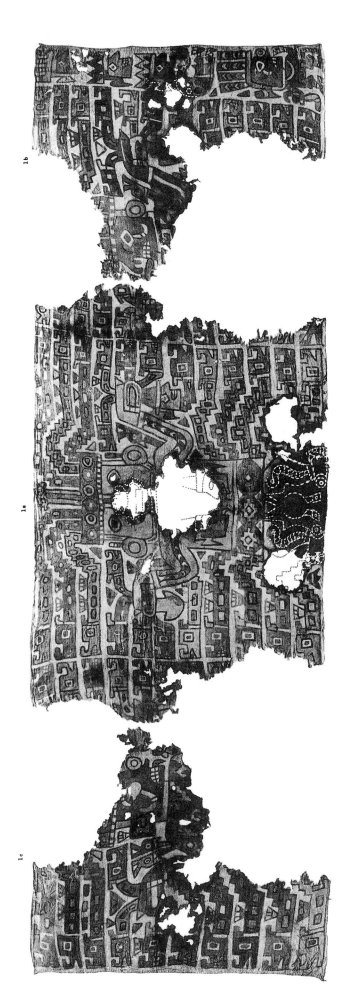

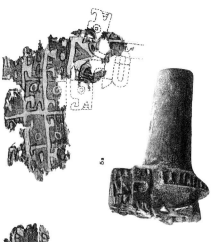

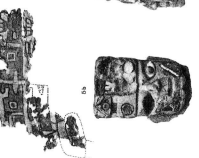

CEMETERY UNDER THE TEMPLE OF PACHAKAMAJ

OBJECTS IN THE STYLE OF THE MONUMENTS OF TIAHUANACO

FIGS. 1a-e : ⅓ N. S.; FIG. 2: AB. ⅔; FIGS. 3, 4 : ⅜ ; FIGS. 5a-b : N. S.

Plte. Pachacamac

4

1 2 3 4 6a 6b 7 5 8 10 11 9 13 15 12a 12b 16 17 14 18 19

CEMETERY UNDER THE TEMPLE OF PACHAKAMAJ

OBJECTS IN THE STYLE OF THE EPIGONE PERIOD

FIGS. 1-11, 13: ⅓ N. S.; FIG. 12: ¼; FIGS. 14, 15: ½; FIGS. 16-19: N. S.

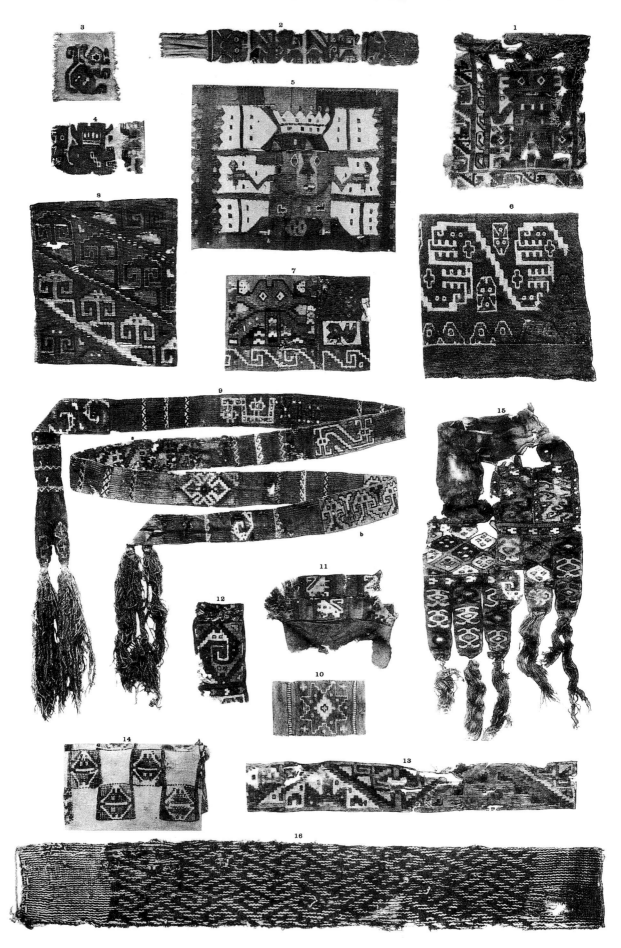

CEMETERY UNDER THE TEMPLE OF PACHAKAMAJ

TEXTILES OF EPIGONE PERIOD

ALL OBJECTS: ½ N. S.

6

Uhle, Pachacamac

FIGS. 1-9—GRAVES IN DÉBRIS OF BUILDINGS UNDER THE TEMPLE OF PACHAKAMAJ, ABOVE THE ORIGINAL CEMETERY. OBJECTS OF THE LATER PRE-INCA PERIOD

FIGS. 10-21—OBJECTS FROM INCA GRAVES IN FRONT OF THE TEMPLE OF PACHAKAMAJ

FIGS. 22-23b—OBJECTS FROM THE CEMETERY OF LA CENTINELA NEAR LURIN

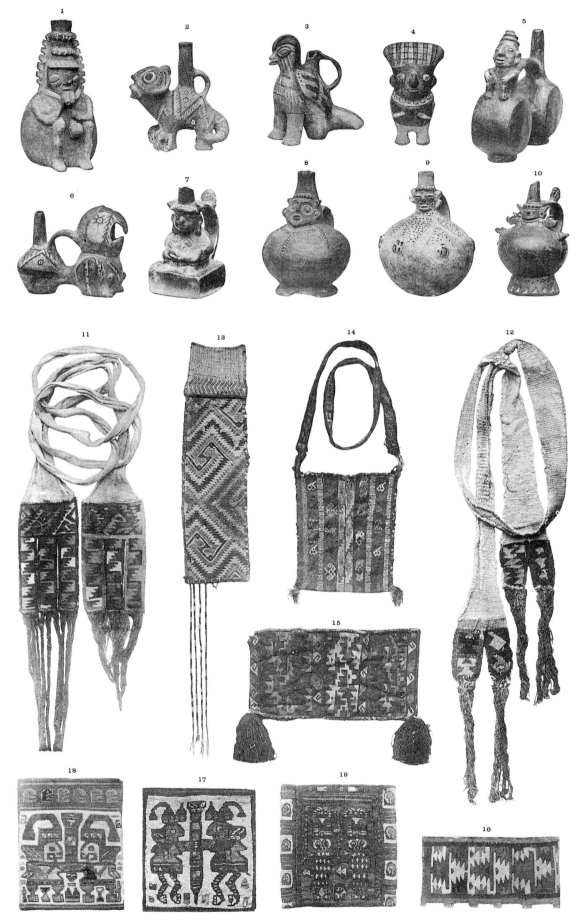

CEMETERY SURROUNDING THE TEMPLE OF PACHAKAMAJ

OBJECTS OF THE LATER PRE-INCA PERIOD OF PACHACAMAC

FIGS. 1-16: ⅓ N. S.; 17-19: ⅓ N. S.

8

VIEW OF THE OLDEST PART OF THE TOWN

FROM THE NORTH

VIEW OF THE SOUTHWESTERN PART OF THE TOWN

FROM THE NORTH

ENTRANCE TO THE PRINCIPAL PALACE OF THE TOWN

2

RUINS OF A PALACE WITHOUT TERRACED FOUNDATIONS

4

THE EASTERN STREET OF PACHACAMAC

FROM THE EAST

1

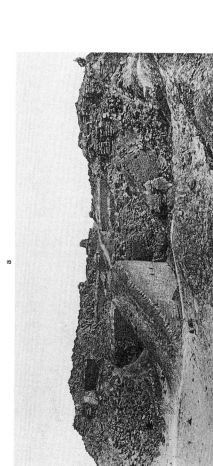

RUINS OF A TYPICAL PALACE OF THE TOWN

3

Uhle, Pachacamac

10

2

TERRACED SLOPE OF THE HILL WITH WATCH TOWER IN THE
NORTHWESTERN PART OF THE TOWN

1

VIEW OF THE NORTHERN PART OF THE TOWN

FROM THE WEST

4

SUNKEN CHAMBERS IN THE SOUTHWESTERN PART OF THE TOWN

3

Uhle, Pachacamac

PALACE WITH SUNKEN CHAMBERS IN THE EASTERN STREET OF PACHACAMAC

11

1

VIEW OF THE SUN TEMPLE

FROM NORTHEAST

2

VIEW OF THE SUN TEMPLE

FROM SOUTHEAST

12

Uhle, Pachacamac

CEMETERY OF THE OUTER CITY. TOWARDS THE NORTH

OBJECTS IN THE STYLE OF THE INCA PERIOD OF THE TOWN

FIGS. 1-8, 10-15: ¾ N. S.; FIGS. 9, 16-18, 21-26: ⅙; FIGS. 19, 20: ⅔ N. S.

13

2

THE SOUTHWEST FRONT

FROM THE SOUTH

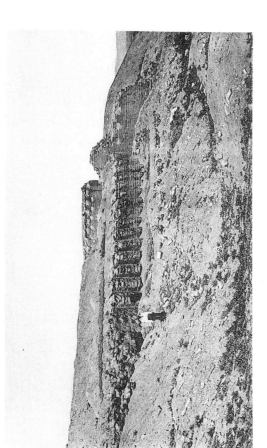

1

TERRACE OF THE LARGE NICHES

FROM THE WEST

4

ENTRANCE TO FIRST TERRACE

SEEN FROM ABOVE

3

NICHED WALLS OF THE SOUTHWEST FRONT

SEEN FROM THE PLATEAU

VIEWS OF THE SUN TEMPLE

14

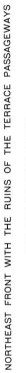

NORTHEAST FRONT WITH THE RUINS OF THE TERRACE PASSAGEWAYS

SEEN FROM THE THIRD TERRACE

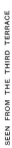

TERRACES OF THE SOUTHEAST FRONT WITH THE CEMETERY OF THE
SACRIFICED WOMEN

MOUND BUILT OF ADOBES. TO THE NORTH FROM THE TEMPLE

VIEWS OF THE SUN TEMPLE

15

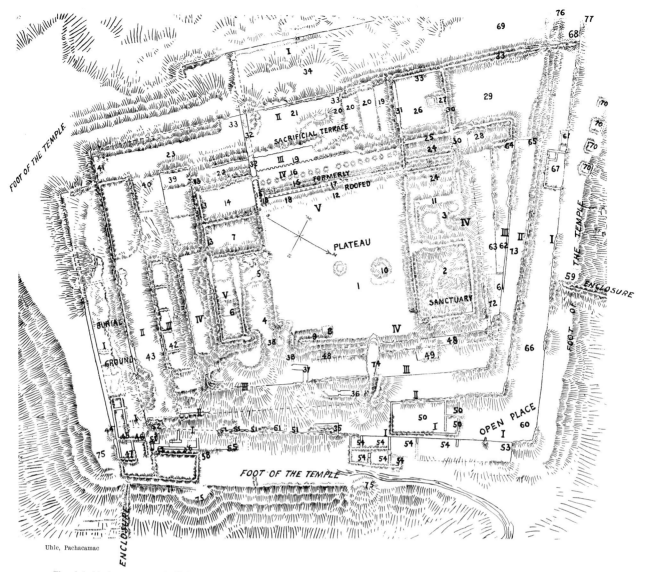

Uhle, Pachacamac

*The red Arabic figures correspond with those used
in the description of the Temple; the red Roman
numerals mark the height of stories.*

PLAN OF THE SUN TEMPLE

Scale   1 : 1000

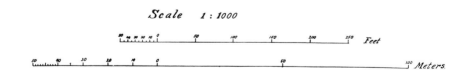

1. South-western Front

2. North-western Front

3. North-eastern Front

4. South-eastern Front

ELEVATIONS OF THE SUN TEMPLE AT PACHACAMAC

17

Uhle, Pachacamac

CEMETERY OF THE SACRIFICED WOMEN. SUN TEMPLE

OBJECTS OF POTTERY, WOOD, ETC.

FIGS. 1-8, 10-12, 15, 16, 18, 19: ⅓ N. S.; FIGS. 9, 13: ¾; FIG. 14: ⅖; FIG. 17: N. S.

18

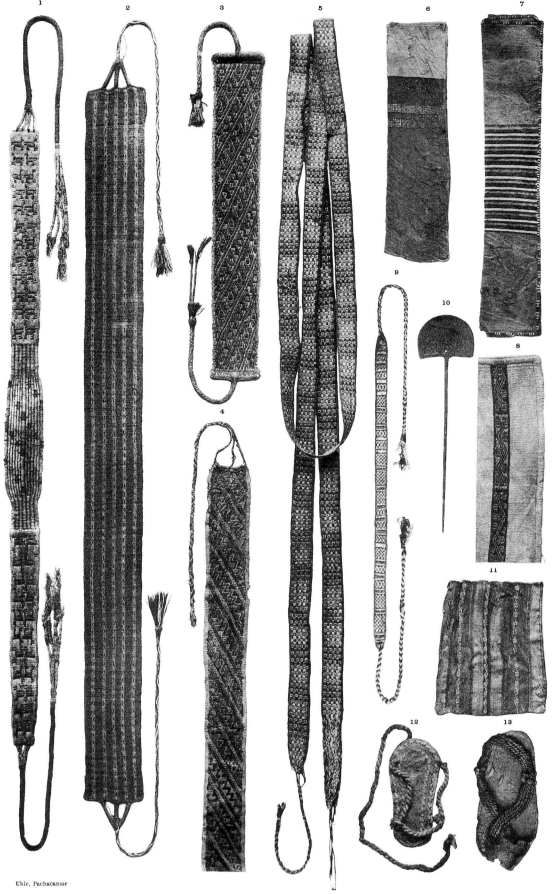

Uhle, Pachacamac

CEMETERY OF THE SACRIFICED WOMEN

ARTICLES OF DRESS

FIGS. 1-4, 6, 7: ⅛ N. S.; FIGS. 5, 9, 11-13: ¼; FIG. 10: ½; FIG. 8: AB. N. S.

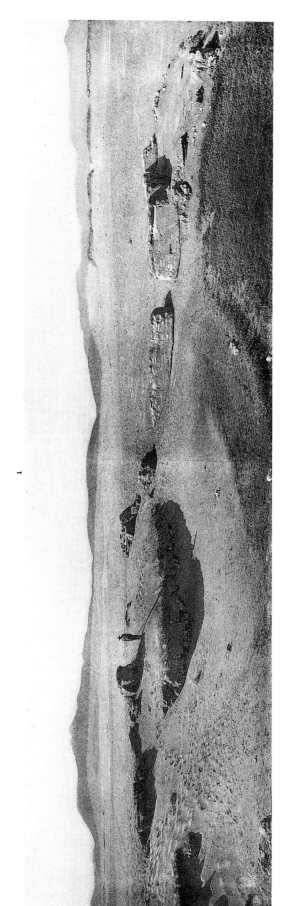

1

VIEW OF THE NORTHERN AND EASTERN PARTS OF THE RUINS OF THE CONVENT

3

WALL TWENTY FEET WIDE IN THE NORTH OF THE EXTENDED TOWN

2

FRONT WITH LARGE NICHES. CONVENT

SEEN FROM THE COURT

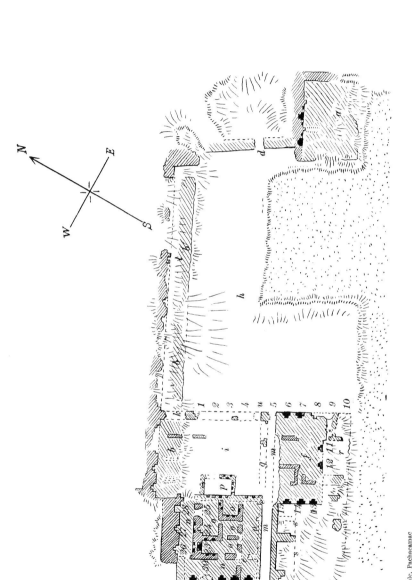

N

E

S

W

Uhle, Pachacamac

Scale 1 : 500

The letters correspond with those used in the
description of the Convent, in the text.

PLAN OF THE RUINS OF THE CONVENT. PACHACAMAC

21